Writers at Work

Writers at Work

Russian Production Novels and the Construction of Soviet Culture

Mary A. Nicholas

Lewisburg
Bucknell University Press

Associated University Presses
2010 Eastpark Boulevard
Cranbury, NJ 08512

The paper used in this publication meets the requirements of the American National Standard for Permanence of Paper for Printed Library Materials Z39.48-1984.

Library of Congress Cataloging-in-Publication Data

Nicholas, Mary A., 1954–
    Writers at work : Russian production novels and the construction of Soviet culture / Mary A. Nicholas.
        p.   cm.
    Includes bibliographical references and index.
    ISBN 978-0-8387-5739-0 (alk. paper)
    1. Russian fiction—20th century—History and criticism.
    2. Production (Economic theory) in literature.   I. Title.
    PG3098.4.N53 2010
    891.73′40912—dc22

                                                    2009035714

PRINTED IN THE UNITED STATES OF AMERICA

"Ia govoriu, chto mne starshii inzhener stroitel'stva skazal, chto nel'zia etogo sdelat'. On otvechaet, malo li chto nel'zia, a my poprobuem."

I told him that the head of construction had said it was impossible. But he answered "Who cares what's impossible? We're going to try."

—Valentin Kataev, Metrostroi rally, 1934

Contents

Acknowledgments

As AUTHORS OF RUSSIAN PRODUCTION NOVELS UNDERSTOOD QUITE well, every book is a collective endeavor. Over the years I have been helped in my study by many individuals and institutions, and I am grateful for their assistance. My first teachers of Russian, Christopher Wertz, Felicia Wertz, and Lew Bagby, taught me to love this language and the great culture it represents. I am grateful for Kit's enthusiasm, Fela's friendship and her cooking lessons, and Lew's Dostoevskian costume parties. The bus that Kit and I rode from Wyoming to Middlebury College in Vermont marked a new stage in my Russian journey.

I am deeply appreciative of the FLAS scholarship that allowed me to study at the University of Illinois and grateful for the friendship of Andi Dunn, Floyd and Elsa Dunn, Steve Askins, and Mary Stuart that allowed me to thrive in the Midwest. Gera Millar was a warm and wonderful presence in the classroom in Urbana. She, too, gave me more than she will ever know. The late Jim Millar was a constant source of inspiration, who taught me how to run a meeting and why it mattered. I am grateful to him for precious opportunities at the SIP project and the *Slavic Review*. It was a honor to work at the journal with Jim and, later, Dave Ransel.

Profound thanks go to the Kosciusko Foundation for a scholarship to study at Jagiellonian University. My time there was unforgettable, and I am truly grateful for the support of the Foundation and the friendship of my fellow students and residents of Krakow. I thank Dr. Dan Davidson and the American Council of Teachers of Russian for their support as well. The chance to spend ten months at the Pushkin Institute in Moscow was a dream come true and changed my life. Tom Garza and Lisa Choate provided particular support during our time at the institute, and I am grateful. I remember the instructors and support staff at the institute and the staff at the Lenin Library where I spent countless hours in *chital'nyi zal #1* with fondness and gratitude. Thanks go as well

9

to the *redkollegi* at Mir Publishers in Moscow, who taught me so much about how Soviet work was really done.

I am sorry that my dissertation adviser, Dr. Elliott Mossman, did not live to see this book published. His quiet support and guidance at the University of Pennsylvania were essential. I am grateful as well for the advice and assistance of Drs. Gail Lenhoff, Moshe Lewin, Gary Saul Morson, Ron Vroon, and, of course, Anna Pirscenok Herz of both Penn and Lehigh for her encouragement and help. Special thanks are also due to Dr. Maria Lekic for inspiration and unending advocacy. Cynthia Martin traded jobs with me, and Tom Samuelian taught me how to use a computer mouse. I appreciate it. The friendship of Karen McCauley and, especially, Lena Coler and the late Lindsay Watton made those years a pleasure. Both Lena and Lindsay contributed significantly to my thinking about Russian and Soviet literature, and Lena shared her good karma. The financial support of the University of Pennsylvania, the Russian department, the Bryn Mawr Russian Language Summer Institute, American Councils, the Social Science Research Council (SSRC), and the International Research and Exchanges (IREX) board is also gratefully acknowledged.

I am grateful as well for the gracious assistance and professional support of Drs. Gary Browning, Kenneth Brostrom, Michael Falchikov, Igor Shaitanov, and, of course, Kira Borisovna Andronikashvili and the late Boris Borisovich Andronikashvili-Pilniak. Special thanks go to Robert Chandler for collegiality and ingenuity. I hope my friends and colleagues Donna Farina and George Durman also understand my deep appreciation. Part of the introduction appeared in an earlier version as Mary A. Nicholas, "Building a Better Metaphor: Architecture and Russian Production Novels," *Mosaic, a journal for the interdisciplinary study of literature,* 35, 4 (December 2002): 51–68. It is reprinted with permission. Part of chapter 3 first appeared in Mary A. Nicholas and Cynthia A. Ruder, "In Search of the Collective Author: Fact and Fiction from the Soviet 1930s," *Book History,* 11 (2008): 221–44. It is also reprinted with permission. Dr. Jonathan Rose and anonymous readers at *Book History* have my genuine thanks as do the staff and anonymous readers at *Mosaic* and Bucknell University Press. Thank you as well to AUP Managing Editor Christine Retz and Dr. Mary Cicora for their good cheer and careful attention. I thank the staffs of the Slavonic Division of the New York Public Library, Butler Library at Columbia University, including the Manuscript Division, the Slavic and East European Reference Service at the University of Illinois, and the archivists at the Hoover Institution Archives, the Russian State Archive for Literature and Art (RGALI), and the State Archive of the Russian Federation (GARF). Their assistance has been invaluable over the years. Naturally, all mistakes are my own. The friendship of Dr. Jean Soderlund helped me bear the burden of chairship while trying to finish this book, as did the kindness of Dr. Oles Smolansky. Support from both Dean Jim Gunton and Dean Anne Meltzer was essential, and I thank them and the Office of Research at Lehigh University for support. I could not have survived without Pat Ward and the excellent interlibrary loan staff at the university. Help and friendship from Stephanie Merkel, Galina Pasteur, and especially Maia Kvartskhava and Sarah Kadarabeck were a blessing, as was the enduring support of Marietta Efimovna Bagrash. My students too have been a genuine inspiration over the years.

I have been incredibly lucky to have the support and friendship of Yuri Albert, Dzhamal Dzhansugurova, Alyona Kirtsova, Bonnie Phipps, Igor Sopronenko, Nadia Stolpovskaia, Aleksei Vasich, Aleksandr Yulikov, and Vadim Zakharov. I treasure every moment I have been able to spend with them, with my *rodstvenniki* Cappie and Tgor, and with the "S" Club. My colleague from the University of Kentucky, Cynthia Ruder has provided a judicious sounding board and endless advice, counsel, and laughter over the course of our long friendship. I have been truly blessed.

Finally I wish to thank my family for their love and support. Antanas Kazio Skersis and the late Maria Vladimirovna Skersis took me into their home and their hearts, and I am grateful. Thanks as well to the late Anna Turchina, Evdokia Vinogradova, Natalia Skersis, Evgeny Krichun, Vladimir Novikov, and Vitaly Smyslov for countless kindnesses. Tom and Katya Nicholas, Richard Nicholas and Patricia Pearce, Laurie and Rick Bethke, and Joe and Joanie Nicholas are mysterious parts of this work as well. Thank you especially, Uncle Mot, little Dickie Bird, Litius, and Ergun! My parents Tom Nicholas and Betty Ann Craggs Nicholas have been enduring models of decency, grace, magnanimity, and courage. It is to them and to my brilliant husband Victor and my handsome and brave sons Peter, Ian, and Paul that I dedicate this book.

A Note on Transliteration

I HAVE USED THE LIBRARY OF CONGRESS SYSTEM OF TRANSLITERA-
tion throughout, except with names that already have another
standard English form. I have also omitted the soft sign in names
in the text, while retaining it in bibliographical references for the
specialist.

Writers at Work

Introduction

Every age has its grand questions, problems that engage the entire community as society marshals its forces to solve particular mysteries that present themselves to each successive generation. Each era spends its intellectual resources differently; some husbanding precious assets with care while others spend profligately as though only excess and extravagant sacrifice will secure the solutions upon which future generations seem to depend. The way the age understands its essential challenges affects how scientists focus their research, politicians rally their supporters, and artists depict their subjects. Such grand questions influence the very stories that writers are able to imagine, sometimes becoming, for authors in totalitarian regimes, a single master narrative that shapes individual contributions and bends them to a common theme.

This was certainly the case with the Soviet Union in the late 1920s and early 1930s. Intellectuals from this crucial transitional period still felt the potential for a better world was in their hands. The revolution seemed to have given them a chance to control not only their personal destinies, but the shape of their world as well, and their first impulse was to rebuild—in a literal sense—both the physical structures that surrounded them and the individuals that would live in them. Houses, churches, factories, and huts would be remade, not just to facilitate a new way of life but to create it. Buildings would no longer be mere shelter but workers' palaces that would promote and secure the revolutionary development of their communal inhabitants.

The notion of construction was the grand question for everyone in the Soviet Union during this transformative period, a metaphor for those who wanted to change the old system, those who mourned its passing, and those caught in the seeming polarity between "for" and "against." The fact that still unaligned "fellow travelers" turned to the symbolism of construction as often as "true believers" did should alert us to the false comfort of apparently

17

clear-cut dichotomies. The challenge of remaking Russian society commanded everyone's attention, and narratives about the question included a realization of the inevitable losses that accompany such thoroughgoing structural changes. That is true of even the most profoundly Soviet of all available genres, the production novel, or *proizvodstvennyi roman*. This complex and intriguing genre was crucial to the construction of Soviet culture, particularly in the transitional period at the end of the 1920s and the beginning of the 1930s, and it is my subject here.

I proceed in a discussion of this transformational period with a cautionary tale from a very different system in mind. Albert Speer, Hitler's chief architect from 1933 to 1945, was spared the death penalty in the trials that marked the end of World War II, and as a result, he had the luxury of writing about his contribution to the architecture of the totalitarian state he served. Speer's choice of ultimate legacy was unexpected, however. The design that he considered his best work evolved from plans for the elaborate staging of a Nazi rally in 1934. As Speer tells it, the project called for 130 antiaircraft search lights, directed upward into the night sky. In this monument to totalitarian might, the beams from the search lights created the effect of a vast outdoor room with "mighty pillars of infinitely high outer walls." Occasionally, a cloud passed through the light display, creating what Speer identified as "an element of surrealistic surprise" in this work of Nazi art. The resulting "cathedral of light," according to Speer, was his "most beautiful architectural concept" and "the only one which survived the passage of time."[1]

Speer's unexpected account of this early work of fascist spectacle raises fundamental questions about the nature of art in totalitarian systems in general. Nazi art and architecture, like that of other totalitarian regimes, was ostensibly based on notions of symmetry, monumental permanence, and social conservatism. Where do Speer's shimmering cathedral and surrealistic clouds belong in such a history? Yet there they are, effervescent reminders that all may not be as it seems. What appears static and fixed may be dynamic and ambivalent. Although the totalitarian project may appear to rest on the permanence of representative architecture, monumental sculpture, and the staid, official portrait, that foundation may actually be asymmetrical and unstable. Speer's almost whimsical pillars, made of nothing more substantial than light and air, remind us that practice often deviates from theory in significant ways. They serve as a useful corrective to long-held notions of the totalitarian aesthetic.[2]

Speer's memoirs are interesting in another respect too. His service to the totalitarian state suggests the still little understood process by which even thoughtful and cultured individuals can come to participate in distorted causes of monstrous proportions. Speer's architectural castles in the air were beautiful, and he focused on them and on a toy-like model of the great capitol that he would never build instead of considering his own complicity in the perverse reign of the Third Reich. His emphasis on the image of distant, fragile, and ephemeral beauty is shocking in light of the horrors of the Nazi regime, but it is noteworthy. The architect seems to offer his memory as evidence of the better artistic angels to which he failed to pay enough notice in his career.[3]

It is with this example in mind, then, that we enter the treacherous territory of Stalinist literary history. Speer's sparkling temple of light is an important reminder to proceed cautiously with the study of art in totalitarian systems. Habit, ideology, vanity, or fear may influence the conclusions that we ourselves draw, and we can approach the story of the construction of Soviet culture only with care. What seems solid may be ephemeral; what looks cast in stone may be no more than a trick with lights. Cultured, well educated, even well intentioned individuals may make willing compromises that later prove misguided, self-serving, or profoundly unethical. Artists may be laying the foundation for their own demise as they construct what seems to them a shared palace of dreams.

The Soviet production novel, which focuses on construction as a theme and relies on the metaphor of building to make its case, has rightfully been identified as the "most common literary form" of Socialist Realism and the "most common type of Stalinist novel *by far.*"[4] In a definition focused primarily on later examples of the genre, Rosalind Marsh argues that the production novel "deals with the social, managerial, and technological issues of industry currently of concern to the party."[5] But such stark definitions, particularly with their emphasis on the final outcome of the genre, have tended to obscure aspects of the development of the production novel, often telescoping elements from later works onto earlier transitional versions. The situation is complicated further by the fact that, as Katerina Clark notes, Socialist Realism was "not yet fully formulated at the time it was adopted as *the* method for Soviet literature."[6] Genre "requirements" for the production novel and for Socialist Realism itself developed haphazardly as a result, and early transitional works were often retrofitted to vaguely defined and continually evolving definitions of creative orthodoxy.

Writers from the transitional period from the late 1920s to the early 1930s found themselves particularly challenged by demands that they reorganize space without being able to commit to a permanent structure.

Like Speer's surrealistic pillars, early production novels provide powerful evidence of the complex and gradual development of an only seemingly monolithic totalitarian aesthetic. Particularly in its earliest incarnations, the genre of the production novel is more ambiguous, exploratory, and interesting than could be predicted from reading its later incarnations. The history of the earliest production novels suggests, in fact, the considerable extent to which the totalitarian aesthetic can deviate from critical expectations and later historical "certainties." Early production novels provide an important key to the tortuous process of constructing Soviet culture, a process that was both more personal and more organic than has been appreciated. Not merely a "genre from above," the production novel provided contemporary writers with essential creative space on which to build the new Soviet personae they themselves fervently desired. The construction site in early Soviet production novels served as the locus for often surprisingly candid discussions of their authors' ambivalence, disorientation, and doubt about this process of self-construction. Early production novels are, thus, essential documents in the history of the process of (re)building Soviet writers. They are compelling evidence of contemporary authors' evolving responses to the questions of how life was to be interpreted and lived in Stalin's Russia. A more nuanced approach to these transitional works is necessary to understand the problematic and paradoxical transformation of Russian letters into Soviet literature.

More than anything else, the history of the production novel is the tale of writers "at work." Far from their normal routine, engaged in activities unusual even in unpredictable postrevolutionary Russia, writers on the construction site were encouraged to pitch in on the most varied building projects, stirring concrete, laying foundations, measuring landscapes, building socialism. Like brothers and sisters of the pen everywhere, most Soviet authors were impractical people, intellectuals and dreamers more at home behind the desk than on the factory floor, but now they were called to bridge the gap between the intellectual realm and the physical. And they responded, some in fear, annoyance, or distress, others enthusiastically, in the sincere hope that their endeavors would be useful and found worthy. As Stephen Kotkin notes, "the notion of a factory-based community, of social and political life *organized* by and for the factory, was the cornerstone of Soviet mass society."[7] Most of all, then, writers in this transitional period were busy constructing a place in the new world for themselves.

The end of the 1920s and the beginning of the 1930s were tumultuous times for authors across the literary and political spectrum, and writers as diverse as Fedor Gladkov, Leonid Leonov, Andrei Belyi, and Ilia Erenburg were drawn to the production novel genre, which seemed to provide a platform for urgent discussions about the role of authorship and the meaning of history in the new world under construction. Some of this discussion was forced on the authors by hostile critics, impatient leaders, or insistent colleagues anxious for the appearance of "proletarian" themes in literature. Yet even those works that were produced as the result of official command excursions to construction sites approach the topic with vigor, intensity, and genuine concern. Early attempts at the genre, in particular, include authentic explorations of the place of the author in the new Soviet society. Most of these early novels reflect a heartfelt response to authorial and societal concerns that has been largely overlooked in studies of this period.

Many critics, both in Russia and outside its borders, have ignored or disdained the genre entirely. Even some of those who treat the topic at greater length, including Katerina Clark, Irina Gutkin, and others, often approach early examples of the genre primarily in light of its later development in the 1940s and 1950s.[8] In fact, the extension and inevitable evolution of the production novel in the decades that followed its first appearance have profoundly complicated appreciation of early examples of the genre. That is why I concentrate here on production novels from the years beginning in 1927, when Iurii Olesha's novel *Envy*, or *Zavist'*, first appeared, to 1936, when Andrei Platonov apparently finished work on *Happy Moscow*, or *Schastlivaia Moskva*. This period marks the high point of artistic interest in the motif of construction and represents a tantalizing view of how Soviet literature and Soviet culture itself might have developed, if not for the ossification of such models in the years that followed.

This brief transitional period at the end of the 1920s and the beginning of the 1930s spans parts of both the First and the Second Five-Year Plans, thus providing a new and more artistically appropriate angle from which to view the development of early Soviet literature. The artificial economic divisions of the five-year plans and the somewhat arbitrary timetable established by the "Cultural Revolution" are interesting in their own right but have less in common with the development of literature, either organic or arranged, than may be apparent.[9] A close look at a genre that emerged on the cusp of the 1920s and 1930s further undermines the notion that those two decades had little in common and provides access to the evolutionary processes that characterized the times. A generic approach to literary culture has the additional virtue of focusing directly on the work of the diverse authors who experimented with the production novel. My study of the production genre highlights both authors favored by fortune in these years and writers cast aside as unneeded, inappropriate, or hostile. The genre that attracted such a diverse array of authors is a useful tool for appraising the process of building Soviet culture.

In his classic work *The Production of Space,* Henri Lefebvre notes that ideology is primarily a "discourse upon social space." Nowhere is that more true than in the twentieth-century Soviet Union, where the ideology of space and its production served as the foundational myth for generations. No one in the Soviet Union needed to ask the naïve question "is space political?"[10] The very idea of construction was a Soviet call to arms, a metaphor of place that was understood literally. Utopian plans for the construction of a better universe were organized spatially: building a new society meant erecting new edifices in which new human beings would work and dwell. Often, the structure itself was expected to have a salutary effect on the populace. Soviet dwellings and, even more significantly, the process of constructing them would succeed in remaking individuals into that most heroic of all creatures, the "new Soviet man."[11] In the Soviet Union of the 1920s and 1930s, more than any other period, the metaphor of construction played a foremost literary role. "Literature," insisted Aleksei Tolstoy, "is one of the cornerstones of our new home."[12]

Architectural metaphors filled the literature of this period—from mundane, nostalgic, or smug reminders of the life that had been destroyed by the revolution to ambitious plans for towering new Soviet monuments and dreams of a built environment that would change mankind for good. Building was the central creative concern of the era, as Russian poets and prose writers alike sought both to catalog the destruction of the old way of life and to craft a new and more just universe in their writings. As historian Jeffrey Brooks has noted, this metaphor of construction was important from the very beginning of the postrevolutionary period, but gained particular significance in the Russian press and artistic prose beginning in 1927.[13]

Tension and ambiguity marked use of the metaphor since it was related to a redefinition of space that had touched people's lives in direct, often traumatic ways. Theories about the appropriate use of space became burning questions of practice after the revolution, as hundreds of thousands emigrated beyond the new Soviet borders, many more relocated to expropriated housing, and countless buildings were adapted to new uses or abandoned to the elements. According to Milka Bliznakov, for example, over five hundred thousand workers and their families were resettled in this way between 1918 and 1924 in Moscow alone.[14] Constrained resources kept new building projects largely on paper for most of the 1920s, but reduced opportunities for building in the real world only heightened the rhetoric of construction. Discourse about building came to seem as significant as actual construction itself, until writing about the process of building became an end in itself, supplanting the signified with the newly important signifier.

The production novel attracted particular interest during this transitional period for its apparent power to edify. Writers and critics of all political stripes were joined by the hope that projects brought to fruition on paper would have a salutary effect on the reading public as compelling as the one to be achieved by the completion of actual structures. A belief popular from antiquity helped cement that notion: writers and builders alike were thought to bring harmony to the world with their architectural projects. Genuine conviction in the possibilities for writing collective history— what Evgeny Dobrenko has called the "utopia of collective creative work"—coexisted alongside a desire to control that shared narrative. Writer and dean of Soviet letters Maxim Gorky described the "almost geological revolution" he thought he saw taking place. Writing to Stalin in January 1930, he invokes the millions of people who "need to be re-educated in the shortest possible time," admitting that it is the "most insane task" (*bezumneishaia zadacha*). And yet, Gorky argues, "it is practically solved."[15]

Gorky's secret weapon was the collective. Since the early days of the revolution, critics had hounded writers for works impressive enough for their "heroic" times. This perceived crisis of genre left the literary establishment groping for a connection to workers, whom they hoped to reach through organized writers' brigades to narrate collective labor projects. Authors who participated would produce topical works widely accessible to Gorky's untutored public, revolutionizing both Soviet literature and society. A result of this generally held conviction was Maxim Gorky's officially sanctioned initiative for a "history of factories and foundries" in September 1931. A publishing house of the same name was soon founded to produce the books the workers needed.[16] The journal

The USSR under Construction (*SSSR na stroike*) was created as part of the same campaign to document and publicize all manner of Soviet building projects.

Gorky's venture reflected a new national fascination with "building socialism." His series was to chronicle the creation of a new society, which would remake human beings into Soviet citizens. As Gorky often argued, a new country demanded a new literature and an "encyclopedia of our construction in motion."[17] His reliance on a dynamic, perpetually evolving model is telling: such dynamism would become essential to later definitions of Socialist Realism. In a compression of present and future that was typical of the time, Gorky's project called for literature that reflected the world as it would be rather than as it actually was.[18] Well-known authors were to contribute their professional expertise to the endeavor, cooperating with laborers specially identified for the joint project. The benefits were intended to be mutual: established writers would impart essential trade secrets to their worker counterparts while they gained valuable insights into the working class, the significance of construction, the process of "reforging," or *perekovka*,[19] and the essence of Soviet power. The often maudlin Gorky thought the result would be a nation of heroic storytellers; a less sentimental Stalin predicted that writers would swarm to the project.[20]

With the advent of plans for industrialization, the process of physically creating a new world intensified, and the use of architectural metaphors grew with it. Although Russia was still reeling from the long-term effects of the revolution and the civil war, the country was embarking on new construction, and the populace became focused on building. The production novel seemed ideal to describe and direct the process of constructing a new Soviet citizenry. Writers were urged to visit the new building sites and write about their experiences, and a large and varied literature resulted. Boris Pilniak's *The Volga Falls to the Caspian Sea* (*Volga vpadaet v Kaspiiskoe more*) (1929), Marietta Shaginian's *Hydrocentral* (*Gidrotsentral'*) (1931), and Valentin Kataev's *Time, Forward!* (*Vremia, vpered!*) (1932) are well-known, though frequently neglected, examples of the genre. These novels and other works not usually associated with the production novel—*Envy* (1927), for example, by Iurii Olesha, *Chevengur* (1928/1988), *Foundation Pit* (*Kotlovan*) (1930/1987), and *Happy Moscow* (1933-36/1991) by Andrei Platonov, and both *Twelve Chairs* (*Dvenadtsat' stul'ev*) (1928) and *The Golden Calf* (*Zolotoi telenok*) (1931) by Ilia Ilf and Evgenii Petrov—suggest the complexity of both the phenomenon and the period.

Until recently, a binary theoretical framework characterized re-action to this literature and to the Soviet era in general.[21] In an ap-proach that may seem simplistic now, the 1920s and 1930s were established as diametric opposites, with the 1920s seen as a time of freewheeling artistic experimentation and the 1930s cast as the age of conformity and repression. Under this schematic dichotomy, 1929 became a nearly impenetrable boundary, as even literary crit-ics seemed to adopt Stalin's "Year of the Great Break" (*god vel-ikogo pereloma*) as a division between supposedly innovative lit-erature from the 1920s, deemed worthy of critical attention, and re-puted hackwork of the 1930s that represented art of only political or historical interest. Under such a scheme, the literature and gen-res of the 1930s, written by artists under gradually increasing duress, could be discounted as inherently uninteresting and pro-foundly inauthentic. As Hans Ulrich Gumbrecht has pointed out, however, such clear distinctions are often merely theoretical con-structs to "give people the impression that they inhabit a homoge-neous world space." Such inflexible dichotomies make for "stable relations" and a "homogeneous world space," but come with a price in historical accuracy.[22]

The binary approach is convenient shorthand, of course, but it may occasionally tell us more about our own times than about the past we wish to study. That is the point Tony Pinkney makes when he cautions readers to avoid applying dichotomies that seem obvi-ous in our time but may not hold for earlier periods. As Pinkney cogently observes, "whereas today revolution and the commodity, political activism and technological novelty, responsibility and 'post-modernist' hedonism are a rigid binary opposition we can hardly think our way out of, for the early-twentieth-century me-tropolis they fruitfully interbreed: mass-production is 'democratic,' technology sweeps away vestigial feudal survivals, and socialism will liberate a dynamism that capitalism fetters."[23] Pinkney's point is well taken, particularly when we approach such a complex period as early Stalinism, in which "obvious" values may be quite differ-ent from those considered normative in our own time. A closer look at the Stalinist era, particularly at the transitional period between the 1920s and 1930s, and at the production novel, the favored genre of that period, makes it clear that binary oppositions are in-adequate to describe the construction of this culture.[24]

In Soviet cultural history, Vladimir Papernyi's compelling archi-tectural study, *Kul'tura Dva*, is the most consistently argued application of the binary model.[25] Papernyi describes an open, dy-namic, utopian, and horizontal "Culture One" of the 1920s opposing a static, closed, hierarchical "Culture Two" that, according to him, reigned from the 1930s to the 1950s. Others have implicitly challenged a rigorously binary approach, particularly in recent years, but the model is still influential. Although Papernyi himself suggests that the early 1930s were actually a transitional period and notes that the "two cultures clashed in the most obvious and dramatic way between 1930 and 1932," the conceptual neatness of an approach that divides the 1920s from the 1930s has continued to make a rigid binary framework attractive.[26] The oppositions involved are easily recognizable—dynamism vs. stability, innovation vs. conservatism, chaos vs. order, and so on—and the polarities can be reversed or renamed at will, depending on the orientation of the critic.[27] As a result, the transitional period and the hybrid production novels that complicate easy conclusions about the construction of Soviet culture have been slighted.

A less dichotomized approach is more difficult to apply, perhaps, but it is necessary if we are to understand the range of responses to the process of constructing Stalinist culture. As Tzvetan Todorov argues in his nuanced study of morality in the concentration camp, an approach of "Us vs. Them" succeeds in "taking only the two extremes of what is really a continuum."[28] Work by Stephen Kotkin and others has made it clear that the need to reevaluate easy dichotomies is particularly acute in dealing with totalitarian regimes. This is especially the case when approaching highly significant, but often overlooked transitional periods in which both societal values and the bases of power are changing. Steve Pile's aphorism is apropos: "there is never one geography of authority and there is never one geography of resistance." There are, instead, many modes of both accommodation and acquiescence, and "the map of resistance is not simply the underside of the map of domination."[29] A study of the production novel, then, will allow us to trace some of the paths that run through these many landscapes, leading authors to willing compliance and unexpected resistance with nearly equal frequency.

Certain aspects of Russian political and cultural life in this period may seem to fall into a neat binary scheme, but other phenomena resist that categorization, and we must ask, as Svetlana Boym does in another context, whether binary theories "*describe* Russian culture or *perpetuate* its cultural mythology."[30] In fact, one of the surprises of the post-Soviet period, as archives are opened and previously forbidden manuscripts returned, has been the extent to which certain familiar dichotomies lose their utility. Sarah Davies's study of popular opinion and opposition in this period, for example, suggests that obvious binary pairs such as "us vs. them" were more capacious and fluid than imagined in the Soviet Union. Writing in this very transitional period, Andrei Platonov even argued that such dichotomies were actually a holdover from the past, when "we divided people into enemies and comrades according to metrics and all sorts of methods."[31] Closer study of the construction metaphor in Soviet production novels, then, reveals both our own reliance on familiar organizing principles and the complexity of the history of this period.

When Russian writers used architectural metaphors during this period, they had more in mind than the science of building. Architecture was an instrument of social justice, and larger questions beckoned. What constituted the new world under construction? Were old cities acceptable, asked an article in 1931, or "must new cities be built in a completely new way?"[32] Could old buildings be preserved, or was the material culture from the past a hostile environment for the new Soviet man? If old spaces could be reconfigured, perhaps old selves, too, could be reconstructed, as questions of self-worth and identity became entangled with evolving notions of Soviet space. Should traditional dichotomies—public and private, outside and inside, spaciousness and confinement, and so on—be reversed, retained, or rejected? These questions and others like them provided rich philosophical underpinning and a certain political imprimatur for writers of the era. Part of the difficulty they faced, however, was the challenge of shaping a landscape in which they themselves had lost their way.

The material culture of a society always reveals something about the values of the individuals and groups that make up the fabric of that society. This is perhaps particularly true of totalitarian societies, even those in their infancy. As Boris Groys has argued, in such a society "the creation of any image, the erection of any building, the composition of any literary text could never be a neutral aesthetic act."[33] This is especially the case in Russia and the Soviet Union where questions about the moral significance of the way people lived and the items with which they surrounded themselves received special attention both before and after the revolution. As Stephen Hutchings has pointed out, the issue of quotidian existence, or *byt*, had special resonance for members of the Russian intelligentsia, especially Russian writers, throughout the early part of the twentieth century in particular.[34] Part of the debate about *byt* undoubtedly stemmed from a desire to overcome the perceived dichotomy between the world of things and the world of ideas. Those writers who felt this dichotomy most keenly were anxious to resolve the conflict, although their attempts to do so were often them-selves one-sided and unsatisfactory. Symbolist attempts to dwell in the realm of the spirits and Futurist rejection of the prosaic world were two of the most prominent responses to this dilemma, still of common concern in the late 1920s.

After the revolution, hopes for a speedy resolution to the prob-lem grew as the struggle for a new material culture and the subse-quent emergence of a new Soviet man seemed about to become a reality. Calls for change in the fabric of everyday life in Soviet Rus-sia led writers to scrutinize their surroundings in an unprecedented way, questioning familiar settings and developing enthusiasms for unfamiliar terrain. The new context, which these writers were to help imagine, valorized certain everyday objects while rejecting other, equally common items. In all their work, the focus was on overcoming a perceived gap between reality and desire as writers struggled to make sense of the new world they were building.

One of the most puzzling questions that faced engineers of the new *byt* was what to do with the old world while the new one was being constructed. Most of the housing stock, public infrastruc-ture, available furniture, and even the decorative details of every-day life had been inherited from the old regime and thus seemed unsuited for attempts to remake the populace. This created an ob-vious problem for those who advocated the brave new world, and it was not at all clear how to solve the dilemma. Old selves, too, were a problem, as writers struggled to resolve contradictions in their own personalities. Early production novels provide ample ev-idence of the difficulties authors had understanding their own be-havior and negotiating the increasing and contradictory demands society placed on them. One of the most interesting aspects of the early production novels, then, is their continual refusal to offer the pat answers to such dilemmas that are usually associated with lit-erature written to order.

Tormented questions about the reuse of "bourgeois" space or the suitability of now outdated selves continued to trouble writers throughout this transitional period. Victor Buchli, who identifies this era as "the height of *byt* activism," has argued that a funda-mental aspect of Stalinism was its retreat from certain attempts to rationalize the domestic realm by manipulating the items of every-day life, including those left from earlier eras. According to Buchli, Stalinism in this period offered permission for "spontaneous and differential performances of socialism in the domestic sphere." Thus, the perception of prerevolutionary material culture "shifted away from a denotative Marxian understanding" to a more contextualized notion in which items deemed "petit-bourgeois" might nevertheless be usefully redeployed in an appropriately Socialist way. The point is a valid one, and it points once again to the problem of a polarized approach to the 1920s and 1930s. Even Buchli agrees that attitudes about which items of everyday culture were socialist and which petit-bourgeois were often "formed by literary social satire emerging before and after the Revolution."[35] As a result, we should expect to see gradual evolution in the treatment of these values over the transitional period, particularly in production novels written "to order." Critical approaches to the production novel genre, however, have downplayed the evolution of taste and contextualized meaning, particularly at the end of the 1920s and the beginning of the 1930s. This fact, again, indicates the need for a reevaluation of the transitional period.

In her path-breaking work on the Soviet novel, Katerina Clark argues that novels "about how the plan was fulfilled or the project was constructed" are "the most highly ritualized" of all Soviet novels, and she includes a schematic description of the plot of a "typical production novel," in this case, Fedor Gladkov's *Cement*. According to Clark, it is with Gladkov's novel that the production genre "more or less originated." Clark's argument relies on her elaboration of the "master plot" of Soviet fiction, a concept she develops at length. Her detailed account of Stalinist literature as formulaic fiction is compelling for a good deal of what was written during the Soviet period, but, perhaps surprisingly, it is not particularly apt as a description of some of the best-known production novels. Shaginian's *Hydrocentral* and Kataev's *Time Forward!*, for example, fail in serious measure to conform to the description Clark provides, and, as Clark herself notes, even Gladkov's *Cement* deviates from the "master plot" in many respects. Clark explains this as a result of the fact that *Cement*, published in 1925, was an early production novel with a plot less "tightly organized" than the "later, full-blown Socialist Realist novel."[36] This suggests that the master narrative is neither entirely predictable nor painfully inevitable from its beginnings. Katerina Clark was one of the first critics to view the production novel as something other than a "disastrous culmination" of Soviet literary politics. How ironic, then, that overly liberal application of the "master plot" to works for which it is poorly suited has had the unintended effect of marking them as purely formulaic and thus unworthy of serious attention.

The situation becomes even less clear when other production novels from the time are included in the survey. Pilniak's *The Volga Falls to the Caspian Sea*, for example, was ostensibly written to curry political favor after its author was targeted in a campaign of harassment in late 1929. The novel might therefore be expected to conform closely to perceived demands for this newly developing Soviet genre, particularly when Pilniak's production novel involved a reworking of *Mahogany* (*Krasnoe derevo*), his officially condemned novella from earlier the same year. Yet *The Volga Falls to the Caspian Sea* presents such an unusual narrative that we are left to wonder in what possible respect the new novel was found to conform to even vague generic standards. Such examples provide graphic proof of the early fluidity of Soviet literature and demonstrate how far from monolithic Soviet culture was in this period.

The astonishing diversity of such early production novels makes it difficult to paint them, as Oleg Kharkhordin nevertheless seems to do, with a broad brush. Identifying a narrative of conversion that "was repeated in *every* Socialist Realist novel," Kharkhordin can proceed to sweeping generalizations that ostensibly characterize all Soviet literature.[37] Yet such wide generalization glosses over contradictions in individual works and significant developments in the early history of what would become the most Soviet of all Socialist Realist genres. Such an approach impoverishes the cultural history of the early Soviet period in particular. Arguments that suggest that the "texts that make up the corpus of Socialist Realism seem to have been written by a single hand" or that treat them "as though they came off a conveyer belt" are simply inadequate.[38] The fact that Pilniak, even in a fight for his creative life, provides only highly contradictory evidence of Soviet successes, indicates how amorphous the criteria for Soviet novels were in this transitional period. Still less do unorthodox works such as Olesha's *Envy*, Platonov's *Chevengur, Foundation Pit*, and *Happy Moscow*, and Ilf and Petrov's *Twelve Chairs* and *The Golden Calf* satisfy early expectations or later generic requirements for the production novel or Socialist Realism. Yet, as we will see, all these novels participated in a significant way in contemporary attempts to create the production novel genre, which was itself an important stage on the road to defining Socialist Realism and constructing Soviet culture.

Part of the problem lies in the fact that the periodization of Soviet literature, like that of Soviet architecture, was oversimplified and polarized for too long. Another well-known commentator on Russian literature of this period, Irina Gutkin speaks directly to this issue in her study of Socialist Realism. Gutkin follows Clark in identifying the production novel as Socialist Realism's "most common literary form," although she refrains from engaging the genre at length. Nevertheless, her historical discussion of the cultural development of Socialist Realism leads her to conclude that the act of "merging social and aesthetic engineering" was a significant aspect of avant-garde theory already in the early 1920s, and she casts doubt on efforts to draw clear boundaries between the two decades.[39] Gutkin's mild skepticism is particularly welcome in a study of Socialist Realism since it makes clear that the creative activity of one decade is profoundly connected to that of the next. Regine Robin makes a similar point in her study of Socialist Realism, pointing, for example, to the "cacophony" that characterized the first Writers' Congress in 1934, a fact she attributes to the existence of "theoretical, aesthetic, and even political" debates that far predated the congress itself.[40]

The idea that the 1920s and 1930s were diametrically opposed is inherently problematic, of course, as Boris Groys, in his study *The Total Art of Stalinism,* has demonstrated for the visual arts.[41] There is little reason to expect that writers in the 1920s were fundamentally different authors by the beginning of the 1930s. Many had accepted, even welcomed government intervention in literature in the 1920s, and, for a variety of reasons, including official intimidation, they continued to do so in the 1930s. The Central Committee announcement of April 23, 1932, that did away with the hegemony of the Russian Association of Proletarian Writers (RAPP) in literature, for example, although later seen as more unwanted governmental intrusion into literary affairs, was initially viewed positively by many authors. Nor should their later fates disguise the fact that many writers, including many fellow travelers, or *poputchiki,* were supporters of the cause, if occasionally ambivalent, doubtful, or inconsistent ones. This is Iu. K. Shcheglov's point in his comment that no matter how skeptically writers might view the details of life around them, "it never occurred to them to question their evaluation of the revolution or to doubt the idea of a radiant future."[42] Authors' willing desire to participate in literary life, even when that participation was only conditional (*po stol'ku po skol'ku*), and the writers' sometimes naïve or overly optimistic expectations for the new literature should prompt us to alter our understanding of the early 1930s in particular.

Blandishments and coercion—the Russian gingerbread and whip—played an obvious role in securing intellectual support for the government, particularly in the bloody second half of the 1930s when the ranks of Soviet authors were decimated. Writers had known at least since poet Nikolai Gumilev's arrest and execution in 1921 that opposition to the reigning political power could be broadly defined and potentially fatal. Even loyal authors were con-

stantly reminded of their precarious positions by criticism in the
mass media and at public events. Continual political harassment,
arrests, and open and veiled private threats made writers aware
that they and their families, neighbors, and colleagues might be in
mortal danger.

Rewards, too, worked well to keep writers trying to stay in line.
They included steady employment and favored status, special housing, overseas travel, and economic remuneration. A confidential
report to the NKVD secret police in 1934, for example, describes
writers' activities after the Writers' Union congress in August of
that year; according to the anonymous informant, writers hurried
off after the meeting to "arrange their personal lives: buying cars,
building summer homes, . . . traveling for business or going on va-
cation, and so on." In a country still cautiously emerging from war,
revolution, famine, and economic collapse, the blandishments detailed in such an account speak of astonishing relative riches. Other
archival materials that have come to light since 1991 underline how
generous authors' remuneration often was in this period. Jealous
complaints from 1933 emerged over writers being paid "significantly more" than the "official minimum" of two hundred rubles
per page. The list of such well compensated authors included
Leonov, Gladkov, Pilniak, Mikhail Sholokhov, Bruno Iasenskii, and
others. In 1936, a report to the Party grumbled that most residents
at the exclusive Peredelkino writers' colony were neglecting to pay
even the minimum rental amount, while other authors lived with
their families for months at Soviet rest homes at public expense.[43]

But not all artistic cooperation was forced or bought. If Soviet
critics were often eager to suppress writers' deviations from an
imagined and continuingly evolving orthodox history, then western
critics have on occasion been equally quick to underplay enthusiastic contributions that favorite authors made to the foundational
narrative. We have tended to overlook excursions into "official literature" or to excuse them as the result of weakness under duress.
There is no doubt that Russian writers were under increasing pressure to conform to a still developing norm. The pressure brought
to bear was often diabolically clever, at other times crudely vicious,
and any one author might be subjected to a variety of tactics to encourage conformity. It is equally clear, however, that many of the
same writers played an independent, sometimes voluntary, if not
completely understood role in the development of that norm. To argue otherwise is to assert that the writers whose work we treasure
from the 1920s had become either tragic victims or compromised
prostitutes by the 1930s.[44] That is an untenable assumption.

Writers as diverse as Shaginian and Platonov rightly believed that their work was a legitimate contribution to the development of Soviet culture, and it is important that we pay attention to all the voices in the long conversation of Russian literature from the Soviet period. The construction site served as the quintessential literary topos from this era, a "common/place" around which a host of profoundly different authors could gather. Construction was the Soviet "magnet," to use Pilniak's term, that even authors troubled by their complicated times used to organize chaotic reality into a coherent narrative. "The contemporary author," Fedor Gladkov told his colleagues in 1931, "needs to build his work, his everyday life subjected to absolutely new methods of work in construction of our economy."[45] To understand the breadth and complexity of that story, we need both to reinvestigate established representatives of the genre and to recontextualize neglected writers whose works elaborate and enrich the history of the Soviet production novel. This is particularly true for writers who were excluded from public discourse in their own time. Writers out of favor for any number of reasons would have been among the most likely to look for common ground on the construction site.[46] It is often on the margins of a general trend that we can see its mechanisms most clearly.

We need to consider as well a more subtle periodization of these difficult times, one that better indicates the gradual though occasionally fitful evolution of ideas from the mid-1920s to the mid-1930s. The production novel, which emerged in the mid-1920s, developed considerably over the early 1930s, and continued into the postwar period, provides an ideal genre for investigating the evolution of Russian writers of all ideological stripes. A better understanding of the emergence and development of the production novel—from an aesthetic, political, and social point of view—is essential if we are to understand how Soviet culture was theorized and built by its practitioners.

It had been a dream from the first days of Soviet power both to give workers a voice and to involve the intelligentsia in production, and writers and literary politicians alike hoped the production novel would finally bring about that longed-for union of brains and brawn. Alienation of the worker from labor and of the writer from the worker was supposed to become a thing of the past as a result of this new genre. Building a new world, then, was tied literally to the process of constructing a new self. The result is that these broadly drawn and socially oriented production novels end by touching on the most delicate questions of identity and self-worth. A closer look at this long neglected genre demonstrates that production novels provide often unexpected answers to such dilemmas.

Chapter 1 of this study addresses the question of self-worth directly in its discussion of the construction of *Envy* by Iurii Olesha, a work usually excluded from critical discussions of the production novel. Its early publication date of 1927 and its quirky narrator make *Envy* an unusual candidate for the official Soviet canon. Yet Olesha's focus on the construction site and his use of the metaphor of building to describe the act of writing and self-affirmation make this an important contribution to the production genre. The novel, despite its difficult, fragmented narrative, dreamlike plot, and alienated hero, was one of the first to treat the construction theme in a substantial way. The importance of this novel to the development of the production genre is further highlighted by Olesha's remarkable speech to the first Congress of the Union of Soviet Writers six years after the appearance of *Envy*. His unexpected return to the theme of building in his speech and the unscripted response that his presentation evoked in other delegates provide fascinating insight into the construction of both Soviet culture and the intelligentsia who created it. Olesha's contribution demonstrates the unexpected and circuitous path that eventually led to Socialist Realism.

Chapter 2 focuses on the process of self-construction in Marietta Shaginian's long neglected production novel, *Hydrocentral*. This fictionalized account of the writer's extended stay at a construction site in Armenia in the mid-1920s describes Shaginian's diligent attempts at remaking herself as well. The work, one of the few of the era by a female author, provides another useful corrective to notions of the Soviet production novel as predictable and staid. Shaginian's experimentation with genre and narrative makes this forgotten classic an argument against the formulaic nature of the production novel, particularly with its emphasis on overcoming the seemingly unbridgeable dichotomies that had troubled Russian thinkers for generations. In Shaginian's work, traditional binary structures—East and West, man and woman, intelligentsia and the people—are tested and often overcome. A colorful, gender-ambivalent hero manages to blend contradictory characteristics while remaining true to essential features of both sides of the dichotomy. Shaginian's theoretical discussion of the genre and her attempts—revealed in recent archival discoveries—to position *Hydrocentral* as an exemplary representative of the production novel expand our understanding of the tangled roots of

Socialist Realism and Stalinist totalitarian art. Her pained discovery of the limits of authorial autonomy in Stalin's Russia rounds out the discussion.

Chapter 3 looks at the role of mapping and material culture in building the Soviet self in its investigation of comic works by Soviet writers Ilia Ilf and Evgenii Petrov. Although *Twelve Chairs* and *The Golden Calf* may initially seem unlikely candidates for a study of the production novel, they too belong to a discussion of the early history of the genre. The authors' studied inclusion of production-novel building blocks—accounts of the construction of a tramline, a visit to the Museum of Furniture, utopian plans for the USSR of the future, and the official completion of the Turkistan Siberian railroad—suggests that both works are important early investigations of themes that would be essential to the genre in later years. Like so many other creations from the period, these two novels reflect the dramatic changes in the culture of everyday life that accompanied the transitional period at the end of the 1920s and the beginning of the 1930s. In fact, much of their humor issues from the disparity between what was attempted and what was actually achieved by campaigns to restructure material culture in this period of Stalinist Russia. In this interpretation, the hero of the novels, Ostap Bender, emerges as a skewed representative of the "new Soviet man," whose wanderings through unfamiliar Soviet space provide both comic relief and guidance to readers struggling to maneuver the changing terrain themselves.

Bender's talent for orienting himself in the new Soviet landscape is particularly impressive in the amorphous space in which production novels transpire, a world of unclear and shifting boundaries. Conflicting maps competed during this period to describe the same space, and the construction of the new world often involved "laying claim" to a location from more than one perspective. This over-mapping—and the confusion that it engenders—is one of the primary sources of humor in these two production novels. Ilf and Petrov's fictional handling of real-life construction dilemmas provides a useful corrective to our view of the genre as overdetermined. Present-day attempts to recreate Ilf and Petrov's famed city "Novye Vasiuki" in contemporary Kalmykia make it clear that the model of the production novel continues to have relevance in our own time.

Soviet literary (re)construction is the subject of chapter 4. The work of author Boris Pilniak provides the ideal test case to investigate the process of (re)building the production novel genre on the cusp of the 1920s and 1930s. Pilniak's attempt to write a production novel by reworking an unacceptable earlier novella into an ostensibly conformist work demonstrates the pitfalls and short-comings of requests for literature to order. The raw material Pilniak used from the 1929 work *Mahogany* changed relatively little as the author crafted *The Volga Falls to the Caspian Sea* from 1930, and this successful reworking of early material into an apparently acceptable production novel suggests the limitations in a strict definition of the genre. Pilniak's experience with *The Volga Falls to the Caspian Sea* demonstrates the erratic and unexpected path Soviet writers took on their way to defining what would become Socialist Realism. Pilniak's continued understanding of Russian literature as a collective endeavor, despite his increasingly precarious status in the field, further enriches our picture of the late 1920s and early 1930s. Pilniak was in official disfavor for much of the 1930s, but his status as literary persona non grata did not prevent him from participating in a much publicized delegation to construction sites on the Belomor canal and in the collective works associated with another famous Soviet construction project, the Moscow subway. The contribution of such "disgraced" authors as Pilniak, Andrei Belyi, Isaac Babel, and others on official works of the regime casts the complexities of the ongoing process of Soviet cultural construction into high relief.

The question of space and its evolving importance in the construction of Soviet reality is the subject of chapter 5. Kataev's classic novel *Time, Forward!* may be the best known of all Soviet production novels, and it demonstrates, perhaps better than any other, the curious method these novels have of focusing on a future perceived as more real than the present. Yet even Kataev's generally straightforward representative of the production genre may confound our expectations with its reorganization of newly Soviet space and simultaneous rejection of clear binary oppositions. Familiar dichotomies of East/West, city/province, teacher/student, and so on are exuberantly abandoned in Kataev's novel, and his handling of the themes of destruction and reconstruction is complex and nuanced. The author's focus on the importance of reconceptualized space in rebuilding both self and construction site enriches our understanding of even the officially sanctioned production novel. Semiautobiographical writings from the end of Kataev's career also cast new light on the difficult and often morally compromised role that orthodox writers played in the development of Socialist Realism and the production novel. In addition to his work as author, Kataev fulfilled the pedagogical role that estab-

lished writers were to play in helping train the working class during this transitional period. The proletariat's entrance into literature was seen as a crucial step in the development of both Soviet
art and a new way of life, and Kataev participated by training
worker-writers, including laborers from the Moscow subway project. His performance with subway builders, documented in archival
materials, gives us fresh insight into the complexities of workers'
participation in the development of the production novel.

Deconstruction of the genre is the unlikely subject of chapter 6.
Some readers will be surprised to find Andrei Platonov featured
prominently in this chapter since his name rarely appears in the list
of producers of this particularly Soviet genre. As a clear-sighted observer of Stalinist totalitarianism and as its victim, Platonov is often left off the list of official Soviet writers. Yet Platonov's works,
including *Chevengur, Foundation Pit*, and *Happy Moscow*, should
be studied as part of the organic development of the production
novel and Socialist Realism in general. To deny Platonov inclusion
in that context is to repeat the actions of literary functionaries contemporary to the author, who labeled him an enemy of the cause
and barred him from publication for much of his creative life. As
an engineer who became a writer, Platonov understood better than
anyone the importance of the construction site in building the new
Soviet man. His neglected contribution to the production novel
and to Socialist Realism needs to be reincorporated into the history
of Soviet literature. The novel *Happy Moscow* is of particular interest in this context since it describes, among many other topics,
the participation of women in the construction of the Moscow
metro. Platonov's artistic treatment of the subway construction
makes a fascinating counterpoint to archival materials from the actual building project.

In her study of myths of the Soviet landscape, Emma Widdis argues that the drive to establish a "single, unified 'national' space"
was the "key Soviet project."[47] Dreams of an inviolate Soviet space
fascinated authors in the late 1920s and early 1930s, even many
who believed that redemptive promises for the territory were at
least partially illusory. Early production novels provided the perfect
place to construct such a Soviet space, bringing elaborate building
plans to fruition in text, if not in fact.[48] This is reflected in the
names of many such works, which seek to accomplish the task they
originally intended only to document: Erenburg's *Second Day* can
finish jobs that were left undone in real life; Gladkov's *Energy* supplies that precious quantity in abundance; and Leonov manages to
tame *The River Sot* just by naming his novel. Thus, the author's

desk turns out to be the real construction site, where writers in the process of becoming Soviet could provide essential blueprints to a better world. Far from being uninspired and formulaic, the early production novels were actually fertile ground on which writers struggled to understand the world that had collapsed, to imagine a better one, and to find a place in it. Most understood their own transitional role in the process, and these early production novels are filled, therefore, with surprisingly candid descriptions of failed projects: bridges that collapse, projects that languish, buildings that can shelter no one. Having accepted the notion that they too needed "reforging," authors knew they were dooming themselves and their literary works to obsolescence.[49] But they accepted that fact in the name of the better future for which they believed they were supplying the building blocks.

We know from hindsight that their imagined universe differed dramatically from the completed totalitarian project. By the end of the Soviet period, millions would have suffered, many sent to unfair, lonely, and painful deaths in the name of the very project these writers seemed to champion. By the time Stalin himself finally took his last breath, four of the authors featured in this study were already dead, the other three spared temporarily to wrestle with their own consciences as time moved on and a new Soviet society dealt with its own set of central problems.[50] The complicated fates of these individual writers should not obscure for us, however, the genuine interest and even enthusiastic support that they and many more authors like them had for such utopian building plans. The obvious issue of complicity is not the only one that arises. Equally important is the question of process.

Even now that many of the contemporary archives have shared their secrets, it remains unclear just how such individuals understood their roles in building the new world they hoped to create. Various scholars have criticized western approaches to this period for their implicit assumption of a "transhistorical subject with a universal response to external challenges of any sort."[51] As Anna Krylova points out in a seminal article on the topic, this "liberal subject" of western discourse is then made normative, as the "Stalinist subject" becomes the dichotomous "opposite of the liberal self."[52] A new approach to both the promise and the ultimate failure of these writers offers us the chance to avoid that methodological pitfall by making clear both what was unique to the Russian situation at the end of the 1920s and the beginning of the 1930s and what other periods, our own included, have in common with that time. One of the key questions underlying our inquiry, then, will be to explain, as architectural critic Selim Khan-Magomedov put it, not "how Stalin managed to impose his politics" but "what social conditions, what reasons brought people and the intelligentsia . . . to support him in the twenties and the thirties and even after the war."[53] The path to a master narrative for the production novel, if such finally exists, is long and circuitous, and we need to follow it carefully, if only to understand how to avoid repeating certain mistakes typical of intellectual endeavor in times of political upheaval and societal unrest. It is with cautious hope that we can better understand the grand questions of both our own and other generations that we begin this investigation of Soviet writers at work.

1

The Cost of Constructing *Envy:* Iurii Olesha and the Soviet Production Novel

ONE OF THE FIRST WORKS TO APPROACH THE SUBJECT OF CONstruction in Soviet literature, the novel *Envy* (*Zavist'*) by Iurii Olesha (1899–1960) is one of the most unusual treatments of the theme. That fact—and the failure of the novel to conform to later expectations for the genre—has meant that it is rarely included in discussions of the production novel, even though various observers have noted the importance of construction to this interesting work of art. Its fragmented narrative and dreamlike plot make this a difficult novel for readers to follow, and workers looking for inspiration in their daily lives on the construction site would have had to struggle with the disjointed story that Olesha offers them.[1] Those who managed to master *Envy*'s difficult form might still have had problems with the work's inconclusive lessons: the building under construction is incomplete at the end of the tale, and the characters themselves have not yet succeeded in the "reconstruction" of self that would become an important part of the genre. Worst of all, the narrator of *Envy,* whose first-person monologue occupies much of the work, is disoriented by, jealous of, and alienated from the construction process.

Olesha himself described the difficulties that *Envy* presents as a production novel. Although the 1927 work was one of the first to treat the construction theme in a substantial way, Olesha argued in a speech to the first Congress of the Union of Soviet Writers in 1934 that official construction projects were not his topic. He insisted that he could have "gone to a construction site or lived at a factory among workers, described them in a sketch, even in a novel, but that wasn't my theme, wasn't a theme that came from my circulatory system, my breath."[2] The slight correction—from "that wasn't my theme" to that "wasn't a theme that came from my circulatory system, my breath"—is necessary: Olesha seems to draw a distinction between themes developed organically, from the writer's "circulatory system," and themes dictated by a social mandate that the author must struggle to make his own. His stubborn insistence that his own use of the theme of construction was independent of official mandates suggests that the development of the production novel was more organic than its reputation as a genre imposed from above would suggest. In his speech to the congress, Olesha contends that he would have "lied, invented" if he had been coerced into writing about such a theme. He notes that "it's difficult for me to understand the worker type, the revolutionary hero type. I can't be him."[3]

The conflict that Olesha describes in his speech to the congress is reflected directly in his novel, which details his attempts to understand both "that revolutionary hero type" and himself better. His method is typical for a young writer; he imagines himself in the role of both hero and antihero. In his remarkably confessional speech to the congress, Olesha admits that "the seedlings of the most diverse passions—both bright and dark—are stored in everyone." He notes that "there is both bad and good in every person . . . , and every person can feel within himself the sudden appearance of the most varied sorts of doubles." Artists are especially susceptible to this, claims Olesha. In fact, "one of the surprising characteristics of the artist" is this very ability to "experience others' passion." These comments, made years after the original publication of *Envy,* are essential to understanding the novel, which relies on a series of such modernist doppelgangers to make its point about the creative process in the new Soviet world under construction.[4] The characters that the author employs in a search for his own role in the new world are projected selves that are essential to this process of (re)construction.

The novel *Envy* concerns the construction of a communal kitchen under the leadership of Andrei Babichev, who, as head of a food trust in Moscow, is consumed with plans for feeding society in the new world. Olesha's narrative describes Babichev's role in both the development of a new type of sausage and the construction of the new kitchen. We see Babichev at work everywhere: the construction site, taste tests, official meetings, at home in his apartment, even in the toilet. His brother Ivan Babichev, an engineer and inventor, is equally consumed with construction plans, but his building impulses are directed toward constructing Ophelia, a machine Ivan claims to have endowed with human emotion. He intends to use this contraption to disrupt his brother Andrei's strictly rational building plans. Ivan's eccentric behavior has alienated Andrei as well as Ivan's own daughter Valia. A member of the new generation, Valia will most likely marry Andrei's adopted son, Volodia Makarov, star soccer player and object of the envy that gives the novel its name. The story is told largely from the first-person point of view of its quirky and jealous narrator, Nikolai Kavalerov.

Kavalerov's self-absorbed monologue is part of what has kept this novel from the ranks of the "most common type of Stalinist novel" for so long.[5] As Olesha himself noted in his speech to the Writers' Congress, Kavalerov was quickly recognized as a largely autobiographical character, invested with some of the author's most personal traits and observations. Admitting that "Kavalerov looked at the world through my eyes," Olesha insisted that the "tints, colors, images, comparisons, metaphors, and conclusions" of this character were the "very freshest, the very brightest colors that I saw." When critics, after initially praising the novel, reacted negatively to this character as a "vulgarity and irrelevance," Olesha admitted to being shaken to the core.[6] He was disturbed to learn that his character was considered out of touch with the times, and he was horrified with the implication such considerations held for him as a writer.[7]

His solution is significant for understanding both the novel *Envy* and the importance of construction metaphors at the time. He develops yet another persona, a "beggar" who has lost everything. Olesha relates in vivid terms how this "concept of a beggar" replaced his own concept of himself as a writer for a time. He describes his use of artistic imagination to place himself in the role of a "person from whom everything has been taken. . . . And I become a beggar, a completely real beggar. I stand on the steps of the pharmacy, ask for handouts, and I have the nickname 'Writer.'"[8] This frightening picture of the "naked idea of social uselessness" must have sounded only too familiar to many of the writers listening to Olesha's speech at the Congress in 1934. They rewarded his presentation with the "thunderous applause"[9] usually reserved for more august personalities. Olesha's sense that he was out of step with his society was clearly shared by others, and his solution to the dilemma reflected a creative construction of individual artistic space that most found compelling.[10]

Olesha continues his discussion of the beggar persona by suggesting that he had reached an artistic dead end at this early point in his young life as an author.[11] The barefoot bum by the name of "Writer" had "sunk to the very bottom" and seemed unlikely to find a way out of his dilemma. His work under fire by "critic Communists," he is left to wander aimlessly in the ruins of his imagination. He describes this outcast state by evoking the image of the beggar writer and his alienation from the events of the First Five-Year Plan: "I walked around the country and passed the construction sites at night. The towers of the construction sites, fire, and I'm walking barefoot."[12] Just at this moment of despair, however, Olesha finds a potential escape from his dilemma, which he solves structurally by building an imaginative refuge for himself. The passage in which he describes this new authorial structure is particularly important for interpreting *Envy*.

This time, the beggar emerges in Olesha's imagination "in the purity and freshness of morning." This metaphorical new beginning finds him suddenly on the edge of an audacious new landscape, one built on the ruins of a past civilization by sheer creative force. The artistic setting that Olesha imagines provides both him and the beggar writer with a means to escape their fate as "vulgar and irrelevant." The beggar, Olesha's speech at the first Writers' Congress continues,

> walks past a wall. It sometimes happens that in a field, not far from a settled area, a half-ruined wall stands. A meadow, some trees, thistles, part of the wall. The shadow on the meadow from the wall is even more clearly defined, more right-angled than the wall itself. I start to walk away from the corner and see that there's an arch in the wall, a narrow entrance (*vkhod*) with a circular top in the shape of an arch, like that found in a Renaissance painting. I go closer to this exit (*vykhod*), I see the threshold. There are little steps in front of it. I peek in there and I see incredible green . . . Maybe goats graze here. I step across the threshold, enter, and then I look at myself and see that this is youth. Youth has returned.[13]

The elements in Olesha's description are essential to understanding the architectural solutions that authors found to their dilemmas of the late 1920s and early 1930s. The importance of past experience is evident in Olesha's discovery of a "half-ruined" wall that has not yet lost its utility. The image of the wall on the meadow is "more clearly defined" than the wall itself; this imaginary structure has more substance than the building fragment it reflects. In a pattern that would be typical of production novels from this transitional period, Olesha sees the possibility for construction as more potent than the completed structure itself. Ready at first to walk away empty-handed, Olesha's beggar writer is struck instead by a chink in the structure, an opening that suggests—in fact, even conflates—both entrance and exit. The aperture ties this humble ruin on the outskirts of some "settled area" to the supreme era of artistic creation. Its location there provides the author renewed access to both creative endeavor and possible fame. The enormous potential of the structure is reflected in the verdant green (*inobychainaia zelen'*) of the small square it surrounds. The endless youth that awaits those who enter the space suggests the immortality of monumental works of literature.[14]

Such space, "transformed—and mediated—by technology, by practice," as Lefebvre describes it, is the destination of the artist in Olesha's world.[15] To reach such a place, at least in the universe Olesha inhabited in the early 1930s, the artist must be ready to undertake a difficult spiritual quest, abandoning past success and past selves, discarding the trivial and corrupting temptations of this existence in favor of a greater purpose in another world. Such, at any rate, are the noble goals of both Olesha and his beggar, who was scheduled to be the hero in a novel the writer planned in 1930. Speaking in diary entries from that year, Olesha notes that he has had thoughts of a novel entitled "Beggar" for some time.[16] The image of that beggar, important to the writer since childhood, has new significance for him now, when it emerges as a symbol of the search for new literary forms that goes hand in hand with Olesha's desire for personal renewal.

Olesha's description of the beggar in his diary comes just after a long passage in which he expresses weariness, even disgust with his current position as overfed and overindulged Soviet writer. In this context, the beggar emerges as a welcome respite from Olesha's steady diet of overly rich "brown swill" (*korichnevye zhizhi*), and the image is clear evidence of the writer's desire for spiritual pilgrimage. "And here in some unseen diary," Olesha notes in his own unpublished papers, "I make a note: there are too many feasts in my life. Return purity to me, I've flung it away . . . It's not clear where or when I will find my lost purity . . . My life is disgraceful . . . I'll become a beggar . . . I'll grab the end of the thread and straighten out the tangle. . . ."[17]

The beggar is not a figure of pity in Olesha's universe, although that is a common interpretation of the author's use of the image in his 1934 speech to the first Writers' Congress. Rather, this is a figure of inner strength. He might wish that circumstance had spared him such ordeals, but he will nevertheless meet the challenges an indifferent fate has set him. Leo Tolstoy is similarly identified as a "beggar" in Olesha's diary, lending the image moral authority and strength. And Olesha's description of himself in beggar's garb seems to draw on canonical images of Tolstoyan moral integrity and simplicity, even on the well-known photographs of Tolstoy dressed in simple dress, setting off on a journey, staff in hand. As Olesha's Soviet (re)incarnation sets off on a similar spiritual quest, his beggar's garb ties current trends to martyrdom of an earlier age: "Christianity—communism—the brink of a new era," Olesha comments, "and I am standing on that brink with a pack on my back, —standing there, leaning on a staff."[18]

Olesha's diary from late 1930 recalls his brief encounter with a beggar on Nevskii Prospect in Leningrad that winter. At first, the beggar is barely noticeable, kneeling in front of a well-lighted store that Olesha is entering. The writer mistakes him for the statue of a lion initially; with his "straight torso," he is "black, motionless, like an idol." A second glance makes clear that this is a beggar, whose upturned face, like the "black surface of an icon," frightens Olesha. Unlike the flighty author, however, the beggar "does not stir, standing just as he has been standing, perhaps, from morning—a bearded peasant, mighty and meek." To underline the tremendous strength of this sober image, Olesha adds, in a parenthetical comment to his diary, "beggars command the respect of the Russian people: wanderers, holy fools, soldiers, Methuselahs, blind men."[19]

It is this powerful image that Olesha imagines will lead him to the appealing space of creative potential that is at the heart of the novel *Envy*. Olesha's struggle to find such a refuge for himself absorbed the author, as we will see, throughout the late 1920s and early 1930s. Olesha demonstrates the significance of the topic by returning to it in his contribution to the Writers' Congress where he ties the creative space he needs to his tale about the beggar writer. The novel "The Beggar" went unwritten, he says, for reasons he understood only later. "At the time I was thinking about the theme of the beggar, looking for youth, the country was building factories," he comments self-critically. Now, that situation has changed: "I believe in the youth of the country. It's not my own youth that I want to return. I want to see the youth of the country, that is, of new people. Now I see them. And I have the proud thought to consider that their beginning youth is, to a certain extent, the return of my own youth."[20]

This sense that the author is struggling with his characters to find a place in the new universe makes *Envy* a compelling and useful example of the early production genre. To exclude the novel from a discussion of that genre is to narrow the definition unnecessarily, to mimic, in effect, critics and party hacks from the time who wished to control which works of literature would be part of the Soviet canon and which would not. Olesha's *Envy*, with its focus on construction as a theme and its reliance on the metaphor of building, clearly belongs in a study of the production novel. V. O. Pertsov, who identifies the work as "perhaps the first novel in Soviet literature" to treat the motifs of industrialization, offers a description that is still relevant.[21] Olesha's eccentric pronouncements in *Envy* about the role of building in contemporary society only emphasize how artificially narrow our inherited critical categories have been.

The need to redefine the production novel is confirmed by an unusual source, the orthodox "proletarian" writer Iurii Libedinskii, who responded to Olesha's public confession in his own speech to the first Writers' Congress. Libedinskii appears to have been genuinely impressed with Olesha's revelations about his creative method, which he calls "one of the most significant events of our Congress."[22] He argues that Olesha's remarks demonstrate the possibility of finding common cause in the Writers' Union. "Is it really possible to relate such unguarded, deeply personal processes from the podium of such a gigantic organization, in front of writers who are occasionally indifferent and often antagonistic to your creation?" Libedinskii asks rhetorically. Noting that Olesha's comments answer his question in the affirmative, he concludes that the process of self-examination Olesha describes is the "process of radical change of opinions of reality that all Soviet authors have undergone." The "gigantic political shift made in Soviet literature in the last four years," Libedinskii notes, involves a change in the model of the ideal writer in the Soviet Union. Gone, Libedinskii argues, is the old model of writer-observer. In its place must come a newer understanding of the writer as activist.[23]

Numerous critics have detailed the many political twists and turns such a change involved, even for stalwart supporters of Party politics, such as Libedinskii, who was himself the author of production literature.[24] What is interesting for us here, however, is Libedinskii's seemingly sincere assertion that Olesha's remarks are part both of the author's genuine attempts at self-redefinition and of a larger movement to incorporate the activity of writing into society as a whole. The attempt to bring workers to literature involved introducing thousands of amateurs to the profession, as the work of Evgeny Dobrenko and others has demonstrated.[25] But what seems to excite Libedinskii about Olesha's speech is its emphasis on the related question—historically important for Russia—of the professional writer's role in relation to the people. Libedinskii argues that the question of the writer's role in society had been a problem for Soviet literature "throughout all of its history."[26] Olesha's description of his doubts about his own work and his struggle to find a place for it and himself in the new world suggests, to Libedinskii at least, that artists are resolving this question. Such a change was inherent to the production novel, with its emphasis on rebuilding and reconstructing both self and society, just as it was to so many such initiatives for joint authorial activity in the early 1930s. Olesha's exploration of this fact in *Envy* makes the work a fascinating and necessary contribution to the history of the genre.

In *Envy*, Olesha creates a world of shifting boundaries and changing perspectives that make it difficult, if not impossible, to establish a definitive point of view from which to observe events of the novel. This modernist technique puts the reader on a par with the work's characters and its writer, as all seek a way to understand their role in the narrative and the world it describes. One of the ways Olesha accomplishes this feat is by altering the physical space in which events transpire: readers are continually disoriented, as unsure of their place in the universe as are the hapless heroes of Olesha's fictional world. Kavalerov's eccentric point of view completes the sensation that this is a manuscript in which the scale of perception can change unexpectedly, leaving readers and characters alike unsure of the ground beneath them. Kavalerov's close and quirky focus reveals that the landscape around us is more complicated and more treacherous than we imagined. His description of a simple domestic scene, for example, is fraught with danger. "Have you ever noticed that . . . man is surrounded by tiny inscriptions, a crawling anthill of little inscriptions: on forks, spoons, plates, the frame of pince-nez, buttons, pencils? No one notices them, but they are engaged in a struggle for existence. They evolve from species to species, all the way to huge sign-board letters! It's an insurrection —class against class: letters on street signs are battling the letters on posters."[27]

Distant landscapes in the novel are no more comforting than closer views. Unsurprisingly, they often serve as metaphors for the utopian future, and, as such, they seem to portend a life more vivid, colorful, and joyful than the one at hand. "I find that a landscape, seen through the distancing lens of binoculars, gains in luster, brilliance, and stereo-opticality. Colors and contours seem to become refined. Items, while remaining recognizable, suddenly seem amusingly tiny, unfamiliar. This arouses childlike notions in the observer. Just as though you were having a dream. Notice that a person who has trained his binoculars on the distance starts to smile with joy"

(63–64). But as characters search for clarity of focus in the world to come, they often lose perspective on events at hand and overlook potential trouble in this world.

This is the case on one of the many occasions on which Andrei Babichev, leader and activist, is harassed by his brother Ivan. Andrei is waxing poetic at a meeting arranged at the site of the future giant kitchen. He stands on the construction site itself, an imposing edifice covered with wooden scaffolding that evokes comparisons with structures and events as diverse as a ship, a tree, a guitar, a mathematical equation, and the siege of Troy. From this symbolic location, Andrei, "like every orator, looked off into the distance, above the nearby masses of spectators, and therefore remained indifferent to what was taking place below, beneath the tribunal, until the very end of his speech" (112). What is taking place, apparently, is sabotage of both his speech and his project; his brother Ivan storms the stage, seeking to inflame the crowd against Andrei before the construction site and its planner are destroyed in a whirlwind brought about by Ivan's invention, Ophelia. When these events are later revealed to have been nothing more than the flight of Ivan's vengeful imagination, readers, already profoundly suspicious of both the close and the long view, are left searching for a stable perspective from which to comprehend events. The confusion of boundaries and points of view is essential to Olesha's realignment of narrative space.

The characters, too, lack clear definition, sharing personality traits, thoughts, dreams, and even physical characteristics that make it difficult to distinguish one individual from another. As brothers, Andrei and Ivan look alike. Perhaps unexpected, though, is their shared resemblance to the pudgy Nikolai Kavalerov, whose physical similarity to both helps blur the lines of identity among all three men.[28] Kavalerov's temporary assumption of Makarov's position in Andrei's household, his longing to replace him in Valia's heart, his confusion of Makarov's correspondence with his own and of Makarov with both the "character" Tom Virlirli and his own imaginary youthful persona are all additional examples of the physical and spatial confusion of the work's many selves. This raises doubts as to each man's identity and role in the novel. In a work concerned above all with questions of self-definition in a new universe, characters are lost in a maze of potential doppelgangers. As we stand with Olesha's characters on the edge of life as new Soviet men, we face the dilemmas they do as they contemplate potential loss of power and identity in the new world that simultaneously beckons and frightens all who would venture within/beyond.

We are participants, as well, in Olesha's own complicated process of building a self in this world under construction. We know from Olesha's comments elsewhere that his biography ties him to both Kavalerov and Volodia Makarov, both of whom link him, in turn, to Andrei and Ivan Babichev.[29] None of this is surprising in an author's first novel, which we expect to draw heavily on personal experience. Nor are we surprised by the implications of the Babichevs' deceased brother, Roman, who is mentioned only in passing in the work. The double entendre—Roman is both a man's name and the Russian word for "novel"—indicates Olesha's organic connection to this brother/work. As *Envy* proceeds in its tortuous way, we witness Olesha's attempts to fashion a coherent Soviet personality from the multiple pre- and postrevolutionary fragments available to him.[30]

The novel itself begins with a confusion of space. Andrei Babichev, who inhabits the apartment in which the story begins, is in the toilet, an unlikely location for a "revolutionary hero." This unorthodox starting point suggests the distorted perspective of space that will characterize the rest of the novel as well. Although Babichev has several later opportunities to adopt the heroic pose on the ramparts that is expected of such figures, Olesha places him first in this most ordinary of sites, thus firmly tying him to the coarse, elemental, earthy side of life and immediately reversing established dichotomies of private and public space.[31] The enthusiastic director of a Soviet food trust, Babichev is master of this prosaic space, breaking into song to urge his intestines to function properly and later parading in his underwear as he performs his morning exercises. Brimming with health and energy, he can barely fit his well-fed pink body into the close confines of the apartment that momentarily contains him. He is associated with dominance from the moment he enters the "room of unclear intent," contested space for which his temporary guest Nikolai Kavalerov will later have to compete.

The contemplative narrator Kavalerov, that writer-observer whose outmoded stance must be abandoned if he is to survive in the new world, acknowledges Babichev's latent power by noting his ease in his physical surroundings. "Things love him," Kavalerov notes enviously, contrasting that happy fact with his own "complicated" relationship with the surrounding world in which "things don't love me" and furniture, blankets, even coins and collar buttons conspire against him (8–9). Kavalerov relates Babichev's attractiveness and power to the director's masculinity by focusing his attention on Babichev's groin as he exercises. The elemental masculine force that Kavalerov imagines in Babichev both fascinates and frightens this passive observer, whose struggle to find a rightful place in the universe that Babichev commands occupies most of the novel.[32] When we first meet Kavalerov, he is an interloper, who has no claim to any space. His location outside the entrance to a beer hall marks him as a transitional figure; he is neither in nor out of the universe that portends the future. His location on the threshold (or the fence, the window sill, or the edge of numerous structures) identifies him as a potentially marginal member of the society under construction. He understands this liminal position and its possible consequences only too well. He is invited into the new world by Babichev, who lets him into his apartment and offers him the chance to take up residence in the new spatial arrangement.

Olesha is careful, however, to avoid establishing a clear binary opposition between the two characters. Babichev's last name, with its feminine root *baba*, undermines pretensions to masculine dominance, as do his overly feminized breasts, which are described on the first page of the narrative. The name of the passive and impotent Kavalerov, meanwhile, hints at a "cavalier" masculine essence that belies his present "feminine" inertia. The attempt to highlight and overcome, rather than rely on, such dichotomous distinctions is typical of production novels of this transitional early period. What critics have imagined as carved in binary stone, then, is actually a feature of later Soviet novels that is largely absent from these transitional works. Early production novels display considerably more flexibility, polyphony, and doubt than has previously been noted.

Babichev's revolutionary goal is to free Soviet citizens—especially Soviet women—from the tyranny of domestic chores. He will do so by creating a "house-giant," the "greatest of lunchrooms, the greatest of kitchens." This invention, called "Two Bits" since two dishes at the cafeteria will cost only a quarter of a ruble, is intended to bring an end to the exhaustion and drudgery associated with everyday chores in the kitchen. The much reviled Primus stoves that characterized early postrevolutionary Soviet life are to become things of the past in Babichev's utopian dream. His worthy Soviet project, however, seems doomed to failure when he first visits the proposed beneficiaries of his intended creative largesse and is unceremoniously driven from their midst.

One morning, he—director of the trust, a very solid citizen, clearly a government representative with a briefcase under his arm—went up the

back entrance to an unfamiliar staircase, and, among all the special de-
lights of such a place, knocked on the first door he came to. . . . He
caught sight of the soot and the grime, the wild furies tearing around
in the smoke, kids crying. They fell on him immediately. He was disturbing everyone. . . . And besides that he had a briefcase, pince-nez,
he was elegant and clean. And the furies decided: "he's obviously a
member of some kind of commission." Standing with their hands on
their hips, the housewives let him have it. And he departed. (12)

Unexpectedly, Kavalerov emerges as Babichev's ally in this "war
against kitchens," providing the inspirational text to accompany
any future attempts to "unite all meat grinders, Primus stoves, frying pans, faucets." The "industrialization of kitchens" that Babichev
has designed can take place only because Kavalerov, like authors of
production novels everywhere, is able to supply the words needed
to enlighten the public and inspire support for the project. Thus,
Kavalerov imagines Babichev declaiming the speech that he himself produces: "Women! We will blow the soot off you. We'll clean
your nostrils of smoke and your ears of discord. We'll force potatoes to peel themselves magically, in an instant. We'll return to
you the hours stolen from you by the kitchen. You'll receive half of
your life back" (12). Babichev is unable to provide such sentiments
since "he has no imagination." But Kavalerov supplies them effortlessly. "He should have said this," muses Kavalerov thought-
fully, before waxing poetic in service to the cause he is only half
certain he supports.

Here, as elsewhere, Olesha establishes the dichotomy—masculinity and action vs. femininity and passivity—only to undermine
it almost immediately. This has the effect not of reversing the binary system, as so often occurs with polarities, but of challenging
its very validity. Olesha refuses to resolve these complexities into
simple oppositions at the very moment that he plays on our desire
to do just that. Babichev is not the one-dimensional Soviet man of
action that later critics would look for in production novels, just as
Kavalerov is more than a marginalized intellectual unable to effect
real social change. Instead, both are part of the complicated construction of self that absorbs both author and reader throughout
this transitional work. Olesha's tortured confession to the first
Writers' Congress only underlines how close he felt his fate and
Kavalerov's to be.

The real construction work of the production novel *Envy* thus
begins where work on all novels does: at the writer's desk. This
construction site—the "green square of a table covered with a glass

top" (14)—is the real locus for all following developments in the novel. This green patch, which was still fascinating Olesha by the time of the first Writers' Congress in 1934, returns again and again to ground events in the work. As the site of creation—present, potential, and failed—the tabletop offers both endless redemption and eternal reproach. In Olesha's description of Babichev's work table and Kavalerov's envy of it, we can see the restless author fighting with himself as he stares at the blank pages of his yet unwritten production novel. The green expanse of the table is littered with both impulsive notes and sober calculations of potential gain. His external and internal critics alike mock him as he sets to work while simultaneously condemning his own inability to generate enthusiasm for the project. Olesha's description of the process in *Envy* is tortuous and self-defeating, suggesting that Iurii Libedinskii was right to recognize in Olesha's later comments the intensely personal struggle for self-definition that writers faced during this time. We can read the following passage from *Envy* as a battle for the process of creation itself between artist, critic, and self-reproach. While the text refers ostensibly to Babichev and Kavalerov, it clearly also reflects the passionate contemporary debate over creative work and Olesha's self-loathing participation in it.

> At home in the evening he sits, shaded by the palm green of the lampshade. In front of him are sheets of paper, notebooks, little strips with columns of figures. He flips through the pages of a desk calendar, jumps up, searches on the shelf, takes out folders, gets on his knees on the chair and—stomach on table, resting his fat face in his hands—he reads. The green square of the table is covered with a glass top. What's unusual here after all? A person is working, a person is home in the evening, working. Nothing unusual. But all his behavior says: you're a plebian, Kavalerov. Of course, he doesn't announce that. It must be that he doesn't have anything like that in mind. But it's obvious without words. Some third party informs me of it. Some third person forces me into a rage (*besit'sia*) while I'm following his moves. (14)

This unnamed third party (*kto-to tretii*) undermines any potential binarity in the text as it mediates between the autobiographical Kavalerov and the coarse man of action Babichev. It is important to note that Babichev is not the source of the reproach that Kavalerov imagines ("it must be that he doesn't have anything like that in mind"). Setting Babichev up as an ostensible example of correct creative activity, this internal voice taunts Kavalerov with his inability to measure up—"You're a plebian"—while simultaneously reproaching him for failing to want to join the struggle. The multilateral battle among the artist's "should, can't, won't, will" suggests how inadequate a binary model is to understanding the dilemmas that writers at work faced in the late 1920s and early 1930s. The green expanse of the author's desk here provides space for a complex process of construction and reconstruction in which the writer attempts to build a social paradise with room (and an escape route) for himself. The problem is as much internal as external: writers under pressure to produce on command were genuinely tortured by their inability to generate the enthusiasm that they themselves believed was necessary. The external pressures to conform were many and often odious. No less significant, however, were the self-reproaches that authors found to motivate themselves long after their initial optimism for the revolution had begun to fade.

The green square of the author's desk is echoed elsewhere in the book, in perhaps unconscious reflection of the creative process itself.[33] Babichev's apartment, which hovers effortlessly in "light space" above a city street, looks out onto a small "garden—heavy, typical for the outskirts of Moscow, a wooded garden, a disorderly collection grown up on the waste land between three walls, as in a stove" (10). This seemingly uninspired landscape plays an important structural and thematic role in the novel. The garden, like the green tabletop in the apartment above it, is an image of the author's creative role in building a fictional universe. At this point, both the garden and the artist's vision are jumbled and disorganized, grown up haphazardly to fill the empty space between structures that threaten to overwhelm it. The location, viewed from a borrowed apartment that provides only temporary refuge for the author, will be transformed by the end of the novel into a vision of the future. Although the artist's claim to the space he constructs will continue to be tenuous, the imaginary location he creates takes on solid form.

Between the overgrown patch at the beginning of the book and the completed refuge that is visible by the end, *Envy* describes a complicated reorganization of space that is connected to the struggle for self-definition and the fear of lost identity that nearly all of Olesha's characters face. This struggle is most acute in the case of Kavalerov, whose confused identity merges at times with those of all the primary male characters in the work. In addition to his intermittent attraction to Andrei Babichev, Kavalerov identifies with both Babichev's adopted son Volodia Makarov and Andrei's brother, Ivan, who is as dreamy and impractical as his brother is prosaic. This purposeful entanglement allows Olesha to describe the problem of self-realization in spatial terms. Kavalerov wanders back and forth across the space of the novel, merging identities with the other characters in attempts to find his rightful place in society. His experiences on the boundaries of the new world that he wishes to inhabit reflect the confusion many others must have felt as they too tried to reorient themselves in a changing universe. Kavalerov's fictional wanderings on the margins of society suggest the difficulty, pain, and envy that accompanied real-life attempts at "self-reconstruction" to fit into the new world.[34]

Kavalerov is seen most often at the boundaries of this new world that all would like to enter. As we have seen, he first appears in the novel in transitional space on the threshold of a beer hall from which he has just been forcibly ejected. His position in the beer hall is mock heroic as he adopts the pose of an orator, speaking from the bar table onto which he has clambered. Like other agitators in Olesha's universe, Kavalerov is out of touch with his audience, and he is quickly ejected from the hall. He is thrown out of the hall by the other patrons, and he lands face down on the grill that covers a hatchway outside. His view from there of another world below the visible universe suggests both his connection to other modes of existence and his downward course in this reality. As an underemployed, misunderstood, marginalized person, he is attuned to the world below the surface of things. Instead of focusing on that indeterminate distance that captures the imagination of other orators, this individual notices instead the secret life of the garbage that has collected in the hatchway (19) and points out a world of meaning that surrounds all those whose focus is close enough to notice it. The garbage that attracts Kavalerov's attention holds special interest for Olesha, and this world beneath the attention of more farsighted inhabitants repeats in miniature the struggles of a larger universe. Kavalerov is one of only a few to notice this level of existence, but his painfully precise observations win him no glory. Far from providing an advantage, the view in close-up merely reflects the observer's inability or unwillingness to see larger, more important societal landscapes. The birds'-eye view escapes Kavalerov, and it will eventually elude even Andrei Babichev. Their closer perspective marks the men as too grounded, too shortsighted to move permanently into the future.[35]

Olesha connected the ability to see things on a small scale with a childlike perception of the world, as we already know from his description of Kavalerov in his speech to the Writers' Congress. Despite his protests there to the contrary, however, Olesha appears to have understood the potential danger of such a trait in the adult observer. Charming in the very young, this close focus may lead to passivity and shortsightedness with age. It is again Kavalerov who provides the best example of this misplaced focus. He has rented a corner of a room from his landlady Anechka, who is the proud owner of a heavy and ornate four-poster bed. This enormous piece of furniture, complete with mirrors, carvings, and arches, is a symbol of the kind of domestic tyranny that Babichev wants inhabitants of the new Soviet universe to escape. Kavalerov, fully aware of the potential traps contained in such bourgeois luxury, is nevertheless drawn to its temptations. "If I were a child," he thinks to himself, "Anechka's little son,—how many poetic, magical structures my child's mind would have created, given over to the power of the sight of such an unusual thing!" As an adult, he perceives "only the general outlines and only some of the details" of the bed. But as a child, he would not have had to obey the rules of "distance or scale or time or weight or friction" that confine the adult imagination. Freed from these spatial constraints, he could have set himself up as a ruler of this imaginary kingdom, receiving delegations to his court among the sheets. As enticing as this brief lyrical digression may be, Kavalerov ends it on a note of caution, realizing as he does that there is potential danger in even the softest of landings. "I would have set off on fantastic journeys over the carved wood—higher and higher—over the legs and buttocks of the cupids, have crawled over them as they crawl over the statue of Buddha, unable to capture it in a glance, and, at the last arch, from a dizzying height, would have fallen into a fearsome abyss, into the icy abyss of the pillows" (104). He ends this flight of fancy well aware that he, like other bugs crawling across the face of the Buddha, may be torn from his spot on the statue without ever realizing its importance.[36]

Kavalerov's limited perspective means that each time he attempts to contemplate the mysteries of the new world from Babichev's height, he is unsuccessful, distanced from his idol by physical separations that reflect the gap in their status and their comprehension of the importance of the overall plan. If he is not too close, he is too far away from Babichev, as when Babichev participates in a ceremony at the airport and Kavalerov is left at the gates. The distance that now separates him from Babichev results in a frighteningly dehumanized vision that makes his estrangement from his erstwhile hero graphic. "The face of Babichev turned toward me. . . . It had no eyes. There were two flat discs, glittering like mercury. The fear of some kind of swift retribution thrust me into a dream-like state. I was dreaming. It seemed to me that I was asleep. And the most terrifying thing about the dream was that the head of Babichev turned toward me on an immobile body, on its own axis, like a screw. His back remained toward me" (42).

When Kavalerov attempts to overcome this distance by following Babichev to the construction site, he becomes confused by the reorganized space and loses his orientation altogether. His thoughts as he ventures onto unfamiliar territory give a sense of how lost writers of this period must have felt on their first excursions to such sites.

> I get closer. Din and dust. I grow deaf and cataracts cover my eyes. . . . Where to look for him? . . . The paths are intricately tangled, as if I'm walking in the inside of an ear. "Comrade Babichev?" They point: "Over there." They're hammering something out. "Where?" "Over there." I cross over an abyss on a girder. I have to balance. Something like the hold of a ship yawns below. Endlessness, black, and cool. It all seems like a shipyard. I'm getting in everyone's way. "Where?" "Over there." He can't be reached. (44)

Even at close quarters, physical obstruction intervenes, and Kavalerov continues to find Babichev inscrutable: half of his face is obscured by the lampshade that separates them; Babichev's head and body appear dissected onto different planes; the light strikes his glasses at an angle that makes it impossible to read the expression in his eyes.[37] Although Kavalerov attempts to emulate Babichev, he finds it more and more difficult to achieve that goal as both the novel and socialist construction continue.

Kavalerov's spatial disorientation continues when he meets Andrei's brother Ivan. Their first encounter takes place on a mirrored surface which renders their resemblance graphic. Despite their obvious affinities, however, Kavalerov is still confused by the optical illusions that surround him and asks Ivan to explain the image they both see in the mirror: "From which side did you come?" he asks Ivan. "How ever in the world did you get here?" Ivan's fanciful reply is eloquent in its simplicity, suggesting a path all creative individuals might take in this new Soviet house of mirrors: "Where? Where did I come from?" he replies, as he searches Kavalerov's face with his own "clear eyes." "I invented myself" (66).

The artistic approach that Ivan advocates is as tortuous as it is whimsical, however, and Olesha makes clear that he understands that fact in Ivan's many impassioned speeches about his own role in the changing world they and other "engineers of the human soul" face.[38] Most significant in this respect is the extended description of Ivan's conversation with an interrogator of the secret police after he is arrested at Andrei's instigation. Olesha initiates the conversation by setting Ivan up as a parody of a martyr; the OGPU interrogator asks him if he has ever called himself a "king." Ivan's answer to his questioner undercuts the biblical parallel: "Yes . . . ," he muses whimsically, "king of bad taste" (86). His focus on newly outdated feelings makes Ivan the bard of sentiment in this new world, and his description of that position is entirely in keeping with the muddled approach of similar characters in other early production novels.

A close reading of his tortured monologues makes clear the difficult position of authors during this time. Relying on metaphors that would become even more popular during the Five-Year Plans to come, Ivan expresses a desire for collective endeavor familiar to students of the period: the "conspiracy of feelings" that will allow him to unite a special group around himself (88) could easily serve as a model for the writing brigades that would soon be organized en masse. His wish ". . . to shake . . . shake the heart of a burnt-out era, the lamp-heart, in order to make the fragments touch . . . and evoke a beautiful, momentary brilliance . . ." (88) uses the industrial vocabulary of the production novel to describe thoughts that Olesha and other writers feared were already outdated and unnecessary.

The tendency to confuse multiple characters in this particular novel and the ever-present temptation to read their sentiments as those of the real-life author is compounded in Olesha's case by his predilection for eccentric punctuation that allows him to include authorial commentary in the primary narrative. The ellipses he uses throughout this passage, in particular, encourage a reading in which authorial asides intrude upon and eventually overwhelm the fictional conversation between Ivan and the OGPU interrogator, which is itself an interruption of Kavalerov's conversation with Ivan. We are invited to read passages in the text as fragments from Olesha's own dialogue with himself, bits torn from the diary form he would soon try to substitute for the *belles lettres* he had been told to despise. ". . . I eavesdrop," he comments in creative desperation: ". . . It's really hard for me to find heroes . . . There are no heroes . . . I peek into strangers' windows, climb up other people's staircases. At times I run after a stranger's smile, skipping like a naturalist after a butterfly! I want to shout: Stop! . . . Stop! I need you . . ." (89).

These comments suggest the difficult inner struggle of a writer at work on his own role in the new society. Used to relying on "a whole list of human feelings," all of which are now "scheduled for destruction" (87), the author searches for new themes to replace old sentiments ostensibly no longer needed by the new Soviet man. Olesha shared this search with most of his contemporaries, as the tortured comments of Mikhail Zoshchenko, for example, in 1927 make painfully clear. Zoshchenko, too, struggles with the sense that it is time to discard his old thoughts and outdated way of writing, in favor of a more heroic and optimistic approach. His torments are recorded by Kornei Chukovskii, who reports Zoshchenko's distress over the "devil sitting inside him" who deprives him of the will to live, alienates him from other people, and robs him of "strong feelings."

"I need to write a different book," Chukovskii records Zoshchenko as saying in the same year Olesha was working on *Envy*. "Not a book like *Sentimental stories*," but "cheerful, full of love toward man. For that, I need first of all to remake myself. I need to become like a person, like other people. For that, I go to the races, for example—and I get excited, and it starts to seem exactly as if it were real [*u menia vykhodit sovsem kak nastoiashchee*], as though I were really excited, and only sometimes do I then see that it is counterfeit." Zoshchenko claims to have read "many medical books" and to have understood "what steps to take in order to become the author of a cheerful, positive book. I have to train myself." The training Zoshchenko imagines is strongly reminiscent of contemporary calls for "reforging," or *perekovka*, which he himself would soon be asked to document in the infamous Belomor Canal volume. The process of remaking oneself, Zoshchenko insists, is even powerful enough to effect physical changes in those subjected to it. Noting that he suffers from a heart defect, he claims to have overcome a recent attack by telling himself "you're lying, you're making it up." He ignored the fit and "conquered my sickness." Noting how interesting it would be to "publish a collection of real letters sent to me," the author continues, "soon I'm even going to start answering letters."[39]

Zoshchenko's sense of his own feelings as strained, false, and opposed to those of other people was shared by many Russian writers in this period. The proletariat was thought to be the only source of authentic sentiment; intellectuals could experience such feelings only vicariously. As a result, many literary accounts from this time have a certain voyeuristic air to them, as authors stifle their own dangerous thoughts and look for sources of "real" emotion in the working class that surrounded them. Acts of eavesdropping and window peeking like that described by Olesha's character are, thus, surprisingly common in these early production novels. An entire generation of authors looked for inspiration from people they met only occasionally and understood poorly, composing their timid narratives in an era whose chameleon-like nature made it a dangerous time to write at all. According to a contemporary observer, Olesha himself shared this "voyeuristic" impulse, commenting, for example, "Ah, how good it would be to peek through a crack to the future."[40]

As Marietta Shaginian makes clear in her production novel *Gidrotsentral'*, observers would not always like what they saw of the "new Soviet man" in transition. When she offers readers of *Hydrocentral* the chance to "peek in the window" of worker barracks, for example, the images that present themselves are decidedly unappealing: "semi-dark corners of the dormitory, cots with dirty rags rolled up into balls, the black soot of the walls, floors where the dirt stands upright like hair on a dog." The quest for authentic voices helped drive interest in the production novel and furthered calls for collectively authored projects, but even established authors were often at a loss to understand their new subjects. On his visit to a Soviet collective farm, for example, André Gide seems utterly baffled by the workers he meets there. Although he was particularly hampered by his inability to speak the language, Gide offers a response that was undoubtedly shared by other writers making ceremonial social calls on the working world. Gide describes the "queer and depressing impression" produced by his visit to "these 'homes'—the impression of complete depersonalization." So unable to imagine life as the working class lived it that he resorts to quotation marks around the very notion of their domiciles, Gide reacts by standardizing the individual workers too. Noting the "same ugly furniture, the same portrait of Stalin," he complains that "every dwelling is interchangeable with every other; so much so that the kolkhozians (who seem to be as interchangeable themselves) might all take up their abode in each other's houses without even noticing it."[41]

The object of such authorial voyeurism, espionage, and perplexity was the new Soviet man, best represented in *Envy* by Volodia Makarov. Kavalerov's confusion of space and identity, evidenced by both Andrei and Ivan, is even more obvious with Volodia Makarov. Kavalerov first elicits Andrei Babichev's sympathy, after all, because Andrei "confuses" the two, noticing a vague resemblance to Makarov in Kavalerov's inert body in front of the beer hall. Kavalerov takes up residence with Babichev in Makarov's stead and assumes his place on the couch in Babichev's apartment while Volodia is away. Like Volodia, Kavalerov is given tasks to fulfill for Babichev, and both adopt a superior attitude toward their mentor, even as they continue to undertake his bidding. We learn of these shared feelings when Kavalerov accidentally reads a letter that Makarov has written to Babichev, mistaking it for his own angry epistle. The mix-up of both the letters and their emotions helps confuse their identities further.

There is little hope that Kavalerov can achieve Makarov's exalted status as soccer goalie, expert gymnast, and "industrial man," but he clearly aspires to do so, and the resulting confusion of their places in Kavalerov's mind is a primary source of the envy that concerns Kavalerov throughout the book.[42] Kavalerov and Makarov first meet in Babichev's apartment, in that contested space—the "room of unclear intent"—that provides the location for these two selves to negotiate their fates. Kavalerov is standing in Babichev's apartment to which he has returned briefly in order to sever relations with the director permanently. His somewhat unexpected decision to do so follows immediately from his trip to the construction site and his unsuccessful search there for Babichev, a trip that has painfully revealed his fundamental ineptitude at the work site. "It's not my fault," he concludes at his inability to measure up at work. "He's to blame" (45). As he stands for the last time on Babichev's balcony, Kavalerov listens to nearby church bells and recalls a previous daydream in which he had imagined himself the resident of a tiny French village, traveling to the capital to make his fame and fortune (54). The balcony with its commanding view of the surrounding area represents a position of strength,[43] and the ringing of the bells Kavalerov hears from there gives a name to the hero of his daydream, as his musings and their music bring "Tom Virlirli" to life. Just then, however, his fantasy is interrupted by a knock on the door. When he opens the space, he is met by the hero of his daydreams, his future replacement, Tom Virlirli/Volodia Makarov.

Kavalerov's confusion—of Makarov with Virlirli and of himself with both—represents the complicated reorganization of self and space that faced Olesha's generation, whose dreams of future glory, nourished in a prerevolutionary landscape, were now being replaced by structures with which they were unfamiliar. Kavalerov refers to this situation when he describes the "barriers" that bar the "roads to glory" (24) in his country. He rejects the path that Babichev offers on surprisingly spatial terms: Babichev's way is architecturally insignificant. Standing on a bridge in the center of Moscow, the House of Labor to his left, the Kremlin just behind him, Kavalerov contemplates hurling Babichev's newly developed sausage into the river. His august surroundings have prepared him for a more exalted form of heroism, he grumbles, making it difficult for him to recognize the accomplishments of this less romantic era: "This is not the sort of glory that biographies, monuments, and history led me to expect" ("*ne o takoi slave govorili mne zhizneopisaniia, pamiatniki, istoriia*"). Has the nature of fame changed everywhere, he wonders, "or only here, in the world under construction"? He ponders this question and the possibility of returning to a previous existence before insisting—in an authorial aside that might come from almost any production novel—that, after all, "this new world under construction is the main one, the triumphant one." He is emphatic in his conclusion: "It's in this world that I want glory!" (37).

To achieve his dreams, Kavalerov imagines a new world that combines features of the old with the new to create a new hybrid existence. The mirage of the future arrives from Kavalerov's own imagination to replace him in the new scheme of things. As Tom Virlirli, this mirage is the personification of Kavalerov's own hopes for glory and fame in the future. Tom Virlirli—the name is part agitational drumbeat, part lyrical fancy—is an onomatopoeic incantation of Kavalerov's view of the universe to come. In Kavalerov's vision, both he and his creation Tom are intended as heroes of the new world, masters of the green landscape they can view from the third-floor balcony of Babichev's apartment and of the green writer's desk that gives access to the world of creation. It is from this very contested space that Kavalerov will nevertheless soon be excluded. Although his youth and his present location in the apartment suggest the possibility of existence, even triumph, in that not-too-distant future being built, Kavalerov already senses his unsuitability for permanent residence there.

Tom Virlirli, the personage he has imagined will inhabit the new world with him, is revealed to be Volodia Makarov instead, a youth as inscrutable and potentially hostile as the new world itself. Kavalerov, who initially sees Makarov as a fellow victim who will soon be evicted from the future paradise, now learns that Makarov is destined to replace both him and, eventually, Babichev in the new environment. Makarov's letter to Babichev, which Kavalerov mistakenly appropriates as he leaves the contested apartment space, reveals the fate that awaits them both at the hands of this representative of the new Soviet man. Chastising Babichev for taking pity on Kavalerov, Volodia criticizes him for his "sentimentality" (*chuvstvitel'nost'*; 58), which he contrasts explicitly with his own forward-looking "industrial" approach. As a member of the older generation, Babichev is doomed to remain mired outside of the new universe that he is helping to construct, while Makarov, a "man-machine" (*chelovek-mashina;* 59) who has freed himself from the encumbrance of emotions, is unquestionably a future resident of the world to come.[44] Kavalerov, who realizes that he too will be left on the threshold of the new world, struggles for a dramatic gesture to mark his space in history.

At home with Babichev, Kavalerov finds himself increasingly frustrated by a society that has unaccountably redefined the meaning of the heroism he seeks. Babichev and his kind have monopolized the new space of creation, and Kavalerov can only look on longingly as Babichev conducts his mysterious calculations at the green-top table Kavalerov covets. He complains to Babichev that in the new country they both inhabit, "there is no route to individual success," but his complaints fall on deaf ears. Babichev and the society have no use for his monologue (24). In a Dostoevskian aside, Kavalerov threatens to commit suicide to prove that the individual approach is still effective even in a communal world. Thinking that he can still have an effect on the new physical environment, Kavalerov imagines overwhelming the space of Babichev's apartment with his self-defining act. "Or how about up and killing myself," Kavalerov remarks, in what he hopes will be a gesture provocative in its individualism. "Suicide without the slightest reason. Just for a lark. In order to show that everyone has the right to self-determination. Even now. Hang myself in your entrance way." Babichev's laconic reaction to Kavalerov's proposal, however, indicates how far Kavalerov has already deviated from the contemporary perspective on space and identity. Babichev is completely unimpressed by Kavalerov's plans to mark the territory and suggests instead a more fitting location for the event. "Hang yourself at the entrance to the Supreme Soviet of the National Economy, on the old Barbarian Square, Nogin Square. That would be better. There's a huge archway over there. Have you seen it? It would have quite the effect" (25).[45]

Shocked into momentary silence by Babichev's suggestion that his place in the new world is at the end of a noose on "Barbarian" Square, Kavalerov attempts to retreat into thoughts of the old world he has temporarily deserted. He remembers the room in which he used to live before Babichev's kindness gave him entry into the new world. This former residence once provided shelter and serenity ("exhilarating sleepiness") (26), but the bed it contains is now "frightening" (25) and has lost its youthful appeal. This bed, a perversion of both the ideal garden and the writer's desk that replaces it, is tied to Kavalerov's past by the blanket that covers the bed. The covering was purchased long before and is tied by association to images of fertility, plenty, and childhood and by its blue color to thoughts of a radiant future.

> On the bed is a blue blanket, purchased by me in Kharkov, at the Blagoveshchenskii Bazaar, in a hungry year. A peasant woman was selling little pies. They were covered with a blanket. As they cooled, not yet having given up the heat of life, they practically burst under the blanket, moving around like little puppies. I lived poorly then, like everyone, and such abundance, such housewifeliness, such warmth exuded from that composition, that on that very day, I made a resolution: to buy myself such a blanket. (25)[46]

What was once a potential source of life and abundance, however, has now become twisted, overblown, empty, and useless. The bed he occupied is now frightening; the potent blanket that sheltered him is now covered with "patterns" that have "already blossomed" (26). Kavalerov must leave behind this childish retreat if he is to enter the future and make a real mark on the world. "Now I sleep on a wonderful couch," he concludes, trying to convince himself of his suitability to the new world after all.

As he drifts off to sleep on the new couch, he seems about to recapture the youthful energy and endless potential of childhood. His reveries suggest a "cultivated garden, thick with grape vines: a path beside the vineyard, a sunny road, heat . . ." (27) Just then, however, he faces yet another moment of doubt in the novel, this time in the image of his father, whom he remembers/meets in the mirror. As he contemplates their shared image and fate, he understands that the system he had seen as one of binary opposites is in fact a circular pattern of identification. The image of his father in the mirror brings him to the realization that he, too, will soon share the older man's fate.[47] As tempting as it is to imagine one generation breaking free from the last, Kavalerov here reflects that he will be unable to do so and sadly comes to the realization that his dreams of a new kind of glory are equally far-fetched. "I'll never go from a small town to the capital," he concludes. "I won't be a general or a People's Commissar or a scholar or a runner or an adventurer. I'll soon just return to my old apartment, to the room with the frightening bed" (27). This return to the past, a return to an environment outdated both personally and spatially provokes both fear and desire in Kavalerov. Thoughts of his father and of the inevitability of generational change, which he too will eventually endure, mingle with images of his landlady at his former apartment. Her sexual advances remind him again of his aging body, of the unlikelihood of a return to childhood. "And now I recognized my father in myself. It wasn't a formal resemblance. No, it was something else. I would say a sexual resemblance, as if I had suddenly perceived my father's seed in myself, in my very essence. And as though someone had said to me: you're done. Finished. That's it. Produce a son" (27).

As Kavalerov's dreams and fate become conflated with those of his father, so too do they join with those of Babichev. The combination is one that reflects on the resemblance the two men share. Sleeping on Babichev's couch, Kavalerov dreams of his ideal woman, a beauty who comes to him as he drifts off to sleep on Babichev's couch. This location carries with it an inevitable price tag, however. His first thought after the arrival of the woman is one of restitution: "how, how will I ever repay her? . . . What in the world will she demand of me?" The beautiful muse reassures him that all will be well, and her explanation ties his dreams and the price tag for them to Babichev and his construction project. "Oh, don't worry," she quiets him. "It's only two bits" (28). As such, the woman serves as a reminder of the inevitable cost of participation in Babichev's communal project: prostitution of one's individual muse.

From here the narrative moves to a dream sequence or a remembered fragment in which Kavalerov and his father visit a wax museum. The famous figures immortalized there remind us again of Kavalerov's dreams of glory. He views the wax representation of a former French president, Sadi Carneau, captured for all time in the throes of death after an anarchist's attack. Kavalerov views the scene in a kind of rapture; for the first time in his short life, he hears the "hum of history" (*gul vremeni* [28]) and realizes the inexorable pull that time has on human affairs, first of all on his own individual existence. This sense that he, too, will one day be nothing more than a memory, that, in fact, to remain in the future as a fleeting wax image is the privilege of only the most famous, spurs the young Kavalerov to vow to become a celebrity. "I swallowed rapturous tears. I decided to become famous, so that one day my wax double, filled with the din of centuries that only a few can hear, would also adorn a greenish cube in just this way" (29).

The temptation to confuse Kavalerov's musings with those of Olesha himself is made even greater by the next paragraph, in which an authorial "I" appears to bemoan his own place in life and eventual mark in literary history. "Now I'm writing the repertoire for popular stage performers," complains this narrative voice, "monologues and rhymed couplets about tax inspectors, Soviet princesses,

NEP men, and alimony" (29). Both the fictional Kavalerov and the real-life Olesha thus express their creative anxiety about the fleeting nature of artistic output. If they miss the chance to participate in this new world under construction, the only one worth considering, they relinquish their chance for fame. Equally painful for both to admit, however, is the fact that any works they do construct will soon be outdated. Once Soviet authors accepted that they and their works were part of a transitional period, they doomed their own creation to obsolescence. In the brave industrial world that they wish to help build but will never inhabit, Kavalerov and Olesha will be, at best, nothing more than museum exhibits, marked by works no longer read or needed. Any space they are granted in the new universe will be in a wax museum, where the exhibit, although it is labeled "Nikolai Kavalerov," resembles all of Olesha's old-world heroes. It figures as a damning self-portrait as well.

> But maybe some time, after all, in a great panorama, there will stand a wax figure of a strange, bulbous-nosed man, with a pale, well-intentioned face, messy hair, childishly plump, in a jacket held together with only one button across the belly. And on the cube will be a little plaque: NIKOLAI KAVALEROV. And nothing else. And that's all. And everyone who sees it will say "Oh!" And will remember some kind of stories, maybe, some legends. "Oh, that was the one who lived in memorable times, who hated everyone and envied everyone, boasted, became arrogant, was tormented by great plans, wanted to accomplish a great deal and did nothing—and ended by committing a disgusting, vile crime." (29)

The wax figure and its importance as a monument to the individual ties the main male characters of the work together in a single space, a space related to the real construction site of the novel —the author's desk. As eccentric and angry as Ivan, as fatuous and plump as Andrei, the figure of Kavalerov emerges as a synthetic vision of the old world, the world in which the hero "was tormented by great plans, wanted to accomplish a great deal and did nothing." This world contains Ivan's irrationality and passion as well as Andrei's sentimentality and self-satisfaction, none of which has a place in the world under construction and is therefore relegated to the small, self-contained "greenish cube" of the museum. This square of green glass is marked only with the name of the individual whose musings make up the narrative "and nothing else. And that's all."

This is the creative process stripped bare, spread out on the terrifying glass space of the writer's desk where emptiness threatens at any minute to engulf the work of constructing fiction. Like all writers, Olesha worried that his work would become irrelevant or forgotten. As a fellow traveler of the late 1920s, however, Olesha had particular reason to fear that his work might disappear altogether. That is why he constructs this writer's space and ties to it both Andrei's pragmatism and Ivan's romanticism. This guarded museum space is safe, but static. As a habitat, it is fit for only one, already forgotten writer, and that is where Olesha leaves this discarded self. Although Kavalerov continues to move through the novel, it is already clear that he will not make it any further than the greenish cube he has been allotted. By the time he returns to his previous residence at the end of the narrative, he is already a former person, relegated to the disinterest of history. Ivan, with whom he will share his lodging, his bed, his landlady, and his fate, urges him to adopt an appropriate mode of behavior, one befitting the museum shelf: "Indifference is the best of all the states of the human brain. We'll be indifferent" (141).

The dispassion that Ivan counsels here at the end of the book is foreign to Kavalerov, who feels his exclusion from the new world intensely. But it is a natural state for his rival and double, Volodia Makarov, who inhabits the new universe with ease. Makarov reveals his pitilessness in his letter to Babichev, whom he chides for being too weak (*"ty slaben'kii"*), too caring (*"podumaesh': nezhnosti!"*), and too feeling (*"Eto u tebia rabota takaia, nastraivaet na chuvstvitel'nost'"*).[48] Makarov describes himself in opposition to this softness as an "industrial man," a fact he relates to their generational differences (*"Ia, ponimaesh' li, uzhe novoe pokolenie"* [58]). Makarov's indifference to the existence of the old world and its complicated "conspiracy of feelings" frees him to move effortlessly into the future, again imagined as an enclosed space conjured from the same green-covered writer's desk that has created the other locations of this fictional world. Volodia exists easily in this future space that is almost, but never quite accessible to those prematurely relegated to the past.

Ivan and Kavalerov travel through the real-world location of Moscow to reach this promised land that only the favored may inhabit. Olesha sets his characters in a familiar location in the center of the city, where they notice that even light and shade have taken material form. Their "charming" walk through this "empty, holiday" landscape leads them to enter a "stereoptical" world in which light and dark assume a shape, a "thickness" uncharacteristic of everyday locations. This magical picture of the familiar world suggests that space itself is gradually being reconfigured. The exceptional clarity of vision that Olesha describes prepares us for the unusual landscape awaiting Ivan and Kavalerov at their destination —a glass structure on an incongruous green patch of grass in the center of Moscow. Olesha locates their position precisely: on a lane between Tverskaia and Nikitskaia streets stands a green hedge (*tsvetushchaia izgorod'* [118]) that marks the entrance to this new world and suggests the fantastic existence that awaits all who enter.

Ivan and Kavalerov pass through gates and climb a staircase to reach a mysterious "glass-enclosed gallery" that is overgrown and "untended" but nevertheless "cheerful." This long, glass structure resembles an abandoned greenhouse with its ivy-covered sides. The fact that the glass walls are missing many individual panes gives the building a faceted aspect and has the unexpected effect of highlighting the view. This space, which is "intended for a happy childhood" (118), transforms the landscape for those who approach it, framing and freeing the view in the varied aspects that its glass façade simultaneously presents to the spectator. The resulting spatial distortion connects this place with others far distant in geographical terms. When Kavalerov catches hold of the "ivy or whatever the hell it was" that is growing into the structure, he notices that glass and plant have become an "invisible structure" that exists "as though in Italy and not in Moscow" (118). From his vantage point high in the air—"the gallery was located at a height midway between the second and the third floors"—Kavalerov is able to look down on to a "frighteningly green square." From this bird's-eye view, "Italy continued" (*Italiia prodolzhalas'* [119]).

If we had any doubts about the significance of this location to Olesha personally, they are removed by a diary passage from late 1930 in which he dreams of a day of rest, a day which "in its perception of life and its relationship to it resembles those that made up childhood and early youth." On such a day, Olesha notes longingly, he will "take a walk out of town along some kind of fallen brick wall—in loneliness and quiet, sweaty, barefoot, in an unbuttoned shirt . . . I'll stride along, seen by no one, forgotten by everyone in a search for immediate sensations . . . Then far, far in front of me I'll see the giant letters on the back side of a factory, a ravine will cross my path, that refuse ditch over which the genius of travel hovered in childhood" (100).[49] Realizing that a ditch full of trash is a most unlikely place for the "dreamiest genius of childhood" to arise, Olesha explains its fascination for him by its location on the forbidden edge of town. The location is dangerous, in parents' view, for its stray dogs, unfamiliar boys, and suspicious looking vagrants.

They haunt the neighborhood to which Olesha, himself now a beggar, wants to return. The garbage that fascinated Kavalerov has now returned as a source of wonder for Olesha too.

This landscape seems to be from the past, but what is most intriguing in it, for both the adult Olesha and his readers, is an incongruously foreign and futuristic figure of a water tower, which "resembles nothing else." This tower, which has nothing at all in common with the "buildings of the city, its roofs, balconies, courtyards, and entrances," serves Olesha as the site of endless potential that only the future can offer. His potent description of the seemingly nondescript location makes clear how much he, and other authors of production novels, had invested in the imaginary landscapes of their manuscripts. "The tower," Olesha notes in his diary, "did not belong to the city, to the order, to all that which was familiar and existed only so long and until such time as the prohibitions and restrictions of childhood existed. It soared up in another location, already in the future. There was an iron staircase around it. An un-Russian something green bloomed at its feet, and there was a round, little, un-Russian window in its high, high, blind body" (101).[50] Although Olesha tries to defuse the power of the image he has just created by following it immediately with a parenthetical disclaimer ("a small portion of *belle lettres*" [101]), it is clear that he invests the symbol with significance far beyond even that normally allotted to a cherished childhood memory.

The future, tantalizing and dangerous, beckons, but Olesha is not at all certain that he will be able to inhabit the fascinating new world it represents. Doubts about his own worthiness torment the author, who engages again and again in a complicated dialogue with himself on the subject. Here the conversation is not the easy one his colleague Vladimir Mayakovsky imagined between the poet and the tax collector, but an emotionally fraught discussion between the poet's old understanding of himself and a newer self-image that the times insist he adopt. "Occasionally I think," Olesha's diary from 1930 notes,

> "Oh, how well I, a bourgeois, would live in a bourgeois society!" I start to hate what surrounds me. And then suddenly I remember and I yell to myself: "How's that? Really? Am I really against this most majestic of ideas? I, having read Wells in childhood, I'm against the idea that will build fantastic technology? I already saw this city of the future in my dreams, the glitter of giant glass, the sparkling blue of some kind of endless summer . . . How's that? I—a Philistine, a property owner? No! No! No! I'm embarrassed even in front of myself!"[51]

As emphatic as Olesha's denials are, however, he ends the passage with the plaintive, yet clear understanding that he will never enter the future he so vividly imagines. "After all," he concludes mournfully, "I won't be around then. After all, I won't live long enough to see technology in socialism." This sober realization is one Olesha shares with most writers of his generation, all of whom were fated, as he was, to feel "mowed down (*skoshennym*) somehow," only "two dimensional" in the elaborate three-dimensional future they were certain lay just beyond the next hill.[52]

This sensation of belonging to a transitional generation during the very years their country was being restructured was tortuous for most writers. Among other torments, most shared the painful sense that the traditional forms of literature they had studied, loved, and practiced were now inadequate to describe the positive changes they hoped they would soon see around them. This explains Olesha's numerous protests in his diary concerning his "hatred" for *belles lettres*[53] and his repeated insistence that fiction had no place in the new world under construction. He describes his "success" with a declaration to that effect to his fellow writers during an evening meal at the Herzen House in central Moscow. "I say: 'Literature ended in the year 1931.' Laughter. My prophecies meet with success. No, comrades, I say, really. Literature in the sense in which it has been understood in the world where . . ."[54]

Olesha's comment, which trails off in an inconclusive ellipsis in the diary entry, is balanced elsewhere by ambitious plans to replace *belles lettres* with a more authentic literature of fact. "Instead of starting to write a novel," Olesha begins a diary entry from May 5, 1930, hopefully,

> I'm going to start writing a diary. The reader is fascinated by memoirs. I will say for my own part that I too find it much more pleasant to read memoirs than *belles lettres*. (I hate the latter.) Why dream up, "create"? It's necessary to note down the content of everything experienced, honestly, day after day, without philosophizing or, for those who succeed, with philosophizing. Let everyone write diaries: office workers, blue-collar workers, writers, functional illiterates, men, women, children—now that's an investment in the future![55]

In Olesha's case such occasional optimism usually resulted in a quick abandonment of the diary form, however, or in the author's sober realization that the act of writing itself was "literary," even when the product was ostensibly "fact." Thus his comment of May 5, 1930, ended just a few paragraphs later with an admission that "sometimes it seems to me that the writing of a diary is just a trick, just the desire to push off from some kind of unusual material in order to find a form for the novel, i.e., to return to *belles lettres*."[56]

Olesha's acuity here is reflected as well in a lengthy criticism he makes of the many organized literary campaigns of the time. He explicitly criticizes even the production novel itself as a prepared form that is irrelevant to the era it wishes to chronicle. "How they cook up novels!" he complains. "How offensive it has become to read these novels! No more than a week passes from the day the latest campaign is announced, and, be my guest, here comes a series of stories with the theme, the hero, the type, with anything needed: collective farm construction, a purge, construction of a new city. It's imperative, supposedly, for literature to reflect the times . . . But is such a form of reflection itself timely? The short story? The poem? The novel?"[57]

Olesha may want to escape the tyranny of such packaged novels to discover a new form, but most often he finds himself in an uncomfortable position between the old and the new. "I'm hanging between two worlds," he complains before adding, hopeful once more, "this real situation is so unusual that a simple description of it could compete against the most cunning *belles lettres*." Confessing elsewhere that "I'm in a state of complete confusion," he continues, "I'm not a bourgeois and not a 'new man.' Then who in the world am I? No one. A function in time. I'm my own thought, born in childhood." His return to an image of the future that he first imagined as a child allows Olesha to be content with a modest goal: a book of the sort he is contemplating about loneliness, he insists, would nevertheless "have the right to exist."[58] It is a sign of the times, of course, that such a humble ambition nevertheless seems utopian in the highly politicized era.

Olesha's tortured confessions about his versifying (*sochinitel'stvo*) reflect the general dissatisfaction with traditional forms that characterized his era. Most of his colleagues were equally convinced that their times demanded a break with the literature of the past. Thus, Boris Pilniak remarks in a "programmatic article" from 1922 "we and I, I and we—and not I and they, I and he—she: — is the new theme." He notes in 1924 that "it's clear to me that more and more I'm departing from those *belles lettres* where 'He entered. She sat down. He said. She said, both about love and the moon shines through the window.' It constantly seems that I'm departing from *belles lettres*, forever, from every kind. It's necessary to write differently somehow." Marietta Shaginian echoes similar sentiments in a diary entry from 1928, insisting on the current need for new forms in literature: "I need to settle in on the new and find the new, my own form" (*ia dolzhna zasest' na novoe i naiti novuiu—svoiu formu*). That conviction leads her, too, to a change in plans: "with that I decided to return to [the book about the hydroelectric construction project] Dzorages (at one time I had firmly decided to break off with it)."[59]

The dissatisfaction Olesha, Pilniak, and Shaginian express over conventional fiction was typical of writers even in the early 1920s. Boris Shklovskii, for example, notes a similar sentiment from Aleksei Remizov, who complained "I can no longer begin a novel 'Ivan Ivanovich was sitting at his desk.'" It is Shklovskii, as well, who notes that Andrei Platonov had decided that it was "impossible to describe a sunset and impossible to write short stories." According to Valentin Kataev, Ivan Bunin, too, was increasingly wary of such literary clichés during this time, and Kataev's own weariness with conventional forms emerges in his sketch "Porogi," where he notes "that's how I should have written, if I followed the traditions of the old literary genre. However, that's completely impossible. The epoch and style have parted ways. The old forms are no longer adequate for the volume and quality of the new content. Just as the landscape that I've had for eleven years is no longer in any condition to accommodate within it signs of its new meaning and place in the world."[60]

Such comments are indicative of the need most writers felt at the time to create a literature that would reconcile new societal demands with their own individual talents. Boris Pilniak explicitly engages this desire for new forms and new themes in a short story from 1925 entitled "An Unborn Tale" (*Nerozhdennaia povest'*). The narrator there interrupts Pilniak's story within a story to describe his own attempts to write something brand new. He mentions looking at the sky, particularly the moon, and wonders if it is possible to write something unique that has never been written before. "I wanted to discover a word for the moon," he notes plaintively, "which has never before been said." He tries out various adjectives in his search for a new way of expressing himself, but he is dissatisfied with them all: "Round, green, full—no, not that. Dry, frozen, icy—no, not that. Indifferent, calm, callous, kind, stupid—no, no, not that . . ."[61]

The narrator's struggles are made more poignant by the fact that Pilniak draws specific parallels between himself and his "fictional" character. As the narrator heads home to the street on which the real-life Pilniak lives, he continues his attempts to hit on an altogether original adjective for the celestial body. He dates his story "Gaspra, May 28, 1925," but he leaves it to future readers to provide a link between this story and Pilniak's other "Tale of the Unextinguished Moon," which provides in its title a solution to their shared search for originality. The moon in "An Unborn Tale" shines "in Moscow, and in Madrid, and in Paris, and in Spitsbergen," the narrator/author notes, and "maybe some acquaintance, a friend is looking at it from London and has thought of me." Maybe the moon is like a ruble, the author comments finally. Yet even this last attempt at originality is interrupted by a quotation that makes the communal nature of literature obvious. "The moon is like a ruble," he notes, "(if the moon is reflected in the sea, then it's possible to say 'the ruble of the moon is exchanged for silver pennies by the water'—that's nicely said, the moon, like a pot—no, you can't think of anything, it's all been said)—no matter what word you dream up—they've all been picked over." Concluding wistfully in the last sentence of the story, the narrator notes "I didn't manage to think up a word for the moon."[62]

Olesha's work, particularly the early work *Envy*, draws much of its charm from precisely this same desire to find completely new formulations for shared sentiments. The alluring yet disturbing location for such literary magic is the construction site we have visited before: the glass-covered, green-topped working table at which Olesha-Kavalerov-Babichev labors to give birth to a new world from his old-fashioned emotions. Unlike the tortured Nikolai, Ivan, and Andrei, however, the alter ego of these characters, Volodia Makarov, has no problem inhabiting this new space of the "pleasant, sweet, and cold" "green of the lawn" (119). Looking on as Volodia trains for a sporting event, Kavalerov and Ivan can see the entire region, which spreads out in all directions, even as it threatens to overwhelm this small "meadow." The small space is crowded, defined as it is by tall, thickly crowned trees that line its edges. This tiny location in the center of Moscow seems about to be overgrown with "Italian" weeds or crushed by the unfriendly structures that surround it. Nevertheless, it remains the focus of our attention—"the little square was all important" (120) —and that of the characters as well.

When Ivan and Kavalerov descend from the gallery to the square itself, however, they find themselves no nearer to the source of their envy. Although Olesha's forbidden patch of earth is now in the center of the city, access to the green expanse is barred: a stone

wall stands in the way of Ivan and Kavalerov, and they are forced
to play the role of spectators rather than participants in this
demonstration of life in the future. Olesha the writer has been here
before. We know that because he tells us so in diary accounts of
encounters that he, the impoverished son of a disenfranchised
landowner, experienced in his youth. Exploring wealthy neighbor-
hoods as a child, the young Olesha peeked over the fences and
walls that separated him from the well-to-do, noting, as he did so,
that "someone else's fence didn't scare me and didn't oppress my
feelings. Just the opposite. I'd put my elbows on the wall, and
peeking into the private garden, I would weigh, as it were, what
others possessed, comparing it with what I would possess." These
early daydreams about future success are accompanied by absolute
conviction in the glories of an individual future. "I was completely
calm about my own future," Olesha continues, "therefore I was
never envious."[63]

What has changed, then, to turn the "never envious" daydreamer
into the author of *Envy?* Only the context for their dreams is different, but, as the writer and his characters learn to their chagrin,
context is essential to meaning. In Olesha's universe, as we have
seen, dreams of glory revolve around the journey of a "young man
from the provinces to the very center to arrange his personal fate."[64]
But what if that "center" no longer holds? "We say: Moscow, Moscow, the capital, the capital," Olesha grumbles in his diary. "But,
after all, the concept of a capital has been destroyed. Where is the
main city of the new world?" The "system has been annulled," he
complains. "All cities are equal."[65]

When Ivan, Kavalerov, and Olesha peek through a gap in the
wall this time to observe their own creative green space, they
find that it is already occupied by the hero of the new world that
is closed to them. Volodia Makarov is a picture of grace and
strength, and he seems to have freed himself from the earthly
bounds that detain others. As he leaps from space to space, he
demonstrates the agility, raw power, grace, and reach that is denied inhabitants of the old world but will serve as the birthright
of the new Soviet man. "They saw jumping practice. A rope was
tied between two poles. The young man soared up, carrying his
body over the rope sideways, almost gliding, stretched out parallel to the obstacle, as though he weren't jumping over, but rolling
through an obstacle, as though through a wave. And as he rolled
through, he kicked his legs as though he were a swimmer cutting
through water" (120).

Such harmony is ultimately denied to Ivan, Kavalerov, and even Andrei, who look with envy on the future they will never successfully enter. The rope Kavalerov has contemplated using for his suicide is now a barrier over which Makarov soars effortlessly. The physical wall that separates Kavalerov and Ivan from Makarov is now a chronological and psychological one as well, as Olesha and his characters begin to doubt they will ever be able to take advantage of the chinks the walls offer to those who would like to enter. This dilemma, which Olesha shared with many of his generation, is what allows Violetta Gudkova to conclude that creative individuals as diverse as Vsevolod Meyerhold, Boris Pasternak, Osip Mandelstam, and Iurii Olesha "lived and thought, felt and perished as anti-Soviet people, having convinced themselves to become Soviet and then been unable to do so."[66]

That intense desire "to become Soviet" is clearly what motivated many of the authors of these early production novels. The real fear that they would be "unable to do so" explains Ivan's behavior shortly after he sees Volodia's demonstration of prowess. Clinging to his daughter's legs as she sits on top of the wall that divides them, Ivan piteously begs his offspring to "Pluck out my eyes. I want to be blind." Despairing of ever making the transition to the new world that was required of all artists, Ivan turns away from the vision of near paradise that haunts him. "I don't want to see anything," he continues, surrendering not only his inappropriate feelings but also the battlefield on which he had hoped to defend them, "not meadows, not branches, not flowers, not knights, not cowards. I should go blind" (122).

Olesha fought against such despair with only varying success. He is quoted, for example, in late 1935, complaining that it was impossible to praise "destitution" (*nishcheta*) in the "rainbow colors" that were apparently more and more frequently required for publication.[67] Anguished by the sense that he was not serving the revolution he had chosen to support, Olesha nevertheless continued to work for its shared goals in the only way he could. He subjected himself to criticism more severe than any others directed his way, confronting himself, for example, with continual accusations of the sort found in his autobiographical writings from this period: "On the day of the twelfth anniversary of the October Revolution, I, a Soviet writer, ask myself the question: What have you, a Soviet writer, done for the proletariat? For the proletariat, I have done nothing."[68] Excruciating self-analyses of this sort seem to have tormented Olesha for the rest of his career,[69] but he nevertheless con-

tinued working and writing even after it became clear that his eccentric contributions to Soviet literature were largely unwelcome.
He was sensitive to claims that he had stopped contributing,[70] and
his stubborn attempts to write in an otherwise hostile environment
suggest his continuing belief that his view of the society he helped
create was still valid.

His famous story "The Cherry Pit" presents a final scene from the
Soviet landscape as Olesha pictured it. That work, which gave its
name to a collection of short stories from 1931, explicitly engages
the Five-Year Plan in its elegant and nuanced discussion of the role
of the artist in the new world under construction. In this story, we
see Olesha continuing to search for a creative space for himself between the old world he rejects and the new one he has not yet entered. As he often does, Olesha combines an image of unrequited
love and sexual frustration with the notion of artistic endeavor. The
hero of the story longs for a kiss from Natasha, the young heroine
whose own sexual desire is directed elsewhere. Instead of a kiss, the
hero is left with only a cherry pit in his mouth. It is that pit, and its
creative potential, that allows the writer to find an artistic path for
himself in an unfamiliar environment. As he leaves Natasha's summer home with only the cherry pit, he sets off on a now familiar
journey toward a green space that represents creative endeavor. "I
am traveling in an invisible land," the hero tells us.

> I'm completing a two-pronged path. One fork is available for everyone
> to see: anyone meeting me would see a person walking across a deserted
> green location. But what is going on with this person walking along
> peacefully. He sees his own shadow in front of himself. The shadow
> moves along the ground, stretched out far ahead; it has long, pale legs.
> I cross the empty space; the shadow climbs up a brick wall and suddenly
> loses its head. No one meeting me would see that. Only I see that.[71]

The path, the green meadow, the wall, and the artist are the same
images to which Olesha has returned again and again, and here he
names their location specifically: "this all takes place in an invisible land," he tells us. "The invisible land is the land of attention
and imagination."[72]

Here, then, is the location of all of Olesha's creative work, the
birthplace of stories that delight and trouble, of production novels
that find acceptance and works that are denied publication. "So,
what is going on, after all?" the story continues. "Does this mean
that in defiance of everyone, in defiance of order and society, I create a world, which doesn't submit to any laws, except for the illu-

sory laws of my individual sensations? What does it all mean? There are two worlds—the old and the new—but what world is this? A third world? There are two paths, but what sort of third world is this?"[73] Olesha's clear rejection here of the world of binary oppositions should give those who study the history of Soviet literature food for thought. His insistence on the existence of a third world with myriad other options makes it clear that he still hoped to find a way to express the personal in shared societal terms. This was a desire Olesha shared with the authors of other early production novels, but it is particularly obvious in "The Cherry Pit" since Olesha takes such care there to locate his creative nexus at the very center of the first Five-Year Plan.

The hero of "The Cherry Pit" plants his seed in the middle of the deserted space he has identified as the location of his creative endeavors. He does this intuitively, forgetting, as he informs Natasha in a letter never sent, "the most important thing: the plan." "The Plan exists. I acted without having consulted the Plan. On that spot, where right now there is a vacuum, a ditch, useless walls, in five years a cement giant will be erected. My sister—Imagination— is a rash figure. In the spring they'll start to lay down the foundation—and where will my stupid little cherry pit go then!"[74]

Just at the moment his creation seems doomed, however, Olesha finds a way to combine the old and the new in a creative gesture that saves the individual face in the group portrait that the production novel represents. The hero of the story is trailing a guide around the future construction site, listening as the guide explains to a group of visitors how ambitious plans for an enormous complex will transform all that they see. "The visitors will come up to the concrete giant," the hero concludes, adding sorrowfully that "they won't see your tree. Is it really impossible to make the invisible land visible?"[75] Just as he is about to concede, however, the artist hears the guide make a comment. These overheard words convince him that his vision is entirely consistent with plans for the new world: "This building," notes the guide, whose name, Abel, suggests that even historical antagonisms can be overcome, "will be laid out in a semi-circle." And "the interior of the semi-circle will be filled with a garden," he adds, resolutely. "Do you have an imagination?"[76]

The hero's answer, with which Olesha concludes his 1931 short story collection, is nearly ecstatic in its response to the notion that individual creativity can be incorporated into a communal plan. Olesha's profound conviction that his version of the production novel is a legitimate example of that genre informs the end of this story too. Quirky, eccentric, incomplete, the tree that grows from Olesha's imagination nevertheless belongs in the garden of the future, and his conclusion to "The Cherry Pit" is both affirmation of that belief and prayer that others will agree. "I do" have an imagination, "I say." 'I see, Abel.' I see clearly. There will be a garden here. And on that very place where you are standing, will grow a cherry tree."[77]

2
How She Worked on *Hydrocentral:*
Marietta Shaginian and the
Changing Soviet Author

*H*YDROCENTRAL (*GIDROTSENTRAL'*), THE MASSIVE WORK ON SOVIET construction that Marietta Shaginian (1888–1982) produced about her beloved Armenia, is one of the most fascinating examples of the early production novel. This dense, generically complex, and episodic narrative is a broad account of the many setbacks involved in building a hydroelectric plant in the mid-1920s in newly Soviet Armenia. Meant to depict a slice of life from a generous section of society, *Hydrocentral* is a fictionalized retelling of Shaginian's own observations and personal experiences on-site at a similar project on the Dzoraget River between 1926 and 1928. An intrepid traveler, faithful diarist, and tireless correspondent during this period, Shaginian left a rich record of her involvement in the building project that makes it possible to track her development as a writer both on site and off.[1] As a former Symbolist poet, whose experience involved training in German philosophy in western Europe and whose acquaintances included a wide array of the best known turn-of-the-century Russian authors, including Zinaida Gippius, Dmitrii Merezhkovskii, Marina Tsvetaeva, Aleksandr Blok, and Andrei Belyi, Shaginian was an exceedingly incongruous cataloger of the Soviet laborer. Yet for that very reason, she is perhaps the perfect person to test the hypothesis of Soviet cultural construction. If Marietta Shaginian could learn from the workers and remake herself on the construction site, then surely it would be within the reach of other writers to do so.

According to accounts from the author herself, Shaginian's interest in the topic of construction predated official attempts to engage writers in the actual process of building socialism.[2] The notion that writers and other members of the intelligentsia had much to

learn from the working class was common throughout the postrevolutionary years, but the first organized calls for authors to take up
positions in the country's new factories and plants came after
Shaginian had already spent time on-site. Jeffrey Brooks notes that
the topic of construction, important from the early days of the revolution, increased in significance and frequency in the Soviet press
beginning in 1927, and Evgenii Dobrenko details official delegations of "writers to the factory" in the early 1930s. Shaginian was
at pains to date her own trips to a time before that and to describe
her venture into the workaday world of the Soviet laborer as a self-
directed enterprise.[3]

In her diaries from 1926, she details an excursion, one of many
from this peripatetic period, to a hydroelectric plant outside of
Yerevan. She notes that she is interested in both the progress and
the history of the project, which has brought German engineering
specialists to the area and promises to provide a significant amount
of electrical power to the region. The site itself is beautiful, and
Shaginian makes plans on this day in January 1926 for a longer visit
to the office since she has "taken up the idea of building (*vozymela
ideiu postroit'*) my new novel on the theme of that hydrostation."[4]
Her schedule that spring keeps her busy with trips and reporting,
but she finds time to think about the novel and plan its first chapter, a description of an employment bureau that, in fact, finds its
way into the final version of the completed work.[5] A short time
later, Shaginian is planning a weeklong visit to the office and a
study trip to the Council of People's Commissars (Sovnarkom) to
view the archival history of the plant.[6] Her work in the State Planning Committee (Gosplan) archives about the station's construction inspires her even further,[7] and this incident, too, ends up as an
episode in the novel, when one of the main characters is hired as
an archivist on-site.

That character, Ryzhii, or Red, is a proxy in many ways for Shaginian herself. Ryzhii engenders a certain amount of mistrust on
the construction site, and it is clear that Shaginian received a similar reception on her own visits to the building project. She notes at
several points in her diaries that her motives were often the subject
of skepticism during this era. As a woman, she stood out in the
largely male hierarchy on construction sites.[8] As a journalist, too,
Shaginian would have made builders and administrators leery of
her propensity to report inadequacies in the building projects. Her
willingness to learn all she could about this and almost any other
new subject was undoubtedly endearing to some, but such charms

would not have completely made up for the fact that Shaginian was an outsider whose intrusive presence was bound to make the actual work go slower.

Her diary entry about a 1928 research trip to Abkhazia demonstrates her intruder status. She describes an encounter she has there with a red-headed engineer, who tries to block her access to the site she wishes to visit. He "told me that it was 'impossible to get through there' and with great contempt for me allowed himself to doubt that I needed to go there any way. I always meet with such contempt in the beginning of my work and I'm not even surprised by it since people sit for years on their 'subject,' know it down to the last detail, [and] in the 'center' see constant obstacles and ignorance and inevitably look upon a person who flies in from outside as an 'incompetent.'" Shaginian was, nevertheless, able to conclude that day's entry with a more consoling anecdote. The arrogant engineer of the morning had since realized his mistake and sent her a note of apology: "Forgive me my sarcastic tone in our conversation. I've just realized that you are not any old female correspondent, but Marietta Shaginian herself. Welcome!" Shaginian appears to fall for the flattery completely, commenting that it delighted her to know that she had the reputation of a "powerful newspaper employee."[9]

The writer reports that it was initially difficult for her to arrange further visits to the construction site. Her determination to move forward on the project finally paid off, however, and she was successful in visiting a second site in the spring of 1927. She moved to that site, a remote location seven kilometers from the nearest railroad, in the fall of 1927 and spent much of the winter there during a crucial time in the construction project. The result of this extended stay was the novel *Hydrocentral,* published serially in 1930 and then separately in 1931.[10] The work provides a fascinating glimpse into the early stages of the development of the production novel as a genre, and Shaginian's diaries and her extended journalistic description of her work in the booklet *How I worked on "Hydrocentral"*[11] provide us with additional sources of information about the unusual process of constructing self and society in the new Soviet Union.

Shaginian's personal experience in researching and writing the novel suggests the need to modify our notions of the production novel as a "genre from above." This former Symbolist's interest in the most esoteric details of heavy industry was evidently genuine, her "exile" to the remote construction site apparently voluntary. Her notebooks from this time are full of detailed, if somewhat school-girlish, accounts of industrial facts, descriptions of chemical processes, and predictions of projected yields, as though she has set out to "learn industry" in her whirlwind tours of a few factories. As S. V. Laine notes in an interpretation of Shaginian timed for the writer's centennial celebration, "there was no book about concrete, about the ways to mix it, that she would not have studied."[12] A diary comment from Shaginian's visit in June 1926 to the Red October metal factory in Stalingrad reveals her changing aesthetic sense during this time, as well. She notes her fascination with the factory and mentions with evident pride that she has "become acquainted with heavy industry this year." Her recent experiences with mining and metallurgy have taught her how "incredibly plastic and beautiful" industry is "in the process of work." In general, Shaginian concludes emphatically, "labor is the most beautiful and most graceful thing that human beings have."[13]

Shaginian was an outsider on the construction sites she visited, but she did her best to overcome this situation by throwing herself wholeheartedly into accessible areas of the process. She notes in *How I worked on "Hydrocentral"* that she felt it necessary to "prove [her] right to existence." She did this by helping where she could—in the drama club, the chess club, and the "club to raise political awareness," for example—and by listening to the workers' complaints in order to "make it possible to arrive at the root meaning of construction."[14] Although she lacked official authority to intervene, Shaginian was often connected in the workers' minds with an all-powerful central authority, and she usually took the workers' side in conflicts that arose on-site. Her diary from 1926 is full of instances in which she finds herself surrounded by workers who want her to intercede for them with the higher authorities.[15] She remarks with chagrin elsewhere that it is impossible to get anything done in the current situation "without throwing a fit"; luckily for her, she is a born "scandal-monger."[16] On-site at the Dzorages hydroelectric project in Armenia, she was apparently instrumental in bringing problems to the attention of the Workers' Inspectorate (*Rabkrin*), an episode that is fictionalized at some length at the end of *Hydrocentral.*

Shaginian's description of her extended stay at the site lists a host of problems associated with life around the project. Extant diaries and brief passages in *How I worked on "Hydrocentral"* allow just a glimpse into the most prosaic aspects of the hard-scrabble existence that characterized early Soviet construction sites. Shaginian's passing comments on leaky barracks, malfunctioning stoves, treacherously icy paths, inadequate food supplies, and primitive hygiene hint at, rather than highlight, the dreadful working conditions that true believers and conscripted labor alike had to endure while building a new universe. Nevertheless, Shaginian discounts these problems as insignificant, de-emphasizing such details in the novel and arguing that "all these everyday (*zhiteiskie*) inconveniences didn't poison life in the least." *Hydrocentral* is a "harsh document," she continues later, "a monument of the negative phenomena on the construction site. All the same, it gives a positive charge." This "stern and harsh history" gives a "better picture of the positive meaning of the construction than if I had smeared over what was experienced and castrated the truth."[17]

Worse than such temporary inconveniences, according to Shaginian, were the doubts and ill will that characterized certain factions' attitude toward construction in general. The sense that many of those involved in building the new world were mired in the old emerges frequently in her diary entries, particularly after a disaster at the Dzorages project forces her to conclude that "99% of everyone at Dzorages took cruel pleasure and rejoiced"[18] at the unfortunate turn of events. As disheartening as such reactions may have been, Shaginian's response is one of enthusiastic action in the face of what she sees as temporary setbacks, an approach that was common in this era of seemingly endless possibilities and new beginnings. When the author on one of her numerous study trips during this period describes the nearly hopeless situation of farmers in Nagorno Karabakh, for example, earnestly transcribing their antiquated methods of horticulture, inadequate average land holdings, and so on, she continues to project the sense that all such "everyday inconveniences" will soon be understood and corrected.[19]

During this period in the Soviet Union, enthusiasts like Marietta Shaginian believed that, even in the face of catastrophe, their optimism could outweigh the pessimism of the naysayers. Hardships and setbacks seemed to spur such individuals to greater effort, in the conviction that their efforts would allow a better way to triumph. That fact is difficult to comprehend or even appreciate in hindsight, but it is an important point to grasp if we are to avoid an approach to the Soviet period that divides the populace into cynical opportunists and hapless victims. As curious as it may seem now and as damaging to our notion of shared values, it was possible in the late 1920s and early 1930s for well-meaning observers to comprehend the enormous human costs needed to impose the new Soviet system and still express willingness to pay. The early production novels, *Hydrocentral* included, are compelling evidence that their authors understood the risks involved in the enterprises they chronicled and agreed to the costs. If they underestimated those costs, or miscalculated the price they themselves would have to pay, they nevertheless endorsed the proposed end result.

Thus it is that both in her diaries and in her novel, Shaginian emphasizes her endorsement of Soviet construction efforts, despite occasional misgivings. In 1926, for example, she notes that she is having difficulty making herself work, commenting laconically "I don't want to turn completely to creation."[20] In 1928, as she sits at work on-site, working on a version of *Hydrocentral,* she receives a copy of Symbolist poet Aleksandr Blok's diary. The volume reminds her of the past, a prospect which is far from cheering: "I began to remember my past, the milieu which I had left." Confronted with these memories, she notes cryptically that only "unconsciousness (*bespamiatstvo*) saves her." She continues: "I have terribly little strength" and "I guard it and instinctively travel lightly, without memory (*bez pamiati*). And when you are reminded, there's instantly a weight of many years on your back." Claiming that she's becoming a bore, she notes "I'm ruining the fourth chapter [of *Hydrocentral*]. On Sunday I crossed it all out, wrote it over again, but I still think that the novel is coming out flat."[21] Reading Blok's diary "again!" a few weeks later, she notes that "it's so frightening, as though you see a film of your past."[22] In the middle of a search for the source of "magnetic and electric force" during the same period, Shaginian identifies power as "gender—female and male, the division of the initial *'unikum,'* the first act of symmetry, from which flows the mutual activity of divided particles" before immediately rejecting her own conclusion. "That is metaphysics," she concludes unhappily, "and I need physics! I've stepped away from the novel and grown cold toward it."[23]

It was Shaginian's hope that these personal doubts could be countered, however, with greater individual effort. Her "stubborn and thorough attempts to work"[24] are exactly the response typical for this period, when uncertainty was seen as a failure of will and commitment. Doubts in the ultimate rightness of the undertaking were anathema, but worse still was the possibility that individual weakness could lead to a more general and devastating loss of faith in the cause. This makes Shaginian's admittedly elliptic comments about a conflict on-site in March 1928 somewhat surprising. She alludes in the diary to the "stupidest story," a conflict with someone on-site that has interrupted work. The "confused lesson" she draws from the encounter details a host of conditions that might doom the best construction project, regardless of builders' fervent belief in its righteousness. "Our construction is set up abnormally, wildly, absurdly!" Shaginian concludes angrily. "We are spinning our wheels in the mud, a disgusting principle, who is to blame for that—unknown. Spying, mutual surveillance, intrigues, slander, denunciations, idiocy after idiocy, no honest social atmosphere."[25] Such a conclusion was dangerous to her notion of the power of collective effort, and Shaginian carefully downplays such ideas in the novel she eventually produced. Shaginian's challenge, which she shared with other authors of such early production novels, was to reconcile her personal commitment to the Soviet project with a clear understanding of the many obstacles that stood in the way.

This was a considerable challenge since Shaginian and observers like her could obviously see that in this early period of socialist building, initial construction efforts were remarkable as much for their haste and shortsightedness as for the enthusiasm supporters brought to them. Although Shaginian minimizes some of the problems with early Soviet construction and almost entirely ignores issues like the use of conscripted labor, for example, her account in *Hydrocentral* is nevertheless noteworthy for its relatively frank portrayal of building efforts. Early socialist construction was a poorly planned, underfunded, and badly organized affair, and the resulting chaos, which leads in the novel to the collapse of an inadequately engineered bridge, is one of the essential topics of Shaginian's novel. This aspect of *Hydrocentral* will surprise readers who expect it to conform to later notions of the production novel as exemplary Socialist Realism. The novel's refusal to "lie on the Procrustean bed of the [proposed Socialist Realist] Master Plot" challenges the picture of the production novel as a fully formed genre handed down to authors from above and impervious to development or deviations from a centrally controlled story line.[26]

Shaginian begins *Hydrocentral* with an architectural metaphor, the first of many in this work with its emphasis on the formative effect that structures and building have on human consciousness. The first chapter, entitled "Employment Bureau," opens with a detailed picture of the building that houses this *birzha truda*. The long wooden barracks has floor-to-ceiling windows that allow a full view of the activities inside. The resulting tableau suggests a museum display, as it provides readers the opportunity to peer in to the life of the bureau, which resembles "thousands just like it."[27] Like an architectural drawing that cuts away the side of the structure to reveal the mysteries of the interior, Shaginian's description opens the workings of the bureau to our inspection. In so doing, Shaginian reveals a surprisingly fantastic and decidedly unpleasant side to life in this bureaucracy.

She focuses first on the "live participants of the bureau," who unexpectedly turn out to be the tables that stand "expressive and important" in the middle of the department (7). This focus on the tables, with their unwieldy piles of documents and "purple tide" of ink, suggests an unhealthy structure in which the trivial effects of material culture have gained the upper hand over the human inhabitants. People are added as an afterthought. "Anxious additions to the tables," they have grown so used to their positions that they seem to move about on the insect-like, four legs of their chairs. In Shaginian's telling, then, the employment bureau is an isolated space, an island of stilted, abnormal, "everyday existence that is still not completely Sovietized."[28] This grotesque parody of life reigns on one side of the bureau, which is divided by a small window from those on the other side who seek employment.

Shaginian drops her comparisons to both material culture and the insect world when describing supplicants on the other side of the barrier, "people of both sexes" and "all ages." Instead of bugs and flies, they are "machines of unknown intent, instruments for a thousand jobs." Shaginian is careful to avoid an overly mechanistic view of this yet untapped resource, however, referring to their very human "skills, tricks, habits, methods, experience and personal resourcefulness" as powerful energy to be tapped. Even when these would-be workers have no particular skills to apply, their "human force" is equal to that of water, steam, and coal. Shaginian's attention to this human natural resource, the powerful pent-up longing to work that is found in those who are unemployed, suggests her sympathy toward the idea that everyone should be involved in the business of building socialism. She expands on this notion by having the "conventional hero" of the novel, Ryzhii,[29] create a stir in the employment bureau by trying to shame officials there into finding work for people from all walks of life. The examples that Ryzhii uses of those who should be gainfully employed— an old man with years of experience in bookkeeping, an elderly lady schoolteacher, and a chauffeur—make it clear that Shaginian includes even "former people" in the list of those who can help construct socialism.

Ryzhii himself is a study in contrasts, uniting in his own person many of the seeming contradictions of the time. Identified as a person of "extraordinary appearance" (9), he is a blend of the dichotomies that had troubled Russian thinkers for decades, the seemingly unbridgeable gap between East and West, man and woman, intelligentsia and the people. Here, as in other early production novels, those binary structures are overcome, united in a single figure who manages to blend contradictory characteristics while remaining true to the essential features of both sides of the dichotomy. His "fine Aryan nose" rests easily above the "thin lips of an Asian." His "very large" stature is complemented by a "surprisingly soft" step (9). Part German, part Armenian, Ryzhii appears dressed in a pair of patched galoshes and a woman's riding habit from the secondhand store. This huge masculine figure is then compared to the "Muslim dancing girls" (10), coquettishly lifting the ends of their scarves, whose profiles graced the boxes of cigarettes at the time, and this gender confusion is repeated in a later plot device in which Ryzhii is misidentified as a women's hairdresser. Unemployed and nearly starving, he visits the employment bureau every day, his fondest dream a "working lunch during a break from work" (13). Even his desires for employment bridge seemingly disparate areas of activity, combining a need to catalog and preserve with a sense of artistry, an interest in disguise, and real devotion to political activism: at the bureau, he scours the lists of work for "archivists, violinists, hairdressers, and club workers" (12).[30] In a final gesture of synthesis, Shaginian has her character represent both the disruptive power of mocking laughter and the conservative thrust of institutional knowledge by naming him Ryzhii, a term that alludes to his red hair but hints at a clown's wig. In his pocket, we are told, this comical figure carries the diploma of a "doctor of philosophy" (12).

This richly synthetic figure serves as either the catalyst or the foil for most of the action in Shaginian's novel, and it is a tribute to her narrative skill and a comment on the diversity of the era that the eccentric Ryzhii emerges as a fully drawn and believable character. Ryzhii and an artist by the name of Arshak Gnuni, whom Ryzhii meets outside the employment bureau, have one of the most interesting discussions to be found in any Russian production novel on the role that housing plays in the construction of socialism and the new Soviet citizen. Arshak, who approaches Ryzhii after the latter's outburst in the employment bureau, introduces himself as a leftist artist (*khudozhnik LEF*), one of an influential group in postrevolutionary Russia that saw art as a weapon and a utilitarian tool in service to the cause. Shaginian's description of Arshak in her diary accounts of 1928 is a telling indictment of the figure of the artist during this time. Intellectuals who are separated, as Arshak clearly is, from the genuine proletariat are clearly problematic. The artist Shaginian pictures is "the city,—a creative type, doesn't know how to live, personal death, although it's a terrible shame, non-adaptability, scandal-monger."[31] The only thing that can save

this partly autobiographical character, then, is the potential for redemption through construction. In this sense, Shaginian notes to
herself in the diary, the artist is "bohemia in the guise of antithesis, but through him, the problem of building material, struggle for
cement, etc."[32] Arshak invites Ryzhii, who has been camped out at
an abandoned shooting range in the town square, to move in with
him, and it is this move to Arshak's home that provides Ryzhii with
the opportunity to combine thesis and antithesis to special effect.

The conviction that true creation involves the acceptance and mastery of contradiction was vivid for Shaginian and other writers of this
period. In an era of harsh choices and passionate partisanship, the
idea of resolving contradictory evidence seemed a logical goal for
many artists. In a diary entry from 1926, for example, Shaginian
speaks with studied longing of the need for the artist to "absorb contradictions like a sponge, without suffering or even taking cruel pleasure in it, in order to embody them in creation, like a movement of
life." She is clearly providing herself with advice about reaching a desired destination. "It's necessary," she continues in a third-person address to her diary, "to put one's self above (or below) the wind and
not sway from impressions, but, just the opposite, grow thicker and
heavier from them, just the way that a vessel grows heavier while taking on water."[33] The telling interaction between the left-leaning artist
Arshak and the composite figure of Ryzhii provides Shaginian with
a gripping platform on which to wrestle these demons.

The word Arshak uses to describe his "private residence"—*osob-
niak*—evokes a prerevolutionary universe of privacy and privilege.
The reality, however, is quite different and suggests that Shaginian
sees the area as contested space. Arshak has taken up unofficial residence in the remains of the "Persian" part of town. This "oriental"
designation seems to mark the area as part of the past rather than
the future, and the neighborhood is deserted and run-down. Nevertheless, this unusual setting provides a unique perspective on the
entire city, seen from this low-lying neighborhood, looking up from
below. This is a noticeable reversal of the traditional bird's-eye view
of urban landscape, best represented in Russian letters by the vow
to the liberal cause that Herzen and Ogarev took from the vantage
point of Sparrow Hills in Moscow. Shaginian's inversion of that inspirational perspective presents her with the potential opportunity
to command space from the bottom up.

The landscape Shaginian offers is decidedly less triumphant than
its nineteenth-century counterpart. It borders, in fact, on the grotesque, in Shaginian's portrayal of a bloated and outdated city that
is dying.

From here, all of that city was visible, not from above looking down—
the Persian part lay lower—but from below looking up, like the corpse
of a drowning victim that has surfaced. The city strained upward
(*puchilsia*) with the indescribable precision of an outline, the kind in
museums of cartography, on old city plans. Flat-topped, the color of a
faded sepia-toned engraving, under the direct rays of the sun, it took
shadow as its bride, and faithful shade became a constructive part of
the landscape, deepening the archways, outlining the columns, underlining the cornices, darkening the ribs of the houses. (13–14)

Shaginian's description is pointedly old-fashioned, and she resorts
to comparisons that are also used in other production novels to depict the world of the past.[34] "Old city plans" from "museums of
cartography," all done up in the "color of a faded sepia-toned engraving," mark this landscape as forgotten territory. Even the natural world seems outdated here. Mount Ararat, or "Masis," as the
residents in Shaginian's novel call it, is described as an "archaism"
(14). "Water from the destroyed irrigation ditches flowed between
dead little houses somewhere—the thread-like pulse of a dying
man" (14). The earth itself here is old. The skirt of a passing woman
disturbs the volcanic ash that covers the land, "the epidermis of a
face, of which there is none more ancient in geography" (15).

The neighborhood has clearly been the victim of the ravages of
revolution and war, although this is implied rather than directly
stated.[35] Only roofless shells of the original housing stock remain,
broken frames rising forlornly from foundations in an atmosphere
thick with the lime that once served as whitewash and is now
turned to dust, the same lime used to inter victims of such cata-
clysms from the past. In this seemingly inhospitable atmosphere,
the artist has taken up residence, his house serving as an extended
metaphor for the task of reconquering outmoded space and building socialism with art. Arshak makes the role of the artist in construction graphically obvious by reconfiguring his artist's canvas to
create a roof over the four walls of an abandoned building (13).[36]

Shaginian uses the structure to argue for a link between the desire to create art, the need to refashion both oneself and the surrounding environment, and the imperative to build new physical
structures in the devastation that faced this generation of writers.
The activities of art, self-definition, and construction thus become
intimately entwined in the conversation between Ryzhii and Arshak. The artist's "private residence" links the act of creation—
until now an individual act of self-definition—to the communal act
of building. The tarp Arshak pulls over the structure serves as both
roof and canvas for his creative works; he cuts pieces off as needed

for individual paintings. When Ryzhii asks to see one of Arshak's creative works, he is surprised to find that the paintings themselves are completely blank: "On the tarp, which was unwrapped and carried over to Ryzhii, there was nothing, absolutely nothing—not so much as a line or a squiggle" (15). Arshak explains his work as a search for forms that are comprehensible without the clumsy process of transmission. "This is how I draw," he remarks as he displays the empty canvases to Ryzhii. "The old expressionism is dead. I'm searching, I put down a smear, I see that it's worse than nothing. So I wash it off. Up until now I haven't found anything that's better than nothing" (16).

Part of Shaginian's message is the familiar modernist argument that the reader shares responsibility for the creation of meaning in a work of art. In this context, part of the artist's task is to remove obvious artistic connections that would otherwise restrict the viewer's freedom to make them individually. Arshak's attempt to find a form that is "better than nothing" suggests art in which the sun takes "shadow as its bride," absence plays as much a role as presence, and subtraction is as useful as addition. Repeating a comment he attributes to writer Viktor Shklovskii, Arshak notes approvingly "Shklovskii said . . . 'If I don't like a phrase, I simply cross it out' . . . To simply cross it out, that's great" (16). Arshak's search for this unencumbered form leads him to long for a "form like a wireless telegraph. Without transmission. . . . What's the point of a transmission belt in the form? . . . That's my problem" (16). Here, too, Shaginian conflates the quest for artistic expression with a need for self-definition in the amorphous, not-yet-Soviet space that this generation of writers faced. Arshak's creative crisis has a personal dimension since his unsuccessful search for form leads him to self-doubt and despair. "I'm in a terrible position, maybe from old age," says this young man.[37] "I can't do anything right— everything is trash, trash, worse than nothing, emptier than nothing" (16).

Ryzhii's response to Arshak's creative dilemma re-situates the discussion on a societal level. In his view, the battle for personal and artistic expression reflects a larger change in the way space is understood and knowledge is transmitted. "We are currently changing over to a different system of communications," Ryzhii explains. "The transfer of forms from person to person," he says, is now merely a question of "process" as civilization moves "from letters to hieroglyphs." This change in communication styles involves a "fundamental break" (*korennoi perelom*),[38] Ryzhii notes, for the "second time in the history of humankind. The first time from the hieroglyph to the letter. And now again—from the letter to the hieroglyph." The process involves the relatively simple use of metaphor to express—and then replace—meaning. "It's an analogy, a hieroglyph," explains Ryzhii. "The thing [itself] is dying" (17).

With this deft argument, Ryzhii relocates Arshak's search for a satisfactory form of expression. His struggle for self-definition now becomes part of a larger context that includes the need to define "Sovietness" and to create a space in which the ongoing process of building Soviet socialism can occur. Like it or not, Arshak and others are part of a universe in which the signifier replaces the signified, crowding it out as unimportant to the process of making meaning. Actual objects become irrelevant or, to those unable to make the transfer to the new world, actively hostile. This recalls Shaginian's reference to Arshak's "non-adaptability" and her prediction of his "personal death, although it's a terrible shame." He can save himself from this fate only by understanding and mastering this new communicative process.

In this new world of the production novel, the final product becomes irrelevant to the actual act of building the new man of the future: the metaphor becomes what it strives to represent. If society is working toward an anticipated project, then that fact becomes as meaningful as if the building, the planned neighborhood, or the new city of the future had actually been constructed.[39] Ryzhii's definition of the new communicative style as a "transfer of form from person to person as a process" (17) recalls socialist realism's well-known emphasis on the depiction of reality in its "revolutionary development." "Look for the form in action," Ryzhii advises both readers and the artist Arshak (71).[40]

Literary historians of the Stalinist period will surely recognize the familiar in the movement Ryzhii describes. The process that he iterates—away from letters and toward the potent image, away from the reflective text and toward a text in motion—characterizes the development of Socialist Realism as well, as writers moved from thoughts about building to production novels that "finished" the act of construction. Present at one of Stalin's first meetings with writers to announce Socialist Realism, Valerii Kirpotin recalled that the "artist using this method had to see not only the excavated foundation pit, but [also] the high walls of the future building. And when Stalin said 'Write the truth!' that's what it meant—to paint the high walls of the future building."[41]

"Action," "process," and "revolutionary development" all rely on the power of analogy, as Ryzhii makes clear. He describes the use of analogy in a Soviet film, "The Traitor," in which he identifies this "new" form of art in the "first simple symbols of the cinematographer, play in process, analogies" (17–18). Ryzhii's reference to "still crude analogies" (17–18) recalls Shaginian's own text, of course, and that of most of these early Russian production novels, which apply the metaphor of building directly. This straightforward approach was considered unavoidable in appeals to a mass audience, but it also reflected a revolutionary sense, shared with modernism itself, that older forms of expression were now inadequate. Shaginian's determined comment from her diary in 1928 makes this clear. Frustrated by her unsuccessful attempts to progress on the manuscript of "Kik," a work she eventually published in 1929, Shaginian describes her "sudden, complete loathing" for that novel. "I ripped up everything that had been done," she notes emphatically, "and decided not to return to that work in the next few months." Having closed, at least temporarily, that path toward her former creative life, Shaginian concludes that "I need to buckle down on the new and find the new—my own form" in a comment that displays some of Arshak's desperation. It should come as no surprise to learn that the very next statement in the diary entry concerns her intention to finish *Hydrocentral*.[42]

Arshak's objections to the extravagant "overhead costs" of the older forms, their "lack of economy, un-justifiability" (17) are less focused. Tired of the "syntax," "grammar," "range," and "spectrum" of classical art, he fantasizes about giving "Leonardo's palette" to a dog that will lick the slate and memory itself clean (17). This cleared space is alarming, however, "emptier than nothing." Even Arshak backs away from his own vision, reacting to Ryzhii's prediction of the use of direct analogy with shock. "That's terrible!" he exclaims in response to Ryzhii's claims. "Everything wants to be an activity and not a thing . . ." Still not ready for the new world he must help build, the artist can only cry "that's awful" (18).

The dilemma, then, which the two share with the authors of these transitional production novels, is the fundamental one of organizing space without committing to a permanent structure. The moving, changing image—action itself—is essential to convey meaning in this universe, and Ryzhii, in particular, understands that fact. He demonstrates this comprehension by "building socialism" the very next day, promising to add a roof to Arshak's hut in exchange for ten potatoes. As he sets to work the next morning, he explains that he learned to build as a result of his work with a "logging party," in what seems to be a veiled reference to a stint of incarceration and forced labor that initially puzzles Arshak but not, presumably, contemporary readers. Shaginian, in fact, invites

readers' speculation with her cryptic comment "a logging party—
the meaning is obvious" (*lesoustroitel'naia partiia—smysl podra-
zumevaetsia*) (20).

The idea of reform through labor was a progressive notion of the
time. Though far from humane in practice, the theory of *perekovka*,
or reforging, was intended to make productive members of society
out of criminals, "former people," and intransigent peasants, many
of whom Shaginian would undoubtedly have encountered on her
own visit to the construction site. *Perekovka* was still considered
a positive term in the late 1920s, unlike the negative concept of "rebirth," or *pererozhdenie*, which referred to the process of losing
one's revolutionary sentiments and being reborn or returned to
anti-Soviet ideas.[43] Shaginian's character, a German Armenian
who has been back in the Soviet Union for only a short time, seems
to have undergone this process of reforging and emerged *ryzhii*, a
confirmed sympathizer of red, or at least reddish, Soviet power.

Ryzhii's Sovietizing experience "near the Persian border" (20)
has taught him how to create a new Soviet space, and he under-
takes the task with confidence, drawing Arshak into the process by
example. Nothing is more elemental than building a roof for shelter, but when Ryzhii begins that process in *Hydrocentral*, the activity is initially described as "incongruous." The artist first objects
to Ryzhii's project, since the plan to add a roof to his "private residence" turns him into a property owner with Ryzhii as hired
laborer. They find a solution, however, by working together, incor-
porating Arshak's canvas/tarp into the thatched roof they are creating. Both then experience the dignity of labor and the pleasure of
creation as they build a roof on the ruins of the old civilization and
create a work of art simultaneously. This perfect extended metaphor has both a traditional and a Soviet meaning, according
to Shaginian. Ryzhii and Arshak have just relived the formulaic
beginning of "eastern fairytales," which "always begin this way:
There was once a fine young fellow, who lived on the outskirts.
He invited a passerby, who came to work for him. [Then] he became jealous of him and asked [the worker] to take him on as a
helper" (21).

This is precisely the situation in which Arshak and Ryzhii have
just found themselves, and it is the psychic location of Shaginian
and her fellow authors as well. As a result, we need to tread lightly
in creating a model to explain the production novels of this era. Perhaps the reason it is hard to fit Shaginian's comments into a neat
binary structure is that they do not belong there. Shaginian and
other authors of early production novels make it clear that they

would have rejected any paradigm that was theoretically pleasing but sacrificed historical richness. Can a series of dichotomies really describe a novel in which an unemployed Armenian German, dressed in women's clothing and fresh from a spell in the labor camps, emerges as a spokesman for official doctrine? Yet it is this odd character and his honest toil that lead the leftist artist Arshak to understand the redeeming power of labor.

If Ryzhii's activity provides one way to build collective consciousness, another is demonstrated by the elderly schoolteacher whom Ryzhii first notices in the employment bureau at the beginning of the novel. Shaginian returns to this woman with a muff, Anush Malkhazian, in chapter 3 of the book. Malkhazian, too, is consumed with the metaphor of building, and her emphasis on the theme in her new job as a replacement schoolteacher means that the new generation, these "children of the *vydvizhentsy*,"[44] will soon understand its significance as well. Displeased with the existing textbooks, Malkhazian decides to structure her first lesson around a miniature society, which she encourages the children to build with the toy houses, barns, spinning wheels, and dishes she pulls from her trusty muff.[45] She realizes that she is educating the next working class. "In front of her was an actual social element, not an imagined one. She enjoyed beginning with an actual definition of the fact: 'So far we have no proletariat. Our peasant class is too poor; it can't educate children in the city. These are the ones we have to train. These are in our hands. And it's necessary for them, once they grow up, to pull those up and not block the road for them with their own bodies'" (54).

She informs the children, this "actual social element," that they must learn to work collectively, and she divides them into three zones of "pastures," "orchards," and "grain fields" to facilitate that. They are assigned to "develop collective farms, with common forces" (58). She herself will be the city, she says, placing her hand on her faithful muff, which serves as the center, the source, and the model of the new universe she imagines these children inhabiting. Once she has pulled from there the building blocks of the miniature world they are constructing, she uses the muff as a relief map of Armenia itself, encouraging her students to see the mountains, plains, and grasslands of the country in the folds of this worn article of prerevolutionary fashion. "In the mysterious bowels of the muff, her own hand slid around and gave the muff the necessary outlines as needed. That's when the old muff with its threadbare, yellowish-brown, plush fabric justified itself. The teacher spoke and, along with her lips, yellow waves moved on the table, now

straightening out, now bulging up, and the storyteller helped herself with her left hand, indicating the outlines of the muff" (55).

By the time the lesson ends, Malkhazian has won the children
over, enchanted them with the magical world that emerges from her
imagination, her muff, and her own two hands. This enchanted universe in miniature is a metaphor for the real one that this next generation will have to build. They have a considerable distance to
travel in order to reach the imagined reality, of course, as even the
children realize. The youngest pupil in the class understands the
metaphor of construction intuitively, it seems; when asked how
morning in Armenia begins, he answers "With the houses." His
naïve explanation captures the essence of the metaphor: "it was
more difficult for the houses than for anything else in the city. They
rose earlier than everyone. There were very few houses. For eight
schools—only a single house with three rooms" (51–52). This in-
tuitive understanding of the problems that face them is coupled,
however, with the childlike belief—common enough even among
adults during this period—that merely describing the new universe
would already make it a reality.

Desperate to engage her unruly class, Malkhazian decides to use
the map of Armenia as a basis for her lesson plans. The contours
of the country become the staging ground for her attempts to re-
shape the students, just as the land on which they stand is reconfigured. The teacher acknowledges an existing binary system that
has divided the country into a mountainous and wet north and a
flat and dry south. Society, too, is compartmentalized and hierarchical with rural and urban dwellers distinct and alienated from
each other. The hydroelectric project of the novel, however, will
share water between the north and south and, thus, erase these binary divisions as it redraws the map of the country.

This rich metaphor of the map relates to the changing perception
of national space that accompanied the expansion of Soviet power
during these transitional years. Emma Widdis has described the
drive to establish a unified national space as an essential Soviet
project.[46] Defining the shape of Soviet space and describing its
contours was a key task of the production novel as well. This is why
the metaphor of maps is charged with such particular significance
during these transitional years. Authors were challenged during
this period to mark the borders of the Soviet universe, while simultaneously downplaying or ignoring events on the other side of
the line they drew in Soviet sand. In this era of re-situating the universe, boundaries were blurred or erased as often as they were es-

tablished, and maps predicted future landscapes as frequently as they reflected current ones.

Shaginian interrogates the notion of maps directly in *Hydrocentral* when one of her characters, a geologist by the name of Lazutin, turns his house into a geographical museum.[47] Pride of place is given to

> A ma-a-p! A lithographic map of the Trans-Caucasus. The first attempt in the Union. . . . On the canvas was an extremely detailed map of the location of raw mineral resources in the Trans-Caucasus region. Every mineral had its own color, symbol of strength, quality, use. It was a remarkable work. Whoever was able to be a geologist—so Lazutin said—for them, a map like this would be almost like Mendeleev's Table: filling in the gaps with a trained eye, tectonically traveling to the sources, weaving seemingly random threads into an elegant arrangement of deposits, you have learned to guess the secrets of earth's protective cover, to inhabit the void, to predict correctly . . . (244)

Both the map and the museum that houses it function unexpectedly here. Rather than merely describe the environmental status quo, the map invites those who read it to change it. "To predict correctly," Shaginian advises, "that's the talent of our brother." Her unusual reference to the second-person plural pronoun, inviting "you" to make yourself useful and read the map, indicates that she is already using the metaphor that would become the stated goal of Socialist Realism: her map shows geography in its "revolutionary development." The leap Shaginian makes is hardly surprising. As J. B. Harley notes, maps are "part of the broader family of value-laden images." Shaginian already clearly perceives the situation that Harley would outline only five decades later: maps are not "inert record of morphological landscapes or passive reflections of the world of objects" but "refracted images contributing to dialogue in a socially constructed world."[48]

The magical power of the map in the construction of Stalinist culture can be seen in a variety of publications from this era, including, for example, in the volume Soviet writers dedicated to the Belomor Canal. The frontispiece of that volume is a map of the world on which each of the most significant canals is marked in red.[49] The Panama Canal is the only feature delineated in the Western Hemisphere. The other side of the map, however, shows three sites worthy of notice: the Suez Canal; the Kiel Canal; and, of course, the White Sea–Baltic Canal. One of the first pages of the book is a schematic map of the canal itself, as imagined from its northern origin, across both Lake Onega and Lake Ladoga, to its southern termination in the Gulf of Finland. This largely fantastic route is marked in red on the map. The canal, as Cynthia Ruder makes evident in her book on the project, was never fully functional. It never even joined the two points intended, but stretched, instead, from the White Sea only as far as Lake Onega. But the map in the book, given pride of place opposite the elaborate title page for the first chapter, helps give the canal a mental reality more solid than its physical incarnation would ever attain, and the red line links geographical features on paper that were never joined in life.

In fact, geography is one of the reigning metaphors in the Belomor book as a whole. The canal itself is the most significant architectural feature in the new political landscape that was being drawn for this reading public. Design, construction, and, naturally, reforging are essential to the progress of the narrative. But other notions from architecture are important as well. One of the most significant is the idea of boundaries. Since the canal was being constructed by forced labor, we might expect the first boundaries to refer to barbed-wire fences that keep people in. In fact, the boundary that emerges first is a much larger conceptual one that includes all of the borders of the Soviet Union.

This boundary is established in the title of the second chapter of the Belomor volume, "The Country and Her Enemies." The first words of the chapter spell out the location of the narrative. The authors define an area "from the Pacific Ocean to Turkestan, from Murmansk to Baku." This enormous area—mapped out on a trip on "overcrowded trains" in 1931—marks the beginning of the metaphorical journey the authorial collective is preparing to take. This is the Soviet Union, we are told, but one "without Magnitogorsk, without Dneprogez, without KhTZ." These gargantuan building projects were only beginning in 1931, the narrative continues. "At the place where [those places] would be built," the story goes, only "foundation pits are visible, the frameworks of intersecting girders, the glow from welding."

These construction sites form the basis for the narrative to come. They serve as centering devices for the activity that takes place within the larger framework of the Soviet Union. These hot points act as beacons that draw "from all points" of the country to this "renowned construction site." The image is one of frenetic activity on an inert background. If life is going on elsewhere, it seems insignificant in light of the compelling work being done at these locations. "The map of this year," note the commentators, "is full of movement." And "this map is an instant photograph of the space of the Soviet Union in 1931."[50]

Back in Armenia, the teacher Malkhazian, like the author Shaginian, is under no illusions as to the current landscape of the country. Returning home from her successful lesson, she is confronted with graphic evidence of how far reality is from the one she extracted from her muff.

> Her muff was almost empty. Her hands lay in it, and one convulsively squeezed the other. Entering the courtyard, she saw the usual picture of disorderly and insultingly crowded human accommodations. Downstairs, freshly washed clothing was flapping on three strings radiating from the balcony. The fat wife of a Communist was yelling at the kerosene vendor, who was standing with his pails and cup. The fumes from outdoor grills, together with the blue smoke, rose up to the sky, distributing the tasty smell of cooked meat. The children—there were five—were running around the courtyard, yelling, and discarded gray slop, trickling off the stones, added its own tedious smell of rotting steam to everything else. It was necessary to pass through all this, to get to the steep, wooden staircase and scramble up for a long time to the second floor where teacher Malkhazian lived in a tiny little room with her niece or, rather, found refuge with her niece, the Central Committee inspector, Comrade Mardzhik Malkhazian. (60)

Shaginian's description manages to capture the Soviet landscape at the end of the 1920s in just a few images. The humiliating overcrowding, dirt, Party privilege, and envy that characterized the period are all visible here, from the inevitable clothes on the line to the arrogance of the Party member's fat wife. But her description captures, too, the willingness of many to overlook their surroundings, to see them as a temporary stage on the path to eventual communism. It is necessary, Shaginian assures us, "to pass through all this." Malkhazian's muff is "almost" but not quite empty, and her busy hands, "one convulsively squeezing the other," won't be idle long. In a turn that would become characteristic of Socialist Realist style, she imagines the future not as a finally realized state but as a process of becoming. Her goal is movement, rather than the destination itself. "When there's a pull under foot, when you know that you've gotten up right and you're being led now, led to exactly where you should go—we'll still do battle, my dear, for the real thing!" (62).

Like so many other authors of production novels, Shaginian found it considerably easier to criticize the structures of the old world than to imagine the shape of the edifices of the new. Although it is far from clear what kind of buildings will replace those in the old world, it is quite obvious that confining old structures must go. Shaginian notices the destructive effects of old architectural habits, even once she moves the narrative to the construction site itself. There, the Soviet building project suffers from a work site that is poorly organized, laid out, as it is, to retain mistaken hierarchies between workers and bosses. This unfortunate division is reflected spatially on a steep mountainous site where the workers are housed at the bottom of the hill, closest to the work. The farther one goes up the hillside, however, the higher the rank of those housed there and the more distant they are from the actual site of labor.

Shaginian is careful not to idealize the laborers; the workers' barracks are dark, filthy, and disorderly. These are seasonal workers, and they profoundly need the salutary effects the building process is supposed to have on them. The barracks for skilled workers with families are an improvement with their air of semipermanence and domestic culture. Although this group—"skilled workers, the mechanic, the maintenance man, Party and union intellectuals"—could have provided Shaginian with the opportunity to criticize the effects of middle-class existence, she avoids the blanket criticism of everyday life, or *byt*, that was so popular with many other writers of the 1920s, particularly Mayakovsky and authors related to LEF, the Left Front of Art. Unlike the authors of the avant-garde who saw "little curtains and lace gardenias," the "bedsteads, featherbeds, and Viennese chairs" as evidence of abandonment of the revolutionary cause, Shaginian equates them here with the "simplest truth of life." Through these windows, her characters and readers alike can already see the civilizing effects of Soviet power: the face of one of the inhabitants, whose beard marks him as a recent transfer from rural life, is sitting by his window reading, his moving lips a clear sign of the success of recent campaigns against illiteracy.[51] Shaginian refuses to classify the material objects of *byt* as charged symbols of a bourgeois culture that needs to be rejected. Like other authors of production novels from this transitional period, she adopts instead a nuanced approach to the question.

Completely unambiguous reappropriation of the objects of bourgeois life was unusual for this time, however, since material culture provided such tangible evidence that the old world had not yet been fully swept away by the revolution. And, indeed, Shaginian notes elsewhere that the trappings of bourgeois life—silverware, tablecloths, goblets, and knickknacks—hold an engineer from the site, Levon Davidovich, hostage, sterilizing and poisoning his existence.

The figure of the engineer—well educated, often foreign trained, and usually bourgeois in background—is ambiguous in most of these early production novels, and Shaginian's *Hydrocentral* is no exception to this rule. Most engineers in positions of authority in the late 1920s and early 1930s had received their training in either tsarist or foreign institutions, and that fact, coupled with a certain arrogance ascribed to the profession, made engineers and other such specialists, or *spetsy,* the object of endless suspicion.

The notion that a class enemy might be lurking within the specialist's well-appointed interiors is clearly part of Shaginian's none-too-subtle message. As Gaston Bachelard has eloquently put it, "an empty drawer is unimaginable,"[52] and this was certainly the case in postrevolutionary Russia. Sergei Zhuravlev provides a compelling real-life example of the contradictions inherent in the lives of such specialists. He treats this *"byt spetsialistov"* in a masterful history of foreign workers at the Moscow factory Elektrozavod in the 1920s and 1930s.[53] Zhuravlev recounts the story of an apartment on Malotrosskaia Tishina Street in Moscow that had previously been occupied by a skilled German worker and his wife, but appeared to have been left vacant in the early months of 1933. Anxious to find out if the apartment had indeed been abandoned, an official delegation from the housing administration decided to enter the premises, accompanied by citizen witnesses and urged on, no doubt, by jealous neighbors. The resulting archival record of the delegation's visit offers a detailed account of the contents of the apartment, which had not, in fact, been abandoned but was briefly unoccupied while its residents were traveling. Instead of an empty apartment, the visitors found a veritable treasure trove of "bourgeois" material culture, whose relative riches stood in sharp contrast to the penury and real hunger that characterized life for most citizens of the Soviet Union during this period. The dressers, chests, and closets of this particular skilled worker contained clothing, tools, supplies, and food in such Teutonic order and relative abundance that it must have shocked the sensibilities of the underfed workers who made up the search party. Lists enumerating "20 cans of fish," "41 pieces of regular and face soap," "24 fish hooks," "10–kilogram sack of peas," and so on suggest a determination to record in detail every deviation from the revolutionary aesthetic.[54]

Most incredible of all for these observers from the workers' state in 1933, however, must have been the discovery of a carefully tended tuxedo in the closet of this German specialist who had seemed so devoted to the construction of a new world. "Somewhere in the corner, behind the shelf, was a roll of paper used in making wall newspapers" at the factory; the owner of the offending tuxedo was known to have played an active role in such Soviet morale building.[55] The archival documents do not record exactly how observers reconciled this polarizing image of the oppressing class—the tuxedo—with its appearance in the apartment of one of their seemingly sympathetic foreign colleagues. And, yet, such contradictions were inherent in a society that was still partly in the old world as it struggled to become the new.

The need to find a way to overcome such inherent contradictions was part of the discussion at a meeting of writers and subway shock workers, or *udarniki*, that took place on January 11, 1934. One of many such meetings organized by the publishing house "History of Factories and Foundries," the evening brought some of the best workers from the Moscow subway construction site together with writers and literary workers, or *litkruzhovtsy*. The groups were to join forces to create an authentic history of the construction of the subway, but before they could do so, they needed to agree on the meaning of the project itself. One of the crucial issues was how to incorporate the technical experience of old-fashioned engineers, whose connection to the Soviet building plan was suspected of being quite tenuous. According to an archival record of the meeting, the question of the revolutionary commitment of the older engineers arose quickly, and some were immediately critical of the established engineers. Complaining about their "noticeable conservatism" on the project, a certain comrade Volynskii noted that engineers were opposed to a "new method" proposed for the project "because it went against their habits." Engineers who do not have to "drag forty-meter beams through a narrow opening with a colossal expenditure of labor" of their own are unlikely to be sympathetic to the idea of changing the process. "There was talk among us of one engineer," Volynskii continued incredulously, "who came to the site in white trousers and, naturally, he didn't ask himself how to lighten the work load" for the manual laborer.[56]

Writer and true believer Sergei Budantsev was also at the January meeting. He had just participated on the Belomor canal project, which was to be presented at the Seventeenth Party Congress at the end of the month, and now he was turning his attention to the subway project. Budantsev was proud of the work he and others had done on the Belomor volume, but he pointed out that one of the problems on that project had been the fact that writers had worked, for the most part, "from transcripts, from history, from paper documents," while their access to the actual laborers was "severely restricted." The subway project would offer a real advantage: here "for the first time in a book, mass labor will be available, the authority of the engineers and so on, just the very theme that has been so poorly illuminated previously." Budantsev points out proudly that this approach will result in the depiction of real life as it is lived, "an understanding of reality" that until now had been found only with "the great writers, like Balzac, Tolstoy, Dostoevsky."

In a final comment about the supposed power of the working class over that of established authority, Budantsev notes the death of Symbolist author and intellectual Andrei Belyi, who had passed away just three days before this meeting. Remarking on Belyi's participation in Switzerland on another construction project, Budantsev notes that Belyi and a "group of writers" in that country were building "mysticism." Budantsev compares the current project to the efforts by "followers of the so-called philosophy of Ioann's building," which Belyi had helped construct in Switzerland, that "most Philistine country." Belyi's involvement in that project had, in fact, ceased some twenty years earlier, and he had long been interested in Soviet building projects, even, apparently, working on a production novel of his own,[57] but Budantsev is insistent. The project in Switzerland reflected a conviction that "human rationality was powerless to subject the forces of nature to itself" and thus marked a completely different approach from the "great thing that is being built in our country." Under conditions like those in Switzerland, Budantsev asserts, "history is powerless." Belyi was wrong, and "if the results of such a distorted idea of aesthetes-intellectuals like these are compared to the enormous deed that we are building, then we will understand the difference."[58]

Shaginian was not in attendance at this January meeting with Moscow subway workers, but she had participated on the official delegation of writers to visit the Belomor Canal, and Budantsev's conclusions about the hopelessness of Belyi's philosophical projects would undoubtedly have reminded her of "mystical" moments in her own biography. Her attempts to "understand the difference" involved a similar struggle to escape her own Symbolist past, and Shaginian would likely have sympathized with Belyi's delicate position as he struggled to remake himself and his writing. In fact, before Belyi's untimely death, Shaginian apparently provided the author with a cogent example of the path to such "understanding."[59] Belyi and his wife, K. N. Bugaeva, visited with Shaginian in 1928 while she was still hard at work on the hydroelectric project, and Bugaeva's diaries from that time bear witness to the fact that Belyi was himself already engaged in documenting the process of

Soviet construction. An entry from May 22, 1928, for example, notes Belyi's visit to "Narkompros" in Erevan, Armenia, where a secretary "courteously gave instructions on what to see in the area of Soviet construction: a new building site in town, a cotton factory, a carbide factory, and a factory school."

Their visit to a factory the next day reveals the many contradictions that Shaginian, Belyi, and any other would-be authors of production novels faced. Their tour guide, for example, already knew Belyi; this trained engineer had met the writer in Paris in 1907. Such a sophisticated, intellectual guide was perhaps the only familiar element on-site, however. Bugaeva describes her near astonishment at her "first time to see a 'factory' before me," the quotation marks reflecting her continued inability to process the experience fully. Part of the "enormous impression" she takes away from the visit is an almost stunned apprehension of the working class: "Here it is," she notes in amazement, "'physical labor'" (*vot on: "rabochii trud"*). Shocked by the noise and repetitive nature of the industrial process, Bugaeva suggests that "it is necessary to add the adjective 'heavy' to the word 'labor,'" and wonders how it is possible to bear such conditions. "The smell is overpowering, heavy. After a few minutes you want to get to fresh air. But 'they' spend years in it."[60]

Shaginian's own diaries from that month in 1928 further document the visit from Belyi and his wife. Their unexpected meeting allowed the two old friends to renew their acquaintance and gave them plenty of opportunity to discuss the future of literature.[61] Shaginian's diary entry, dated May 14 through May 24, for example, notes that "Andrei Belyi arrived Friday evening and departed on Thursday. He had lunch with us on Monday, and we talked without stopping from 2 in the afternoon until 9 at night." Shaginian's retelling of her "conversation with Boria" provides powerful evidence of the sweeping philosophical generalizations for which both authors were known. Their discussion of the role of rationality in the universe has all the marks of one of Belyi's literary-philosophical essays, in particular, with its scrupulous attention to metaphor and wild flights of imagination. According to Shaginian's diary, Belyi offered the image of a pianist who trains intensively to perform a particular piece. This sort of intense training takes considerable attention and rational thought (*razum*). Once the piece of music is learned by heart, however, the rational mind is no longer needed. Repeat performances produce something like "the process of sclerosis in our minds." Just so, Belyi's argument continues, does the universe—physical matter—operate.[62] Rationality is present, but not needed since repetition itself provides what was formerly the result of the rational mind. Belyi proposes a hierarchical structure to this scheme, moving from 1) man and the rational mind to 2) the animal kingdom and habit to 3) plants and instinct and, finally, to 4) physical matter and the elements.

Shaginian, no stranger to the pleasures of such speculative thought, noted her agreement with the idea that "each cell carries in it a degree of consciousness," but objected to the fact that at the fourth stage of Belyi's hierarchy, this degree of consciousness would veer dangerously close to a level of muteness (*nemota*) in which knowledge overflowed into chaotic existence. Under such a scheme, Shaginian protested, nature is above man, who appears only as the "original limitation, only as a cry from without." Nor could Shaginian agree with Belyi's solution to their common problem: how to escape from a world of such strict determinism. Belyi's suggestion, which Shaginian deems "banal," would have sounded familiar to many avant-garde artists of both his and Shaginian's generation; he argues that it is necessary to "battle" with the sclerotic process of repetition by means of continual "resurrections of Christ." Such an approach, Belyi contends, turns death itself into a process that is no longer final but rather a stage to be overcome.[63]

Shaginian's diary entries suggest that she is skeptical of Belyi's conclusions. His ill-defined reliance on a kind of martyrdom was by no means foreign to Shaginian or to other authors of production novels during this transitional period.[64] The temptation to "sacrifice one's self" for the "people" was a notion common to Russian authors of both this and earlier generations, and the opportunities to do so—by traveling long distances to unfamiliar places and participating in strange activities in the name of the "folk"—were numerous throughout this era. Shaginian, however, is much further along in her attempt to remake herself along contemporary lines than is Belyi, and, as a result, she rejects his terminology, if not the concepts behind it. "I feel that I'm really becoming an atheist," she notes. "I look at Christ and God with some kind of different eyes. I feel revulsion toward the old terminology."

Her need for approval in her own contemporary "martyrdom," however, is reflected in the very next diary entry, when she notes that "Belyi comforted me a great deal, extravagantly praising my latest works. He said that I have a transparent style. Everything I am writing about is visible, remarkably distinct." Explaining this comment to herself after Belyi's departure, Shaginian decides that it is her "didacticism" that is responsible for the clarity Belyi has perceived. "I always understand what I want to say to someone else

to the maximum extent," she notes approvingly of her own ostensibly clear use of language, "and also I want the other person to understand to the maximum."[65]

Heavy-handed didacticism does characterize some of *Hydrocentral,* and that pedagogical bent is part of the reason Shaginian can
set herself the mission of composing a production novel, a task for
which she was otherwise poorly suited. A warm and loving individual, devoted to her family and remarkably capable of sustained
effort in service to others, she is surprisingly deaf to certain aspects
of human behavior, which she seems to think can be effortlessly
eliminated by clear explanation and strong will. Her comments
from a diary entry in March 1929, for example, describe a heart-to-
heart conversation with an acquaintance identified only as "N."
The friend is "offended and therefore an opponent," Shaginian
notes, because he, like other older workers, has been "pushed from
responsible positions." Shaginian, who relates only sketchy details
from this discussion that continued until "2 o'clock in the morning," seems surprised that her interlocutor and others like him "experience [the changes] as a tragedy." In the didactic and overly
clinical manner of someone used to breaking eggs in order to make
an omelet, Shaginian concludes logically though harshly: "but the
people pushing them out are more necessary to contemporaneity
and know how to do the job better." When we see a few lines later
that Shaginian has continued her argument with "N" and finds it
similar to conversations she had ten years earlier to justify the revolution, it seems reasonable to conclude that she has convinced
herself of the righteousness of her opinions.[66]

Shaginian's continual attempts to hold herself to this didactically
established standard of behavior explain in part why she saves her
real ire in *Hydrocentral* for those indifferent to the heroic task of
building a better world because of their cult of prerevolutionary *byt*
and devotion to the material objects of everyday life. Shaginian is
particularly scathing in her indictment of engineer Levon Davidovich's Belgian wife, Marie, whose home reflects an unhealthy devotion to petty material culture and status that separates her from
the surrounding society. Her table is "laid out the way it is never
laid anywhere any more: crystal stands, three kinds of knives and
forks, violet Danish china on the snow-white canvas of the tablecloth, a multitude of goblets and little plates, the significance of
which remained a mystery to the uninitiated."[67] Such abundance
ties the old-fashioned Marie to the deadly hierarchy of the old
world. Her disdain for the great building projects around her leads
to a lifeless existence in which even the food she serves reflects the

hopelessness of her outdated approach. "The entire construction site knew about the Belgian cuisine of 'Madam.' Her lifeless soups had attained legendary status. Boiled chicken that smelled of roses and lavender, all alone on the plate, surrounded by five or six hard, underdone potatoes, tormented the imagination of the engineers and technical workers who were occasionally invited to dinner. Stinginess reigned here" (121).

Marie's comprehension of the world that is being built around her is painfully mistaken, as her confrontation with a visiting German writer quickly reveals. She is too mired in the past and its unhealthy societal distinctions to understand the new forms evolving on the site. The German writer, who is himself undergoing a transformation at the construction site, notices this immediately when she rejects him as a worthy visitor since he is "not from good society" (133), not "comme il faut" (137). Just pages earlier, the writer was himself defending the old world against the new, but he now finds himself unexpectedly but firmly on the side of the system that has resulted in the new construction. Shocked at his hosts' skepticism toward the great building that surrounds them, the writer notes that the new world is a long-term project. "New societal forms are not achieved for free," he tells his hosts. "Oh, new societal forms!" Levon Davidovich comments skeptically. "I guarantee you, Europe is just pretending to believe in all these signposts. But those of us here cannot believe. I don't see new forms. I ran away from them to Belgium 15 years ago: it's the same complete confusion over whom to follow, the endless fear of being shouted at, and the first guy to come along, the first one with a gullet is the one who shouts" (134). Their conversation reveals such profound disagreement about the significance of life in the Soviet Union that the writer leaves their home in genuine distress, fleeing this unhealthy environment for the better air of a public meeting on-site. By the time Levon Davidovich returns home after escorting the German, his wife has returned their living quarters to the orderly, soothing, and yet utterly lifeless state of existence she finds unthreatening. "The dining room was already empty; the china was washed, the service put away, all the disorder of the entire day, the unsuccessful duties disappeared in the cupboards and drawers, in order to fade coldly in the old, oil-cloth tablecloth left on the square table" (137).

Equally damaging is Shaginian's depiction of Zakhar Petrovich, the head of the clerical office, and his wife Klavdiia Ivanovna. Shaginian's diaries identify Klavdiia as a "developing parasite, from nothing becomes a big figure, evil," and the author's disdain for the character is obvious from her first appearances in the novel. Klavdiia's lush sexuality, her devious behavior, and her complete incomprehension of the importance of the work around her make Shaginian's description almost cartoonish in its negativity. Once again, the physical environment in which this monster develops helps both to create her unhealthy attitudes and to reflect them. The surroundings in which Zakhar Petrovich and Klavdiia Ivanovna live make their moral depravity unavoidably clear. "The smell of the chief clerk's living quarters was loathsome. The den smelled of a beast living in its own filth. The corners covered with cobwebs, the stains on the wooden wall that spoke of bedbugs and shoe leather, the dirt of the windowsill where a moldy glass stuck out from a saucepot full of trash, footwear and discarded socks, a half-unraveled basket in the corner" (182).

To counter such attitudes, Shaginian describes a series of public spectacles, both planned and unexpected, meant to lead her characters and her readers to a proper comprehension of the world under construction around them. The "trial of the worker" that takes up chapter 6 of the novel, for example, serves as a formative experience for readers who are learning what significance Soviet construction will have in their lives.[68] Orchestrated by Ryzhii, who plays a leadership role in organizing the event, the trial is initially imagined as just one part of a public meeting that will combine entertainment with education. The plan is to combine a general meeting with a "social lesson" (132), followed by a celebration of International Woman's Day, which happens to coincide with the meeting, and an official welcome to the German writer who needs "to be shown worker communal spirit" (132).

The focus of judicial scrutiny in this case is the activity of a seasonal worker by the name of Grikor Sukiasiants, who has been caught in the act of removing boards from the construction site. Identified from the beginning of the proceedings as a "thief," Grikor admits to the act, committed ostensibly in order to get wood to make himself stools. Eyewitnesses abound to testify to his activity, and he himself offers nothing in the way of justification or rationale for his illegal acts. When asked what he can say in his own defense, Grikor "answers sullenly: 'Nothing'" (152). Yet Shaginian uses this seemingly open-and-shut case as an opportunity to air a lively variety of issues that surround the construction of Soviet culture, and the presentation of her characters and situations is multidimensional and nuanced. Unlike many of the better-known show trials of the 1930s, this public demonstration of Soviet justice from the late 1920s allows for considerable ambiguity and disagreement.[69]

First to look for a lesson in the public hearing is Ryzhii, who, as unofficial master of ceremonies, struggles to understand his own role in the creation of Soviet meaning. His extended musings on the significance of that role involve a comparison of the frivolous nature of life in Germany and the didacticism of life in the Soviet Union. Here as elsewhere, Shaginian rejects the sharp division of a binary approach, however, in her search for a happy medium between empty frivolity and heavy-handed seriousness. Using what he calls a "moment of defamiliarization" (140), Ryzhii analyzes public spectacles in the West and finds them wanting in their studied avoidance of serious issues. But he is equally critical of the "intolerable didacticism of our time," the tendency to "be serious no matter what" so that "every reflex is organized into a poster" (140). Ryzhii notes the absurdity of too many directives in the current climate and laughs, along with Ostap Bender, at the tendency to subordinate every act to a social imperative. "Isn't there too much concern," he wonders to himself, "about [proper] mastication of food?"[70]

Sitting on stage before the meeting begins, Ryzhii notes the division of the crowd into obvious camps. Groups of tow-headed Slavs can be easily distinguished from the swarthy Armenians; the big bosses in the front row are clearly separate from the workers in the back. Such dichotomies, Ryzhii concludes, reflect "unhealthy and improper relations" (143), and his initial impulse is to reverse the arrangement so that master and man change places. Ryzhii ends his reverie on the role of master of ceremonies (Shaginian uses the borrowed word *konferans'e*) with a commitment to overturn the obvious binarity he sees in front of him. "Our master of ceremonies should make social divisions and enflame socially: to shake up those who are in the back, to lift the lower level. . . . If you are the director, don't make those sitting all by themselves in the front carry the melody, but those who are all together in an amorphous mass in the back. Class is the owner of the melody" (143).

As soon as the trial begins, however, Ryzhii sees the error of his ways and blushes with the recognition of his mistake. By simply upending the binary division between boss and laborer, he has ensured that the workers will perceive the "thief" as an innocent victim of an unfair system stacked against them. "That's not the way to go about things," Ryzhii thinks ruefully to himself (145). With the subtleties of this beginning, Shaginian can present a trial that is devoid of easy dichotomies, and she does so with genuine flair. Her talent for quick characterization makes the glib volunteer prosecutor, the kindhearted but self-congratulatory volunteer defender, the clever young woman judge, and the mostly befuddled older writer, a stock character in such transitional production novels, fully drawn participants in this modern morality play.

Shaginian is careful, however, not to let anyone's arguments carry the day completely. The prosecutor's point of view, for example, is standard and expected: "From whom is he stealing?" he asks rhetorically. "He's stealing from himself, from his class, from our, comrades, future order" (153). And the obligatory parts of an oratory against class enemies are certainly present. "While we are dragging along a board to build socialism," the prosecutor continues, "they are quietly, comrades, right under our noses stealing those very same boards and dragging them all over, they are dragging them away, if you'll permit me, to build a coffin for socialism! Yes, for a coffin for socialism!" (154). But the words of his speech ring somewhat hollow: Shaginian disparages them as "typical teeth-sharpening" and "little words" (154), and she frames the prosecutor's entire speech with the pointed disapproval of one of the most sympathetic members of the audience, the lovely Central Committee inspector, Comrade Mardzhik, who has already caught Ryzhii's eye. Mardzhik's "internal objection" (153) to the proceedings leaves readers, if not skeptical of their outcome, then at least highly attuned to the possibility of skepticism.

The presentation of the defender is also complex, balancing, as it does, a picture of the thief as poor and disadvantaged with evidence of Grikor's prior convictions for social crimes. The defender suggests that the theft of boards to make stools is defensible as evidence of cultural progress; up until now, after all, the uneducated Grikor has been sitting on rugs on the ground in "barbaric" eastern fashion. But such evidence fails to sway the judge, and the defender's satisfaction with his own performance—"an inner voice confirmed to him: good guy, good going" (157)—leaves the reader, too, suspicious. Shaginian even undermines her own efforts with the production novel here by her studied overuse of the idea of teaching by example. The defender's suggestion that the thief can learn from his experience on site—*U nas svoego roda shkola* (We have our own type of school) (156)—is treated as a cloying platitude stripped of meaning by such performances.

Grikor himself is largely unsympathetic. His extreme poverty lends his case a certain complexity, but this is undermined by the evidence that he has committed other crimes. His unacceptably bold behavior as he awaits his verdict also casts doubt on the picture of the man as a helpless victim. When the thief plops down unceremoniously next to the German writer, he appears in a different guise. No longer the country bumpkin dazed by his encounter with Soviet construction, he appears to understand the system, which he has tried to manipulate, quite well. The contrast between the German writer's enthusiastic embrace of workers' justice in theory and his disdain, even horror, of the worker himself provides Shaginian with the final irony she needs to end the scene.

As nuanced as her portrayal of the show trial is, however, it is clear that she believes in this kind of public spectacle. The event, which displaces the planned celebration of Woman's Day and the official welcome to the German, has, for all its contradictions, served its purpose. When Ryzhii looks out onto the scene after the judge has passed sentence on Grikor, he no longer sees a sharply divided audience, in which binary oppositions are the rule. Instead he faces as rich and diverse a populace as could be found on the Soviet construction site, and now the easy divisions that seemed to separate Slavs from Armenians and bosses from workers have disappeared. "Having found places here and there, helter-skelter," the crowd "had demolished the little barriers that had separated them earlier, and now everything flowed together: the white-blond Russian heads with the wooly caps of the Armenians, the headgear of the technical worker with the modish short haircut of the lady janitor, the office itself found in the thick of the Party intelligentsia—in a word, it was already impossible, just by glancing from the stage, to identify groups of people defined by a single category who had chosen their own spots" (160).

The verdict—six months in jail and a fine of twenty-eight rubles and forty kopecks damages—leaves some in the audience dissatisfied, including both Mardzhik and Ryzhii. "The form of the court is, in essence, outdated," Ryzhii comments quietly. "It's a bourgeois form," he notes. "Not only is the court to blame, but our entire system of the stage, grandstanding, falsity" (159). But Shaginian poses, rather than resolves, these lingering doubts, relying on her own and the reader's faith in the virtue of movement and the cleansing process to bring eventual closure to the issue. "Nonsense," the judge interrupts, "the dialectic! We do our thing, the masses do theirs, and a positive result is achieved. You'll see!" (159).

The meeting continues in a widely ranging discussion of the many problems on-site: workers are disappointed that their expertise is discounted; failures in "discipline" vie with waste and disorder to impede the progress of the project. Ryzhii's timid comment that "work on the construction is badly organized" (159) even elicits a secret confession from Zakhar Petrovich that the estimates and plans for the project have not been formally approved (171).

But Zakhar's insistence that such disorder is evidence of a "systemic flaw" (*organicheskii porok*), which "you are helpless to touch" (170, 171), meets quiet resistance from Ryzhii. Shaginian relies on Ryzhii's "calm" and "meek" but, nevertheless, fervent skepticism of Zakhar's cynicism to suggest that things can, in fact, change for the better (171).

It is Ryzhii, after all, who is able to see the great potential inherent in the construction efforts. In his confident hands, even the dusty and incomplete archive of events on-site emerges as a work of art. From his very first glimpse of the disorderly piles of archival material that sit forgotten and neglected in an office on the site of the building project, Ryzhii has had the creative passion and imagination to make a thing of beauty from the records. "Ryzhii looked at the papers and, hot damn, how he looked at them! That's how a literary maniac would look at a shipment of old novels in translation, the kind with murders, where an investigator tramps through the pages, slowing down the denouement, he and she hate each other, just right to torment the reader languorously, in a word, with everything needed for a tasty sauce to spice up an otherwise drab and ordinary life" (121). Ryzhii's fascination with the archival material is clearly autobiographical in its reflection of Shaginian's own work in Gosplan archives, which she had visited in 1928 in preparation for her work on-site in Armenia and on *Hydrocentral*.[71]

Inclusion of this archival episode in Shaginian's own novel makes the passage a wonderfully wry comment on the genre of the production novel itself. Mention of the detective story is a clear allusion to Shaginian's own success with that genre in her novel *Mess-Mend* and her "play" with conventions of the genre in *Kik* as well. Her "deconstruction" of the author's craft in the passage about Ryzhii is telling. So, too, is her comment in passing on outmoded exchanges between bourgeois hero and heroine. Such "he said/she said" passages had long been a target of disdain for revolutionary critic and modernist author alike, and Shaginian wastes no time in establishing that she is not going to weary her reader with such outdated literary techniques. Her suggestion that Ryzhii finds the archives as compelling as such previously popular genres highlights Shaginian's own desire to move away from "old borrowed" forms to more organic and uniquely Soviet modes of expression.[72]

Shaginian reproduces excerpts from the fictional archive, which includes material from a previous project to build a small textile factory, in her own novel.[73] The material that Ryzhii has approached with such passion and interest turns out to be detailed job descriptions, equipment inventories, and obscure tales from the life of the factory project. Working with files that have otherwise been consigned to the waste bin as "outdated and unnecessary" (194), Ryzhii crafts a new way of viewing the past that makes present gains and future possibilities comprehensible. Calling his abstract of the archive a "novel" (196), Ryzhii weaves a creation intended to be worthy of its new hero, the electric equipment building trust El'mashtrest. "Read the description of this hero," he asserts boldly. "What kind of a poet would imagine saying so little and so much at the same time?" (197). Despite all the contradictions, the "dialectic" that faces every undertaking, "the engineer in Ryzhii's telling was magnificent" (197). Pushing himself and his listeners to a dramatic conclusion, Ryzhii announces breathlessly, "We build better than before!" (198). Suspicious of Ryzhii's conclusions and stunned by the passion Ryzhii reveals to his largely indifferent coworkers, the chief clerk Zakhar Petrovich can only comment balefully: "People here work for a piece of bread. It's not good, you know, to stand out from the rest of your crowd. . . . But, you, brother, well, it seems that you aren't working [just] for a piece of bread. . . . That's not very collegial" (200).

Thus it is that Shaginian can arrive at a production novel in which the main event is the collapse, rather than the building, of a bridge on-site. At the end of the 1920s, the task of remaking society by engaging writers in the work of construction was just gaining steam, and Shaginian's first visit to the construction site came at a time when she and other contemporary observers seemed to feel real hope at the prospect for free exchange of ideas in the world of cultural construction. Both the first version of Shaginian's manuscript and her second attempt after the original was stolen were finished well before the literary campaigns against Zamiatin and Pilniak, for example, had established that writers' participation in the creation of Soviet culture would be obligatory. These facts are forgotten when we treat the theme of construction and production novels in general with an approach that is more apt to the dead end of the genre than to its hopeful beginning. It is important to remember the transitional early production works in order to comprehend fully how writers understood their own activity in this crucial period of literary history.

Indeed, in this world, construction becomes the end, rather than the means to it. This curious impulse makes it possible for characters to overlook the physical world surrounding them and replace it with a landscape better suited to their dreams. On his way to take up employment at the construction site, Ryzhii has the opportunity to consider his own place in the collective history that society was writing about these times. His musings on the train reveal the powerful contemporary impulse to see beyond the failings of the past into a glorious future. When he looks out the train window at night, a landscape already relocated to the past is what appears. "They say," comments an authorial digression, "that there will come a new, squeaky-clean time, when the sky will spread out like a window freshly polished for Easter, and the outlines of things, their colors will appear with a clarity and brightness never seen before." That may be, continues the passage, "But I, to tell the truth, will miss the age of noisy breathing, the age of soot and steam" (103). With the appearance of the authorial "I," the text takes on the rhetorical flourish of historical memoir. "[I] miss the enormous smokestacks, whose rows of columns announce a working-class neighborhood, miss the smoky watercolor of the sky touched with grey-blue and the disturbing city sunsets, muddied with soot" (103). By implicitly abandoning the future tense, Shaginian shifts the architectural focus from an admittedly grimy present to the ever-nearing future in which grit, discomfort, and loss will be the object of fond nostalgia.[74]

This authorial digression echoes Shaginian's own reveries from a trip she made in March 1926 to an industrial center that caught her fancy. Her diary entry on her initial view of the factory landscape is telling. "As you approach, you feel the industrial center, an incredibly beautiful place. In general I feel more sharply the beauty of industrial locations, which in my opinion are absolutely a substitute for the beauty of medieval castles and their surroundings." Shaginian notes that industry, like castles, demands scenic locales, and she argues that the very constructions themselves "demand a certain decorative element—giant smokestacks, for example." Besides that, she continues, industry is beautiful. "Smoke is a very beautiful thing, since it creates a certain picturesque color and gives all colors in it a special synthetic tint."[75]

This perception of the ever-present future is common to other characters and to the early production novel in general. Daydreaming about her next lessons, for example, the schoolteacher Malkhazian moves on to the topic of water, thus tying her class plan to the tale Shaginian is spinning for her readers. The miniature windmill Malkhazian plans to build on a ditch in the schoolyard leads her to think of "the wheel, the turbine, the main principle . . . Then an excursion to the power plant, an understanding of electricity" (66). According to Shaginian, who described the months of study she put into this narrative in *How I worked on "Hydrocentral,"* the teacher herself still has much to learn: "Anush Malkhazian herself understood electrical energy and how to build stations only vaguely, unclearly" (66). This is a learning process that she must undergo, just as Shaginian herself already has and as the reader will as well. It is no surprise, then, that Malkhazian and her pupils reappear on-site at the end of the novel to provide the perfect pedagogical end to the work. Like buildings, Shaginian informs us, books are built from recognizable materials, one literary brick at a time.

Shaginian was proud of her construction, as a letter she received from Stalin in May 1931 makes clear. In an epistle retained in the archives, Stalin appears to be replying to Shaginian's request that he write a foreword for the upcoming publication of *Hydrocentral*. He declines, citing overwork—*"sverkhsmetnoi peregruzhennosti tekushchei prakticheskoi rabotoi"*—but promises to help with her petition to expedite the publication and to protect her against "attacks from overly 'critical' criticism." He ends with a chilling request of his own: "Just tell me specifically on whom I should apply pressure in order to start the job moving again."[76] Shaginian apparently kept a letter from Stalin, perhaps this one, carefully wrapped in cellophane in her purse, and Clark and Dobrenko cite this fact as evidence of Shaginian's naïveté. But such special pleading was common among writers during this era. If Shaginian still harbored illusions about what Clark and Dobrenko call her own "safe conduct," she would soon abandon them.[77]

For the time being, she continued to prove her own ability to adapt and learn the lessons her society was teaching. In August 1933 she wrote to literary functionary Valerii Kirpotin about her intentions to work in the "best kolkhoz region in Ukraine." By September she had moved to an "automobile-tractor station" in "the most catastrophic and backward" part of the region and was requesting Kirpotin's assistance in formalizing her activities there. She asked Kirpotin to inform "dear Fedor Vasilievich Gladkov" that "as usual" she was challenging him to friendly socialist competition (*sotssorevnovanie*). She hoped to serve as "an example for the creation of cadres of volunteer-activists from the [ranks of the] writers."[78]

Evidence of the evolution of Shaginian's understanding of the individual writer's role in constructing Soviet culture is provided in a letter she wrote to Valerii Kirpotin just a few months later, in May 1934. She describes there a surprising decision to refuse membership in the Writers' Union. The unexpected nature of such a move is reflected in the author's use of an exclamation mark to seal her declaration that she is "forced to refuse initiation into the Union!"

Reminding Kirpotin that she had continually argued against the formation of a writers' union, she repeats her conviction that what Soviet writers need is not such an "*Academie française*" but rather "dissolution into a mass production union" (*rastvorenie v massovom proizvodstvennom soiuze*). Although she regrets the loss of certain "moral and material privileges" that will result from her action, she nevertheless describes her decision as "absolutely firm," concluding her letter with a request that Kirpotin not force her to express her refusal in a public forum since "under our conditions that might not sound very good."[79]

Shaginian's plans did not remain private for long. A secret police report from July 1934 about ongoing preparations for the upcoming congress of the Writers' Union reported the sardonic response of Boris Pasternak to Shaginian's intended principled stance. "It turns out that heroic measures are fashionable now," the NKVD report quotes Pasternak as saying. "I became Soviet [*sdelalsia sovetskim*] at the wrong time." Comparing his own behavior two years earlier to that of Shaginian's current actions, Pasternak notes "I should have stayed the way I was two years ago. At that time I was seething and boiling; I was capable of all sorts of gestures. Then it started to seem to me that that was a false position, that I was a rotten intellectual, that everybody around was reconstructing themselves [*perestraivaiutsia*] and that I also needed to reconstruct myself. And I did sincerely reconstruct myself, and now here it turns out that it was possible to get around it all."[80] Alluding to a recent conversation he has had with a "certain person at the top," Pasternak claims that now "the fashion is for a different type of writer." The writer's comments, ostensibly spoken partly in jest, make it nevertheless abundantly clear just how problematic it was for authors to toe a continually shifting line. "When I spoke with this person in the normal Soviet tone," Pasternak continued, "he suddenly told me that it was impossible to converse like that, that it was toadying [*prisposoblenchestvo*]." Concluding ruefully, Pasternak remarked that "I feel that now many at the top would like it more if I were the way I was before reconstruction."[81]

Despite her convictions, Shaginian did join the Writers' Union, although she was soon to make another misstep regarding that organization that would provide her with an additional lesson on the narrowing limits of authorial discretion in Stalin's Russia. Shaginian's continued doubts about the usefulness of the union led her to resign her membership in mid-February 1936, calling the organization "pointless." She was convinced that "the farther it goes, the more [the Writers' Union] will separate us from the common task and development of the country." Her proposed solution to the problem was for authors to be deployed among the various state ministries, where they would find both "material and theme" for their next books. The day after her momentous decision to abandon the official union, Shaginian wrote to Sergo Ordzhonikidze, who was in charge of the country's heavy industry, to ask that she be included "as a foot soldier in the marvelous army of workers of the Ministry of Heavy Industry" (*Narkomtiazhprom*). Maintaining her customary modesty and revolutionary enthusiasm, she asked "Comrade Sergo" to sign her up for duty "without pay, since I earn a great deal with my books." Shaginian noted her plans to work in Baku and asked Ordzhonikidze to "look on me as your man there, to give me assignments, to demand from me informational work as needed." Already hard at work on a "book about the second law of thermodynamics based on material about oil in Baku," Shaginian commented that she had made arrangements with colleagues in that city and "had begun to participate in their battle for oil." In a final emotional flourish, she signed herself "Your Marietta Shaginian (the first writer to be attached to a ministry, if you will allow that)."[82]

Ordzhonikidze's response was harsh and direct. He expressed surprise that Shaginian could have left the Writers' Union. After all, he remarked pointedly, "it is *our Union*, a SOVIET Union. It was organized, you know, by the Central Committee of our party. Yet you call it 'pointless.' That's strange, incomprehensible." In case Shaginian had failed to understand his meaning, Ordzhonikidze made his stance even more obvious: "You are making a huge political mistake, and my advice is to fix it as quickly as possible." Warning that Shaginian's actions, whether intended or not, were aimed directly "at our party, at Soviet power," he noted with a certain amount of condescension that her action "just won't do." Under such circumstances, Ordzhonikidze remarked, it would be impossible to fulfill her request for assignment to the area of heavy industry. "Excuse me," he concluded definitively, but "help you in this affair is something that I simply can not do."[83] Underlining the seriousness of Ordzhonikidze's devastating response, an article criticizing Shaginian appeared in the newspaper *Pravda* the very next day.

It was a painful lesson, but Shaginian was an excellent student, and she needed no further instruction. In a graphic demonstration of just how far the changing Soviet author had evolved, she replied to the head of heavy industry just a few days later. This handwritten letter was no longer the chummy epistle to "Comrade Sergo," but a devout appeal to "Dear Comrade Ordzhonikidze," whose advice has "saved" her by forcing her "to understand how far things have gone" and helping her "to admit fault honestly." She noted that she would have contacted Ordzhonikidze even earlier, but claimed that she was "still under the influence of what has been done." Apparently in shock at her discovery of the limits of authorial independence in Stalin's Russia, this once hopeful author of one of the first production novels now noted that "it is difficult to write and speak." She had gained from the experience, she assured her interlocutor, and her "terrible action" and the "retribution that followed" have "sobered" more writers than one. In fact, she noted, she could derive some cold comfort from the knowledge that "others will understand the lesson" no less than she does.[84] As a result, "work will continue more honestly and seriously." There are "already symptoms of that." Her letter continued with Shaginian's promises to pay back her debt to the Party and to "Comrade Stalin." Noting that she had already begun that process, she begged their temporary indulgence. In a plea that discredited authors of other production novels would later echo, Shaginian noted how "difficult" it is to work under the circumstances. Her "voice has been torn away," and she "can not find a faithful tone." Confessing her "shame before the country," Shaginian concludes with a final request that suggests her shaken but continued belief in the possibilities that the production novel had initially seemed to offer: "Give me time to improve."[85]

Shaginian, like other authors from Stalinist Russia, would spend the rest of her life in this unending process of self-construction that she had begun with her early production novel. A July 1938 epistle from Party administrator A. A. Andreev to Joseph Stalin demonstrates just how treacherous and incessant that process would be. Although Shaginian had been recommended for an award that year, Andreev cautioned Stalin that the secret police had "compromising materials" on her and some thirty other writers that might preclude their receipt of official laurels. The list of tainted writers included Valentin Kataev, Leonid Leonov, Lidiia Seifullina, Konstantin Fedin, and Viktor Shklovskii. With the help of Stalinist henchman Lavrentii Beria, Andreev had already removed Vera Inber and four others from the list, who were allegedly too compromised by the material to warrant further consideration.[86] Shaginian was in trouble for her work *Bilet po istorii,* an account of the Ulianov family, which would soon earn its author a "severe reprimand" for its "politically harmful, ideologically hostile," and "distorted impression of the national face of Lenin." Outrage over the manuscript resulted in official Politburo censure of both the author and Lenin's widow Nadezhda Krupskaia, who was criticized in August 1938 for her "unacceptable and tactless" assistance with the work, which she undertook "behind the back" of the party, "without [its] knowledge or approval."[87]

Andreev's caution notwithstanding, however, Shaginian, Kataev, Leonov, Seifullina, and Shklovskii all received awards in January 1939, although only Kataev was awarded the prestigious Order of Lenin, the others having to make do with the Order of the Red Banner. Even the particularly compromised Vera Inber received honorable mention with a medal of distinction.[88] The message was unmistakable, and Shaginian, who lived fifty years beyond the publication of her production novel, undoubtedly understood it completely. Reforging, like Soviet construction itself, was a journey to an endlessly receding final destination. Once the process of remaking the author had begun, it continued unabated in a graphic and unending demonstration of the construction of Soviet culture.

3
Building "Novye Vasiuki": Ilf and Petrov Map the Production Novel

ILIA ILF (1897–1937) AND EVGENII PETROV (1903–42) AND THEIR
famous novels *Twelve Chairs* (*Dvenadtsat' stul'ev*) and *The Golden
Calf* (*Zolotoi telenok*) may seem unlikely candidates to include in
a discussion of the Soviet production novel. These two wildly popular and comically rich works from the end of the 1920s and the
beginning of the 1930s seem far from common notions of the
proizvodstvennyi roman as formulaic, predictable, orthodox, and
trite, and like other transitional production novels, they predate the
formal establishment of Socialist Realism with its later embrace of
the genre. Yet both works belong in a reevaluation of the development of the production novel. Like so many other creations from
the period, they reflect the proposed changes in material culture
that accompanied the end of the New Economic Policy, first introduced in 1921, and the beginning of the era of industrialization. In
fact, much of their humor derives precisely from the disparity between what was attempted and what was actually achieved by campaigns to restructure everyday life in this period of Stalinist Russia.
Both works concern the transformation individuals must undergo
to survive in the new world being built, and the character Ostap
Bender, the focus of both novels, serves as a curious blend of classic picaresque hero and imperfectly "reforged" Soviet man, the
quintessential foil in the ongoing process of remaking Russian *byt*.[1]

Bender's talent for orienting himself in the new Soviet landscape
is particularly impressive in the amorphous space in which the
early production novels transpire, a world of unclear and shifting
boundaries. As T. M. Vakhitova notes, writers in this transitional
period often played the role of ethnographers, traveling to the distant land of the factory to explain customs with which they themselves were still unfamiliar. Conflicting maps competed during this
period to describe the same space, and the construction of the new
world often involved "laying claim" to a location from more than

118

one perspective.[2] Ilf and Petrov exploit this over-mapping—and the confusion that it engenders—as a primary source of humor in these two transitional production novels. The utopian plans for the USSR of the future that Ilf and Petrov included in *Twelve Chairs* and *The Golden Calf* make the works important documents in determining how life was to be lived and interpreted in Stalin's Soviet Union. Ilf and Petrov's fictional handling of real-life construction dilemmas provides a useful corrective to our view of the late 1920s and early 1930s, as well as a necessary reevaluation of the early generic history of the *proizvodstvennyi roman* itself.

Although *Twelve Chairs* predates the start of the First Five-Year Plan, it contains many of the elements of production novels that followed the announcement of the plan in 1928, a fact that again suggests the genre was not entirely mandated from above. The story concerns a comic search for jewels that an aristocrat has hidden in the seat of a dining-room chair, one of a set of twelve, after the revolution. When the aristocrat confesses the location of these family heirlooms on her deathbed, she sets off a frantic search for the treasure that pits her son-in-law, Ippolit Vorobianinov, and his unwelcome partner, Ostap Bender, against a former Orthodox priest, Father Fedor. The dining set, like other furniture of the dispossessed classes, has been requisitioned by the state after the revolution, and the chairs, like the characters in the story, are dispersed to all ends of the new Soviet Union. Popular with readers from its first printing as a serial in the journal *30 dnei*, the novel includes the construction of a tramline, a visit to the Museum of Furniture, utopian plans for the USSR of the future, and a "happy ending" in which society's needs take precedence over the selfish desires of certain individuals. Recognizable elements of the later production novel are included in this rambling and disconnected picaresque narrative, full of comic turns that do nothing to advance the primary story line but provide humorous commentary on a variety of aspects of life in Russia just before the beginning of the press toward industrialization.

Ostap Bender first enters world literary history as an ethnographer, explorer, and surveyor of the new Soviet landscape that he and his readers must navigate. In his first appearance in *Twelve Chairs*, he carries with him the tool all stargazers need to find their way on long expeditions, an astrolabe. This instrument, used by astronomers from around 200 BCE until the invention of the sextant in the eighteenth century, allowed early travelers to chart a course on long sea journeys by helping them take relatively accurate readings of the altitude of the sun and stars. In the hands of an experi-

enced traveler, the astrolabe could be used to find longitude and lat-
itude and to survey land, and, while the instrument is amusingly
incongruous in this novel from the late 1920s, it also symbolizes
Bender's ability to navigate the confines of the new Soviet space.
"The young man carried an astrolabe. . . . He squeezed into the line
of vendors selling their wares spread out on the ground before
them, stood the astrolabe in front of him and began shouting: 'Who
wants an astrolabe? Here's an astrolabe going cheap. Special re-
duction for delegations and women's work divisions!'"[3]

In early manuscript versions of *Twelve Chairs,* Bender carried a
long roll of heavy paper in his hands in addition to the astrolabe,
an image that heightens the impression that Bender is preparing an
actual map or creating a text that will plot the course of future developments for the novel and real life in the late 1920s. Soviet reality at the time evinced a fascination with maps that Ilf and Petrov
reflect naturally here and throughout, but in this instance Bender
quickly sells the instrument to a plumber, whose work in the bowels
of the Soviet city will benefit from the navigation the device provides.[4] This suggests the attempted extension of previous boundaries, as the Soviet universe expands from endless sky overhead to
the mysteries underground in a process that is presented as natural and inevitable. Finding a course is easy, Bender suggests as he
exchanges the astrolabe for the plumber's three rubles: "It measures by itself," he notes, "provided you have something to measure" (35). As Bender, Vorobianinov, and Father Fedor canvas the
Soviet Union in search of hidden jewels, readers, too, are trans-
ported to a universe in which the unlikely becomes possible.

Bender himself no longer needs the navigation tool. As we soon
learn, he can find his way just about anywhere, and his ability to
chart a path in any situation is a defining characteristic in both this
early novel and *The Golden Calf* from 1931.[5] Bender's talent for
orienting himself is particularly impressive in the amorphous Soviet space these characters must navigate. Sheila Fitzpatrick has
argued that Bender's role as trickster or "confidence man" is the
flip side of the building metaphor that is "at the heart of prewar
Stalinism," and, clearly, cynicism and deception did play a well
documented role in the formation of Soviet culture and the "self-
construction" that citizens of the new Soviet Union underwent
during this period. Oleg Kharkhordin asserts a similar argument in
noting that "Soviet dissimulation was instrumental in constructing
the Soviet individual."[6]

What has been less well documented, however, is the sincerity of
many writers' belief in the Soviet experiment and their desire to en-

gage in the process of remaking the world. Evgenii Petrov describes his own early and unwavering belief in the revolution in notes for a biographical piece he was preparing after Ilf's death. "I began to walk in step with the revolution instantly," he comments in writing about his own early career as a criminal investigator in Odessa. "I had no doubt whatsoever that I should perish for the happiness of future generations." In difficult times, fidelity to the cause must have been a challenge even for true believers, but a sense of humor helped the stalwart in their struggle. Petrov notes this in his comment elsewhere in his autobiographical writings that he and others often relied on "irony instead of morals" to survive trying times. A finely honed sense of irony, Petrov contends, helped "to overcome that post-revolutionary emptiness when it was unclear what was good and what was bad."[7] Certainly, Ilf and Petrov had reason to hope that the revolution was rendering scam artists like Bender amusing relics of the past, and their work reflects that belief in its "laughter of the victors."[8] Bender's ability to navigate the treacherous, constantly moving landscape is part of what makes him a compelling Soviet hero. Despite constant setbacks, he, like the best Soviet enthusiast, is full of the requisite fervor for continuing the journey. Only a true believer could make the bureaucratic phrase "the session continues" (*zasedanie prodolzhaetsia*), with which Bender initiates each new stage of his journey, into an inspiring battle cry.[9]

The very name of the novel emphasizes the mundane aspect of everyday life and suggests the importance that material culture will play in creating (or stymieing) a new mode of existence. The twelve chairs of the title serve as landmarks in this universe, elusive signposts that seem to point the way to a new way of life and, yet, are endlessly shifting markers in the search for a constantly moving target. Bender, Vorobianinov, and Father Fedor all see the chairs in this light, as each forms elaborate plans about what he will do once he acquires the treasure hidden in such an unusual, constantly changing location. The elusive location of the treasure alludes to the Russian expression to sit "between two chairs," a pejorative cliché for political opportunism.[10] Ilf and Petrov refer to the phrase in passing as they proceed with an imagined census of the number of chairs in the Soviet Union.[11] Setting their characters on a journey to all ends of the Soviet Union, they succeed in creating both an elaborate, though disorganized survey of the country and an extended treatise on choosing the correct political "seat." As amusing as the variants with which Bender, Vorobianinov, and Father Fedor provide us may be, we are never in doubt as to where Ilf and Petrov are located.

There are many chairs. The census calculated the population of the Union Republics at a hundred and forty-three million people. If we leave aside ninety million peasants who prefer benches, boards, and earthen seats, and in the east of the country, shabby carpets and rugs, we still have fifty million people for whom chairs are objects of prime necessity in their everyday lives. If we take into account possible errors in calculation and the habit of certain citizens in the Soviet Union of sitting on the fence, and then halve the figure just in case, we find that there cannot be less than twenty-six and a half million chairs in the country. To make the figure truer, we will take off another six and a half million. The twenty million left is the minimum possible number. (142–43)

The novel *Twelve Chairs* begins at a moment in time that is remarkable for its specificity: April 15, 1927. The time is established meticulously and maintained consistently throughout the novel,[12] a fact that makes the ambiguous spatial location of both the fateful chair and most of the action even more noteworthy. Ilf and Petrov's reference to the unnamed provincial town that is the setting of the beginning of *Twelve Chairs* recalls countless nineteenth-century Russian narratives set in anonymous rural locations. It has the same effect it does in those earlier works, suggesting that the events about to transpire are specific to a particular location that could be named, if only censorship would allow it. Readers suspect that they can identify the very place under discussion, again allowing the authors to create the sense of a space that is at once apparently empty and yet potently full.[13] The allusion to this literary tradition is complicated further by the fact that the manuscript refers to the provincial town as *uezdnyi gorod*, making this particular location, if not a complete anachronism, then at least part of a distant and rapidly shrinking past. As Odesskii and Fel'dman point out, reforms remaking *uezdy* into *oblasti* began in 1921 and were largely complete by 1927.[14] Thus, the remote provincial town in which Vorobianinov has found temporary refuge is both historically and physically removed from a rapidly encroaching Soviet universe.

The town itself is vaguely described, notable mostly for its two competing funeral parlors and a nondescript town square. The monument to the poet Zhukovskii that marks the public space is remarkable less for its artistic merit or its poetic inscription—"Poetry is God in the Sacred Dreams of the Earth"—than for an additional layer of oppositional culture that overlays the bust and rivals it in longevity. The "rude word" that first appears in chalk on the statue on "June 15, 1897" (15) suggests that the impulse that erected the statue must continually vie with a competing response.

Invoking Vladimir Papernyi's categories of two opposed cultures here, we note that the vertical hierarchy of the statue is neither a sequential nor a totalizing response to Culture 1 but appears instead in perpetual battle with the leveling effects of an irreverent, horizontal opposition.

Other "triumphal" architectural moments in this ubiquitous town are dismantled altogether, often literally, as is the case with an arch from the era of Catherine the Great that one of the town's leaders has removed, ostensibly because it impedes traffic. In this forgotten corner of the new Soviet universe, traffic is not yet a concern, however, and the authors' attitude toward the removal of the arch is mocking.[15] More significant, for believers in the Soviet project, however, is the fact that the arch has not been replaced with a different monument. The space it occupied remains empty, but the site is a pregnant emptiness, filled, first of all, with the memory of the edifice that once stood there.[16] This is an important point for scholars of the late 1920s and early 1930s to grasp. This period brought the reorganization of space to the forefront of Soviet public consciousness. As plans for expansion of the industrial sector reached new areas across the Soviet map, it became newly apparent which places had yet to be affected and which space still needed to be reorganized. This is why so many of these early Russian production novels devote their pages to describing the end of an old spatial division as they chronicle the imminent imposition of the new.

Little wonder, then, that the former aristocrat Ippolit Vorobianinov is disoriented in Soviet space even before he leaves the initial site of the novel. His disorientation is something Vorobianinov undoubtedly shared with countless other Soviet citizens, even writer-intellectuals, but as a government official in the nameless provincial town, Vorobianinov initially believes he understands his place in the Soviet way of life. His job in the Registry Office (the well-known ZAGS, or *zapis' aktov grazhdanskogo sostoianiia*) in town even suggests that he is responsible for describing and codifying that new existence. But we soon learn that his understanding is faulty; his spatial orientation in the new universe remarkably tenuous. Once he leaves the familiar "town of N," in particular, he loses the relative equanimity he has managed to establish there with an unvarying daily regime, orderly existence, and noncommittal approach to the new political situation. He departs the provincial town for his old hometown, Stargorod, but even this once-familiar location, literally the "Old Town," is unrecognizable. Walking around Stargorod, he finds the place confusing and disorienting. "As one who had spent the whole of his life and also the revolution in Russia, he was able to see how the way of life was changing and acquiring a new countenance. He had become used to this fact, but he seemed to be used to it only on one point on the globe—the regional center of N. Now that he was back in his home town, he realized he understood nothing" (67–68). His confusion of space in Stargorod is heightened by its newly christened "Red Army Street," a "Cooperative Street," and two different "Soviet Streets" (35).[17] Now the "whole town was a different color; the blue houses had become green and the yellow ones gray" (68). This "old town," no longer recognizable but still to be navigated, is the place most readers found themselves.

Vorobianinov's inability to orient himself in the world is not simply a personal failing. It reflects, as well, the shifting universe in which the boundaries between old and new are unclear. Part of the confusion arises from the fact that the characters are perpetually in motion, on a journey for most of the novel and thus continually exposed to a changing and partially unfamiliar landscape. The authors refer to this fact in a digression about rail travel that accompanies the description of Father Fedor's departure from the town in search of Vorobianinov's treasure. In this world of shifting boundaries and changing terrain, the traveler's special status frees him or her from the quotidian concerns of everyday life, which are left behind as soon as an individual enters that unique space, the "right of way," or "zone of estrangement," as it is known in Russian (*polosa otchuzhdeniia*). According to Ilf and Petrov, the notion of such a zone, separate from but trespassing with impunity on the territory it crosses, encompasses all railroad stations. Once an individual enters this special area, "his life is completely changed" (30). Eating at odd hours, passing the time in a hedonistic cycle of tea drinking and joke telling, people—no longer citizens now but "passengers"—exist apart from their normal concerns.

This is the liminal state in which Father Fedor, Vorobianinov, and, of course, Ostap Bender spend much of the novel. Their transitory existence in the space of neither-here-nor-there gives readers a different perspective as well as critical distance on events as they occur. During this era of continued upheaval and genuine trauma, many, perhaps most, of the moves individuals made were involuntary, the result of personal disasters or societal catastrophes, quixotic but completely unrealistic plans to resettle the country. Lynne Viola, Stephen Kotkin, and others have demonstrated in shocking detail how ill conceived such grandiose utopian gestures for travel, resettlement, and new world order could be in the early Soviet period.[18] Ilf and Petrov lived through the era and witnessed some of the hardships firsthand. Yet their status as committed writers made them immune to some of the catastrophes, and they choose to focus on the idea of travel as liberation. Their universe is one in which movement is a virtue, and even fixed points may shift on a continuum that makes binary schemes of old/new, town/country, and natural/man-made humorous but meaningless abstractions.

Elements of the old way of life continue to exist, in Ilf and Petrov's work, in the midst of the "new" universe. This orientation toward the similarities between the old and new is characteristic of their work, and it is the source of much of their humor. As the former nobleman Vorobianinov, for example, wanders through his old hometown, "at one moment Ippolit Matveyevich felt he had never left Stargorod, and the next moment it was like a place completely unfamiliar to him" (68–69). In this confused state, he arrives on the ideologically significant corner of Marx and Engels Street. This is where he meets Father Fedor, and they engage in a fight over material culture, in this case, the first of many chairs to cause havoc in the novel.

The battle suggests Ilf and Petrov's disparaging attitude toward material culture and its destructive effects. The passage, in which the two men fight over the chair until it is destroyed along with their dignity, demonstrates that the authors share the disdain for such quotidian objects that was common among Russian intellectuals even before the revolution. The notion that everyday reality and the objects of everyday life were undeserving of notice was typical of the Symbolist generation and shared by many in the generation that followed. Ilf and Petrov seem to have shared, as well, the Symbolist belief that quotidian existence could have a deadening effect on human potential. The Symbolist poets bemoaned the destructive influence that the commonplaces of everyday existence had on spiritual life, while the avant-garde writers who followed, Mayakovsky primary among them, complained that the petty concerns of *byt* sapped energy needed for the class struggle. Ilf and Petrov clearly agree that relentless pursuit of worldly goods diverts people from more important societal concerns.

As always, their approach is humorous. Nevertheless, they advocate firmly for an end to the cult of material possessions and poke fun at a host of characters in the novel who put material culture above more vital interests. Vorobianinov and Father Fedor are just two of the more obvious examples of characters skewered for their unholy devotion to *byt*. The unscrupulous Aleksandr Iakovlevich, head of an old folks' home housed in Vorobianinov's former residence, Liza, the Moscow student seamstress with a fondness for meat, and, of course, the colorfully named Little Ella the Cannibal (*Ellochka Liudoedka*) are just a few of the individuals in *Twelve Chairs* whose dreams of creature comfort take unhealthy precedence over more useful pursuits.

A lyrical digression halfway through the novel serves as humorous warning of the dangers implicit in domestic life that threaten to overwhelm more important aspects of existence. The passage follows a visit Bender and Vorobianinov make to the communal house where Bender's acquaintance, the young draftsman Kolia, lives with his new wife Liza. Their lodgings are located in the very heart of Moscow, in a pink house with a mezzanine, just off Arbat Square, down Prechistenskii Boulevard, on Sivtsevaia Vrazhka. Such an exact address, however, leads the travelers not to a clear destination but to an architectural void. The building, once a dormitory for chemistry students, "had long been lived in by people whose connection with chemistry was somewhat remote" (146). The original students have either graduated or been dropped for poor scholarship, and it is the second group that has "formed something between a housing co-operative and a feudal settlement" in the house. The tenants refuse to give up their spaces, and even the house itself is declared "wild" and "has disappeared" from all the institute's plans. This "remapping" is strictly superficial. It no longer exists officially, "as though it had never existed," the authors comment. "It did exist, however, and there were people living in it" (147).

Their visit to Kolia begins shortly after Bender has been unceremoniously fired from his job as an artist on a government cruise ship on the Volga. The cruise itself provides ample opportunity for the authors to depict Soviet life, and the travels Bender and Vorobianinov make down the Volga are rich in humor and irony. One of the best vignettes of life in Russia during this period is found in the writers' description of a provincial town by the fictional name of Vasiuki. The picture they provide is taken in part from a contemporary guidebook to travel on the Volga, and Odesskii and Fel'dman argue that the description refers to the real-life town of Vetluga. Although later versions deleted reference to the date of the description, the original manuscript of *Twelve Chairs* noted that the guidebook was from 1926 and therefore completely up to date with events in the novel.[19] Bender reads the brief description of the town, which serves as the official portrait of the place. "On the high right-hand bank is the town of Vasiuki. Timber, resin, bark, and bast are dispatched from here, while consumer goods are delivered for the region, which is fifty miles from the nearest railroad. The town has a population of 8,000; it has a state-owned cardboard factory with 320 workers, a small foundry, a brewery, and a tannery. In addition to the normal academic establishments, there is also a forestry school" (*Dvenadtsat' stul'ev,* 1998, 368; my translation).

Far from the romantic view of endless potential that is typical of literary cityscapes depicted from a bird's-eye view, the guidebook offers a dry catalog of the modest offerings of provincial Russia. Bender's response is uncharacteristically sober and surprisingly disheartening: "The situation is more serious than I thought," he comments bluntly. Nevertheless, the "Smooth Operator" never lacks inventiveness, and his visit to the town recalls the extent to which the real and the imagined were able to overlap in Russia during this era. He arrives in the provincial town as a self-appointed grandmaster of chess and is warmly welcomed by the gullible local chess enthusiasts. Their receptive response inspires Bender, who experiences a "flood of new strength and chess ideas" (321) and proceeds to draw a picture of the possibilities for the small provincial town so impressive that its residents find the vision irresistible. The fact that Bender is posing as a grandmaster gives his proposals an aura of logic and rational thought that temporarily masks their utopian nature. "Chess!" he exhorts the club members. "Do you realize what chess is? It advances not only culture but also the economy! Do you realize that 'The Four Knights Chess Club,' given the right organization, could completely transform the city of Vasiuki?"[20]

The transformation Bender envisions appears to involve nothing more than decisiveness and force of will, qualities that Bender urges on his listeners in the chess club. The leap from present-day reality to an imagined future appears to be effortless, and the breadth of Bender's fantasies suggests a model of the world in which space is infinitely expandable as the boundaries of the provincial Vasiuki extend to Moscow and beyond. Bender's elaborate plans for the provincial town reach in all directions of the compass.

First of all, the river transport will not be able to handle such a large number of passengers. So the Ministry of Railroads will build a mail line from Moscow to Vasiuki. That's one thing. Another is hotels and skyscrapers to accommodate the visitors. Third, improvement of agriculture over a radius of five hundred miles; the visitors have to be provided with vegetables, fruit, caviar, and chocolate candy. Fourth, a palace for the actual tournament. Then, fifth, construction of garages to house motor transport for the visitors. An extra-high power radio station will have to be built to broadcast the sensational results of the tournament to the rest of the world. That's number six. Now about the Vasiuki railroad. It undoubtedly won't have the capacity to carry all the passengers wanting to come to Vasiuki. A "Greater Vasiuki" airport will be required with regular flights by mail planes and airships to all parts of the globe, including Los Angeles and Melbourne. (*Dvenadtsat' stul'ev*, 1998, 371–72; my translation)

Bender's inspired description, which continues for nearly five pages of the novel, has a hypnotic effect on the members of the chess club. Their fascination with the plan is expressed spatially as the expansion of the surrounding horizons.

Dazzling vistas unfolded before the Vasiuki chess enthusiasts. The boundaries of the room expanded. The rotting walls of the stud farm collapsed and in their place a thirty-story glass palace of chess thought rose into the sky. In every hall, in every room, and even in the lightning-fast elevators thoughtful people were playing chess on malachite-encrusted boards. Marble steps led down to the blue Volga. Ocean-going steamers were moored on the river. Cable cars communicating with the town center carried up beefy foreigners, chess-playing ladies, Australian advocates of the Indian defense, Hindus in turbans, devotees of the Spanish gambit, Germans, Frenchmen, New Zealanders, inhabitants of the Amazon basin, and finally Muscovites, citizens of Leningrad and Kiev, Siberians and natives of Odessa, all envious of the citizens of Vasiuki. (*Dvenadtsat' stul'ev*, 1998, 372)

In deft defiance of the opposition between province and urban center that was supposedly inflexible during this period, Bender relocates the country's capital to Vasiuki, which he renames New Moscow. This new city, "the most elegant city in Europe and, soon in the whole world," will finally stretch its boundaries to the limits of the universe and "in maybe eight or so years" be the site of the first "interplanetary chess tournament" (*Dvenadtsat' stul'ev*, 1998, 375). The plans are outlandish, of course, humorous in their bombastic audacity. Yet part of what lent the passage its humor was its similarity to the rhetoric that accompanied real-life plans in the 1920s and 1930s.

Bender's scam to remake Vasiuki is utopian, but how much more realistic was it to expect the largely agrarian Soviet Union with its untrained, semiliterate workforce to become an industrial power? Surely thousands of Soviet citizens called upon "to make this fairy-tale come true" found themselves in the position of Bender's one-eyed chess player, who listens carefully and trustingly to Bender's elaborate plans before timidly asking "how are we to put the plan into effect, to lay the basis, so to say" (326). A willingness to see endless vistas, to accomplish the impossible by overcoming perceived dichotomies between the manageable and the unattainable was a required characteristic for those wanting to believe in schemes like the First Five-Year Plan. In this sense, the Four Knights Chess Club looks like any other committee formed to ensure the success of one of Stalin's industrial blueprints. When the one-eyed chess player asks the rest of the group "Well, what do you say?" the only possible response is the expected "We'll build it! We'll build it!" that he receives.[21]

Ilf and Petrov insert the Vasiuki episodes as one more example of Bender's cunning, and naturally he has no intention of developing his plans, which are hatched to earn him breakfast and a few more rubles on which to continue the search for real riches. When his lack of expertise is revealed, Bender has to run through the darkened provincial streets to escape his pursuers, and we learn that "on account of the interrupted transformation of Vasiuki into the center of the world, it was not between palaces that Ostap had to run, but little wooden houses with outside shutters" (333). But the novel does describe a more traditional building project, and it is worthwhile looking at that description for what it reveals about construction and the production novel during this transitional period.

According to the narrative, the idea for the project—to build a tramline in Stargorod—dated from before the revolution. Despite this considerable history, however, the beginning of construction is shrouded in mist: "no one knew exactly when they'd begun to build the tramline" (*Dvenadtsat' stul'ev*, 1998, 147; my translation). Perhaps the early starting date frees the authors from the need to describe the project in glowingly heroic terms. There is nothing heroic or even very sensible about this act of building, which arises almost accidentally and is plagued from the beginning by disorganization and waste.

> Sometime back in 1920, when volunteer Saturday work started, railroad workers and rope makers had marched to Gusishe to the accompaniment of music and spent the whole day digging holes. They dug a great number of large, deep holes. . . . The next Saturday they continued at the same spot. Two holes dug in the wrong place had to be filled in again. . . . Then fresh holes were dug even bigger and deeper. Next, the bricks were delivered and the real builders arrived. They set about laying the foundation, but then everything quieted down. (*Dvenadtsat' stul'ev*, 1998, 147–48)

The champion of the plan, Treukhov, is purposefully depicted in modest, almost unattractive terms. His moustache is "withered," his face marred by a "snub" nose. The project itself languishes for

years "approved by one and rejected by another; passed on to
the capital, regardless of approval or rejection, it became covered
in dust, and no money was forthcoming" (110–11). Treukhov approaches Gavrilin, the new chief of Stargorod's public services, for
support. The new director has just been transferred from Samarkand and is "deeply tanned from the Turkestan sun" with a flat
face that resembles a "smoothly peeled turnip" and "cunning" eyes
(112). He listens indifferently to Treukhov's plans before noting that
"in Samarkand, you know, we don't need a street railway. Everyone rides donkeys." "But that's Asia!" Treukhov exclaims before
running from the room, slamming the door in frustration (111–12).

This play of dichotomies—Europe and Asia, educated and prag-
matic, prerevolutionary and Stalinist generation—dissolves quickly,
however, when Treukhov and Gavrilin join forces to set the plan in
motion by creating a stockholders' association which will loan the
needed money for a percentage. The ironies are obvious, but the
message is also clear. Only by joining together opposing forces can
the new regime "create the material base"[22] needed for real change.
The fussy prerevolutionary Treukhov and the crude Gavrilin, whose
authoritarian excesses earn him official rebuke, are both needed for
the undertaking. Treukhov is shown washing his own underwear
as a way to calm a fit of nerves associated with the project, while
Gavrilin is called before the provincial control commission for
"using his position to exert pressure," but "everything came out all
right" (113).

When work on the tramline actually begins, the problems that
emerge are considerable. The town lacks qualified personnel and
the necessary machinery for the project. The available shaped iron
is the wrong size or the wrong kind. Most of the cast pieces they
originally intend to use are substandard. The wood they get is wet.
The rails they need are fine, but they arrive a month late (113–14).
The picture Ilf and Petrov paint is of a project nearly paralyzed by
disorganization, lack of coordination, waste, and incompetence.
This is no surprise to those familiar with the history of Soviet building projects, but it is somewhat unexpected in a novel published
just before the beginning of the First Five-Year Plan. A closer look
at the production novel genre, however, reveals that such relatively
candid discussions of the numerous failings of Soviet construction
were typical of these early transitional novels, most of which include numerous such examples of the problems with Soviet building projects. In fact, the critical light in which Soviet construction
is presented in *Twelve Chairs* seems to have puzzled contemporary

literary critics; unsure of the proper response to the book for a number of reasons, they avoided mentioning its appearance for some time.

The picture of Soviet construction in the novel is candid, though by no means complete. A long description of the problems associated with financing the building project was censored, for example, including a discussion of the trip Gavrilin and Treukhov had to make to the "center" to ensure that the central bank fulfilled its obligation. And certain aspects of the building project go unmentioned altogether. Although numerous scholars have detailed the use of conscripted labor on Soviet construction sites, there is no hint of that here.[23] Nevertheless, the novel includes enough critical material to suggest that what is presented is intended as a relatively realistic depiction of the undertaking.[24] Ilf and Petrov add further realism to their own account by contrasting it to accounts of the project from the local newspaper, "Stargorodskaia pravda." The sarcastic columns of a muck-raking local correspondent "Prince of Denmark," which grace the newspaper with evidence of bureaucratic waste and individual incompetence, are shown to alternate with more optimistic reports the same journalist provides under a different pseudonym. This writer, known as the Flywheel, or Makhovik, provides Ilf and Petrov with a humorous opportunity to scoff at glowing official accounts of Soviet construction, which they mock for overly "sunny and encouraging" as well as ill-informed depictions of the building process (114). By including examples of the made-to-order headlines that became so common during the First Five-Year Plan—"How we are living and how we are building"; "Giant will soon start work"; and "Modest Builder" (114) —Ilf and Petrov suggest that their own account is free of such false enthusiasm.

The excerpts from an exemplary article in the "Stargorod Truth" irritate the engineer Treukhov both with their grandiose comparisons and with their lack of real understanding. Overreaching references to Pushkin and Peter the Great that Treukhov finds in the provincial newspaper—"It brings to mind Pushkin's poem: 'There he stood, full of great thoughts, on the bank . . .'"—fill him with "disgust for the brotherhood of writers" (114).[25] The technical illiteracy of the published accounts of the building project annoys him even more, so much so that he even writes a letter of protest to the paper (115). All of this indicates that Ilf and Petrov wish to position their manuscript as a meta-narrative, a truthful account that gains in verisimilitude by including and parodying similar but less reliable reports.

A related approach marks their description of the official ceremonies surrounding the opening of the tramline on May 1.[26] When
they include a comic description of the press coverage of the affair
by the local journalist, whose treatment of the events exactly mirrors that of his Moscow colleague in its "hackneyed, second-hand,
dust-covered phrases" (117), we are invited to laugh along with
them at the formulaic way in which other writers describe such
heroic events. While encouraging readers to see the façade behind
such prepared statements, Ilf and Petrov effortlessly serve up another, ostensibly more authentic picture of the same ceremonies.
Gavrilin is the first speaker, and he, "without knowing why himself, suddenly switched to the international situation. Several times
he attempted to bring his speech back on the rails, but, to his horror, found that he was unable to. The international words just
flowed out by themselves, against the speaker's will" (117). When
Treukhov's turn to speak comes, Ilf and Petrov provide the "authentic" text—a virtual wish list of projects for the First Five-Year
Plan—that lies behind his humorously shopworn words.

> Treukhov wanted to say a great deal. About voluntary Saturday work,
> the difficulties of the work, and about everything that had been done
> and could be done. And there was a lot that could be done: the town
> ought to do away with the horrible market; there were covered glass
> buildings to be constructed; a permanent bridge could be built instead
> of the present temporary one, which was swept away each year by the
> ice drifts, and finally there was the plan for a very large meat-refrigera-
> tor plant. (*Dvenadtsat' stul'ev*, 1998, 156)

Instead of this genuine speech, however, Ilf and Petrov depict
the flustered engineer delivering a formulaic statement unrelated
to the problems that face them. "Treukhov opened his mouth and,
stuttering, began. 'Comrades! The international situation of our
State . . .' And then he began to mumble such boring truisms that
the crowd, now listening to its sixth international speech, lost interest. It was only when he had finished that Treukhov realized that
he had not said a word about the tram" (156–57). The contrast
that Ilf and Petrov thus create between official pronouncements on
the project and the unspoken truths that they have ostensibly
recorded provides their manuscript with the gloss of authenticity.[27]
The device has the effect of taking the reader into the authors' confidence, thereby creating an alternate space from which the events
of the narrative can be admired from within. This can hardly be
called a critical distance since the effect is to undermine rather than

enhance readers' tendency to find fault with the official record. The reader emerges instead as one of the initiated few who "speak Bolshevik," to borrow Stephen Kotkin's phrase, by understanding and appreciating both the hyperbolic official discourse and the unspoken dialogue behind it.

The same effect is achieved in a number of other scenes in both this novel and *The Golden Calf,* scenes in which the authors goodnaturedly point out the discontinuity between recorded images and the reality that remains unseen behind the official record. This is clear, for example, in their depiction of the film crew that visits Stargorod to record the official opening of the tramline. The crew arrives too late to film the actual ceremony, but, as the filmmakers clearly understand, that fact is no obstacle to their work. The set of available images makes it simple to recreate reality on the run. "But, anyway, we'll manage" (122), notes the young director, who confidently and immediately begins to craft his film: "Nick, lights! Close up of a turning wheel! Close-up of the feet of the moving crowd! . . . Now we'll take the builder. Comrade Treukhov? Would you mind, comrade Treukhov? No, not like that. Three-quarters. Like this, it's more original! Against a streetcar . . ." (122).

The filmmakers continue their work on the "documentary" by giving stage directions that are as formulaic as the images they accompany. "Now you're talking to the first passenger. Liuda, come into the picture! That's it. Breathe deeper, you're excited! . . . Nick! A close-up of their legs! Action! That's it. Thanks very much. Cut!" (122). The film they are creating is a silent one, of course, which enhances the impression of an authentic experience that the director is supplanting with his officially supplied text. When the director notices Gavrilin's "oriental" features, he instantly casts this head of the city's public services in a minor role. "'Over here! A marvelous character type! A worker! A streetcar passenger. Breathe deeper, you're excited! You've never been in a streetcar before. Breathe!' Gavrilin wheezed malevolently. 'Marvelous! Sweetheart, come here! Greetings from the young Communists! Breathe deeper, you're excited! That's it! Swell! Nick, cut!'" (122–23). Although Gavrilin is irritated, he complies; the need to conform to those expected images is essential to the victory itself. "Aren't you going to photograph the tram?" Treukhov inquires shyly. But the actual tram is irrelevant to the official story line, and the filmmakers depart with promises to take any additional scenes they need in Moscow itself. As authors of the transitional production novel, however, Ilf and Petrov use this obvious gap between rhetoric and reality not to caution readers about the dangers of symbolic representation in general but to convince them of the authenticity of their own depiction of life.

In a further blurring of "real" life and its representation on the silver screen, Treukhov starts smoking out of nervousness (123) shortly after the filmmakers depart. The simulated emotion captured on film is now reflected in the real emotion of the narrative by Ilf and Petrov. This device of offhandedly displaying an authentic truth after first depicting an artistically crafted one is used repeatedly in the novel to create a sense of realism that readers can presumably share.[28] We are invited to laugh at the inaccuracies and exaggeration of official accounts without having to deny the real heroism and passion they imperfectly represent.

Ilf and Petrov identify this technique as the focus of their work in a preface to *The Golden Calf*. "Our goal," they comment there, "is satire of precisely those people who don't understand the reconstructive period."[29] Their implied readers do comprehend the situation—the pathos, the setbacks, the necessary sacrifices, and the inevitability of victory—and can look with amused tolerance on those who do not. The ease and humor with which Ilf and Petrov treat such people in their novels suggests the bemused attitude of writers completely secure in their convictions, confident enough to resurrect their hero, murdered at the end of the first novel, and set him newly adrift in a vast Soviet environment. If Bender had to be punished in *Twelve Chairs*, he could now be reanimated and let loose to roam the secure Soviet state. This implied position of strength must have appealed to Soviet leaders as well.

Bender and his three travel companions spend *The Golden Calf* looking for Koreiko, a legendary but elusive illegal Soviet millionaire. Their search takes them, as it did in the previous novel, from one end of the country to the other, in travels that suggest the expansive Soviet space in which they operate. If Emma Widdis is correct that the expansion of the Soviet map was the premier Stalinist project,[30] then Ilf and Petrov depict a universe in which that project has been successfully brought to fruition. The beginning of the novel establishes this conquered space quite effectively by describing a natural environment that has been completely transformed by the human beings in it. They have "built cities, reared many-storied buildings, installed plumbing and a water system, paved the streets and lighted them with electric lamps. It was they who spread culture throughout the world, devised printing, invented gunpowder, flung bridges across rivers, deciphered Egyptian hieroglyphics, introduced the safety razor, destroyed the slave trade, and determined that one hundred palatable, nourishing dishes may be prepared out of soybeans."[31]

The creators of all this abundance are "pedestrians," human beings in their natural state, free of mechanical encumbrances, and shorn of the trappings of ordinary *byt*. This nomadic creature is the essential Soviet citizen of the First Five-Year Plan, an activist who lives out his days traversing a heroic path "from Vladivostok to Moscow" (4). This journey of exploration reverses the traditional European path of discovery from west to east.[32] Here, movement flows from east to west as this "Soviet pedestrian-physical-culturist," armed with a banner exhorting "Let Us Reconstruct the Life of Textile Workers," makes his way across space that is no longer contested. The ignoble end of his journey, in which he is hit by a car at the "very gates of Moscow" (4), suggests the inevitable fate of pedestrian Russia if it fails to accommodate both east and west in its plans for the future.

Having established this ultimatum and the geographical landscape on which it will unfold, Ilf and Petrov immediately insert their hero, Ostap Bender, into the situation. As a pedestrian, Bender belongs to the group Ilf and Petrov humorously identify as the "greater and best part of humanity" (5). As a visitor to those "small Russian cities" in which the "pedestrian is yet respected and loved" (5), Bender straddles east and west, old and new, reality and potential. In this sense, Bender's comments on the appearance of the provincial Russian town in which he finds himself at the beginning of the novel can be read as one more point for action in the First Five-Year Plan. Nearly his first words in the novel are both a statement of fact and a call to action. As he enters the town along the optimistically named Boulevard of Youthful Talents, he notes with disappointment that "This is not Rio de Janeiro. This is much worse" (6). He has reached this weighty conclusion by passing "with tolerant curiosity" (5) through this provincial town of unremarkable architectural features, which he catalogs for us as he passes. The multiple structures—a dozen or so "azure, mignonette-colored, and pale rose bell towers"; the "molting Caucasian gold of the church cupolas"; the flag which "snapped over the official building"; the "white-towered gates of the provincial Kremlin"; the church itself, which he renames the "cathedral of Christ, the Savior of Potatoes," to acknowledge its current use as a storehouse; a plywood arch newly whitewashed with a patriotic greeting—combine to create the image of a stagnant society in need of initiative and repair (5).

Bender's reverie on the city is interrupted by an encounter between an engineer and an official from the local factory. The engineer, Comrade Talmudovskii, is making his way to the train station, having abandoned his post at the factory because of the poor condition of the town: "The apartment—a pigsty. No theater. The emolument . . ." (7). The factory official wants to put an end to the kind of sophistry that Talmudovskii's behavior and his evocative name imply, and he invokes professional, religious, and societal reasons for staying on the job. But even his threat of legal action fails to stop the engineer in his escape from the task of helping to turn the provincial backwater into a place that can rival the exotic world capital of Bender's dreams. After Talmudovskii's hasty departure as a "deserter from the labor front," Bender can only conclude that his first harsh evaluation of this particular space was correct: "No," he comments again laconically, "this is not Rio de Janeiro" (7).

Bender repeats this negative evaluation a few moments later when he enters the office of the local chairman of the executive committee where it becomes clear that here, as in Ilf and Petrov's earlier novel as well as in other early production novels, physical surroundings serve as both historical place markers and ideological statements. The description of this provincial leader's office is telling because it indicates how much has changed since the revolution. It also makes clear, however, how much progress still needs to be made in the reorganization of Russian everyday life. Use of interior landscapes to reveal the political state of the country is a common technique in literature of this period, and Ilf and Petrov manage their inventory of ideological furniture humorously and efficiently.[33]

They begin by establishing the previous landscape, a state in which there was a place for everything and everything was in its place. "A long time ago, in the days of the Tsar," the novel informs us, "the furnishing of public spaces was standardized" (9). A "special pedigree of official furniture" was bred: "flat wooden benches with six-inch polished seats, tables on billiard legs, and oaken parapets that separated the officials from the restive outer world" (8). Ilf and Petrov give no explanation for the nearly complete disappearance of this type of furniture, although we know what happened to it from other accounts. Some, for example, was burned as fuel in the difficult revolutionary years, as Viktor Shklovskii's account of life with Mayakovsky, Brik, and other members of LEF makes clear. Shklovskii mentions an occasion in Mayakovsky's apartment when he was freezing. Into the fireplace went the cornice, which had been hacked to pieces, and some frames that had showcased a pre-Revolutionary butterfly collection. "Maybe this was not just the desire to get warm," Shklovskii offers in a moment of insight into his younger self, "but also the thirst for destruction."[34] Other furniture was refashioned for unusual uses, as Sergei Eisenstein notes in his memories of sleeping during the war years on a mirrored wardrobe of the very type Ilf and Petrov mention. "In Dvinsk," Eisenstein comments in his autobiography, "I slept on a mirror in a hurriedly evacuated apartment—after the Red Army had taken the town. There were no beds left, and camp beds were not yet available. But a mirrored wardrobe stood proudly in the empty room. This wardrobe was laid on its back, and onto the mirrored surface of its door, which reflected the world, a straw mattress was laid. And onto the mattress—me."[35] As we know from copious other sources, many such pieces of furniture were traded for grain and other essential supplies and disappeared into the vast Russian landscape. Boris Pilniak's graphic descriptions of his own excursions into rural Russia in search of supplies record the barter experience of such early *meshchochniki,* or petty barterers. Pilniak's catalog of postrevolutionary furniture debris takes up a good part of both *Mahogany* and the production novel Pilniak crafted from it, *Volga Falls to the Caspian Sea.*[36] Although the emphasis they give to old-fashioned furniture in their work differs, Pilniak and Ilf and Petrov alike seem to agree with the humorists' conclusion that "the secret of its construction" has now been "lost" (8).

The material culture that replaces the world of conventional furniture reveals a complex universe in which previous stereotypes and obvious boundaries between office and external world, public and private life, West and East, even good taste and kitsch are blurred. The description Ilf and Petrov offer of this transitional world of Soviet officialdom suggests that here, too, reality leaves a great deal to be desired. "People forgot how the quarters of official personages should be arranged, and there appeared in the offices of civil servants objects that until then had been the inseparable property of private apartments" (8). The blend of public and private is complete; individual apartments have official sounding "inseparable property," while offices are furnished in increasingly idiosyncratic and diverse ways. "Government offices now boasted the divans of lawyers, with springs and a mirrored shelf for seven porcelain elephants which presumably bring luck, cupboards for dishes, little cabinets, special leather chairs for rheumatics, and azure Japanese vases" (9).[37] This particular office described at the beginning of *The Golden Calf* contains, in addition to an ordinary desk, "two small pillows upholstered in pink silk," a "striped settee," a "velvet screen with a picture of Mount Fuji Yama and a cherry tree in blossom," and "a cheap, machine-made Slavic cupboard with a mirror" (9).

Bender, whose comprehension of the significance of material culture to politics is admirably precise, is even able to identify the amount of money he can con from the official in question by glancing at the furniture with which he is surrounded. "The cupboard is of the type 'Hey, you Slavs!'" Bender notices unhappily, perhaps, like Eisenstein, remembering his own uncomfortable rest during the war years. "There isn't much to get here." Thinking longingly of more up-to-date offices in which "new Swedish furniture of the Leningrad Lumber Trust" has supplanted this uncomfortable provincial montage, Bender again states his First Five-Year Plan slogan with finality: "No, this is not Rio de Janeiro" (9).

Bender's negative definition of this location as "Not-Rio-de-Janeiro" suggests, first of all, the potential ubiquity of the space he inhabits. Like the unnamed provincial town in which *Twelve Chairs* begins, this is a spot that resembles all others. The exotic reference to Rio de Janeiro, however, and Bender's insistence on that as his destination add a comic utopian note to the narrative. Bender's companion Shura Balaganov knows nothing of such "world homes of culture, in addition to Moscow, he knew only Kiev, Melitopol, and Zhmerinka," and since he is in any case "convinced that the earth was flat" (24), he views Bender's plans to relocate to Rio de Janeiro as completely impractical.

Bender's attraction to the Brazilian city, not surprisingly for this period, is as a model for urban development. Claiming interest in the city "since I was a child" (24), he pulls an article from a well-known Soviet encyclopedia to bolster his case, and the description he reads from there hints at a fairytale existence in a utopian city of the future. "Here!" he exclaims, having found the passage he needs in his cherished clipping from the Malaia Sovetskaia encyclopedia. "Here! '. . . in the wealth of stores and the grandeur of buildings its main streets rival those of the largest cities of the world.' Can you imagine that, Shura? Rival!" (25).

This utopian dream is what Bender wrongly substitutes for the much more demanding aspirations of the First Five-Year Plan. Called upon to sacrifice for the country's larger goals, Bender refuses. "I want to go away from here," he complains. "In the course of the last year grave differences have developed between the Soviet government and me. The government wants to build socialism, and I am not interested. The building of socialism bores me" (25). His rejection of the Soviet project, his identification of "the last year" as a problematic period, and his desire to substitute an unrealistic fantasy—"mulattoes, bay, export coffee," even "the Charleston" (25)—for the triumphs of Socialist construction mark Bender as one of those very "people who don't understand the reconstruction period" that Ilf and Petrov had identified as the object of their satire in *The Golden Calf*. One of the intentions of the novel, then, will be to redirect the type of utopian energy that Bender exhibits to the practical task of creating a Soviet heaven on earth. Part of the message of *The Golden Calf* is that while the process of remapping the universe to reflect new Soviet structures is inevitable, it nevertheless requires the efforts of everyone. The physical boundaries of the new universe of Sovietness are extensive and expanding, and Bender will discover by the end of the novel that it is impossible to transgress them.

The character Fedor Nikitich Khvorobev demonstrates that the psychological dimensions of Soviet consciousness are unlimited as well. Khvorobev is a humorous figure, a monarchist whose visceral hatred of Soviet power results in such distaste for the world around him that he develops an antipathy for the very terms of geometry itself. "He grew to hate the word 'sector.' Oh, that sector! Fedor Nikitich, who valued everything refined, including geometry, had never imagined that this splendid mathematical concept, which signifies part of the area of a curvilinear figure, would ever be so debased."[38] This dissatisfaction with the new order, even with the units of measurement the new order uses, leads Khvorobev to seek refuge in an imaginary space of his own creation.

Khvorobev longs for a psychological reinstatement of the physical images of the prerevolutionary world but is soon devastated to learn that Soviet *realia* have invaded even his dreams, as psychological representations of the physical world of socialism impress themselves upon him. He lives on the psychological and physical edge of the world, having moved out of the city in the hope that "a new life would start." But his new location, at the edge of a ravine with a view of the city in the valley below, only confirms what we already know: "there was no place anywhere to escape the Soviet way of thinking."[39] Since his physical retreat from the Soviet city, he has only become more convinced of the reach of the new Soviet *byt*, which has now overwhelmed his dream world as well: "He, Khvorobev, would have liked, for a start, to dream of the tsarist procession from Uspenskii Cathedral. Having calmed down, he fell asleep again but instead of the face of the beloved monarch, he instantly dreamt of the representative of the local party committee Comrade Surzhikov."[40] Always ready to help if he can see a personal advantage, Bender promises to cure his new acquaintance "according to Freud." Noting that "the principal cause is the very existence of the Soviet regime," he concludes that he cannot remove Soviet power since he simply doesn't have time. In the meantime, however, he offers a sound bit of advice: "You're in a bad way," he notes "sympathetically. As the saying goes: 'Being determines consciousness.' Since you live in a Soviet country, then your dreams should be Soviet."[41]

As Khvorobev's example illustrates, the process of becoming Soviet occurs inevitably with the change in material culture. And changes in material culture, Ilf and Petrov remind us, are part of a natural evolution in images in the "small world" of everyday life that parallels, rather than opposes, developments in the "big world" (*Zolotoi telenok*, 98; my translation). The structure the authors imagine is not of a dichotomy between a big world of ideology and invention and a smaller private universe in opposition to those ideas. They describe instead a small world of praxis in which the ideas that drive the larger universe are inevitably reflected. This small world is petty and coarse, as we might expect from two writers steeped in a tradition of disdain for *byt*. The big world is characterized by an elevated "striving to improve mankind," while the small universe is full of vulgar and superficial interpretations of the big-world politics that drive it.

> Small people hurry after the big ones. They understand that they have to be in tune with the epoch and only then will their wares find a market. In Soviet times, when ideological foundations are created in the big world, then the small world becomes more animated. The granite base of Communist ideology is laid under all the petty inventions of the ant world. . . . And when there's a fierce discussion in the big world about the formation of a new way of life, everything is already ready in the small world: "Dream of the Shockworker" ties, Gladkov vests, little plaster statues of the "Bathing Female Collective Farm Worker," and ladies' cork underarm protectors called "Love of the Worker Bees." (*Zolotoi telenok*, 98; my translation).

This "kitschification" of big ideas is one of the most fundamental sources of humor in Ilf and Petrov's work, and it allows them to stay on the side of orthodox ideology while poking gentle fun at those whose understanding of the "big world" is still imperfect. This approach makes it possible for the authors to reject a binary model in which "those who are not with us are against us" and to substitute instead the notion that "those who are not *yet* with us are fair game for satire." Such is the fate, for example, of the old-fashioned and politically illiterate puzzle maker Sinitskii, whose bumbling attempts to use that "popular word 'industrialization'" in his puzzle result in his hapless creation of a humorous neologism "industrializaktsiia"[42] instead. We know this sort of "wordplay" often had unexpectedly dire consequences in the Soviet Union, but Ilf and Petrov were allowed to portray such political illiteracy as a passing problem that their satire would help solve. Their big world and the small are not diametrically opposed but tied to each other by bonds of shared culture and responsibility.

Political neutrality and even bald hypocrisy in the political arena are depicted here as nothing more than opportunities for Ilf and Petrov to unleash their well-known wit. Thus, the incidental character in *The Golden Calf* Bomze, an "employee of the noble mien" (116), expresses diametrically opposed opinions during his lunch hour at the office, where he works with the secret millionaire Koreiko and a number of other bureaucrats. Bomze has no political convictions of his own, but he is an expert in reflecting the concerns of the "big world," as he understands them. "That's it! There's no room for individuality," he agrees with one of his colleagues who has just been criticizing life in the Soviet Union, "no incentive, no personal prospects. My wife, you know, is only a housewife, but even *she* says there's no incentive, no personal prospects" (117). When he joins a different colleague, however, his opinions effortlessly change so that he now expresses an opposing point of view without losing his reputation as an "honest man and, what is more important, a man of principle" (118). His new insistence on an opposing viewpoint implies that for those in the small world, questions of ideology are primarily stylistic.[43] "That's it! The will of the collective!" Bomze argues emphatically to another colleague. "The Five-Year Plan in four years, even in three—Here is an incentive which . . . Take even my wife—just a housewife, and even she gives industrialization its due. . . . The devil take it, a new life is growing up before our very eyes!" (117).

Ilf and Petrov allow themselves such liberties since they imagine a world in which real contradictions of policy and ideology have long ago been resolved. The space in which their characters operate is already uniformly Soviet, and remaining questions of space utilization—whether they concern the use of office space, the division of a communal apartment, or the final resolution of property division after a divorce—are trivial. Much more important, Ilf and Petrov imply, is the larger picture on a national scale. In this world in which all of the Soviet Union has been transformed into a construction site, fundamental contradictions have dissolved, as have artificial divisions between public and private, East and West, urban and rural, past and present, even foreign and native. The space of the early production novel, shown by Ilf and Petrov in triumphal bird's-eye perspective in a lyrical digression halfway through *The Golden Calf*, is the end of such binary structures.

> Night, night, night lay over the entire country. In the port of Chernomorsk the cranes turned easily, dropping their steel feelers into the deep holds of foreign ships and turning again to the quay to deposit, with the loving care of a mother cat, pine boxes with machinery for the tractor factory. Rosy-tailed flames spewed from the high chimneys of silicate plants. Here gleamed the gathered stars of Dneprostroi, Magnitogorsk, and Stalingrad. In the north the star of Krasnoputilovsk had risen, and behind it flared a great multitude of other stars of first magnitude. There were factories, here, combines, electric stations, new construction; the entire Five-Year Plan, blazed forth blocking out the old sky which once shone for the Egyptians.[44]

The uniform distribution of the stars across the plane of Soviet space helps erase distinctions between north and south, as well as such chronic divisions as urban and rural. Even home and abroad become blurred as the Soviet Union becomes an exporter and foreign resources are used for socialist ends. And when this panorama of nature's glory is harnessed by the working class, then sky becomes land, and present and future subsume and overwhelm the past. This is the message of the end of Ilf and Petrov's lyrical digression, in which an electric map of the Five-Year Plan brings heaven to earth while abolishing distinctions between private concerns and public initiatives. Two young workers in love plan their individual futures in perfect concert with society's master plan in front of the starry map, which they themselves illuminate. "And the young man, who had sat for a long time with his sweetheart in the workers' club, quickly lit the electrified map of the Five-Year Plan and whispered: 'Look at that red light. There is where the Sibcombine will be. We'll go there! Want to?' And his beloved laughed quietly, freeing her hands" (160).

This touching scenario contrasts with a later scene in which Bender abandons his love interest, Zosia, on the steps of the Museum of Antiquity, in order to follow Koreiko to the Far East where he has fled to escape Bender's clutches. Bender makes his decision reluctantly, but he is driven forward by the same utopian dream as before. "No," he concludes, as he turns away decisively from Zosia. "This is not Rio de Janeiro" (278). Koreiko has now found temporary refuge with a group finishing the "Turk-Sib" railroad between Turkistan and Siberia. Even his new address, which Zosia unwittingly shares with Bender, suggests the transitional nature of his stay there. "He has a job as a switchman in the northern rail settlement," she reveals. "But it's only called that—a settlement. It's actually a train. . . . That train lays the rails. You understand? And then rides on those same rails. And coming to meet it, from the south, is another settlement just like it. They'll meet soon. Then there will be a solemn joining. It's all in the desert, he writes, camels . . . Isn't it interesting?"[45] Ilf and Petrov, as well as Shaginian and, as we will see, Kataev and Platonov, use the railroad motif in their writings to describe changes in life during this period. The idea of traveling cities expresses the notion of dynamic, moving space that is particularly suited to this transitional era of utopia in practice.

Zosia's genuine interest in the railroad project and Bender's self-serving journey there allow Ilf and Petrov to provide their readers with a detailed description of the railroad construction project that fulfills generic requirements while moving the plot forward nicely. Thus, the authors are able to continue their comic treatment of Bender and his antics while simultaneously providing the requisite report from the field that construction novels required. Part Two of the novel ends with the destruction of the faithful automobile Antelope-Gnu, which has taken Bender and his companions across nearly the entire Soviet Union before disintegrating on one of Russia's notoriously bad roads. The death of Panikovskii, one of the original four members of this band of con men, casts an even deeper pall over their trip. The miraculous appearance of a special train of journalists headed to cover the joining of the two ends of the Turk-Sib railroad thus serves as Soviet "deus ex machina" to drive the plot ahead. This vision of a well-appointed train in the middle of nowhere inspires Bender to split off from the remaining members of his group and set out for the railroad construction site in the company of its official chroniclers.

This clever plot development allows Bender to join his creators on a train that the real Ilf and Petrov actually rode from Moscow to the Far East. Sent to cover the union of the rails for the journal *30 dnei*, Ilf and Petrov rode in the special car that they describe as Bender's new home in *The Golden Calf*. Many of the pictures that Ilf, an amateur photographer, took on the journey were published in the journal in 1930, and one can almost discern Bender's presence in the group photographs there. Here, too, the narrative takes pains to erase the obvious dichotomies that seem to surround the journey. The train car is filled with a striking mix of western and Soviet journalists, but the "meeting of the two worlds," we are told, "ended satisfactorily. No quarrels resulted. The coexistence of two systems in the special train, the capitalistic and the socialistic, had to continue willy-nilly for a whole month" (301).

Ilf and Petrov reject the obvious binary comparisons that flow so glibly from the pens of their fellow journalists. Just as they did in *Twelve Chairs*, here they use the device of contrasting official rhetoric to give their own account verisimilitude and authenticity. Thus, they laughingly portray the western journalists who are fascinated with the pseudo-exotic they find in the camels, the desert, and the Kazaks that surround them. They spare none of the feelings of their Soviet counterparts, either, as that group falls into predictable raptures over the first female tractor driver they encounter. By mocking stereotypical images on both sides of a perceived dichotomy, Ilf and Petrov salvage a place for their own work that avoids the easy comparisons of a binary system.

> But if the camel had his picture taken with full consciousness of his right to fame, the female tractor driver turned out to be more modest. She endured about five photos calmly, then blushed and went away. The photographers then fell on the tractors. By a stroke of good luck, a line of camels could be seen on the horizon behind the machines. All of this, tractors and camels, would fit nicely into a picture entitled "The Old and the New" or "Who Will Beat Whom?"[46]

In place of such easy contrasts, Ilf and Petrov offer more complex images that suggest the richness of reality beneath superficial appearances. The thumbnail descriptions Ilf and Petrov offer of both western and Soviet correspondents on the train go beyond easy stereotypes of either East or West. The western delegation includes such colorful characters as "a provincial from New York, a Canadian girl . . ., a Japanese diplomat . . ., a young English diplomat . . ., the German orientalist . . ., an American economist, a Czecho-Slovak, a Pole," and so on (301). The Soviet group—defined by profession since they share a nationality—is no less diverse with its "shock-brigaders," "prosperous" journalists, "a builder from the Stalingrad tractor factory," a "weaver from Serpukhov," "metal workers from Leningrad, miners from the Donets Basin, a machinist from Ukraine" (302). A vignette the authors offer in which East meets East also works against the familiar binary comparisons.

> The Japanese diplomat stood two steps away from the Kazakh. They regarded each other in silence. Their slightly flattened faces, stiff mustaches, polished yellow skin, and swollen, narrow eyes were exactly alike. They would have passed for twins if the Kazakh had not worn a sheepskin coat belted with a cotton sash, while the Japanese wore a

gray London suit, and if the Kazakh had not begun to read only last year, while the Japanese had graduated twenty years before from two universities, one in Tokyo and the other in Paris. The diplomat stepped back, bent his head to the sights of his camera, and clicked the shutter. The Kazakh laughed, jumped on his rough little horse and galloped off into the steppe. (*Zolotoi telenok*, 276)

This passage and others like it make the irrelevance of the question "who will win?" seem clear: any such battle would have to take place not between binary opposites but between nearly "identical twins." By casting the model of facile dichotomies into doubt, Ilf and Petrov offer their own narrative as a legitimate substitute for the superficial system it aims to replace.[47]

Just as they did in their depiction of the opening of the tramline in *Twelve Chairs*, here Ilf and Petrov present their version of the official ceremonies to join the ends of the railroad as more authentic and realistic than the stereotypical reporting available from other sources. The authors lampoon the accounts of their fellow correspondents, which have become so hackneyed that the journalists must resort to a collective vow to avoid certain phrases. Needless to say, the very phrases the writers have promised not to use appear almost immediately in the reports filed by several of their fellow journalists. This problem is so widespread that Ilf and Petrov laughingly reveal formulae that can be effortlessly applied to create a news story for any occasion, a "Complete Celebrator," replete with all the phrases any journalist needs for creating a story to order. The product of Bender's restless imagination, this "indispensable manual for the composition of articles for gala occasions, feuilletons for state holidays, odes, hymns, and also poems for parades" (319) includes a useful list of appropriate vocabulary, images, and even punctuation help for the beginning author. By making these trite phrases the focus of their own account, the coauthors manage to undermine clumsier purveyors of the production novel while simultaneously creating one themselves.

Ilia Erenburg uses the same technique in his own production novel *Den' vtoroi* (*Second Day*, also translated as *Out of Chaos*).[48] Erenburg is insistent in his argument that reality on the construction site is unlike its literary and cinematic depictions. He pointedly compares the normally distorted artistic representations of other works to the ostensibly unvarnished truth of his own work in a scene from *Second Day* in which two of the characters see a construction site in a movie. "Irina went to the movies with Kolya. They were showing some kind of silly picture: shock workers in brand-new little shirts were building a factory, just exactly as if they were playing a game of ball—'one-two.' They sang in unison and, without even skipping a beat, they taught some bespectacled American a lesson. Kolya frowned: 'Bunch of hacks! They don't have the foggiest idea of a construction site'" (117). Kolya objects to the filmmakers as a "bunch of hacks," second-rate artists whose artistic sense is poor, as Erenburg links the question of verisimilitude to one of aesthetics. Production literature, then, becomes an aesthetic education in which participants literally relearn a system of values by reinterpreting the view of the space around them.

Erenburg uses the trope of a figure at the window in a later love scene between Irina and Kolya to reinscribe the new landscape on his readers' consciousness. By comparing landscapes of the past with the new depiction, Erenburg hopes to undermine the traditional idyll while simultaneously reinscribing it on a construction site from the First Five-Year Plan. Irina and Kolya have just expressed their love for one another. "Look at our story," comments Irina. "You can't even write a novel about it. . . . I think that our life is wonderful and we love each other truly. But you can't stage a tragedy [about us]—'Irina and Kolya.' My nose is too stubby for that . . ." (214–15).

This seeming rejection of the literary possibilities for their life is countered, however, by a passage in which Erenburg reintroduces them as real-life heroes of a new novel, the one the reader is holding. The setting, naturally now, is the construction site, and Erenburg frames the lovers at the window as they gaze out onto this new world they will both build and inhabit. The reader is inside the building with the young lovers, looking out on to that new landscape. Their gaze is now ours, as the world becomes comprehensible, beautiful, and so familiar that only a few details are needed to evoke it for us completely. "They went up to the window," Erenburg continues, and "from the window the whole construction site was visible. The smokestacks and fires said the rest. Irina and Kolya were at the right place. They knew exactly what to do" (215).

Ilf and Petrov make use of this same device to complete their description of the final phase of construction of the Turkistan Siberian railroad. When the actual union of the rails takes place, it is late at night and most of the journalists' corps is fast asleep. Once again, this allows Ilf and Petrov to present an account of the event that has been purposefully stripped of rhetorical excess and empty gesture. The authentic note they strike allows them to present their narrative as more genuine and more profound than others.

There were no lights in the cars. Everybody was asleep. Only the large square windows of the headquarters' car were lit up. Its door opened quickly and a member of the government jumped down to the ground. The chief of the railroad took a step forward, saluted, and delivered the report which the entire country awaited. The Turkistan Railroad, which connected Siberia and Central Asia by direct line, was finished a year ahead of time. When this formality had been carried out, the report given and accepted, the two middle-aged, unsentimental men kissed each other. (*Zolotoi telenok*, 291)

The heartfelt emotion that overcomes these two "unsentimental" officials at the completion of their strategic mission is left in the story that Ilf and Petrov tell. That makes their account ostensibly more personal, more believable, and more honest than the official version from which this emotion is deleted. Ilf and Petrov manage to offer the "real" production novel by explaining what happened to its expurgated cousin: the editors back in Moscow decide to publish the "first part of the telegram" that a journalist sends about the union of rails, but "the kiss was eliminated. The editor said that it was improper for a member of the government to kiss" (*Zolotoi telenok*, 291).

The description Ilf and Petrov present of photographer Menshov's attempts to document the historic moment on film raises similar questions about images of such important events. Hours after elaborately arranging a staged photograph of the train in front of a wooden arch built just to mark the occasion, Menshov realizes that he snapped the photograph without film in his camera. Only the lack of enough magnesium to illuminate another shot keeps him from insisting on the train's return to the original site for the picture he had planned (318). By telling such tales, Ilf and Petrov succeed in suggesting that their account depicts the reality behind the official version of truth normally offered for public consumption. Readers and viewers are not invited to question that official truth, which seems to the coauthors to need no justification or proof. They are encouraged, however, to understand its complexity and appreciate the human element involved in such heroic undertakings.

The union of the rails serves as the final link in the project to extend Soviet space from European Russia to the far eastern borders of the country. Bender, too, seems to achieve a personal goal by succeeding in his project to extract a fortune from Koreiko's illegal fund. The two underground millionaires then strike up a friendship of sorts and even decide to travel together. Unfortunately for them, the universe in which they set off on their adventure has changed beyond recognition. Denied space on the train that now unites East and West, Bender is similarly unable to secure a seat on the airplane departing at the end of the ceremonies. The "special flight" (344) no longer has room for unofficial passengers of his ilk. He and Koreiko are finally able to secure passage out of the area only by buying the camels that have earlier been used to represent a way of life left in the past. After riding eight days through the desert on their way to a town that they hope will "rival Baghdad," they arrive instead at an ancient cemetery of "semicircular graves stretched in waves of stone" all the way "to the very horizon" (348). This forbidding stone landscape suggests the ultimate destination of their illusions.

When they reach the actual oasis, they find it no less disappointing. Bender has promised to show Koreiko a wonderful bar in which they can indulge their illicit desires. The name of the establishment, "Beneath the Moon," suggests a limitless nocturnal landscape in which the two con artists can operate. Instead of the "semi-darkness" that Bender has imagined, however, they find that the bar has disappeared, as has the street on which it stood, replaced instead by a "straight European street," (349) which is being rebuilt along its entire length. The notion of western rationality and logic superseding the supposed chaos and disorder of the East is familiar from other production novels, especially, as we will see, Kataev's *Time, Forward!* But Ilf and Petrov forestall critics who might see this as just another example of colonial hubris by including a spokesman from the indigenous population who supports the building efforts. The young director of a museum that has sprung up on the site of the former bar is unequivocally in favor of the changes. In his hurry to point out the achievements of the past few years, he rushes to indicate the "buildings that were already up, buildings in the process of construction, and places where buildings were going to be erected" (352). When Bender and Koreiko object to these intended projects—"And aren't you sorry to lose this exoticism? It's Baghdad!"—the young man "becomes angry," pointing out that "it's beautiful for you, the tourists, but we must live here" (352). This exchange underlines the fundamental assumption of this production novel: building projects and the progress they imply are, in and of themselves, desirable and inevitable. To imply otherwise is to adopt the viewpoint of the heartless privileged, who would thoughtlessly allow others to remain in their picturesque squalor while enjoying the advantages of civilization themselves.

It is no surprise, then, that Bender is ultimately unable to escape from this space. His newly found fortune cannot release him from a universe in which the transformation to Soviet reality is already complete. Everywhere he goes, Bender finds that an irreversible process of Sovietization has already taken place. This is brought home to him in the very next location he visits as an independently wealthy citizen. He is unable to secure even a single hotel room in the city because more important citizens have reserved them all in advance. The symbolically significant "Congress of Soil Experts" (*kongress pochvovedov*) (357) has preceded Bender at the hotel, in the restaurant, and even at the theater. Only specialists who understand this space and comprehend the very texture of the soil on which they stand will be allowed to inherit the earth. Bender travels aimlessly from train station to train station in this Sovietized space, unable to find a landing place anywhere. The authors hammer away at their point: no matter what your destination, you always arrive in the Soviet Union.

This unsettling experience even causes Bender to lose faith in his utopian world of dreams. "The devil take it!" Bender answers with "unexpected anger" in response to Balaganov's question about the possibility of traveling to Rio de Janeiro. "It's all a figment of the imagination! There is no Rio de Janeiro! And there is no America! And there is no Europe! And there is nothing! The waves of the Atlantic Ocean break on Shepetovka" (360). Bender has been stripped of his last dream of an alternate space, but the coauthors use this as an occasion for a one-liner about the world beyond the real borders of the Soviet Union. "The rest of the world is a myth about life beyond the grave," Bender continues. "He who goes abroad never returns" (360).

Of course, the end of the novel demonstrates that the Smooth Operator is wrong. He does make it abroad at the end of the book, and yet he returns, forcibly reinjected into the space he has been intent on leaving from the beginning of the narrative. In preparation for his flight abroad, he creates one final structure, an overcoat that he "had been building for four months, building it like a house" (398), filling it with treasures—watches, medals, gold and silver plate—to support his life in the briefly resurrected Rio de Janeiro. Bidding the Soviet Union farewell on the spot, he resorts to familiar construction metaphors to describe his desire to move outside of the boundaries that have measured his activity until now. "I'm a private person" (*chastnoe litso*), he comments just before stepping across the river into Romania, "and not obliged to evince enthusiasm for silos, trenches, and towers" (398).[49] Continuing defiantly, Bender insists "I'm not really interested in the socialist problem of remaking man into an angel."[50] The construction motifs are familiar by now, as is the link between rebuilding the physical environment and reforming the humans who inhabit it.

When Bender steps across the Romanian border, however, he finds that passage to another world of illusions is impossible. If life is to be remade, as Bender hopes it will be, then that process must take place in the Soviet universe. He is quickly stripped of his wealth and beaten back inside the Soviet border, and the phrase he has used throughout the novel to describe a new development in one of his schemes—"The ice is breaking!" (401)—becomes a realized metaphor as the actual ice on the river beneath his feet starts to crack, sending him scurrying onto the Soviet embankment to continue his search for the perfect existence.

Bender has been deprived of his ill-gotten material wealth, but he retains the more valuable possession of continued enthusiasm. Weak and bloody from his brutal encounter with foreign border guards, he notices that he is still gripping a medal from the Order of the Golden Fleece in his hand, the only item of value to remain from the overcoat he "built" to protect him on his journey. The Golden Fleece medal suggests Bender's willingness to continue his search for the ideal world and provides a new platform on which to construct that edifice. Since the path to Rio de Janeiro has proved elusive, he must now find fulfillment within the Soviet universe, the only world accessible to him or to his readers. Bender's return to the Soviet Union, his narrow escape from the thin ice at the edge of the world, can thus be presented as a welcome return to safety and potential redemption. It is funny, of course, but also fitting that Bender immediately imagines himself in the new career of house manager (*upravdom*).[51] Where else, indeed, can a man just back from the dead turn?

Ilf and Petrov, too, are left to wander through the Soviet world they helped construct, albeit with an extended trip to "one-story America" in the offing.[52] They noted in a newspaper article under the heading "Our Third Novel" that "we are often asked what we plan to do with Ostap Bender. And while we were considering this question our third novel turns out to be already written, completed and published. This happened at the Belomor Canal."[53] They participated, as well, in the construction of the Moscow subway, providing a relatively small written contribution to a projected volume in honor of the metro. Their essay, approximately one manuscript page in length and entitled "Subway Line Ancestors" (*Metropol-*

itenovy predki), was envisioned as a set of "satirical sketches of the history of Moscow transportation and modern transport (tram, taxi, horse cab drivers)."[54]

Exploring the contrast between the old and the not-quite-new was favorite territory for Ilf and Petrov, and transportation provided the authors with a familiar topic on which to exercise their well-known wit. Their description of a horse cab on Moscow's "exemplary kilometer" of asphalt, for example, provided them with the perfect opportunity to contrast prerevolutionary streets with the successes of a relatively well-paved Soviet capital.

And this is where the daredevil cabdriver comes out onto the straight path of the highway . . . , and his lively little horse kicks up the fresh snow, under which lies asphalt, the so-called exemplary kilometer. Not very many years ago, Moscow was able to boast of only a single kilometer of completed roadway. People drove specially to this kilometer to try it out. Photographs of the kilometer were printed in the newspapers, and filmmakers shot urban scenes from American life on this very spot.[55]

When the manuscript strays into more recent history, however, to describe taxi drivers from the period of the New Economic Policy, or NEP, their humor is no longer welcome. The NEP period, when petty capitalism made a brief reappearance in the Soviet Union, had previously provided the two authors with some of their best material as they focused on the foibles of fallible human beings making a clumsy transition to the new world. In the manuscript for the subway volume, however, their text is thoroughly edited to erase all traces of shady businessmen, their blowsy girlfriends, and the low-level criminals who surround such undesirable types. With the excision of such comically drawn figures, however, what remains is a dry and pedantic manuscript largely atypical of the two humorists, a fact that highlights the difficulty writers of transitional production novels would eventually have with the move toward a more orthodox and centrally controlled narrative. Without their characteristic comic touches, the essay Ilf and Petrov produced is politically acceptable but impersonal and dry. The drabness of their doctored contribution makes it hard to agree with its conclusion that what is "great" about the building of the subway is that "human cobblestones are disappearing together with cobblestones from the pavement. Along with the city, the people who live in it are being perfected."[56]

The collectively authored volume to which Ilf and Petrov contributed was intended to convey a sense of history in the making, but also to serve as a road map of sorts, by which both common folk and sophisticated authors could navigate the path to becoming new men and women. A strange yet compelling logic piloted the endeavors: the lessons of history they documented were focused not so much on actual events as on modes of behavior, and it became clear that even mildly eccentric voices were to be replaced with a central narrative. Soon enough, the Moscow subway volume, along with other collective histories of the time, including the *History of the Civil War in the USSR*, the *Great Soviet Encyclopedia*, and the Belomor volume itself, began to sacrifice authenticity in the name of conformity, distorting many of the activities they proposed to cover, in some cases even "documenting" events that had yet to occur. Initial trust in authentic worker responses transformed over time into a concerted effort to shape, control, and finally suppress the spontaneous and naïve reactions of real laborers on the job. As Frederick Corney puts it in another study of Stalinist historical projects, "the objective needs of the revolution in the present" were quickly seen to outweigh "the subjective vanities of the individuals who recalled it."[57]

Yet even sophisticated writers agreed to participate in this process of compiling Soviet "history." Some of the most talented contributed to this kind of collective endeavor precisely because it offered a way to respond to monumental events. Such literary enterprises provided even the nonconformist an opportunity to participate in the construction of Soviet culture. Ironically, there may have been no one better to relate such tales of grandiose building feats and construction achievements than modernist writers well versed in the art of relativistic storytelling. In their quest to find a role for themselves in an increasingly unfamiliar world, Soviet authors from this era demonstrated not "how life writes the book" but "how the book should write life."[58]

It was unclear how two humorists whose career was based on the foibles of individuals not yet fully adapted to Soviet life would manage in a society that expected to achieve the goal of complete conformity.[59] A sketch published by the two authors in *Pravda* in February 1935 makes it clear, however, that they thought the process of reaching uniform perfection might take some time. In "M," which appeared in the newspaper with a variety of other materials relating to the new subway line, Ilf and Petrov offered a humorous account of the extreme politeness that previously irritable passengers would now be using on their subway, "incalculably the best" in the world. The subway's spacious "palace halls," dressed in marble and mosaics, would be the site of exquisite behavior.

Workers from abroad, where the only concern of their "stock market society" was to "increase dividends," could suffer in silence. The Russian laboring classes would be riding in comfort. The authors ended their sketch with advice that all the authors of production novels understood: it will be so wonderful underground, they warn us, that "comrades on the surface will have to shape up!"[60]

4
(Re)constructing the Production Novel: Boris Pilniak, *Mahogany,* and *The Volga Falls to the Caspian Sea*

ONE OF THE MOST COMPLICATED EXAMPLES OF THE USE OF CON-struction themes in Russian literature is the case of *The Volga Falls to the Caspian Sea (Volga vpadaet v kaspiiskoe more)*, the production novel that Boris Pilniak (1894–1938) published in 1930. Pilniak's American biographer calls the work the "first of the Soviet five-year-plan novels," and a prominent Russian scholar notes that before Pilniak began to write the work, he "spent several months at Dneprostroi." Shortly after its publication, the author recommended the novel to Stalin himself. He tendered the work as important and thoroughly compelling evidence of one of "my bricks that are in our construction." Pilniak offered the volume to the country's leader as a convincing sign that he could be trusted, explaining to Stalin that he "never imagines my fate outside of the revolution."[1]

With such an impeccable pedigree, *The Volga Falls to the Caspian Sea* should have provided contemporaries with a convincing model for literary orthodoxy. Pilniak, after all, was one of the fathers of Soviet *belles lettres,* a fact he himself pointed out in claiming status as the author who "published the *first* book of stories about the Soviet revolution *in the RSFSR.*"[2] With interest, preparation, timing, and desire on his side, Pilniak should have been able to write an exemplary production novel. It is all the more surprising, then, to realize that *The Volga Falls to the Caspian Sea* is a contradictory and tortured narrative that deviates from later representatives of the genre in nearly every way possible. The reasons for those deviations tell us much about the author, the early development of the genre itself, and the contradictory milieu that produced them both.

Pilniak's narrative is remarkable by almost any measure, but it is particularly surprising in light of later claims that the production novel was the essential Socialist Realist genre. The central conceit of *The Volga Falls to the Caspian Sea* is the construction of an enormous dam that will reroute the flow of the Volga, reverse and rationalize the flow of the Oka, Kliazma, and Moscow rivers, make the Russian capital more accessible to seaports, and provide a workable set of canals to serve Russia's largest metropolis. This orthodox topic is nearly overshadowed in this early version of the genre, however, by a number of outlandish subplots that deviate significantly from any hint of a master Stalinist narrative. These include the stories of Evgenii Evgenievich Poltorak, a bourgeois engineer who is unfaithful to his wife and infects her dying sister with syphilis; the engineer Laslo, a Hungarian specialist who betrays his lover, Maria, thus precipitating her suicide and triggering a crisis on the construction site; the unsightly local patriarch Iakov Karpovich Skudrin, who harbors counterrevolutionary plans; the Bezdetov brothers, an unsavory pair of antique dealers; and the mysterious foreigner Sherwood. Intimately tied to these stories are narratives about more appealing characters, especially Pimen Sergeevich Poletika, the aging professor who heads the engineering project and represents the prerevolutionary generation; his daughter Liubov' Poletika, an archeologist who is conducting excavations near the construction site; and the worker-engineer Sadykov, who generously frees his unhappy wife Maria before he himself finds love with Liubov'.

A very pronounced secondary theme is the conflict between the new system and the *okhlomony,* a group of old Bolsheviks on the construction site. These aesthetes from the sterner time of War Communism are portrayed here as holy fools who speak the truth that no one will heed. It seems incredible that Pilniak would not only write such a book but point to it in 1930 to demonstrate his loyalty to the official revolutionary cause. Re-situating *The Volga Falls to the Caspian Sea* in its rightful place in the early tradition of the production novel demonstrates the need to rewrite this chapter of Soviet literary history. The fact that Pilniak published such a work, considered it worthy of acclamation, and was vilified in the West for the same novel reveals the unpredictable and counterintuitive nature of Soviet literary politics of the late 1920s and early 1930s. Evidence that has emerged in the post-Soviet period casts new light both on Pilniak's career and on the significance of the production genre in general.[3]

Pilniak's production novel was written between February 14 and August 28, 1929. We have the author himself to thank for such an exact chronology. He notes those dates scrupulously in a letter

about the work that he sent to *Literaturnaia gazeta* at the end of
August 1929, when a scandal erupted about his publication earlier
that year of a novella entitled *Mahogany* (*Krasnoe derevo*). Textological analysis confirms Pilniak's insistence in his letter to *Literaturnaia gazeta* that *The Volga Falls to the Caspian Sea* is a partial
reworking of material from his earlier novella. The close textual relationship of the two works suggests that Pilniak saw the later
novel as an organic development of his earlier work, a fact to which
he purposely calls attention in his public statement that *Mahogany*
had been reworked as part of *The Volga Falls to the Caspian Sea.*[4]

    Mahogany itself was under suspicion in August 1929 since it had
first appeared not in the Soviet Union, but in an émigré publication
in Berlin. It was common practice during the early 1920s for Soviet writers to preserve copyright on their works by publishing
them abroad before they appeared in Russia, but when Pilniak took
such a step with *Mahogany,* he was unexpectedly accused of anti-
Soviet behavior for the "slanderous" work and criticized for the action. The exact dates Pilniak quotes in his letter to *Literaturnaia
gazeta* are thus significant: the author needs them to establish that
he had already decided to rework *Mahogany* into a new production
novel before it was ever branded "forbidden" by Soviet publishers.[5]
Pilniak's approach to the material in his work indicates that, for
him at least, the production novel genre would develop from the
same roots as his previous writing.

    The sudden attack on Pilniak in 1929 seems to have caught both
the writer and his colleagues by surprise. An initial article in *Literaturnaia gazeta* by B. Volin challenging Pilniak was followed
soon by numerous others, and the incident served as the pretext for
an extensive and acrimonious campaign against Pilniak, with "an-
tisocial actions," "White-Guardism," and "emigrantism" among the
charges. Criticism was directed at Pilniak's friend, fellow author
Evgenii Zamiatin, as well, and much to Zamiatin's dismay, his at-
tackers held him newly accountable for his novel *We*, even though
that work had been written nearly a decade earlier. Zamiatin was
excoriated along with Pilniak, despite the support offered to them
by no less a personage than Maxim Gorky. In a letter to his wife,
Zamiatin noted the "general panic" that surrounded the attacks.
After all, this was one of the first organized campaigns against Soviet writers, and it had an unsettling effect on all authors, particularly "fellow travelers" like Pilniak and Zamiatin, whose standing
in regard to proletarian literature continued to be shaky. The scandal, which lasted until early 1931, ended Pilniak's tenure as head

of the All-Russian Union of Writers (*Vserossiiskii Soiuz Pisatelei*) and Zamiatin's leadership of the Leningrad sector of the union.[6]

Because Pilniak was under such intense political pressure at the time he was writing *The Volga Falls to the Caspian Sea*, his re-working of *Mahogany* in creating the later production novel has usually been seen as an unhealthy political compromise.[7] In both the East and the West, *The Volga Falls to the Caspian Sea* has frequently been approached as nothing more than an attempt by the author to curry favor and save his literary political skin. Max Eastman's contemporary reaction is typical. Eastman argues, for example, that "no work in the world's history was ever completed in more direct violation of the artist's conscience, or with a more unadulterated motive of self-preservation than" *The Volga Falls to the Caspian Sea*. Sympathetic critics, for their part, often pass over the work in relative silence, as though skirting an embar-rassment better left undisturbed. Editions of Pilniak's work by his family, for example, dedicate loving attention to nearly all of Pilniak's oeuvre, but usually leave the issue of the produc-tion novel largely untouched. Eastman's hyperbole is telling: the affair caused many critics in the years that followed to denigrate Pilniak's subsequent output or to disregard his work after 1929 as inauthentic.[8]

Such a categorical approach may satisfy the desire to pass over-all judgment on an era marked by many acts of brutality and ac-quiescence. But it does little to illuminate how authors subjected to such pressure understood their own behavior or how they actu-ally negotiated the increasing demands made upon them. This is an especially rich field of investigation with regard to Pilniak, whose literary output was suffused with revolutionary themes and who actively sought a leadership role in the literary politics of the time. Pilniak, like so many of his fellow writers, saw his role as helpmate to a shared cause, and he accepted the many twists and turns that their mutual goals required of him and other creative intellectuals. His first unvarnished responses to the effects of the revolution make it clear that he understood the cost he and others might have to pay to make changes in Russia; his early *Naked Year* (*Golyi god*), for example, like many of his prose works, is graphic in its depic-tion of revolutionary violence.

Nor did Pilniak shy away from using literature as a political tool, and this, too, is an attitude he shared with many of his contempo-raries, at least those who came to creative adulthood in the fiery light of the revolution, as he had. This generation of writers was

compelled by circumstance to make a conscious choice to support
the new revolutionary order. Even those who answered definitively
to the original question of support were required to demonstrate
and re-acknowledge their devotion to the Soviet cause again and
again.[9] Pilniak's production novel, like those of his fellow writers,
is thus both an authentic individual response to the times and another political "brick" in the common building he thought he and
like-minded Soviet writers were constructing. As we will see, Pilniak saw his role as an author in unequivocal, determinist terms:
he was "fated" to write, and his works were small but essential
contributions to the larger social processes in the world that surrounded him.

There is no doubt, of course, that Pilniak was under political
pressure throughout much of his creative existence. Such pressure
continued during the affair with *Mahogany*. In some ways, in fact,
the attack in 1929 must have felt like a reactivation of the disapproval Pilniak had experienced following the publication of "The
Tale of the Unextinguished Moon" (*Povest' nepogashennoi luny*)
about the death of Army commander Mikhail Frunze in 1925. The
political dimensions of Pilniak's art had been made unmistakably
manifest during the affair over that story, which gave shocking fictional voice to accusations that Stalin had murdered Frunze to con-
solidate political power. The drama of that earlier incident must
have left an indelible impression on the author: it resulted in the
physical destruction of the journal issue that contained Pilniak's
offending narrative, and the work was not published again in Russia until 1987.[10]

Worse than anything for the writer was the fact that his involvement with the Frunze story left him temporarily unable to publish
in official channels. This is clear from a letter Pilniak wrote to I. I.
Skvortsov-Stepanov, the editor of *Izvestiia*, in November 1926.
He admits there that the tale, which described Stalin's alleged murder of Frunze in fairly graphic detail, was "essentially tactless" and
he requests that he once again be allowed to publish: "I want to
publish," he notes insistently. "I want to have the rights and responsibilities of a Soviet writer." This exchange with the editor of
Isvestiia is fascinating for what it reveals about Pilniak's understanding of his position at the time. In retrospect, we can see that
the writer was in mortal danger from the moment he accused Stalin
of complicity in Frunze's death. Yet Pilniak himself seems largely
unaware of the gravity of the situation, and, in fact, he was soon
able to resume publication and continue his tireless efforts as both
writer and man of letters.[11]

"Tactlessness" would be the least of the charges leveled against him in just a few years, yet in 1925 Pilniak would admit to little more. In fact, his private letter to Skvortsov-Stepanov indicates that the writer still strongly believed that his contribution to Soviet literature was as valid as any. The political twists and turns that made his story a political gaffe were hardly his fault, he insists; after all, if the Party leaders who had published the work couldn't anticipate problems, how was he, an unaffiliated *"pisatel'-neparti-ets,"* expected to do so?[12]

What is clear from Pilniak's letter to Skvortsov-Stepanov is his acceptance of the power of political authority over his activity as a writer. "All the years of the revolution and until this very day, I felt and feel myself to be an honest person and a citizen of my Republic," Pilniak continues, "and a person who does everything he can to do work that is needed by the revolution." Reminding the editor that the only person who never makes a mistake is the person who does nothing, Pilniak emphasizes that he is "a writer, whose name was born with the revolution and whose entire fate is tied to our revolutionary public spirit [*obshchestvennost'*]." Noting that he apparently has the legal right to publish in other venues, he expresses his intention to ignore such juridical niceties (*ne xochu byt' "iurkim"*). His only desire is to "submit to the will that forbade me to publish" (*podchinit'sia toi voli, kotoraia zapretila mne pechatit'sia*).[13]

His acceptance of that unnamed "will" reflects a pattern that would be repeated in the years that followed, but it is important to note that Pilniak's behavior on this occasion was not solely a response to the pressure bearing down on him in 1925 and 1926. Rather, his willingness to submit to the unnamed authority was part and parcel of a more general attitude he had toward the nature of art and the process of creation in the Soviet Union. Pilniak's conviction that art was an ongoing public conversation was one he shared with many artists, particularly in nineteenth- and twentieth-century Russia, where the notion of the writer as a public figure with moral responsibilities toward society was well established. Pilniak's understanding of those responsibilities, which he shared with many of his generation, included a sense that the artist was obligated to speak to and for the crowd. Giving voice to the people, the *narod*, of Russia was a moral imperative for many writers in the nineteenth century; it continued to be so, even after that same *narod* "came to power" in the twentieth.

As a modernist, too, Pilniak subscribed to the notion that the terms of artistic conversations were determined not only by the artists who recorded them, but also by the readers who helped generate and sustain such dialogues. In this sense, the insertion of politics into the creative dialogue was not an imposition, but an inevitable, at times even desirable, state of affairs. It seemed unavoidable to Pilniak and his generation that writers would relinquish absolute control over their narratives, although they often did so with a certain nostalgia for the time when artistic certainty had been an author's prerogative. To writers from Pilniak's generation, however, complete authorial power was an illusion. They were convinced of the need to share the process of creating meaning, and doing so was made even easier when it both assuaged their consciences and paid their bills. Such an approach to the artistic dialogue was only highlighted by the unique circumstances in Soviet Russia after the revolution, when the avant-garde unexpectedly found itself in a position to dictate many of the terms of the conversation.[14]

Pilniak's off-the-cuff comment in a personal letter from 1924 indicates just how familiar this process was coming to seem to him. He mentions in a quick note dashed off to his acquaintance D. A. Lutokhin that "we are living quietly. People are writing little, disjointedly [*narod pishet malo, vrazbrod*]. There is no theme, I guess, or else it is absolutely necessary to retune your lyre from scratch—again from scratch!" (*netu temy, chto li, ili uzh ochen' nado nanovo—opiat' nanovo!—perestraivat' svoiu liru*).[15] Pilniak's language is characteristically communal, even in this 1924 note: "we" are living; "people" are writing; he speaks of only one "theme," which has not yet appeared. When it does, clearly, everyone will set to work on that single, shared topic. The need for artists to adapt or retool is also taken for granted—*nado perestraivat' svoiu liri*—in a process that is annoying not in its essence but only in its frequency (*opiat' nanovo!*).

In this and other postrevolutionary correspondence, Pilniak describes a Russia in which everything has to be rediscovered and redefined. The task is daunting, but exhilarating, too, for those with the strength to maneuver. He explains in a letter from 1923 to his colleague and mentor Aleksei Remizov that the "geological layers haven't settled yet" in Russia. "There are no norms. Everyone is like an explorer on the ocean, when every day it is necessary to discover a new America, always a tortuous one when it is in the area of morality."[16] In a letter from the same month to Lutokhin, Pilniak complains that all his time is being devoted to frenetic public activities. Thus, in April 1923, he notes "I'm all 'in a whirl,' doing things, arranging, organizing—'questionnaire-ing, culturally-enlightening, commanding'" (*anketiruiu, kul'turnopro-svetitel'stvuiu, komandiruius'*).[17]

Such social engagement and active involvement in Moscow literary politics were important aspects of Pilniak's activity throughout the 1920s and 1930s, but he balanced that work with periodic departures from the whirl of the capital to the quiet of provincial Russia. Solitude seemed to offer a respite: "How great it would be to sit down somewhere like Krasnokokshaisk," Pilniak notes wistfully, "over manuscripts, papers, thoughts: I've got an enormous theme, for a novel."[18] Much anticipated retreats to the relative isolation of provincial Kolomna, the even greater seclusion of the forest beyond Saratov, the splendid austerity beyond the Arctic circle, and so on gave the writer both time to reflect and a vital connection to an authentic rural Russia that he prized for his creative work.[19]

Pilniak's frequent swings from active participation to temporary disengagement were typical of the 1920s and early 1930s, as he and others sought the right balance of political involvement and creative independence. Just a few months after his description of frenetic political activity, for example, Pilniak would claim in another letter to Lutokhin that "last winter I tried to get involved in public affairs [*pytalsia bylo obshchestvennichat'*]. I'm abandoning that now. It's necessary and possible only to write, and then history will sort it out." His invitation to Lutokhin in May 1922 encourages his friend to "come and see me in Kolomna. My place is quiet, good, and primeval." But a year later, he is complaining that it is "boring to feel like an inhabitant of a monastery in Kolomna, at Nikola na Posad', in the heroic act of seclusion."[20]

Pilniak sought to unify such divergent desires with his writing, which he saw as a joint project to be completed collectively. This explains his organizational efforts to benefit what he saw as the common goal of creating a new Russia. He writes to Voronskii from Berlin in 1922, asking him to have writers send their material for publication in Germany. "Tell all writers, regardless of party affiliation or 'name.' The demand here is enormous," he insists, and "it's necessary to display our Russian wares."[21] He shared this purpose, Pilniak thought, with a variety of groups, all of whom were focused on Russia, particularly on Moscow. Just returned from the trip overseas in 1922, Pilniak describes the Russian revolution as a uniting force: "*russkaia revoliutsiia—eto to, gde nado brat' vmeste vse.*" Only the revolution is capable of bringing together the many disparate energies—"*i kommunism, i es-erovshchinu, i belogvardeishchinu, i monarkhovshchinu*"—that exist within Russia today. "All of these are chapters in the history of the Russian revolution," Pilniak concludes decisively, "but the main chapter is in Russia, in Moscow."

This comment, from a letter to Lutokhin in May 1922, explains much of Pilniak's long career to follow. The revolution has overwhelmed all of Russia, he notes, and each political movement is just another chapter in the lengthy and complicated history that he and his colleagues must write. Russia is the center of this activity, the "main chapter," and Pilniak's duty is to explore all of its territory, no matter how difficult or contradictory the stories that he collects on that journey may be. "From Germany," Pilniak notes, "Russia seems like the *Pamirs*, lice-ridden. And it is *she*, lice-ridden, with cannibals, that is bringing something to the world."[22]

Insisting on an impartial approach that will allow him to capture all of what he observes, Pilniak claims he wants "to be a *historian* in the revolution. I want to be an indifferent spectator and to *love everyone.*" Little suspecting, apparently, that the unaligned approach would be impossible to maintain in the years that followed, Pilniak notes that "Communism is foreign to me (although Bolshevism is another story) because it castrates my—national—Russia." Nevertheless, he is ready to believe in the existence of and to welcome Communist passions. In fact, he likens them to those of religious fanatics, unhinged but fervent in their beliefs. "I had a great-grandmother, an Old Believer," Pilniak explains, "and she showed me, she saw little devils in the corners, and both she and the Communists have faith. I bless faith."

Pilniak's stunning comparison would soon become anathema, of course. His own leather-coated Communists wanted nothing to do with the superstitions of Russia's religious grandmothers. Yet Pilniak continued to insist that both were part and parcel of the complex story writers were telling about revolutionary Russia. Pilniak's analogy throws his own approach to the problem into high relief. Communism is just one more manifestation of the fervor that has always clutched Russia in its iron grip. It is an aspect of his culture that he honors, claiming that "I love Russian culture, Russian —even the ridiculous—history . . . I love the Russian, peasant, rebellious—October, in our revolution the little snow storm, the mischief,"[23] and he sees it as his job is to recite that contradictory narrative. "I was nineteen when the war began," he comments. "And I accepted Russian culture, its dead ends and wood-burning stoves [*lezhanki*] in the everyday life of war and revolution. That everyday life is my quotidian everyday life [*Etot byt—moi povsednevnyi byt*]. I know no other. I'm used to it to the point of automation."[24]

Pilniak imagines himself as a force for unification, standing outside the "two literary fronts" he sees in literature and arguing that the way of the new "everyday life," his way, is the path of the future. Thus, he writes to Lutokhin in 1922 that two literary camps exist. One is organized along traditional, prerevolutionary lines, "raised on 'before the revolution,' with old wine, perceiving life in the old existence [*v starom byte*]." The other literary front is decidedly "Soviet, Communist." Although he admits it with "shame and embarrassment," Pilniak notes that "I don't belong to either camp." He imagines that there are other unaligned authors like him, wondering rhetorically if "perhaps we will run together into a group?" His primary concern, however, is not membership in a particular camp, but, rather, the objective truth.

Although he is adamant about his own devotion to objective reality, he notes parenthetically that such truths may evolve over time. "We have a different *everyday reality* [*inoi byt*]," he proclaims, and "*never in my life have I distorted my conscience* in signing my name Pilniak: what I thought, what I knew, what I saw, that's what I wrote." Yet at the end of that brave sentence, Pilniak adds the other verity that he has understood equally well: "(well, of course, much of what I wrote previously, I would write differently now, in particular, several chapters of the novel.)" He ends his letter to Lutokhin with a plea that demonstrates his awareness of the elusive nature of his quest for impartiality: "Don't publish my letter, please, or else my apolitical stance will turn into politics."[25]

Despite his apparent realization of the difficulty of his approach, Pilniak continued to cling to it, although the problems associated with such a stance would become more and more obvious as time passed. Thus, in August 1922, he writes to Maxim Gorky with news of plans to organize a new publishing house. "So it has somehow turned out that in Russia a new public spirit [*obshchestvennost'*] is springing up, has sprung up," Pilniak informs the older writer.

It's difficult for me to say: is life intelligent or useful? Is it harmful or pointless to eat, drink, sleep, die? These concepts are outside of that framework. The communal spirit taking shape now in Russia—biological, like life—doesn't fit into frames, forms, or parties. I see it crawling out everywhere. On a personal level, it is made up of people, who grew up, took shape in the revolution, who have seen nothing but revolutionary Russia, but were still able to patch themselves together, sew it up, ferment the real way, *invigorated* and strong.[26]

In a gentle nudge to Gorky in emigration, Pilniak reminds him that "anyone who hasn't seen Russia in six months won't recognize it." The new communal spirit is best reflected in literature by those on the ground. Writers like Pilniak and his colleagues Vsevolod Ivanov, Nikolai Nikitin, and Konstantin Fedin can see for themselves that "in Russia there is a lot of vigor."[27]

Here too, though, Pilniak insists on an inclusive approach, one outside of the petty politics and generational gap that otherwise threaten to divide those who must capture the spirit of the new Russia together. A new communal spirit means that "we somehow haven't attached ourselves to the old [writers] or to the new or to the RKP [Bolshevik Party], but we are drawn to each other, and others are already being drawn to us," Pilniak continues. Their new publishing house will publish works of "the young," of course: "many new [writers] have arrived, very talented" ones. But there is room for the "old men" too, at least for those works "that will teach us and, yes, 'elucidate' us." As one of the "old men," Gorky must have read the letter with a mixture of amusement and irritation: Pilniak's request for a contribution to the new publishing venture—"from all of us (the publishing house is already organized) —give us your things—maybe your 'Hermit'?"—gives the wrong title to Gorky's work.[28]

The minor gaffe notwithstanding, Gorky must have been gratified to read the assertion that "right now Moscow and Petersburg look no worse than Berlin." Pilniak assures Gorky that writers' fees have improved "by tenfold." There are "many publishers."[29] Nevertheless, he continues, life in the new Russia is difficult and the authors who came of age with the revolution need guidance. "But this new life," Pilniak explains to Gorky, "the birth of this new communal spirit, alive, as prickly as nettles, as insistent as a poplar pushing through the newly paved sidewalk in Nizhnii Novgorod, often prickles the hand and hits the forehead, and we are still inexperienced and have too little culture to keep from getting tangled up. We get tangled up and we often do the unnecessary." Admitting that he himself has made many mistakes, Pilniak insists that he, at least, would rather be in Russia than elsewhere. "After Germany," he notes, "life in Russia is much better, more interesting, and more necessary [*kuda luchshe, interesnei i nuzhnei*]." In a last pitch for Gorky's assistance, Pilniak comments leadingly that "we don't have the kind of moral guide that is essential for us."[30]

Pilniak's letter to Gorky was sent as a joint epistle, and, as such, it is particularly revealing of the general hopes writers held for Soviet literature at the time. "Vs. Ivanov, Fedin, Slonimskii, Lunts were here. Nik. Nikitin came from the Urals," Pilniak notes, and the group had been "wandering around in a herd, organizing the publishing house" for three days. Full of hope for the future of Soviet letters, they turn instinctively to Gorky, nearly appointing him a member of their "workshop" (*artel'*) without even asking. Then, Pilniak continues, "we decided that it was necessary to get permission first and to make a request of you. To request that you arrive as quickly as possible, to help us."

This insistence on the need for moral leadership is particularly noteworthy in light of other claims Pilniak makes in the same letter. Political freedom, he assures the older writer, is abundant in the new Russia. "The political freedoms can't be compared" with earlier life, he notes, as he asks for Gorky's spiritual guidance for their endeavors. "It's much easier, more intelligent, to breathe, and not only in Moscow, but also in Kolomna." The break they had all hoped for has taken place (*perelom proizoshel*), he assures Gorky, and although they are currently enduring the effects of the New Economic Policy (NEP), "that communal spirit, that healthfulness that I see is moving—*not with NEP*."[31]

Pilniak's letter—alternately bold and imploring, audacious and humble—reveals the distinctive mix that characterized Russian literary life during this early period. Authors like Pilniak were genuinely thrilled with the possibilities newly available to them, and many held on to that early optimism long after any objective reason for it had disappeared. Certainly, all of literary life must have seemed open to the group of young writers "wandering around in a herd" in the summer of 1922. They would publish what had never before been published, amazing the world with their daring teachings about the new society they were building. Combined with a profound sense of endless possibilities, however, writers of this generation seem to have felt an equally strong need for spiritual guidance. Provide us with a "moral guide," Pilniak implores Gorky. "We get tangled up" and need works that "will teach us."

Such an amalgam may seem strange at first, but the artists' conviction of their own capacity and their simultaneous desire for edification are actually two sides of the same coin. Both impulses are intimately related to an understanding of literature as an educational tool. The hope that they might change society was tied directly in the minds of these Russian writers with the thought that they themselves might need instruction. Pilniak and his colleagues turned to Gorky and the "old men," but others saw the Party, the workers, or the youth of the country in the same role of instructor. Pilniak points directly to this fact in 1923, writing to A. K. Voronskii, his colleague at the publishing venture "Krug," that "Russian literature always was and is (in its healthy branch) public spirited [*obshchestvennicheskaia*]." Parenthetically, Pilniak adds that "from the point of view of a European that [fact] is a deformity, but that very deformity, as a matter of fact, is [Russian literature's] main charm."[32]

Even in 1923, Pilniak already guessed that their group call for moral leadership might be problematic. Thus, he notes in his comments to Voronskii, that "in this day and age, it is difficult, after all, to speak about [literature's] public spirit [*obshchestvennost'*], since writers—forgive me, but it is so—have, on the one hand, public spirited government-mindedness [*obshchestvennicheskaia gosudarstvennost'*], and, on the other, not only censorship and nonfreedom of speech [*nesvoboda slova*], but also moral management [*moral'noe rukovodstvo*]." Pilniak's subtle shift in terms—from the "moral guidance" he requests of Gorky to the "moral management" he resents with Voronskii—suggests a slowly dawning awareness that the authors' call for assistance may bring them more than they expected. Pilniak indicates as much in a remark to Voronskii. The "moral management" under which Russian artists are laboring, he patiently points out to his colleague critic, "isn't needed by everyone, maybe not by me either."[33]

At the time of this declaration to Voronskii, Pilniak was already deeply involved in the affairs of the new publishing venture, and his activity there highlights important aspects of both his career and little known Russian literary politics. A letter to his colleague Evgenii Zamiatin in the same year makes it clear, for example, that Pilniak was seeking a middle ground to unite the many forces that threatened to tear creative Russia apart. This is true of both his own work and his endeavors in literary politics. Zamiatin was already intent on emigration at this point in April 1923, but Pilniak advised his colleague to proceed with caution. He and fellow publicist Voronskii had hatched a scheme to allow Zamiatin to live abroad without breaking all ties to Soviet Russia. In the plan they had devised, Zamiatin would reside outside of the country, since that was his wish, but he would still contribute regularly to the publishing house "Krug" and their journal *Krasnaia Nov'*. Such an arrangement would allow Zamiatin a steady source of income and assure the publisher exclusive rights to his writings outside of Russia, but Pilniak emphasized another advantage to the plan. "Do you understand?" Pilniak asked Zamiatin. "Decide what will be most convenient for you. But one way or another—we live in such times (and, I think, it was always like this) when you can't survive without compromises—it's not advisable to break with Russia, *for Russia's sake.*"[34]

Pilniak's comment is telling, particularly in light of the common perception of him as an opportunist who sacrificed his creative integrity on the altar of Soviet political power. Here he reveals a different set of priorities, in which he urges Zamiatin to make a personal compromise in order to perform a more significant public duty. Pilniak seeks, as he would throughout his career, a balance between the excesses of political fervor and the uncompromising nature of creative endeavor. It is typical of the writer that he frames this stance as the appeasement of western sensitivities for the ultimate benefit of Russia. Such compromises, usually portrayed in Pilniak's case as lack of will or concession to political conformity, emerge in Pilniak's own telling as necessary "for Russia's sake." This same impetus for Russian unity leads Pilniak to request that Zamiatin do his best to mend literary fences while he is overseas. "When you are abroad," he implores Zamiatin in his letter from April 1923, "and they start to criticize me, defend me: I'm not guilty *in my conscience* before very many, and—you know—I'm a good person. Politics (not mine, because I have absolutely none) is separating us, and that really wounds me."[35]

At this point in the game of literary politics, it was still possible, at least for Pilniak and writers like him, to imagine a world in which there was only one Russian literature. They saw a universe in which writers both at home and abroad would compose the shared "main chapter" of Russian literature together. Little wonder, then, that Pilniak wrote in September 1923 to ask the recent émigré Lutokhin for help with his new novel, the work that would eventually be published as *Machines and Wolves* (*Mashiny i volki*). It seemed natural to the author to turn to colleagues abroad for assistance, even when it concerned such delicate questions as the current economic situation in Russia and its connection to events in 1918. Such collegial friendliness across international borders would become nearly unthinkable with time, but, for the moment, Pilniak could imagine Russian letters as a shared concern. Some of his well wishers were people he had known since childhood, after all, and he knew that he could rely on both such individuals and the good offices of those in the Russian missions overseas to help with his research.[36]

A similar sentiment characterizes the letter that Pilniak and others composed to the Central Committee of the Party in May 1924.

Pilniak's version of the epistle, which survived in family archives, gives eloquent testimony to the desire of self-identified "Russian writers" to find an inclusive approach to the shared problems of literature in postrevolutionary Russia. Denied official status at an upcoming meeting of the Press Section of the Party, the group nevertheless insisted on the necessity of a common response to shared quandaries. Their goals were remarkably modest. "Literature should be a reflection of that reality which surrounds us, on the one hand," they commented diplomatically, "but, on the other hand— on that basis—a creation of an individual writer personality [*individual'noe pisatel'skoe litso*], who in each case perceives the world on his own terms and reflects it in his own way." Insisting that "a whole series of Communist authors and critics" agreed with their conception of the writer's task, the correspondents described their belief that the "talent of a writer and his resonance with the epoch —each writer has specific value—is part of the understanding of the literary mission."[37]

Pilniak's letter takes specific aim at "several critics" and a number of journals like *Na postu* (On Guard), which have "adopted a tone" that they attempt to pass off as the opinion of the entire Party. The "attacks on us," Pilniak insists, ignore the fact that fellow-traveler writers are as close to the goals of the revolution as any: "the paths of contemporary Russian literature—and that means our paths—are connected to the paths of the New Russia, being built in accordance with the bidding of October 1917." Pilniak is quick to point out that he and experienced colleagues like him "welcome writers who have emerged from the ranks of the workers, the peasants, and the revolutionary intelligentsia, and in no way do we oppose them to ourselves or consider them antagonistic or foreign to ourselves." Each of us, Pilniak emphasizes, "strives to help [such colleagues] in every way with our knowledge and skill."[38]

Pilniak and his colleagues insisted on their willingness to help draw more workers into literature. In fact, Pilniak comments in the letter to the Central Committee, "our practice already confirms it." Such a stance underlines just how broad the groundwork for mass literary collaboration was. As Pilniak's letter makes clear, the intellectual underpinning for such ventures was already laid by 1924. From this point of view, the cooperation of Pilniak and other fellow travelers in such episodes as the Belomor Canal volume, the volumes on the construction of the subway, and other such joint projects was already inevitable by the middle of the 1920s.[39] The willingness of experienced writers to cooperate with their worker colleagues would only increase over the next decade, although questions remained about the speed with which inexperienced individuals could actually be taught the fundamentals of literature. Pilniak in 1924 notes, for example, that "the right to bear the title of writer—an impressive title—is given not on the basis of membership in this group of that or for any literary understanding, not by administrative fiat, but on the basis of enormous work and culture (it goes without saying that talent and understanding of the epoch must be present)."[40] Despite such cavils, Pilniak was one of many established writers who accepted the necessity of bringing workers' voices to the printed pages as a given.

Pilniak continued to insist on quality as the primary criterion for judging a writer's work. Thus, he notes in a letter to Voronskii from 1924,

> I was considering what literature means to me, and I can't explain it, just as I can't explain human life, young blood (which in its chemical composition differs not at all from old blood, and yet . . .), or how the sun makes us cheerful, while twilight makes us melancholy. What does our literature need? I don't know that either. I know only one thing. Good things are needed, and everything else will fall into place. And that these things must be tied to the new Russia; to write about that is the same thing as writing that a table is a table, and not an airplane. And these good things are Mayakovsky's and Pasternak's and mine and Nikitin's and Artem Veselyi's, no matter how different we all are.[41]

Pilniak's use of the word "thing" (*veshch'*) to refer to works of literature is revealing. No longer viewed as the exclusive prerogative of an elite group of aesthetes, literature is real, physical, concrete, its materiality an essential link to the broader public these writers saw as their eventual readers. Literature is real and essential, as vital as life itself. And all good writers have the right to exist, to create "good" literature, and to contribute to the communally told story of Russia itself. The notion that "good" will automatically entail the "new Russia" is too obvious, in Pilniak's mind, to warrant serious discussion.

Yet Pilniak is forced to acknowledge that there is dissension among the storytellers, even in the ranks of writers of "good things." His reaction to that fact is closer to regret than any other emotion; at this point in 1924, Pilniak seems to have little reason yet for anger or fear from his dabbling in literary politics. Thus, he remarks to Voronskii, "Mayakovskii has good things, Pasternak, others, although they are all different, foreign to one another and (that is incomprehensible to me since we are poor as it is, and everyone is necessary, and there's room for everyone, and—you could put everyone in a single railroad car to launch to the moon) of warring schools." In this passage, too, Pilniak recalls his great-grandmother's "devil." Tied to a string under the old woman's control, the creature was invisible to everyone around her, and yet, Pilniak notes earnestly, "she was an honest old woman, good, kind. Let Mayakovsky, Artem, Arosev—each sees his own devil. I respect their ability to see (as long as it is honest, of course)."[42] Pilniak had yet to realize how wide the search for demons would eventually become or how rare his respect for others' devils would soon be in Stalin's Russia. And Pilniak's already "poor" group of writers would soon become even smaller, as more and more of their colleagues were loaded onto railroad cars heading to the moonscape of Kolyma.

For Pilniak and many of his colleagues, however, a belief in the need to respect the contribution of other writers still included all of Russia. "Russia is one," Pilniak insists to Voronskii.[43] Thus, in his opinion, the necessary expansion of literature's reach to workers, peasants, and the new "revolutionary intelligentsia" goes hand in hand with a desire to engage the older generation of writers as well. Pilniak writes to Voronskii and Vsevolod Ivanov with a discussion about the possible inclusion of a manuscript by Ivan Novikov in an almanac they were planning for "Krug." Noting huffily that he is not in charge of "political censorship," Pilniak explains his evaluation of the older writer's work as follows:

> Of course, this is a writer of the older generation, but a good writer, thoughtful, and one who knows how to drink from his own cup considerably better and more honorably than many, many of us, the contemporary ones. Since we had planned to have one hundred pages and thus monopolize all of literature, I found it necessary to attract some of the old guys to us too. Because I believe that they have no less right than we do to make literature . . . and they are making it.[44]

Pilniak's comment comes in the context of a disagreement over the acceptance of Novikov's manuscript, and he ends the discussion by choosing to recuse himself from the final decision.

Nevertheless, his defense of the right of all authors to contribute to the creation of Russian literature is eloquent. Pilniak's offer, in the very next paragraph of his letter, to help a different author with his submission to the publisher suggests that he means what he says. The manuscript of a certain N. Iuvenskii has been threatened with rejection for "careless" use of language; Pilniak requests that the author call him to discuss the matter at length. This kind of generosity was typical for some writers of the era, and it helps to explain some of Pilniak's numerous coauthored works as well. Pilniak's willingness to help inexperienced authors get a start seems to have extended even to those about whom he knew almost nothing. Thus, he writes to the critic Viacheslav Polonskii at the end of 1926, "the person who brings you this note is comrade Skopin. I haven't read his play, but I read reviews of it and I see that the man is struggling and getting confused. Help him, please, straighten it out."[45]

The fact that Pilniak's note to Polonskii was written just about the time he was preparing a public apology for his "Tale of the Unextinguished Moon" is significant. Pilniak, whose remorse over that story was begrudging at best, would eventually learn how unusual his own liberal stance was. But at the time, and apparently for years after, Pilniak seems to have found the concept of a harsher approach unthinkable. The thought that his work might be excluded from the joint tale he and others were crafting about Russia was incomprehensible to him, and he continued to behave as if such a notion was absurd. Such disbelief, which Pilniak shared with a number of his contemporaries, seems to have colored his perceptions until the day of his arrest.[46]

Persistent disbelief provides motivation for Pilniak's behavior during the affair with *Mahogany* in 1929. Pilniak might simply have apologized for the novella; few of the critics and virtually none of his readers had seen the foreign edition, after all. A quiet apology might have directed at least some of the critics' venom away from a now chastened author. He might also have helped the furor die down by vociferously distancing himself from the work. Such an approach had helped other artists avoid serious consequences for their mistakes, at least temporarily.[47] Instead of that, however, Pilniak drew careful public attention to the unacceptable work by detailing exactly how it was to be used in a new novel. "On February 14," he points out with certitude in his letter to *Literaturnaia gazeta*, "I began work on a novel (now nearly complete), in which *Mahogany* is being reworked into chapters."[48] The fact that he incorporated the old "slanderous" work almost wholesale into his new novel suggests that Pilniak saw *The Volga Falls to the Caspian Sea* as the continuation of his oeuvre, not a departure from it. Pilniak reuses the text of *Mahogany* itself to demonstrate that he and his manuscripts are continually being remade. This process of "reforging" aligns Pilniak perfectly with official demands for the remaking of Soviet writers.

Pilniak's creative method up to that point made such a stance easier. Under pressure over the publication of *Mahogany*, Pilniak found that his habit of reusing passages from earlier works in the construction of later pieces was ideally suited to the production novel. Pilniak had been continually criticized in the past for the technique of recycling entire segments of his previous work in new contexts.[49] But Pilniak's use of building blocks from earlier works in constructing *The Volga Falls to the Caspian Sea* is more than a modernist affectation or the habit of a lazy imagination. *Mahogany* and *The Volga Falls to the Caspian Sea* share a number of characters and themes, and large sections of the texts are virtually identical. Together they give us an unparalleled opportunity to study the process of rebuilding the Soviet author, who both chronicles and experiences the transformation of physical and psychological space during this transitional period. How well Pilniak succeeded in the process of reworking his material and remaking himself serves as illustration for the artistic method itself. Pilniak's example, like that of the other authors under consideration here, suggests that remaking the world—or even writing about it—was a complex problem.

Pilniak speaks about this difficulty in a passage from the foreword to his 1925 novel, *Machines and Wolves*. In an apparent response to criticism of his tendency to reuse images and passages from previous works, Pilniak argues that such a technique is a natural part of the artistic process. Art, in Pilniak's understanding, depends precisely on such individual reworking of shared images. "It's not for me to judge my virtues," he notes in the foreword to his 1925 novel, "But I do have the right to speak about my deficiencies. My things live with me in such disorder (*tak nesurazno*), that when I start to write a new thing, I take the old ones as material. I destroy them in order to make the new better. What I want to say now is much dearer to me than my things, and I sacrifice old labor, if it is useful to me."[50] Here, too, Pilniak's approach demonstrates his reliance on both modernism and the evolving Soviet aesthetic. His insistence on the pliability of old "material" is modernist, but his belief in its utility for new creations suggests, as well, a society optimistic about the possibilities of wide-scale "reforging."

Pilniak continues his discussion in a way that blurs the lines between such binaries as old/new and I/we. Thus he explains in the foreword to *Machines and Wolves*, "it is not important what I (and we) did. It is important what I (and we) will do." The Russian original makes Pilniak's point even more emphatically by confusing the grammatical endings for the otherwise separate categories of "I" and "we." Pilniak's understanding of the literary process completely rejects such a binary distinction: *Ne vazhno, chto ia (i my) sdelal, —vazhno, chto ia (i my) sdelaem)*. The "communal nature [*sobornost'*] of our labor is essential," Pilniak continues pointedly. "It was and is and will be."[51]

Pilniak's insistence on such joint effort is striking, particularly in the context of 1925 when notions of originality and innovation were still dominant in Russian avant-garde aesthetics. Remarkably for the time, Pilniak argues that his reuse of old material extends not only to his own work but to that of other creative artists.[52] In his view, the individual work is significant and valuable only insofar as it partakes of a larger, shared body of work. Individual manifestations of the general are parts that retain their separate integrity while nevertheless comprising the more important whole. Pilniak identifies older writers Andrei Belyi and Ivan Bunin as particularly important influences on his work and insists on his right to borrow wholesale from them and others. "I emerged from Belyi and Bunin," he points out in the foreword to *Machines and Wolves*. "Many do a lot better than I do, and I consider myself justified in taking that 'better' or what I can do better. It's not very important to me what I will leave behind, but it has fallen to us to do Russian literature communally [*soborno*], and that's a big obligation."[53]

Pilniak's reuse of *Mahogany* as raw material for *The Volga Falls to the Caspian Sea* demonstrates the suggestive power of the metaphor of construction and its rhetorical resonance for this period. For Pilniak, and for other writers to follow him, the construction site serves as a general "magnet" around which the many particulars of the Soviet experience can coalesce. The author describes this process in a discussion of the problem of the artistic image published in *Literaturnaia gazeta* in 1934. He argues there that the theme of a work of art is secondary to and dependent on the artistic image. The concrete image organizes material taken from chaotic reality and makes expression of it possible. Reality is made comprehensible and meaningful by the image, which facilitates both memory and art. The image organizes sensory data in a process that seems instantaneous but may actually be years in the making. "I hear this, I see that, and suddenly (actually it seems that it is 'sudden') such a combination of events, something seen, something seen and thought out ten years ago, long forgotten, is now newly returned to the memory, starts to live, to be perceived."[54]

This "sudden" process of organization is a natural one, which Pilniak compares to the physical attraction of metal filings to a magnet. Everything that the artist has seen and experienced in his life serves as raw material. The image organizes that material into a coherent pattern. "In schools, in physics labs they demonstrate an experiment," Pilniak explains in the 1934 article. "They throw iron filings, iron junk on the table and move a magnet over them. The filings start to move, to come into a sort of order, to adhere to the magnet and to each another, to adopt regular graphic forms and formulae."[55] This elemental physical mechanism, Pilniak argues, is reflected in the creative process itself. Just as iron is attracted to the magnet, so thoughts are attracted to an image, which organizes them into regular patterns that bring order to chaos. The organizing image, like the organizing magnet, can give comprehensible meaning to chaotic reality.

In the production novel, that organizing image is the construction site itself, and the artist, like the reader, comes to understand the goal of society by visiting the site. "Each of us moves through the world," Pilniak explains,

> Seeing, hearing, perceiving, and analyzing thousands of things and situations. All of that is like the iron filings or the junk in a warehouse. The image [*obraz*] emerges, . . . and the image works like a magnet: from the filings of what has been seen, heard, and experienced, the necessary is selected. The filings begin to move [*prikhodit v dvizhenie*], sort themselves out, adhere to one another, take shapes, stick to the image and to each other.[56]

With such an approach, the construction of a production novel seems a simple affair. The metal filings the author needs are there for the taking: individual segments from the construction site or from previous works—even those that have been criticized or forbidden—are available for use. The author has only to move the right magnet across the table, and the pieces will assemble themselves. All of the parts can be activated, brought to life, *prikhodit v dvizhenie* around the energizing image of the construction site.

The action of the image reifies and recontextualizes data from the past, from the author's memory, and from the society itself. These images from the physical world become the basis for the artist's understanding of reality, which is created and recreated in an ongoing communal activity. "Literature should be a reflection of that new life which surrounds us, in which we live and work," Pilniak and others argued in their manifesto from 1924. "Art is everything that I took from life and poured into words," he notes in an early work. "Every story is as boundless as life is boundless."[57]

All too soon, of course, Pilniak's inclusive approach was to become anathema. Others wanted to choose the images that artists would be allowed to employ, and many literary politicians were uncomfortable with the notion that any individual whatsoever might thus have access to a creative "magnet." Leonid Leonov, for example, points out that unfriendly writers might attempt to appear sympathetic to the cause by larding their manuscripts with superfluous revolutionary thematic elements. Leonov's caution about such dangers even refers specifically to Pilniak himself: "not everything red is revolutionary," he notes in 1931. "Just look at [Pilniak's] *Red Wood*."[58]

This, in fact, was the primary reason for the eventual failure of such collective literary projects as the one to chronicle the construction of the Moscow subway. The further such projects went, the more obvious it became that not all red workers were revolutionary. Yet initially there seems to have been real enthusiasm for the idea, particularly for the subway project, and real belief in the likelihood that such projects would produce politically acceptable, even inspiring, historical documents. In retrospect, that belief seems utopian, and all the more surprising given the fact that such "suspicious" writers as Pilniak and Isaac Babel were employed to help the subway workers organize their thoughts. Yet such work continued, with what appears to have been authentic optimism, until it was brought precipitously to a halt, in part for deviating too egregiously from the continually evolving Party line. Despite this untimely end, however, it should be pointed out that Pilniak, arrested just two years after the subway publications were finished, worked on a number of the accounts that were included in the final volumes.[59]

It undoubtedly also bears repeating that the Party line for literature was far from clearly established, even well into the 1930s. Matthew Leone, for example, makes some intriguing comments about the continuity of literary doctrine from the late 1920s to the years after 1932. But he overstates the extent to which the early production novels in particular actually conformed to a model that was only vaguely perceived.[60] Most remarkable for students of Stalin's totalitarian Russia, in fact, is just how random and ad hoc the literary politics of the early 1930s actually were. Stenographic records and reminiscences that have come to light since the opening of Soviet archives make it clear that literary policy in this transitional period was developed haphazardly. Even key elements of later Socialist Realist dogma were often invented on the spot, only to be contradicted by other pronouncements and developments. Stalin's much vaunted and often repeated description of Soviet writers as "engineers of human souls," for example, was originally nothing more than a late-night toast the leader offered to a small group of hand-picked authors, many of whom were not even listening carefully.[61]

So, too, with the definition of Socialist Realism, the method that would rule Soviet literature from the mid-1930s until the demise of the Soviet Union. Stalin's off-the-cuff description of that method to a group of Party writers in 1932 contradicts his discussion of the same concept at the better-known meeting held at Maxim Gorky's residence just a week later.[62] Neither meeting presented clear guidelines that willing writers might follow or any indication of how to proceed, even with the genre of the production novel, which seemed to lend itself to the idea of common effort to build a new world. Nor was the confusion cleared up in the months and years that followed. In fact, in looking for rhyme and reason in the construction of Soviet literary politics, we are just as likely to stumble unexpectedly on "elements of surrealistic surprise."

Pilniak's entire career presents numerous such surprising moments. The Party orthodox had been suspicious of the writer for years and had subjected him to harsh criticism and periodic punishment. Despite the clouds continually gathered over his head, however, Pilniak had been remarkably successful by almost any measure. He was able to publish in some of the best venues the country had to offer and to travel abroad with dizzying frequency. He was active in literary politics, nearly up to the moment of his arrest, and his lifestyle and expectations were those of a respected member of the established pantheon of Soviet writers.[63] Is it any wonder, then, that Pilniak blithely proceeded in 1929 to base his novel of "capitulation" on a work that had just been banned?

Pilniak had reason to believe that his approach would continue to serve him well. Remarks from a letter to Voronskii in 1923 make it clear that, even that early, the writer saw the future of Russian literature in spatial terms rather than in terms of narrow political concepts. "The Russian communist party is only a link in the history of Russia for me," Pilniak notes, only a link in the "history of our days. I know that history gave the party an honored place, because the heads of the party—brilliant people—were able to hear the footsteps of history. But the human material of the party is the very same as human material in general. There are good and bad people." Pilniak's reference to human material is significant, of course. This is the "material" from which "things" are made, in the broad shared process of creating art. "Every writer," Pilniak insisted in 1923, as he would continue to do over the course of his life, "if he is honest, should write the truth, without suffering from the 'will not to see.'"[64]

Pilniak repeats his reference to the "will not to see" in his remarkable contribution to the 1924 anthology *Pisateli ob iskusstve i o sebe*. Pilniak's "Fragments from a Diary" included there establish the author's belief that Russian literature is larger and more capacious than the narrower category of communist literature. Noting in one of the "diary fragments" that his mail in Kolomna is again filled with "all sorts of lito-politics," Pilniak observes how "very boring it is that the entire world has come down now to one question: do you recognize [Bolshevik authority] or not?" For him, the question "is as unnecessary as a question of whether I recognize my own life or not." Pilniak continues,

> I am not a Communist and therefore I don't recognize that I have to be a Communist and write in a Communist manner. I recognize that Communist power in Russia is determined not by the will of the Communists, but by the historical fates of Russia and in as much as I want to follow (to the extent that I can and my conscience and reason prompt me to) these Russian historical fates, then I am with the Communists, that is, in as much as the Communists are with Russia, then I am with them.[65]

Pilniak softens the categorical nature of his statement slightly by adding parenthetically that he is with the Communists "now more than ever, as it turns out, since I am in no way with the Philistine [*obyvatel'*]." Despite this slight rhetorical hedge, his position is clear, particularly once he adds emphatically that "the fates of the RKP [Bolshevik Party] are much less interesting to me than the fates of Russia."

Pilniak insists that his duty as a writer is to provide his own best view of the world as he sees it. "I know very well that I simply cannot write differently than I do [*inache, chem ia pishu, ia pisat' ne mogu*]. I don't know how. I won't write [differently], even if I wanted to violate myself. There is a literary law, which does not permit, does not allow the possibility of doing violence to literary gifts, even by your own brain." The best proof of that, Pilniak hurries to explain, is the damage older writers have done to themselves by abandoning their literary talents to serve the god of politics. He cites the examples of Bunin and Merezhkovskii on the right and

Serafimovich on the left as authors who have substituted politics for art. As a result, Pilniak concludes sadly, "their art is not art at all; it no longer resonates."[66]

He advances a similar argument about the work of writers who have been catered to and thus spoiled by their Party masters. "Our government apparatus [*gosudarstvennost'*] has set up incubators these last few years for Party literature and supplied them with regular support, and nothing came of it." In fact, Pilniak continues, "it turned out badly since these people, having come in contact with art, stopped being politicians without having become artisans [*iskusstvenniki*]." The "new literature" that has evolved on its own is wonderfully diverse, Pilniak notes happily; "peasant-like anarchists and broken intellectuals and Communists, they've all come." But they've arrived, Pilniak insists, one by one, "without passports for a particular literary rank or special Party affiliation." Their only recommendation is the one that counts: "the true coin of their own manuscripts, which relate how our life nowadays resonates for them."[67]

Pilniak's ringing endorsement of the value of individual voices became less and less popular with time, but he stuck to it. Thus in his contribution to a 1929 discussion of the social mandate in literature, Pilniak argued that external directives to the artist are unnecessary, harmful, even impossible. To the notion of a societal directive (*sotsial'nyi zakaz*), Pilniak proposes the concept of a personal mandate, or *nakaz*. Each writer, he argues, has his own mandate formed by that person's background, upbringing, education, and favorite images and ideas that he is bound by the shape of his own mind to express. A writer's theme and style are determined naturally for him by these factors. Struggle against them, even self-imposed attempts to change, are pointless. His argument in 1929 continues to echo his brave words from 1924. Individual writers, he notes insistently, write the way they do because they must (*ne mogut inache*).[68]

Pilniak's comments epitomize the creative dilemma for this generation of writers. Increasingly pressured to write works of social relevance, they were tortured as well by their modernist realization that the literature they had seen as a salvation for society was itself highly suspect. Pilniak's numerous stories about the unreliability of authors and the inherent deception involved in the creative process make his torment abundantly clear. Describing his method of creating stories in front of a mirror as a child, Pilniak notes in the anthology *Kak my pishem* from 1930 that "I lied to organize nature and [put] concepts in the order that seemed to me to be best and most engaging. I lied incredibly, I suffered, being despised by those around me, but I could not avoid lying [*ne vrat' ne mog*]." "Disloyalty [*nevernost'*] is life," he comments in a story entitled "Tools of the Trade" from 1927. "It is life to go to the newly discovered, the new, the improved. That's the way each person goes, as long as he has strength, must go, because each will later be discarded on the heap by death."[69] Convinced, then, of both the inevitable need to change and the inherent duplicity of the act of writing, Pilniak and others of his generation looked for ways to be true to their evolving times.

For Pilniak, that involved a continued search for balance. Both the eccentricities of individual talent and the compelling needs of society had to be taken into account. Pilniak raises the issue of this balance between individual writers and society in his contribution to the 1929 discussion of social directives in literature. "Pushkin was the truest son of his century," Pilniak emphasizes, "yet with the exception of a dozen lines, there's *not a word* said about his era: they were exiling and executing the Decembrists, [while] Pushkin was writing 'The Miserly Knight' and 'Mozart and Saleri.' Pushkin evoked his epoch not by *what* he described but by *how he wrote.*" "It's not important if I *describe* the Congress of Soviets or the requisitioning of grain," Pilniak insists, "or if I write about Attila the Hun. It's important *how I write, how* I fulfill the directive given to me by the epoch." The "primary mandate [*sushchestvenneishei nakaz*] for every writer," Pilniak continues, is "to be talented, to husband his own gifts—and only take account of them, since the social directive is stored up [*zakaz zalozhen*] in those gifts."[70]

"Every writer should write in his own manner," Pilniak repeats in an article in *Literaturnaia gazeta* from 1933. "It's good when Pushkin doesn't resemble Shakespeare, and Gogol doesn't resemble Shakespeare or Pushkin or Vs[evolod] Ivanov." Imagining the more perfect world of the future, Pilniak notes that the "future socialist Pushkin won't resemble the socialist Shakespeare, that is, will be individual." Socialism, Pilniak insists, is "the emancipation of individual talents." Pilniak was still proclaiming the artist's inability to write to order as late as 1936. When he was called to task in that year by the presidium of the Writers' Union, he apparently offered no defense but simply repeated his argument that the writer finds it impossible to write differently, "*inache, chem on pishet.*"[71]

Battered by such criticism throughout his career, Pilniak nevertheless attempted to write the truth as he saw it. Like most authors of this period, he had been to real Soviet construction sites and was genuinely impressed with the progress he saw there. His enthusiastic description of a visit to a cellulose plant near Lake Ladoga appeared, for example, in the newspaper *Izvestiia* in March 1928, and his letter to disgraced political operative Karl Radek during the same month gives private confirmation to his public expression of infatuation with the project. "I returned from there completely cheered," Pilniak tells Radek. "I saw colossal things. In place of pine trees, a colossal factory. It is very good, and thoughts are built very well, if machines direct them: I am committed to romanticism forever."[72] Like many other authors of this period, Pilniak saw his own art as a way to overcome the binary strictures that had previously separated mind and labor, work and romance, nature and the industrial world.

Pilniak's insistence on the romance of industry was typical of the times, but quite unusual was the writer's contrary insistence, just a few years later, that writers need not "travel to all the ends of the [Soviet] Union in order to write a novel about the factory." Commenting in an article in *Literaturnaia gazeta* in 1933, Pilniak recalls that Daniel Defoe wrote his well-known account of the adventures of Robinson Crusoe while sitting at home in his study. Russian writers need not be any different. And if authors do want to visit, Pilniak mentions helpfully, "there are enough large factories and foundries in Moscow in order to write a so-called industrial novel. There is no necessity to travel to Magnitogorsk for that. The question isn't about exactly which factory, but about how to write a work of art." And that, insists the normally well traveled and adventurous author, is a "question of the author's talent."[73]

Pilniak's work on his own production novel was apparently influenced by a visit to Dneprostroi, but the relocation of the narrative to a site near Pilniak's beloved Kolomna makes both artistic and geographic sense. This allows Pilniak to situate plans for modernization in the middle of his "primeval" Russia, which plays a role as important to the narrative as the building project itself. Thus, the engineering plan that Pilniak describes in *The Volga Falls to the Caspian Sea* is not fully articulated until midway through the novel in a lengthy passage that begins incongruously "The construction was coming to an end" (131).[74] Although the description continues for several pages and is suffused with the "Tonnenideologie" that Malte Rolf has argued was typical of the Five-Year Plan, its curious placement in the middle of the novel tends to downplay the era's fascination with large-scale projects.

Such an approach has the effect of grounding the grand societal narrative in the many individual stories that populate Pilniak's novel. By thus balancing the particular with the general and the temporary with the historical, Pilniak is able to give his production novel the balance he advocates for all creative projects. His approach is both achingly individual and sweepingly broad, focusing simultaneously on the grand building project that will remake society and on the diseased, warped, and grotesquely individualized characters that the dam project will sweep away. The project will result in a new river, "for the first time in Europe, the first in Europe, made by man" (131). The "new river was rebuilding the geography of the ancient Moscow, Riazan, Vladimir lands, the hydrology of the rivers and the climate" (131), the novel continues. "Geography changed the economy just as man and man's labor insisted, and labor was rebuilding geology." This project, a symbol of the new Russian government and the "Russia of Octobers," had "recreated—with the machine—for the sake of labor—human relations among men, to labor, to nature" (132).

The process, explains Pilniak, is one of synthesis rather than opposition. The man-made "monolith was built just as primeval [*pervozdannaia*] nature was built," he notes, in a statement that underplays binary oppositions of nature and man. The "granite of the earth's crust and the granite brought by human will were welded into geology, in first creation" (133). Here as elsewhere, Pilniak looks for ways to overcome the seeming divide between man and nature. Although there are no straight lines in nature—*v prirode net dvizhenii geometricheski priamykh, nichto v prirode ne dvizhetsia geometricheskimi priamymi* (175) —the natural world does have logic and rules, which must be followed. One of the few sympathetic characters in the novel, worker-engineer (*inzhener so stanka*) Sadykov understands the need to overcome any false dichotomies in his work on the river. He knows that "while building, it's never possible to break these [natural] forces and laws, since in a fight with nature it's necessary to use nature itself" (140). Using nature to build the dam is essential, Pilniak argues, even when that process will result in the destruction of part of nature itself. It is possible to grapple "with these forces" of the water, Pilniak insists, only by "not disturbing them in any way, by not contradicting them in any way, but by coordinating them" (2).

Pilniak's change of title from *Mahogany* to *The Volga Falls to the Caspian Sea* implies the complicated reworking of Russian geography, literary history, and folk wisdom that will be necessary to turn prerevolutionary "mahogany" into Soviet red wood. The phrase "the Volga flows to the Caspian Sea" is already familiar to readers of Russian literature as the leitmotif in Anton Chekhov's short story "Uchitel' slovestnosti," where it serves as the dying utterance of Ippolit Ippolitovich, who "in his delirium says only what is known to everyone." In the *Semiotics of Cinema*, Iurii Lotman identifies the phrase as a truism, a statement so entirely predictable, so saturated with banal truth that it removes uncertainty and therefore conveys no new information. Pilniak plays on such conditioned readings in his committed reconstruction of his own text, where established truths and geographical certainties are no measure of the outline of the future. Vladimir Mayakovsky's play "The Bathhouse" (*Bania*) from 1930 opens with a timely but sarcastic iteration of the truism on which Pilniak bases his novel. "Well," says Mayakovsky's character Velosipedkin, "does the vile Volga still fall to the Caspian Sea?" But Mayakovsky has missed Pilniak's point. In Pilniak's understanding, the truism represents the old that must give way to the new.[75]

Pilniak was fascinated by the texture of material culture and its endurance over time, and this fascination is reflected in the long descriptions he provides in both *Mahogany* and *The Volga Falls to the Caspian Sea* of the detritus of the old world that lingers in the new one. This interest in *byt*—both new and newly outdated—occasionally threatens to turn Pilniak's production novel into a catalog of the material substrate of the old way of life. Thus he begins a numbered section of *The Volga Falls to the Caspian Sea* with a description of the homes that the antique dealers visit and the items they find there. As we will see in Kataev's "chronicle" as well, such an attempt to have their literary cake and eat it too was typical of writers of this time. The Bezdetov brothers travel from location to location, itemizing and categorizing the objects they find in each domicile, allowing Pilniak's text to serve as a permanent record of the *byt* that the author knows will soon be destroyed.

Pilniak's descriptions of these items and the "former people" who owned them are blunt and painful but not devoid of pity, and this approach characterizes Pilniak's account throughout both works. "Well, are you selling or not?" one of the Bezdetov brothers asks his "ancient" client regarding her wishes for the Russian stove they want to acquire. "I don't even know what to do" (*ne znaiu kak byt'*), she replies helplessly. "After all, our grandfathers lived, and our great-grandfathers, and even the times are getting lost . . ." Of course, she does sell; she must in order to live. She, like Pilniak, understands that life means change and inevitable disloyalty to the lives that came before. We must "sacrifice old labor" in order to make "the new better," as Pilniak has reminded us before. The ordered list of such transactions that Pilniak includes in his production novel ". . . 4—5—7—" makes it clear that this process—and the continuing need to evolve—is endless.[76]

No matter how much party officials wished it otherwise, the mahogany furniture being bartered away in the homes and second-hand stores of the late NEP period is thus the literal embodiment of the culture that is to be reconstructed. One conundrum that faced engineers of the new *byt* was what to do with the old world while the new one was being constructed. The housing stock, the public infrastructure, the available furniture, and even the decorative details of everyday life were inherited from the old regime, making it ostensibly unsuited for large-scale attempts at reforging the populace. Utopian projects to change the very texture of everyday life in socialist Russia, like those described by Christina Kiaer in her research, were still relatively limited in their reach.[77] This created a dilemma for reformers since the resources to institute massive architectural changes were lacking. What should be done with the material cultural inheritance from prerevolutionary times? Should it be destroyed as hopelessly outdated and tainted with unhealthy influences, or could it be retrofitted, "reforged," as it were, and reused, at least temporarily? Fedor Gladkov's *Cement* refers directly to these dilemmas when his main character Dasha insists that bourgeois but comfortable furniture be taken out of storage and returned to the Soviet children's home for use by the young proletariat.[78]

More than five years after Gladkov raised the issue, Pilniak saw that the new Russia was still awash in a sea of pre-Soviet Russian history. What Gladkov's Dasha might accomplish unblinkingly in the early postrevolutionary years was more of an embarrassment at the end of the first full decade of Soviet power, and Pilniak reflects the ambivalence of official opinion toward the prerevolutionary cultural heritage in his work. His characters must negotiate a strange no-man's-land between, on the one side, the forbidden luxury of bourgeois Russia and its NEP heirs and, on the other, the stark and equally unpalatable aestheticism of war communism, best represented by Pilniak's characters Ivan Ozhogov and other unrepentant members of the old guard that Pilniak refers to as "okhlomony." Without specifying what will replace these two extremes, Pilniak makes clear that neither approach is acceptable in the new world.

Like the household objects in *Twelve Chairs*, furniture serves in Pilniak's work as a graphic reminder of a past that is no longer recoverable. The dining-room suite of tsarism is deconstructed in

Twelve Chairs, literally taken apart and reused to build a new school for Soviet children. Pilniak's version of the same process shows that deconstruction also involves an inevitable process of disruption and decay, which may take generations. In a painful echo of Ostap Bender's search for hidden treasure in the discarded refuse of the disenfranchised Russian aristocracy, Pilniak's character, herself an impoverished noblewoman, must hunt on her own for a few trinkets to barter for food. Her unsuccessful search for a complete dining-room set ends mired instead in the Homeric mud of the Russian provinces.[79]

Physical objects take on a life of their own in *Mahogany*, as the furniture of the title becomes the measure of a man. The nameless creator of a single piece of mahogany furniture may live and die to finish just one item, which lives on beyond the human lifespan: "the master died, but the things live" (41), Pilniak notes. The author admires the craftsmanship involved in the process—"the art of mahogany is the art of things" (56)—but in *The Volga Falls to the Caspian Sea*, he relegates such objects to the sterile world of the past, tainted by the system that characterized their creation by serf craftsmen. Objects and the buildings that house them can be "radioactive" in Pilniak's world, both dating human life and potentially contaminating it. Thus, a house may be a measure of the length of human existence, as is one described in both *Mahogany* and *The Volga Falls to the Caspian Sea*. Built with axes instead of saws and sited on a plot of land that was chosen before any streets were built, the structure bears witness to the very dawn of man's residence in the area. "The house stood catty-corner to the street because it was built before the appearance of the street, and the house was built not from sawed timber but from hewn logs, that is it was built during the times when carpenters didn't use saws yet, when carpenters worked only with axes, so that was the time before and during the time of Peter."[80]

Yet this house, like all of the structures in the village, will soon be under the floodwaters that the new construction project brings, and those who traffic in such items are doomed. The antique dealers who figure prominently in both *Mahogany* and the production novel are bound for extinction. Their last name, Bezdetov, or Childless, reveals them as sterile representatives of a way of life that is soon to be swept away. They are portrayed in *The Volga Falls to the Caspian Sea* as thoroughly unsavory, and like many other representatives of the old way of life, they are morally suspect. The syphilitic Poltorak, for example, manages to betray women by the name of Sofiia (wisdom), Vera (faith), Nadezhda (hope), and

Liubov' (love) before the end of the novel. He and his Hungarian colleague Laslo, who betrays the aptly named Maria, serve as proof that men are a destructive force and must be aligned with the creative and pure female presence to advance humanity. Poltorak, the Bezdetovs, and the cruelly patriarchal Skudrin are particularly odious since they have entered a sinister plot with the counterrevolutionary Sherwood to foil the construction plan with an untimely explosion on the building site.

Just as suspect in Pilniak's world, however, are the craftsmen of words, and it is here that Pilniak faces the consequences of his own approach most directly. Like the would-be restorers of the past that he lampoons in *The Volga Falls to the Caspian Sea*, Pilniak sees that he, too, and wordsmiths like him everywhere, deal in the world of "things" that threaten to overwhelm individual human existence. "Two million people lived in Moscow," Pilniak notes in *The Volga Falls to the Caspian Sea*, "an enormous human forest, a thicket, where one person and many others never knew about each other, where very many who resonate passed each other by, never knowing about their accord. This forest in the millions had its own loves, affairs, dresses, tables, chairs, bed-clothes. How many beds and towels must there be in a million-peopled city!" (84). The answer, of course, is that there are too many, each item with a story that Pilniak the chronicler wants to tell, each piece the empty shell of a real human life that once animated it.[81] Such outpouring of emotion over the detritus of postrevolutionary Russia comes in the middle of a scene in which the bourgeois engineer comments morosely "we've been discarded beyond everyday life" (*my vykinuty za byt*) (85). This is the complex utterance of a modernist artist: untrustworthy but still burdened with responsibility, emotional but no longer able to feel genuine pathos, the modern artist, too, is doomed. He understands the central paradox of the contemporary work of art, but he is unable either to change or to cease his own activity. As part of life, art is subject to life's inevitable process of decay and death. As part of the "construction" process, the artist's own work will itself soon need to be torn down. Although the author may find some consolation in the notion of the "reconstruction" certain to follow his own demise, such comfort is minimal. Writers of this generation clearly intuited that by accepting the notion of "reforging," they were dooming their own works and the selves that created them to obsolescence.

The authors of most of the early production novels shared this tragic realization that they would never live to see precisely what final meaning their personal sacrifices had acquired. Pilniak acknowledges such awareness in the section of *The Volga Falls to the Caspian Sea* in which he states that the "construction was coming to an end." The imminent completion of the building project leads the author to thoughts about the completion of books and, inevitably, to an understanding of the end of his own individual existence. "Shelves of years are like shelves of books," he notes in *The Volga Falls to the Caspian Sea.*

> Shelves of human years are like books, since every book—isn't that really a human convulsion, the convulsion of human genius, human thought, destroying the laws of death, walking right over death, just like the convulsions of the crematorium? And shouldn't, shouldn't every person once in a while, at night, in his study, in the shelves of books— whether he wants to or not—shouldn't he be terrified in the face of these books, feel that every book is a counterfeit of real human life, every book is a convulsion of thought, deceiving death, be terrified and feel that here, at night, when the books look out from the shelves with huge jaws . . . be terrified and feel that this room and these books are in essence dead men in the mortuary, the morgue . . . (135)

Completion of a mahogany bookshelf—or the books to store on it—signals the end of the individual human spirit that engendered the piece. Cognizance of that fact helps explain Pilniak's decision to include the "slanderous" *Mahogany* in his attempt to create an acceptable production novel. He knows that his own production, his "things," will be replaced by others all too soon. He understands the goal of art as one of endless process, and he supports it, just as he "supports" life since it would be unthinkable not to do so. The engineer Poltorak, for example, "remembered a thought he'd read not long before about the machine, about steel, about construction, in the face of which there is no end to opposing nature and organizing it—it is impossible not to bow to that and it is necessary to write a poem about it" (93). Both engineer and author acknowledge the inevitability of the process—*etomu nel'zia ne klaniat'sia*—and they share the search for a way to use nature to overcome rather than merely reflect established dichotomies. Both share as well, however, a sense of profound sorrow at the loss such progress entails.

Pilniak voices his concerns over the never-ending individual cost of never-ending progress throughout the production novel, but it is in the long digression about the meaning of books that he is most expressive. His musings about classic works of literature are particularly poignant, especially as he evokes them as a childhood legacy that has now been discarded. His thoughts merge halfway through the passage with the thoughts of the engineer Laslo, whose wife Maria has committed suicide just that day. Maria's act of self-murder prompts the women laborers on the construction site to go on strike in female solidarity, and Laslo's confused expressions of sorrow and guilt mingle with those of the author in a sustained condemnation of the destruction that every act of building inevitably entails. Their connection is made even more obvious by the fact that the metaphor of bookshelves as a measure of human life is one Pilniak has used before, most notably in his short story "Spilled Time" (*Rasplestnutoe vremia*). That story by the red-headed Pilniak notes that "there are ever more little books growing on the shelves, you crawl ever higher on the shelves of books, where everything starts to grow lonely. Yeah, and you crawl on the shelves of years. Your hair is no longer reddish, not radish, it loses its color. Every life is monotonous, and I have, like everyone has, monotony."[82]

Construction—whether of new dams or new books—inevitably involves a sense of loss, and Pilniak/Laslo are only partially convinced that the new structure that emerges on the site of building will be worth the cost. "This room and these books are in essence dead men in the mortuary, the morgue," the passage in *The Volga Falls to the Caspian Sea* continues: "from which they took Maria to the cemetery today, where are buried life, the dead counterfeiting the living, thoughts, convulsions as in the crematorium. From this shelf crawl the thoughts of Johann Wolfgang Goethe, the image of the never-having-lived Werther,—friends from a young age, sins from youth along with Pushkin, Tolstoy, Dostoevsky" (135).

Their reluctance to see the past disappear is combined with their guilt at having participated in its demise, Laslo by his work on the construction site and his callous treatment of Maria, Pilniak by the very fact of his work as an author. "All of that," the passage continues,

is left in pre-history, in pre-October [*v doepokhakh, v do-oktiabre*] and out of inertia crawls in boxes of books onto the scales. Marx, Lenin, Plekhanov—the history of the development of the workers' movement in Germany, Austria, Hungary, in Russia, in the world—have become epochs. And the books about labor, books about construction—Alekseev, Akulov, Kandiba, Dubakh, Zbrozhek, Gerardon—the engineer, not the sociologist Engels—is engineering, building, labor. Lenin is dead, but his books grow and grow. Beyond the building, beyond the trenches of earth turned inside out by construction a monolith appears, which is rebuilding nature. (135)

Pilniak's task as the creator of a production novel, then, is to find a synthesis of the destructive and the creative, the male and the female, the future and the past, the intellectual and the worker, the chatter of his bookshelves and the altogether mute silence of the grave. He offers his own complicated metaphors as a way to resolve the limitations for such binary systems. One such attempt at synthesis, for example, is his treatment of the metaphor of the willows that have been planted to secure the fascine of the dam. The individual plants themselves will not survive, Pilniak tells us, but their sacrifice is necessary to ensure the success of the shared project. The pliant willows are essential to anchor the man-made dam, which is rigid and, therefore, unstable in its unyielding logic. Sadykov notices the willows and draws on the implicit connection between their inevitable demise and that of the women workers whose sacrifices on the construction site are given significant treatment throughout the novel.

The worker-engineer Sadykov is one of the survivors of the relentless march of history in Pilniak's novel, and it is Sadykov who suggests that individual surrender to the press of time and necessity is essential to universal survival. He alludes to the willows as an allegory of individual and group sacrifice for the greater good, but he nevertheless refuses to make the connection explicit. "I don't have time for allegories right now," he notes gruffly as he confronts his wife and Laslo with evidence of their clandestine love affair. His decision to "sacrifice" his own feelings for his wife, which will free her to marry her lover, ends up having serious consequences. The wife commits suicide, precipitating a strike of the women workers and the eventual demise of her lover. But Sadykov, who makes his painful personal sacrifice willingly, is able to find happiness after all, and his newfound love represents yet another synthesis of seeming dichotomies. His relationship with Liubov' Poletika, the site's archeologist and daughter of the prerevolutionary head of the project, helps resolve inherent contradictions between the past and the present, prehistoric existence and future industrial development, passion and reason, and even women and men.

Liubov', whose name means love, is an important transitional figure since her activity as archeologist is crucial to Pilniak's attempt to synthesize the contradictions inherent in his society. Liubov' arrives at the construction site as an expert on *kamennye baby*, the crude but powerful stone figures of women that served as totems and fertility figures on the steppes of ancient Rus'. The images of these "stone women" figure prominently in Pilniak's prose, and they would seem to be part of the past that will be swept away with the release of flood waters once the new dam is constructed. Yet, instead of rejecting these remnants from the preindustrial past, Pilniak and his communist heroine Liubov' counsel their embrace. These ancient architectural monuments speak to a primitive and retrograde aspect of life, but Liubov' finds a particular beauty in them, one which she strives to reclaim as a modern heritage. Although these "women were really terrifying, high-cheek-boned, narrow-eyed, cow-stomached, Liubov' spoke of their grace" (89). The decadent Poltorak, who involves Liubov' in a brief affair before abandoning her, proposes a "mystical" explanation for the archeologist's interest in the fertility figures, but this sexual interpretation is rejected flatly in favor of an approach that seeks to appropriate the past for use in the future: "That was in no way true for Liubov'. Liubov' dug around in the centuries in order to give them to the future" (90).

Pilniak's example—here and elsewhere in his work—suggests an organic and cyclical understanding of the texture of everyday life. The stone women that serve as architectural reminders of the past in *The Volga Falls to the Caspian Sea* are equally powerful figures in the present. Pilniak links the preindustrial age to the first Five-Year Plan explicitly when he compares those stone figures to the women workers on the modern-day construction site. His character Nadezhda, or Hope, yet another female victim of Poltorak's depravity, views Maria's funeral procession from the window of her hotel room:

> This ancient town square, this ancient howl of church bells, and these ancient women, these proletariettes. I saw: they are made of stone, these giant broads. . . . They had clothing on them that was 1,000 years old, their ancient wraps and skirts. They were barefoot. They were ancient, these gigantic women. It was a procession of Scythians, whose age was ancient. They carried a coffin in front. What antiquity were they carrying, if they set out behind a coffin, these gigantic women in ancient clothing and in silence? (107)

The past they are burying, Pilniak implies, is the one of contractions that would artificially separate these present-day industrial workers from their elemental and legitimate past.

For Pilniak, this artificial division is associated with Peter the Great, whose reforms, he argues, resulted in an unnatural division between past and present, East and West, nature and man. This explains Pilniak's dogged insistence on the incomparability of Peter's "modernizing" reforms and those that are taking place on the construction site as part of Soviet industrialization plans. He draws a negative comparison between Peter the Great and the builders of this dam. The Soviet landscape of the late 1920s bears no resemblance at all to Peter's activity, we are told: "this landscape, where Poletika and Sadykov stood like marshals in battle with old Russia for new Russia did not resemble in the slightest Serov's painting of Peter marching in Petersburg."

This comparison or, rather, anti-comparison is abruptly interrupted by the women's work stoppage, a fierce, powerful, and silent protest of hundreds of *kamennye baby,* stone women who rise up to offer a heroic alternative to Serov's vision of construction. In case the implied contrast is too subtle, Pilniak makes it explicit in a later passage in which he identifies Peter the Great with the depraved counterrevolutionary Iakov Karpovich Skudrin. Skudrin, who represents the worst of patriarchal old Russia, is discussing his plans to dynamite the construction site with his co-conspirators, the sterile Bezdetov brothers and the engineer Poltorak. They discuss the women's strike but are incapable of understanding its elemental nature or its profound significance. Instead, Skudrin imagines himself as the central figure in the "heroic" landscape. He "saw himself beyond the smoke of the dynamite, beyond the streams of water, beyond the granite debris,—himself, a disgusting little old man, the Bezdetovs, Poltarak—more or less exactly like in Serov's painting, where Peter is tramping around Sankt-Piterburkh. The disgusting little old man was Peter" (58).

For such enduring binary contradictions that can not easily be resolved, Pilniak and other authors turned to the "Moses solution." Just as Moses could not enter the promised land, those who helped build the new world could truly never be part of it. Writers as diverse as Iurii Olesha, Ilia Erenburg, and Andrei Platonov all wrestled with this problem,[83] and Pilniak refers to this idea directly in *The Volga Falls to the Caspian Sea* when he notes the fate of the War-Communist-era believers in the novel. Chief among this group is Ivan Ozhogov, brother to Iakov Skudrin, whose plot to bomb the dam is foiled at the end of the book. Skudrin is a stand-in for the despotic order of Peter the Great, while his brother Ivan, the "hero" of *Mahogany,* symbolizes a more congenial but equally polarizing view of the revolution as passionate anarchy and permanent upheaval.

To these binary approaches, Pilniak posits a middle ground that benefits from both sides of the polarity between order and chaos, science and primitivism, memory and abandon. Skudrin and his side of the dichotomy destroy themselves, while Ivan and the rest of the *okhlomony* are willing human sacrifices swept away in the floodwaters that end the novel and signal a new beginning in a renewed world. Remarkably sympathetic to these survivors and promoters of War Communist ideals, Pilniak nevertheless sees that as inhabitants of the old world, they have no place in the new. Symbolic keepers of the flame, as their fiery names indicate, they have taken up residence in the old brick factory.[84] That location makes it clear that they will serve as building blocks for the new society they will never inhabit, and their destruction in the waters of the new world is perfectly predictable.

Pilniak had mostly abandoned the experiments with typeface and font size that characterized his *Naked Year* and other early works. But he succeeds in breaking the surface of the text in *Mahogany* and *The Volga Falls to the Caspian Sea* by his clever handling of an architectural metaphor of church bells which appears in both works. The incidents refer to a real campaign to assist Soviet industrialization efforts by recycling the metal in age-old church bells for new uses. Bells were removed across Russia to be resmelted and redeployed in construction, though it is unclear how many usable resources this effort actually yielded. Pilniak describes the process of removal as an ongoing one, and his suspension of the clamorous bells over the narrative—always ringing, never finally removed—establishes both an aural and a physical dimension to the tale, as though the bells stretch from the past to the present, from the space of the text to the space of the reader.

Further disturbing the one-dimensionality of the narrative is the "real-life" newspaper that Pilniak includes in *The Volga Falls to the Caspian Sea*. Dated July 13, 1929, the two-page facsimile purports to be a newspaper from the construction site and includes articles about the events in Pilniak's own production novel. This device provides Pilniak's fictional work with the aura of verisimilitude, and it helps, as well, to effect the fairy-tale-like transformation of everyday life that was expected of grandiose Russian industrialization plans from the late 1920s and early 1930s. That favorite Stalinist aphorism, "We were born to make fairytales come true" (*My rozhdenny chtoby sdelat' skazku byl'iu*), was the underlying message for all authors interested in constructing Stalinist culture. This is the essential Soviet production novel, of course, the "text" that made it possible for such an unorthodox narrative as *The Volga Falls to the Caspian Sea* to be considered for the pantheon of Socialist Realism.

In a personal appeal to Stalin in January 1931, Pilniak asks the leader for permission to travel abroad. Acknowledging that he has made "many" mistakes, Pilniak nevertheless ventures to inform his interlocutor that "no matter how paradoxical it may seem, contemplating my mistakes, very often, when I'm alone with myself, I saw that many of my mistakes have emerged from the conviction that a writer of the revolution may only be someone who is sincere and truthful with the revolution." "It seemed to me," Pilniak continues in this somewhat brazen epistle to the man he had accused of murder just a few years before, that "if I was given the right to wear the great honor of a Soviet writer, then there is also trust toward me." Noting that he had already been punished for the *Mahogany* affair, Pilniak describes the "enormous difficulty (they must have been afraid of me)" involved in finding a publisher for *The Volga Falls to the Caspian Sea*. In addition to that novel, Pilniak points out other works, including his writings on Tadzhikistan, which he believes will serve as a "correction for my authorial mistakes." Pilniak goes so far as to include a copy of his latest work, published "in connection with the wreckers' trial" and carefully marked with red pencil to note the most pertinent passages.[85]

Intent on gaining Stalin's support for his travel plans, Pilniak points out that his work has already been translated into numerous languages and he himself has traveled abroad fourteen times since 1921. If he is allowed to venture overseas again, the author mentions, the profit from foreign editions of his works will bring the state bank "1,000–1,500 hard-currency rubles a year."[86] Assuring his leader that he already has an idea for a novel about the "last decade and a half of the history of the world," Pilniak explains that he considers this new project his "first big and real work." The location of the action will be the "USSR and the USA, Asia and Europe." He knows Asia and Europe from previous trips, he points out helpfully, but since he has "not been to the United States," he requests Stalin's assistance in approving the trip. In classic Pilniak fashion, the writer is soon carried away by the eloquence of his own arguments. "Iosif Vissarionovich," he pleads with Stalin, "I give you the honest word of my entire authorial fate that if you will help me now to travel abroad and work, I will pay back your trust a hundred-fold." Insisting that suspicions of his possible desire to flee the Soviet Union are ludicrous ("After all, I can't really run away from myself; [*ved' ne mogu zhe ia ubezhat' ot samogo sebia*] . . . ?!"), he notes that he can only travel overseas as a "revolutionary writer."

If allowed to go, Pilniak assures Stalin, he will "write a necessary thing [*nuzhnuiu veshch'*]."[87]

Pilniak was granted permission to travel to the United States.[88] We have his "necessary thing," the novel-travelogue *Okay: An American Novel* (*O'kei: amerikanskii roman*), as proof that his plea for assistance from Stalin proved successful. But according to archival sources, *Okay* was published only with difficulty, and the intervention of the Party hierarchy was needed once more. The rough draft of a letter retained in Pilniak's family archive reveals that the author considered appealing both to Lev Mikhailovich Karakhan and Lazar Moiseevich Kaganovich before deciding to address his plea for support to Stalin. Pilniak had been allowed to travel to Poland, Germany, France, and America in his seven-month trip outside of the USSR, but he returned home to find that he was "losing the possibility not only of publishing but even of being considered a Soviet citizen." Although his works had been published "many times and were never forbidden by Glavlit, just as they are not now forbidden," a new planned edition had been canceled, he complained, and the contract nullified.[89]

Such scenes were to be repeated frequently over the next few years, as Pilniak turned repeatedly to the Party hierarchy for assistance in an increasingly hostile atmosphere. He turned to Stalin again in July 1933 for help publishing *Stones and Roots* (*Kamni i korni*), his account of a visit to Japan. Although that generically complex work had been declared "a good and very necessary work" by Karakhan and championed by Ivan Gronskii, Pilniak found it "forbidden" by Glavlit.[90] *Stones and Roots* represents the absurd Stalinist end of Pilniak's modernist device of self-quotation; the work consists largely of self-citations from Pilniak's earlier work *Roots of the Japanese Sun,* this time with Pilniak's highly critical commentary on the original work. Despite the author's attempt to preserve much of the original account by surrounding it with a critical framework, he nevertheless includes certain devastating criticisms that are difficult to ignore. Thus, he remarks, for example, that "I must inform the Soviet reader now that 'Roots' is an inaccurate book. I request readers to discard from their book shelves the seventh volume of my Collected Works" which contained *Roots of the Japanese Sun.*[91]

Pilniak thus found himself gradually isolated from the collective that was entrusted with constructing Stalinist culture. In his discussion with proletarian writers on October 20, 1932, for example, Stalin referred to Pilniak directly as an example of a problematic writer. Speaking about the Central Committee's decree of April 23, 1932, that liquidated RAPP and reorganized Soviet literature, Stalin cautioned writers not to misinterpret the implications of the decree. "Some writers, like Pilniak," Stalin noted, "understood our decree as 'okay, now the shackles are off and we are permitted everything.'" Clearly, that was not the case, Stalin assured his audience of true believers. Nevertheless, Stalin continued, in a classic example of his ability to send mixed messages, it was necessary to treat such mistaken individuals with care. "That group of writers doesn't understand everything that is taking place in the country of socialism under construction. It's hard for them to understand it all. They are turning to the side of the working class slowly, but they are turning." Authors like that "should have been helped in a timely and patient manner," Stalin comments, before delivering his criticism of those proletarian writers who were listening, "but you were impatient with them."[92]

Stalin's reassurances about the need for patience notwithstanding, his reference to Pilniak as an author who had misunderstood the new decree was telling. The writer was excluded from a discussion that took place just a week later with another group of writers at Gorky's house. That gathering included Kataev, Leonov, Bagritskii, Libedinskii, and others, but Pilniak's name was not on the list, even though the writer ostensibly had challenged Gorky directly about his exclusion.[93] The next few years would be filled with similar examples. Pilniak considered a place in the pantheon of Soviet writers to be rightly his, and he managed to maintain that position nearly up until his arrest. But there were continual signs that his status was in danger. He complains in his letter to Stalin in January 1932 that "under such conditions it would be easier to abandon literary work, especially since such conditions could even threaten hunger." Nevertheless, he insists, "I want to work, and my fate is forever tied to our revolution and its general line."[94]

The story of Pilniak's final "production novel" adds an intriguing end to his involvement with the genre. The work entitled "Meat" (*Miaso*) that the author published serially with coauthor Sergei Beliaev suggests one of the directions Soviet literature might have taken if it had continued to develop organically. The genre of the production novel itself might have continued to evolve, if Pilniak and others like him had been allowed to continue to play with the genre, forcing it to accept unorthodox methods in staid socialist guise. Pilniak's family biographers call "Meat" a "combination of a

parody of the so-called production novel and historical research."
According to testimony offered by Pilniak's third wife and re-
counted by his son and granddaughter, the author had no initial de-
sire to undertake the project. Assigned the task of describing the
Soviet meat industry, he had to be coaxed into accepting the job by
A. I. Mikoyan himself.[95]

Pilniak's family archives have preserved a unique document from
March 7, 1936, that marks the "completion of the collective novel
Meat." Written in humorously official style and signed by Beliaev
and Pilniak, the "memorandum" notes that the novel was "really
written collectively," inasmuch as "the ideas were dreamed up in
concert," Beliaev "turned these ideas into materials and concrete
principles" (*konkretnosti*), and Pilniak "polished these materials
and concrete principles, along with the ideas, to publication readiness." The authors note in mock-heroic style that the novel is "scientific, highly historical, widely philosophical, and deeply technical,
and, at the same time, truly social and socialist." It was written,
they assure us, for a "wide circle of readers, both feudal-bourgeois,
in order to tweak their noses, and for proletarian readers so that
they can relax while having a good laugh along with the authors,
looking back on the past and taking pride in the present, in natural pride in their labors."[96]

The emphasis the writers put on the collective nature of their endeavor is obviously humorous, particularly since they include a
passage detailing their intentions to sell the novel "on the basis of
fifti-fifti."[97] Their jocular evocation of the notion of collective authorship, nevertheless, points up the continued importance of the
concept for both Pilniak and his times. Valentin Kataev gave voice
to this shared dream of joint authorship in a statement he included
in his work "Grass of Oblivion," written long after Pilniak and
many of their contemporaries had died. Speaking in that odd mixture of future past that such authors found congenial, Kataev notes
that "subsequently—many years ago in the future [*mnogo let tomu
vpered*]—I came to the conviction that in Russia there was, is, and
will be a single, immortal poet, a national genius, who wears different names in different eras."[98]

Pilniak shared this sentiment with Kataev and others of his
tragic, hopeful time, and he expressed this conviction in his published works, his artistic methods, and his creative pronouncements. He states his belief emphatically in the foreword to his 1925
novel *Machines and Wolves.* "With each day," Pilniak comments
there, "it becomes more clear to me that my authorship is, for me,

not the means to gain fame or win glory or live well— authorship is a cheerless task and—practically a mouse's labor" (*myshechnyi trud*). The loneliness, the hopelessness of this thankless authorial task is relieved by thoughts of the communicative nature of writing itself. If even one reader "in thirty or forty years" takes an interest in his scribbling, Pilniak tells us in a foreword to his eight-volume set in 1930, then that individual "will have justified my labor." The job of writing is social, and it is that fact which gives it both meaning and responsibility. The "communal nature [*sobornost'*] of our labor is essential (and was and is and will be)," Pilniak claims in *Machines and Wolves*. "It has fallen to us to make Russian literature communally [*soborno*], and that is a big obligation."[99]

5

Finding Space in *Time, Forward!*: Kataev and Writers at Work

IN ANY STUDY OF THE DEVELOPMENT OF THE SOVIET PRODUCTION novel, long-lived author Valentin Kataev (1897–1986) deserves pride of place: as critic Richard Borden notes with amazement, Kataev published "in all eight decades of Soviet rule" and *Time, Forward!* (*Vremia, vpered!*) is "perhaps the lone masterpiece of Soviet construction fiction."[1] Elder brother to Evgenii Petrov, Kataev was the creative godfather to the novel *Twelve Chairs;* at age thirty, he was already a respected elder man of letters at the newspaper *Gudok* where he, Petrov, and Ilia Ilf were employed, and his literary opinion was highly regarded. In 1927, the same year that he engendered *Twelve Chairs,* Kataev published a novel of his own, *Embezzlers* (*Rastrachiki*), and he was preparing a new comedy entitled "Squaring the Circle" (*Kvadratura kruga*) for its premiere at the prestigious Moscow Art Theater. Kataev's place in the Soviet pantheon would soon become even more secure: *Time, Forward!* was about to become one of the best-known and most telling examples of the production novel genre. This work—and Kataev's later attempted reconstruction of both it and his own role in literary politics—make it clear that the author's path to a new Soviet self led directly through the building site. Kataev's compromised participation in the project to (re)create Soviet literary space makes *Time, Forward!* an essential example of the transitional production novel.

A fictionalized account of Kataev's own trip to a construction site in the Urals in 1931, *Time, Forward!* was first published in 1932.[2] His "chronicle" detailed life at Magnitogorsk, on a gargantuan project to "reconstruct the Soviet Union's strategic steel industry" in the middle of the Siberian steppe that became one of the keys to Stalin's industrialization plan.[3] The novel includes many recognizable components of the later production genre, including shock workers, socialist competition, and "backward elements." It

197

is a classic example of a Soviet "writer at work," and the images Kataev offers there, particularly of an initially disoriented author on the construction site, are useful in a reevaluation of the production novel genre. The example of Kataev's production novel is even more relevant to a study of the genre since Kataev himself played an active role in later attempts to bring the "new Soviet man" to the writing desk. His participation on the Belomor Canal project, his work with worker-writers at the Moscow subway construction site, and his own writing career over a long and complex life provide needed insight into the production novel genre and its later effects on the course of Russian literature.

Kataev's active involvement in organized outreach programs in the 1920s and 1930s comes as no surprise. Like many intellectuals, both East and West, he supported the revolutionary cause as a desired step in the process of remaking mankind and fashioning a more just society. His later autobiographical writings assert that Kataev was intent on a literary career from his early years, and such professional ambition combined easily with his instinct for self-preservation after the revolution. In the hungry years that followed 1917, it seemed obvious for him to lend his authorial talents in service to the greater good, his natural inclination to do so becoming a necessity during the famine that swept postrevolutionary Russia. In fascinating narratives about life in Odessa and Kharkov during the civil war, for example, Kataev makes it clear that his work as a journalist, writer, and propagandist was a way to survive this difficult period. His description of official excursions to the countryside in the early 1920s makes rural life seem an attractive alternative to the privations of a city author. "After starvation in the city," Kataev contends, in the village the author "could have as much as he wanted of the grey wheat buns, the salted pork fatback, cut in cubes, the pickled green tomatoes, soup, grain, and that sort of crude but filling rural food, to which the women treated him, finally accepting the boarder, who had really lost weight in the regional center, where people used ration cards, whose meaning was mostly symbolic since almost nothing could be obtained with them."[4]

Writing about the period decades later, the older Kataev makes the surprising claim that, for urban residents, a trip to rural Russia during the civil war was comparable to an all-expense-paid visit to a Soviet sanatorium in his own era.[5] The famine that struck in 1921–22 would soon give the lie to such sentiments, however, and Kataev admits elsewhere that in comparison to the "terrible summer of Volga hunger in 1921," his current existence as respected

Soviet writer now "seems like Paradise."[6] Reminiscences from that summer of famine in Kharkov suggest that Kataev, his colleague Iurii Olesha, and many others were saved from real starvation only by their status as authors. A colleague from Kharkov, for example, later remembered their "famished and ragged" look as they arrived from Odessa barefoot to take up their new positions.[7] Their work in "agitation and propaganda for the Commissariat of Enlightenment" (*Narkompros*) gave them access to a restricted cafeteria that helped the writers survive.[8] When that official dining hall shuts down unexpectedly for two weeks "for repairs," Kataev and Olesha face the bleak prospect of starvation and death until their creative talents save them once again. Delivery this time comes in the form of a Red Army military man, who wants to order some celebratory verses to honor the birthday of the wife of his commander. Kataev and Olesha are happy to accept the commission, one of many to follow, and they use such requests for their authorial talents to keep themselves in food for a number of "years."[9] Their powerful ambition to succeed as writers makes it easy to believe the eyewitness who describes the authors as "full of creative plans. They wanted to conquer literature. They were cheerful, humorous, despite all the difficulties."[10]

In "Grass of Oblivion," (*Trava zabveniia*), a generically complex, autobiographically inspired "tale" from the late 1960s, Kataev describes the adventures of another such young "journalist," who is empowered by local Soviet authorities to carry the revolutionary word to the deepest recesses of the Russian countryside. Kataev names his fictionalized journalist "Riurik Pchelkin," but in a self-justifying move, he invites us to read through the pseudonym to see a young Valentin Kataev behind the literary pose: "Don't think that I—or, if you prefer, that young man—was on a creative sabbatical in the village," he cautions readers. "The newly born Soviet republic sent its poets on trips of a completely different sort." In addition to this depiction of Pchelkin, "Grass of Oblivion" includes Kataev's often dissembling description of his friendship with both émigré writer Ivan Bunin and loyal Soviet poet Vladimir Mayakovsky during those years. The semi-fictional work provides important insight into Kataev's motivations in the 1920s and 1930s. A self-serving and retrospective account, "Grass of Oblivion" suggests just how important a role the reorganization of space played in writers' attempts to become Soviet authors.[11]

The fictional Pchelkin's task is to enlist rural correspondents to provide the party with daily bulletins on the political situation in the vast Russian countryside. The assignment is a difficult one. The rural population, like that of the cities, was sharply divided in its many political loyalties, and not all such revolutionary agitators lived long enough to carry out their missions. According to Kataev, such "an official trip to the village could, without hyperbole, be compared to being sent to the most forward positions on the front line of the war," and his account in "Grass of Oblivion" lends credence to that claim with its tale of Pchelkin's narrow escape from death.[12] Despite the dangers involved, however, Kataev's literary stand-in accepts his assignment without question, even though to do so means he must leave his regular life and the young woman he is convinced he loves. To do anything other than answer the call is unthinkable: "it never even occurred to him to decline. In those times, any professional obligation was understood to be the fulfillment of a Sacred Revolutionary Duty."[13]

Writing years after the events, Kataev signals both the emotion he ostensibly felt then and his estrangement from those youthful sentiments in his canny use of upper-case letters to describe those "Sacred" feelings. By the time he finished this account in 1967, Kataev was a seventy-year-old man. He had lived through the purges and the Second World War, which had killed millions, including his younger brother Petrov, and he had outlasted Stalin and many of his contemporaries in post-Stalinist Russia. Sitting in his summer home in the exclusive government writers' colony of Peredelkino, Kataev was by now light-years distant from the revolutionary fervor of the propaganda campaigns of civil-war Odessa and Kharkov in which he had taken part so many decades earlier. He had finally reached the fame and material success that his mentor, Ivan Bunin, accused him of desiring while still an inexperienced young poet, and he had paid a heavy price in both personal cynicism and damaged reputation for his participation in literary politics over the years.[14] Nevertheless, writing nearly five decades after his first experiences as a literary activist, Kataev apparently still clings to that early enthusiasm, claiming "I am a son of the Revolution. Maybe a bad son. But a son all the same."[15]

This kind of devotion to the cause, or willing literary pose of such, provides context for Kataev's agreement to serve the state again in 1931. Like so many other authors of the period, Kataev set off for work on the construction site with every intention of locating exactly what he had been asked to find: clear evidence of the emerging new Soviet man. It is not surprising, then, that in the obliging production novel that resulted, Kataev introduces his readers to a significant trope of the genre: the figure of an established writer who visits the construction site and must become newly oriented to a different arrangement of the world. This new orientation in *Time, Forward!* is expressed spatially, as a new geographical configuration; writers must literally orient themselves on a different axis.[16] Built structures frame this process of reorientation, but their role is ambiguous since the existing buildings themselves are often inadequate, confining, or temporary, and they misplace as often as they ground individuals. The role of author in *Time, Forward!* is played by Georgii Vasilevich, an older writer who arrives at the construction site unprepared for what he will see. His search for a connection among the disparate images he views from his hotel window is "chronicled" in "quoted" vignettes, but like any set of photographs without an accompanying essay, these journalistic snapshots lack context.[17]

The hotel offers a panoramic view of the construction site, and the writer views the scene from all points of the compass, moving from window to window in his attempt to understand the landscape in front of him. But this 360–degree view offers the author little in the way of comprehension, and he is hampered by accustomed habits of viewing that are now outdated. The old-fashioned hotel confines him to archaic ways of seeing. "He walked up and down the stairs, coming close to the huge square-paned windows at the end of corridors. He stopped before them, regarding them as if they were magnificent engravings, severe, dark brown, slightly retouched. The windows looked out to all four sides of the world—north, west, south, east. He walked from one corridor to another, from one window to another" (99). His search for a point of view from which to make sense of the landscape yields only a dizzying series of unrelated images that refuse to coalesce. "Around him turned the distant, segmented panorama of the construction site, studded with a multitude of stark, sharply limned fine details. Barracks, tents, roads, posts, insulators, thermo-electric plants, cranes, excavators, trenches, mounds, wagons, scaffoldings, mountains, hills, grass, smoke, refuse, horses . . ." (99).

This list of images from the real-life construction site would soon become a set of required clichés for the production novel itself; beginning writers, even some of those taught by Kataev himself, were encouraged to use the vocabulary of the new Soviet state in "authentic" personal histories. Kataev's later writings suggest his own shrewd awareness of that fact when he makes a similar comment about the clichés of the lyric poetry he fancied as a younger author.

Commenting on his own painfully mechanical, early efforts to become a writer, Kataev notes that he even had

> the idiotic idea that it was possible to compose a list of all the possi-
> ble rhyme pairs in a little student notebook "For Words" and then to
> memorize them all like the multiplication tables. All the possible po-
> etic meters—iambic, trochaic, amphibrach—which wasn't a real big
> deal, by the way, and the thing would be a piece of cake! As for the
> content itself, it was commonly known and completely accessible:
> dreams, daydreams, sadness, melancholy, love, garden, moon, river,
> rendezvous, passion, flowers, autumn, spring, winter, summer (less
> frequently), kiss, night, morning, evening, noon (less frequently), be-
> trayal, bitter fate . . .[18]

As an older writer in the autobiographical tale that he called
"Grass of Oblivion," Kataev appears to mock his own notion that
literature can be crafted mechanically. Nevertheless, he remembers
his own attempts to write stirring poetry with the help of just such
a crib sheet of images and concepts quite vividly. And the episodic
nature of his production novel suggests that, hard at work in Magnitogorsk, he was busy cobbling together just such a series of ready-
made vignettes to capture life on the construction site. Ilf and Petrov
had parodied the approach of such piecemeal literature in *The
Golden Calf*, but Kataev's fictional double uses that very model in
Time, Forward! And it is not surprising that he does: certain images
were essential to the literature of the post-revolutionary period, and
authors could use them to catalyze their narrative.[19]

Kataev's authorial double is a "novelist," or "*belletrist.*" In his
first dispatch from the front line of socialist labor, Georgii Vasilevich provides his readers with another such catalog of the images
and concepts that hopeful writers will need to begin their own
production novels. But Kataev's fictional author, like the worker-
writers who will follow him, must come to an understanding of the
truth as a result of participation in the process of physical labor,
and so his first glance at the new Soviet landscape is initially a
"puzzle." Writing rapidly to capture the scene, he notes,

> "From my window, the world opens like a rebus. I see a multitude of
> figures—people, horses, wicker, cables, machines, steam, letters, clouds,
> mountains, cars, water . . . But I do not understand their relationship.
> But I know that this interrelationship exists. There is some all-power-
> ful interaction. This is absolutely indubitable. I know it. I believe it. But
> I do not see it. And that is exasperating. To believe and not to see! I am

tortured by the thought. I try hard, but I cannot solve the rebus . . ." He underlined the word "believe" and the word "see" twice. (90)

The "rebus" over which the writer puzzles is clear to us in hindsight. The sleight of hand that this puzzle involves would soon become the commonplace Socialist Realist formula for depicting reality in a process of revolutionary development. Kataev alludes to the ease with which such a trick might eventually be accomplished in his early production novel: any experienced writer can turn the desire to believe—the Russian word *"verit'"*—into the ability to see—*"videt'"*—with just a stroke or two.

Such a transition will take practice, however, and Kataev obliges readers with a detailed description of the transformation that his author must undergo on-site. In his struggle for understanding, Georgii Vasilevich first resorts to an outdated framing device—the eighteenth-century engraving—to try to bring order to the chaos he sees in front of him. His attempts to do so, however, only further emphasize his own inability to find what is significant in the landscape that confronts him. By "framing" the construction site as he views it from the hotel, he attempts to use the window as an improvised Claude glass, that marvelous eighteenth-century hand-held frame invented to capture chaotic nature in digestible scenes for the purview of upper-class English tourists.[20] But the new world of Stalinist industrialization is far from the tamed landscapes of England's Lake District, and Kataev's writer finds the device completely inadequate to contend with the unedited twentieth-century chaos he finds outside his hotel window.

The construction site spreads out before the author, but he is trapped in a building from the past, and the outdated structure is filled with objects from a mode of existence that is soon to be irrelevant. The debris of the old world sits motionless and useless in front of the heroic landscape of the building site. The items of a now cast-off *byt*, many already familiar to us from descriptions in Olesha, Shaginian, Pilniak, and Ilf and Petrov, are incongruous and unneeded in the struggle for a new world. "He saw shining Slavic wardrobes with mirrors; iron beds with nickel-plated knobs; shaky oval tables; wash-basins; wooden lamp stands covered with light, round, tautly-stretched, hand-made, colorful silken lamp shades. All of this hotel furniture had been bought at the market for second-hand goods. It was commonplace, prosaic, incongruous and strange in the midst of this ancient, sultry Pugachev steppe . . ." (99). In this short passage alone, Kataev reveals his accomplished mastery of the developing production novel genre. By subtly abandoning the clutter and triviality of the old world, he allows his readers to prepare for a new mode of existence. The new world Kataev imagines is one appropriately distant from the tainted recent past of Slavic wardrobes and tacky lamp shades. In its wisdom, passion, and daring, the world—at once both ancient and new—is now tied to the solidity of a proud and powerful but decidedly ahistorical past. On this ancient site made new, the eighteenth-century rebel Pugachev has been domesticated, "reforged," and deployed to build a new existence for all to enjoy.

Still trying to make sense of the bewildering landscape from his hotel window, Kataev's writer appropriates a more modern tool as an aid. His use of "field artillery" binoculars to try to understand the scene before him evokes the metaphor of war that was popular in much Soviet rhetoric from these years.[21] He now wields German-made prismatic binoculars, but Georgii Vasilevich is still unable to bring the entire scene into focus: "the undulating vista flooded toward him, swelling fabulously and flowing out of his circular field of vision in all directions" (99). Although he attempts to move the binoculars "slowly and smoothly," he can not come to terms with what he sees before him and "the objects—the posts, the roofs, the wagons, the uneven surface of the ground, the cars, the culverts—sped by with a purposeful mad speed, dazzling and flowing together from right to left, merging in the cone of an endless carousel" (100). He is just as unsuccessful with the even more contemporary comparison to photography that he evokes to make sense of what he sees: "Tiny human figures—the further away the tinier—and their microscopic shadows scattered sparsely over the tremendous landscape, seemed completely immobile, like a photograph" (99). The static image of the photograph, while more modern than the engraving with which the passage began, is nevertheless inadequate to the endlessly evolving images of the construction site.

As a result, Kataev's author, like Kataev himself, finds it necessary to leave his own zone of comfort and thrust himself directly into the landscape he has tried unsuccessfully to observe from afar. Georgii Vasilevich's willingness to leave his hotel, which is too hot and uncomfortable to provide real shelter anyway, mirrors that of Kataev and other writers, who were coerced or coaxed into abandoning their writing desks for "direct participation" in "the struggle to fulfill the economic plan of the decisive year of the five-year plan."[22] Writers who wanted to answer the "call of shock-workers into literature" had no trouble finding a way to create the required

"Magnitostroi of literature."[23] They had merely to visit Magnito-gorsk, as Kataev had, or another construction site of importance to the cause, and they too could soon contribute to the shared goal of building Soviet culture. Their success, it was implied, relied pri-marily on their strength of character and willingness to harness their talents.[24] For writers like Kataev, who had been mobilized by the authorities for literary service since nearly the first days of So-viet power, such a call to cooperate would have been natural. And for authors with less seniority in the common cause, enrollment as literary production workers afforded a way to demonstrate their trustworthiness and establish Soviet credentials.

This is not to suggest that the process of creating such literature was easy, even for those writers equipped with the list of requisite nouns and verbs. Experienced authors devoted to the cause and newcomers alike sometimes found it difficult to fulfill the social or-der (*sotsial'nyi zakaz*) as required, and many felt out of place on the construction site and poorly equipped for the technical tasks they were now being asked both to do and to describe.[25] Kataev captures this feeling succinctly in a multivalent image from *Time, Forward!* that initially confronts the writer figure there. The first sight that greets Georgii Vasilevich once he ventures outside of his hotel to explore the new landscape is a jarring, seemingly inexpli-cable one: an elephant being led down the road. This surprising detail—an elephant in the middle of a construction site in Siberia—almost fails to register. Since the writer has no way to make sense of the landscape, the otherwise striking image is just one more in the long list of sights that do not fully register. "Georgii Vasilevich was not surprised," we learn. "Anything might be expected here. He only thought mechanically: Where did the elephant come from? Where was he being taken? Why? Who knew?" Trying to describe these incidents later, he tears the page from his notebook. "Creep-ing empiricism," he comments harshly. (104)[26]

Kataev managed, of course, to save the author's page by cata-loging its contents before "destroying" it. Having accomplished that feat, however, he needed to provide a new frame for his read-ers. As he developed both his own and Georgii Vasilevich's narra-tives, was Kataev thinking of the image of Hannibal's elephants and drawing a veiled comparison to Stalin's own growing empire? Did he have in mind the well-known Soviet prison camp, Solovki, and its official acronym, which formed the Russian word for ele-phant—*Solovetskii lager' osobogo naznachenia*, or SLON?[27] Was he hinting at the "eastern" despotism that made such a huge and, in many ways, brutal project thinkable, or was he alluding, perhaps, to the inappropriateness of such an out-of-place gesture? Any of these interpretations is possible. As these early production novels demonstrate, even committed individuals had their moments of doubt, and the use of Aesopian language to elude the censor had been an accepted technique in Russian literature since tsarist times.

It is possible that Kataev had all these interpretations in mind simultaneously, as he attempted to negotiate the boundaries of the new genre by styling himself as both a committed Soviet writer and an independent thinker. As we will see, that is precisely the stance he would adopt on the official trip writers made to the Belomor canal just a few years later.[28] As surprising as it may seem, then, Kataev's complex motivation in *Time, Forward!* apparently included a veiled reference to autocratic despotism in this "written-to-order" production novel. Kataev negotiates this landscape gingerly, providing an explanation for both the elephant and the overall plan of construction. When we return to the image of the elephant in the penultimate chapter of *Time, Forward!*, it is to learn that the scene with the elephant is ostensibly one of the few fabricated incidents in the book. A letter from "V. K." to a colleague on the "real" construction site that is now included in Valentin Kataev's own production novel establishes the genesis of the image: "I made [the elephant] up. But couldn't it have been? Of course, it could have been! More than that, it should have been" (337). Despite apparent disapproval of Georgii Vasilevich's episodic approach, Kataev has constructed his chronicle from the same blueprint of "creeping empiricism."[29] But unlike his fictional stand-in, Kataev understands the process of construction and can add to the landscape in confidence that his perspective is the correct one. "Perhaps they have an elephant by now," he notes boldly. "If so, please write me about it" (337).

It is the city of Paris that teaches both Georgii Vasilevich and Valentin Kataev this admittedly negative lesson. "Do you remember our talks about Paris?" the character "V.K." asks in a "letter of the author of this chronicle" that Kataev includes at the end of *Time, Forward!* "Imagine! Paris is not what we thought it was. I have not found what I sought, what I dreamed of." What he finds instead is "much greater," however: the link to human memory that Umberto Eco calls the "deeper bond between architecture and literature."[30] "In Paris," Kataev comments, "I have found a sense of history. . . . May not a single trifle, not even the smallest detail of our inimitable, heroic days of the first Five-Year Plan be forgotten!" (340).

Here, too, Kataev ties the fictional to the real as he attempts to press both into service for the production novel he is faithfully constructing. First in Kataev's list of connections between "fact" and "fiction" is his friendship with Mayakovsky, who originated the title *Time, Forward!* and ostensibly presented it as a gift to the younger prose writer. Kataev mentions this episode in his autobiographical "tale" about the poet. Mayakovsky has just composed his own work, "March of Time," and he recites it for Kataev as they walk down the street in Moscow together. Kataev is enchanted by the piece and remarks that it contains the "very essence of contemporary life. Time, forward! A brilliant name for a novel about the Five-Year Plan." In Kataev's account, Mayakovsky's reported response is both generous and insistent: "Then you will write it, that novel. About Magnitostroi if nothing else. The title *Time, Forward!* is my gift."[31]

Interwoven among such fragments of memoir in "Grass of Oblivion," Kataev includes several fictional story lines that buoy the historical material and subtly question the division between the actual and the invented. In a complex and sophisticated narrative, Kataev is able to combine elegiac passages about his real life with pronounced regret for certain of his own fictional characters. As he mourns his own inability to provide favorite characters with the rich and complex life they deserve, we can sense a palpable feeling of regret for his own missed chances and for his failure, as he sees it, to save either Ivan Bunin or Vladimir Mayakovsky from what he perceives as their tragic fates. Kataev struggles to accommodate stories of both the émigré Bunin and the revolutionary Mayakovsky in his own complex narrative written decades later. Still affected by calls to adopt an unforgiving "us vs. them" approach, Kataev looks, instead, for a way to integrate more of the richness of history—with its contradictions and compromises—into a single biography.[32] Just as he managed to save Georgii Vasilevich's page in *Time, Forward!* while ostensibly destroying it, here, too, Kataev succeeds in recreating his own versions of both Bunin and Mayakovsky, as he recounts his life without them.

His sketch of the life of a favorite, fictional revolutionary heroine is similarly ambivalent. Even as he writes her fictional life and demonstrates the method by which such a character is created, Kataev simultaneously regrets his inability to do so. His invented heroine, who eventually receives the name of Klavdiia Zaremba, appears first in "Grass of Oblivion" as a little girl Bunin instructs the young Kataev to describe. Her story and her narrative importance then grow with Kataev's own personal history and with the account of revolutionary Russian history that he weaves from both "factual" and "fictional" details. We can read a complicated literary history in the evolution of Klavdiia's image. She moves effortlessly from life as an incidental figure—used as a writing exercise in Kataev's schoolboy notebook—to a variety of the many literary poses her author and her country need her to adopt. Thus, she evolves over the course of Kataev's highly fragmented narrative into a young student with notions of political reform, a love interest for both the writer and his competitive young colleague, a steely revolutionary who is willing to betray her own lover for the cause, and, finally, a matronly grandmother who is facing old age heroically, if somewhat wistfully, in the town of Magnitogorsk.

The twists and turns of Klavdiia's fictional life intertwine with both Kataev's treatment of his own day-to-day existence over the decades and his professional life as a developing Soviet writer. When he needs a foil for his propagandistic excursions into the Russian countryside, for example, Klavdiia appears as the girlfriend whose own understanding of the revolutionary cause is just developing. Soon Kataev is reminded of the calls his real-life "old comrade and friend" Sergei Ingulov made for writers to produce a new revolutionary heroine, and Klavdiia assumes a new personality, made to order for the era. "Authors and authoresses, tragedians and poets, Acmeists and neoclassicists, about whom are you telling us?" Ingulov entreats Kataev and other writers of the time. "Poets and poetesses, you were able to proclaim the love of Dante and Beatrice. Can the tragic love of a staff officer and a young woman from the Party School really be beyond your grasp?"[33] No sooner has Kataev remembered Ingulov, than, as if by fortunate happenstance, Klavdiia arrives to fall in love with a captain, whose secret counterrevolutionary intentions will make it necessary for her to betray him. Ingulov, whose reputation as literary politician was as compromised as Kataev's,[34] was already dead by the time "Grass of Oblivion" was being composed, but the revolutionary heroine he inspired lives on in Kataev's manuscript.

It is only a matter of time before Klavdiia mutates into the "leader of a brigade of cement mixers," tanned and fit, as she stands on the steppe near Magnitogorsk in the "old leather jacket" and "red kerchief" that mark her as a true believer. Kataev offers the now overused images of Party membership almost apologetically in "Grass of Oblivion," his seeming reluctance explained in part by the fact that he has already tread this ground at length in his earlier production novel. What makes the Magnitogorsk episode in Klavdiia's life unusual, however, is that Kataev insists that she is the fictional descendent of both the émigré Bunin and the revolutionary Maya-kovsky. "Describe a sparrow," he recalls Bunin advising him. "De-scribe a little girl." Yet the result, Kataev complains, is completely unexpected: "But how did it turn out? I described a little girl, and she turned out to be the 'young woman from the Party School,' a heroine of the Revolution. But Mayakovsky taught me the Revolu-tion. 'Describe Magnitogorsk. Time, forward!' And the young woman from the Party School, having returned from Mongolia, turned into the leader of a brigade of cement mixers."[35]

Despite her complicated heritage, then, Klavdiia is clearly a So-viet heroine, and, as such, she must be depicted as ultimately op-posed to the world that Bunin represents. Kataev's understanding of that point explains his motivation in creating Klavdiia, his own production novel, and the many other works he wrote to order over a long, productive, though decidedly compromised career in Stalin's Russia. Near the end of "Grass of Oblivion," Kataev notes laconically that "I learned to see the world from both Bunin and Mayakovsky . . . But that world varied."[36]

Kataev identifies that variation as the essential difference be-tween Bunin's life and his own. As Kataev describes it, the path Bunin took is the path of irrelevance, "childish illusion." Hoping to become a "completely independent, pure artist," Bunin turns his back on society, but that stance wrongly frees him from the "moral pressure from outside" that is actually necessary, according to Kataev, to all great artists. Although he was able to reach the "high-est level of technical mastery" by the end of his life, Bunin "stopped choosing points at which to apply his skills, his spiritual strengths." As a result, "artistic creation stopped being a battle for him and turned into the simple habit of representation, an exercise of imag-ination." To avoid such a fate, Kataev implies, the writer should ac-cept engagement with the world around him, embracing "moral pressure from outside" and stoically fulfilling every task that "so-ciety" and the "motherland" assign. To refuse to do so is to risk falling victim to the "thousand-headed hydra of empiricism" that both Goethe and Georgii Vasilevich in *Time, Forward!* urge writ-ers to slay. Without societal pressure, the writer risks becoming a deep-water fish that, according to Kataev, will be "torn to pieces" when it finds itself in only shallow water, no longer subject to the healthy pressures of the deep sea.[37]

Kataev's handling of his material is complex and skillful, and his adroit use of fact and fiction makes the position of a Soviet writer—torn now this direction, now that in the 1920s and 1930s—more understandable and more sympathetic, as Kataev clearly intends.

The semi-fictional, semiautobiographical approach allows Kataev to provide accounts of Bunin, Mayakovsky, Russian émigré life in Paris, and the everyday life of the creative intelligentsia in Moscow in the 1920s and 1930s in the context of his own creative method. Thus, a trip Kataev takes to Paris allows him to meet and converse with real individuals he remembers from his youth in Odessa at the same time that it unexpectedly puts him in touch with the fictional Klavdiia's former lover. That man, sentenced to death by firing squad in Odessa on the basis of Klavdiia's testimony, has managed to escape his fate in a coincidence worthy of the best of Kataev's fiction. The author's explanation of the character's overly theatrical escape from righteous Soviet retribution, however, is much like the one he gives to explain the elephant in Magnitogorsk: "And, really, why not, after all? There were such cases in that era." Now reduced to selling flowers outside a Parisian cemetery for a living, the former counterrevolutionary can barely recall the name of his former lover, Kataev's fictional Klavdiia, but he knows that his life is nearly meaningless without the cause she represents. As Kataev departs, he buys a bouquet from the man to place on Bunin's real grave, a monument to both literary creation and real lost dreams.[38]

Kataev weaves this sophisticated narrative to include both real events and episodes he seems only to wish had taken place. He is writing, after all, in the late 1960s, long after the deaths of both his mentors, and his memories of those two men are touched with the melancholy that attends thoughts of lost communication and missed opportunities. Elegiac is the tone he eventually adopts toward his fictional character Klavdiia, as well. She scolds him, for example, for not looking her up on a recent trip to Magnitogorsk. Over the course of the narrative, which is developed in fits and starts, she gains weight and loses her teeth with advancing age. Ailing in retirement, she is soon reduced to babysitting her grandchildren and giving lectures on the history of the Party for the local housing authority. Nevertheless, she retains her youthful enthusiasm and her complicated but unwavering devotion to the cause. In a letter to Kataev, she confesses both her true love for the spy she betrayed and her unending belief that her actions were correct: "I loved him and I have never forgotten about him for a moment my entire life. . . . But my conscience is clear before the Revolution and before my self: I didn't betray him. He betrayed the Motherland. And we punished him. It was only fair. I don't regret it. He deserved death. But I loved him nevertheless. And if you want to know the truth, I still love him."[39]

Klavdiia's "deathbed" confession reflects, then, Kataev's own complicated relationship to the demands made of Soviet writers in the 1920s, 1930s, and beyond. Convinced of the righteousness of their positions, they are nevertheless tormented, not by remorse ("I don't regret it"), but by feelings of loss and grief for the loves, friendships, and lives that their own actions had "inevitably" destroyed. Not surprisingly, Kataev redeems both himself and Klavdiia by returning to the notion of creative fervor in service to the cause that joined them initially. Another trip to Paris finds him working feverishly on the manuscript of *Time, Forward!* which Mayakovsky inspired shortly before his untimely suicide in 1930. Kataev now "misses Mayakovsky" in Paris, but communes with his spirit by working on his production novel in the very café the poet had frequented. Mayakovsky's figure, Kataev tells us, "stood invisibly near my little table." As Kataev writes the work that Mayakovsky and the times had demanded of him, the poet's "'March of Time' thundered over the Soviet land, which had begun the unheard-of feat of labor of the first Five-Year Plans. I was completely filled with the rhythms of socialism being born and couldn't tear myself away from my chronicle, and I wrote and wrote and wrote wherever possible on anything that came to hand—a notebook, paper napkins, packs of cigarettes . . ."[40]

This belief in a shared cause is more important than the individual, whose contribution is valued but inevitably insufficient. The goal, like time itself, presses relentlessly forward, leaving poets and revolutionaries—both in Russia and émigré Paris—far behind. In no time at all, Kataev finds himself burying the "young woman from the Party School" he has just reanimated. Her moment has passed, and she will be laid to rest in the city of Magnitogorsk, which Kataev can now call the "city of realized dreams." He finds solace for his sadness over both her death and his own impending fate by adopting an Olympian perspective: "I soon learned that she had died and I imagined . . . no, not imagined, but created a view of the Urals from several kilometers up." The marvelous bird's-eye view he imagines elides smoothly into a landing he is soon making at the Magnitogorsk airport, where "every tree and every bush—elm, lilac, poplar, linden—which I had seen as saplings" is now "a miracle of winter beauty." This mature landscape is "as beautiful as a fairy-tale in its imperial Russian ermine trimmings." It appears miraculously out of the winter steppe to accompany Klavdiia on a journey to her final resting place in the city. As Klavdiia is interred in this realized metaphor of her own and Kataev's revolutionary dreams, the old world is also laid to rest, like the "mysterious city of Kitezh," as Magnitogorsk arises out of the winter steppe to replace Russian folklore and Pushkin's literary fantasies with a triumphant communist reality.[41]

> Every tree and every bush—elm, lilac, poplar, linden—which I had seen when they were still saplings was now a miracle of winter beauty: some of them looking like magical creations of Russian lace makers, others standing alongside the creamy and rosy multi-storied housing complexes, like white marble sculptures, still others remarkably similar to the delicate branches of the lime-coral of a bluish, underwater kingdom . . . and the city of Magnitogorsk, sinking in clouds of sunny mist, was as beautiful as a fairy tale in its imperial Russian ermine raiment—the city of realized dreams . . . (274)

Hand-in-hand with the story of the construction of the new city, then, goes the tale of the end of the old. This is a process that Kataev treats at length in his fictional work, and it consumed much of his daily activity at the beginning of the 1930s as well. *Literaturnia gazeta*, for example, noted Kataev's participation, along with that of Vsevolod Ivanov, in the "All-Union Day of the Shock Worker" in October 1930 where the authors visited the opening of the Soviet government's first watch factory and shared their enthusiasm about that achievement with the workers themselves. Just a month later, the newspaper carried word of plans by the workers from the "Red Proletariat" factory to "adopt certain authors" in order to bring their creative endeavors closer to the process of production. The proposal was intended to be of mutual benefit: factory workers would read and discuss the authors' work before publication, carefully "following every step of their creation"; writers, in return, would have complete access to the factory, its shock workers, and the production process. Authors, including Kataev, Olesha, A. Bezymenskii, and others, would "be incorporated into the life of the factory, into cultural work, into the real battle to fulfill the Five-Year Plan in four years."[42]

In that year and the next, Kataev visited the construction sites of a hydroelectric station at Dneprostroi, a factory for agricultural equipment, Rostsel'mash, near Rostov-on-Don, and Magnitogorsk in the company of well-connected proletarian poet Demian Bednyi. Like so many other authors in these transitional years, Bednyi traveled to a number of building sites throughout the Soviet Union to "see what was being built, everything that is being done in the country." Bednyi's excursions took place in a private railroad car, which, Kataev reports, he was always happy to share with his friends. Kataev's later reminiscences describe Bednyi as almost a force of nature in the 1920s and early 1930s. "He had enormous stature then," Kataev noted in a private conversation with biographer L. Skorino in 1962. "He didn't hold any official position, had no particular rank. He was . . . Demian Bednyi. That's who he was."[43]

Bednyi's special status included a residence in the Kremlin itself, which Kataev viewed with awe. "I visited his home," Kataev told Skorino. "It was interesting. He wrote out a pass—they were already checking very strictly—and I walked along the long, white corridor that led to the other apartments—Voroshilov's, Molotov's, and others . . ." Clearly impressed even years later, Kataev views Bednyi in almost mythic terms. Engaged in the great shared cause, he nevertheless seemed above the petty literary squabbling that tormented less independent writers at the time. "He wielded colossal authority in literary circles," Kataev confided in Skorino, "but he wasn't a member of RAPP and took no part in the administration of writers or journals."[44]

Kataev's nostalgic memories of Bednyi are part of the complicated context he imagines for his own activity, and they gain a peculiar piquancy in light of the fact that Bednyi himself was later toppled from his literary perch.[45] Despite the fall from grace, Bednyi provided the older Kataev with the image of an authorial figure powerful enough to incorporate the contradictions of the revolution. This notion must have been appealing to Kataev as he struggled to make his own peace with the moral contradictions of life as an "engineer of human souls." Kataev's personal commitment to the greater cause would be frequently tested in the years that followed publication of his production novel, and his attempts to justify the violence of the revolutionary struggle were part of an effort in the post-Stalinist period to understand his own complex role in constructing Soviet culture, even its Stalinist chapters.

Kataev's participation in an official trip to the Belomor Canal in northern Karelia in August 1933, for example, required that he sing the praises of both forced labor and Stalin's autocratic rule. That journey, made in the company of 119 other officially sanctioned Soviet authors, resulted in a massive, lavishly produced, and collectively authored history of the construction of the canal, which was built, as was Magnitogorsk in part, with the labor of prison camp inmates. The Belomor volume, meant to publicize the canal, demonstrate the rehabilitation of its prisoners, and lionize its "architect," Joseph Stalin, appeared in January 1934. A first pressrun of four thousand was triumphantly distributed to delegates at the Seventeenth Communist Party Congress, the "Congress of Victors."[46]

Kataev's participation on the Belomor trip was allegedly marked by a principled stand he adopted in conversation with canal boss Semyon Firin. His ostensibly pointed questioning of Firin was reported years later by Aleksandr Avdeenko, a shock worker and newly minted author from Magnitogorsk who had been pulled from relative obscurity and asked to join the writers' brigade on the Belomor Canal. Kataev's reported conversation included just a few inquires as to the likelihood of prisoner deaths on the canal and the possible location of the cemeteries that held their bodies. The questions seem mild, almost innocent in retrospect, but they allegedly caused Avdeenko and others real unease at the time. "Looks like your humble servant has done something foolish [smorozil glupost']," Kataev is reported as saying, after his inquiries have caused the normally "cheerful and hospitable Firin" to "grow stern" and walk away. "That happens with me," Kataev confesses. "I'm nonparty, after all, not properly reined in [ne podkovan]. Haven't yet mastered the dialectical unity of contradictions. What can you expect from me?"[47]

Kataev's reported decision to stay longer than the other writers on the canal similarly pits him against Firin in a seeming battle for control of the real story. As the organized group of authors heads back to Moscow on their specially appointed train, Kataev suddenly challenges the Chekist boss, asserting that they have been given too little opportunity to see the canal. "Too little!" Avdeenko reports Kataev as saying. "You need a week, a month to see such a marvel. And not in such a huge herd either, a crowd of 120 strong, but alone, sensibly, compassionately, deliberately." Asked by Firin to explain his meaning, Kataev notes that "such a holiday train doesn't give a true impression of the life of the canal soldiers."

In Aleksandr Avdeenko's account of the incident, Firin fixes Kataev with a chilling stare before replying. "You seem to want to say that right now they are turning off the parade lights on the canal, taking down the decorations, washing off the makeup?" Kataev backs away from a direct challenge: "Of course not. Of course not. I had nothing like that in mind. I've said what I wanted to say. Nothing more." But Firin insists: "I'll give you the opportunity to see Medvezh'gorsk [the location of canal construction headquarters] as it normally is. I'll send you back. This very minute! Will you go?" According to Avdeenko, Kataev's writer colleagues expected him to extract himself from the situation with a well-placed jest, but they are deceived. Looking "impertinently" at the Chekist, Kataev accepts the offer: "And you think I will refuse!? I'll go."[48]

Kataev's insistence seems to have struck the younger Avdeenko much as Demian Bednyi's example impressed the older writer. According to Avdeenko, Kataev had "conquered" his heart and could capture the "portrait of a man, the landscape of construction in two or three lines." *Time, Forward!* was incomparable, in Avdeenko's opinion, worthy of both the single fevered reading and the later careful study that he had given it. On the canal trip itself, the author was "noisy, always jolly." "Narrowing his eyes," the author "spoke sharply" and "listened to others impatiently, frequently interrupting." It is supposedly such decisiveness that leads the writer into conflict with Firin. When the train stops at a nondescript station in the middle of nowhere, Kataev departs "briskly," leaving the "warm, bright car" for a wet and windy return trip to the prison camp in the company of the secret police. Although Avdeenko's essay offers no further clues as to what Kataev's extended trip taught him, he notes that Firin has supplied the stubborn writer with vodka and sausage for the trip. The author's final word on the venture, as Avdeenko himself points out, was his "rapturous" participation in the volume itself.[49]

Avdeenko's own example suggests how genuine enthusiasm might have been possible, despite the costs of such endeavors, which were so obvious that even Firin's strenuous efforts could not camouflage them all. A working-class orphan (*bezprizornyi*) in postrevolutionary Russia, Avdeenko was the very personification of the downtrodden masses the revolution was meant to emancipate, and his personal experiences on the construction site in Magnitogorsk seem to validate the fictional picture of Russia remaking itself. Here was a character from Kataev's *Time, Forward!* made flesh and blood, and Avdeenko's testimony that he "had been infected with construction zeal for life" appeared to add depth and verisimilitude to that portrait. With his own disadvantaged childhood and experience as a laborer in Magnitogorsk as background, Avdeenko saw the construction site as deliverance for his entire society. "Every building site seemed to be the center of the world," he notes in his description of a "rally of shock-worker canal soldiers" he and other writers were asked to attend shortly after the official trip to the Belomor canal. "What is most interesting, life-affirming is being created right now on countless of our construction sites, full of conflict, courage, heroism." With such heroic testimony by a willing cast of characters is it any wonder that Gorky himself was moved to tears?[50]

Writing years later, Avdeenko attempts to describe the events in question through the eyes of his younger self, who believed then "that the Belomor Canal and the future Moscow-Volga canal were a marvel of creation." Even in retrospect, Avdeenko explains his own understanding at the time as a complicated mix of "self-deception, self-blinding and, along with that, legitimate pride in what had already really been accomplished by your nation and yourself."[51] As such comments make clear, writers were often swept along in these years on successive waves of enthusiasm and terror, overcoming or abandoning their objections in a broader context of unwavering support for the regime. In his own retrospective account, author Konstantin Simonov tries to explain his relative indifference to the arrest and execution of his beloved aunt in 1937: "perhaps I thought: 'You can't make an omelette without breaking eggs.' This acceptance seems more cynical today than it felt then, when the Revolution, the breaking up of the old society, was still not so distant in people's memories."[52]

The stance of clear-eyed but ultimately loyal supporter of the regime would be more and more difficult to maintain as the decade continued, of course. If Kataev was really fashioning such a pose for himself with his behavior on the canal trip, it was a precarious position he adopted. His attempts many years later to (re)write his own creative history and to explain, for example, his friendships with both the émigré Bunin and the committed revolutionary Mayakovsky left the author all too aware that even mild objections could place him "on the edge, and it's a very dangerous edge."[53] Demian Bednyi's example must have helped Kataev to come to terms with his position in the overlapping roles of writer and government employee. His comments to a biographer in his later years suggest an author who has overcome any perceived dichotomy in such a stance. "In his creative life," Kataev tells B. E. Galanov,

> an artist always perceives himself to be a government man. Otherwise what kind of a creator is he! They impressed upon us: there's a scale for government people. A table of ranks. Who is a government man? Stalin, of course. His closest comrades-in-arms, the ministers. And there's a place for the artist in this system—as an executive (*ispolnitel'*). To depict what the "ranked" government people want from you. They thought for you and decided for you, along government lines (*oni za tebia i podumali i reshili po-gosudarstvennomu*).[54]

The sympathetic biographer, publishing his study of the "Master" Kataev in 1989, is not entirely certain how to handle such an admission. In the heady days of perestroika, Kataev's depiction of writers as obliging servants to Stalin's will was shamefully dated, and, as a result, Galanov includes it only as a stray, de-contextualized comment near the end of the biography he is crafting. And yet the image Kataev conjured of an author in service to a greater cause was the one he had worn proudly for decades. From his early sorties as an agitator for ROSTA to his late semiautobiographical musings as a mature writer, Kataev had been enrolled in government service, wearing his rank with genuine pride.[55] As a Soviet writer, Kataev, like so many of his colleagues, was willing to follow orders, and he saw no contradiction to his authorial responsibilities in that.

This explains Kataev's participation on March 30, 1934, in a literary evening that had been organized by the publishing house "The History of the Metro." Kataev would be playing the part he had written for his own character Georgii Vasilevich in *Time, Forward!* The fictional portrait there of an aging writer who finds new creative inspiration on a Soviet building site rang true to life, even for Kataev, who was still relatively young at age thirty-seven. The March "rally," or *slet*, brought Kataev to share his authorial expertise with a large group of workers engaged in the construction of the Moscow subway. The subway site was one of Russia's most prestigious building projects, and Kataev's visit at the peak of the country's drive to industrialize was heavily invested with political significance. Kataev's presence at the rally was part of a much larger campaign orchestrated to capture and publicize the history of Soviet construction. The author was one of many who would be called to serve.[56]

Although this March meeting was taking place only months after the Belomor volume was published, it was Kataev's experience far from northern Karelia, beyond the Urals at an industrial construction site in Siberia that seemed to be of most interest to the audience gathered. *Time, Forward!* was one of the best examples of the early production novel, and it was expected to provide would-be proletarian authors from the subway project with an appropriate model for their own soon-to-be-composed versions of Soviet construction. The semi-fictional approach that Kataev had adopted in his "chronicle" must have seemed ideal for this latest experiment in collective authorship, especially with its emphasis on the many ways individual stories contributed to a shared project. Kataev's close focus on a single brigade in Magnitogorsk and his belief in the importance of that individual story to the larger Soviet mosaic made his approach appear both ideologically palatable and artistically achievable.

The individuals who packed the auditorium to hear Kataev that evening were themselves a respected, if motley group. They had been specially chosen to provide worker voices to the joint history of the subway construction that was now being planned, and some of the laborers were no doubt recent transplants from the trauma-tized Russian countryside. Often only semiliterate themselves, many workers were drawn to the city and to the project by the promise of work, advancement, better food, or housing. Male and female, Russian, Ukrainian, Georgian, and Kazakh, young and old, the workers on the Moscow subway construction site were as di-verse as all of the Soviet Union itself.

Most of the laborers on the Metro site, however, had been mobi-lized by the Communist youth organization, the Komsomol, from institutes of higher learning for the dangerous but highly valued task of building Russia's first subway system. These enthusiastic but mostly untrained students comprised many of the over seventy-five thousand workers who made the Metro project the largest con-struction site in the Soviet Union at the time.[57] Others on the site were experienced workers, who brought technical skills otherwise in painfully short supply as the Soviet Union entered the middle of its second Five-Year Plan. Still others, including engineers and in-tellectuals trained under the old regime and, perhaps, peasants es-caping an even more hostile rural environment, were undoubtedly looking for a way to remake their pasts by participating in this vis-ible symbol of the country's future.

Moscow Party boss Lazar Kaganovich captured the all-encom-passing nature of the subway enterprise with his slogan, soon ubiq-uitous throughout the capital, "The entire country is building the Metro!" Some of the audience that night in March might have been released from the day's physical labor in order to participate in this literary meeting, a clear sign of the importance awarded the ven-ture. For others, the discussion came at the end of a long working day in the subway shafts, where conditions were almost unimag-inably difficult, wet, and dangerous. For some of those workers, participation in a literary event must have been an unwelcome bur-den at the end of a tiring day or still more evidence of administra-tive caprice, just one more campaign dreamed up by meddlesome managers.

This was not the first such meeting nor would it be the last. The upcoming congress of Soviet writers, the first for the new Soviet Writers' Union, was scheduled for August, and that meant that most of 1934 would be given over to organizational meetings of just this sort.[58] The "rally" of March 30, 1934—the term is indicative of the promotional nature of the event—was just one of a series of organizational meetings intended to turn the planned public history of the subway into reality. The main event of the March 30 rally was a question-and-answer session at which newly enlisted working-class writers could quiz established authors for help in writing about the construction of a new society. The entrance of the authentic proletariat into literature was seen as a crucial step in the development of Soviet art and a new way of life, and Kataev was one of many who would be asked to assist in ensuring its success.[59]

The call for workers themselves to enter the ranks of literature was "one of the most important pages in the history of establishing Soviet culture," according to Evgeny Dobrenko, particularly for the Russian Association of Proletarian Writers (RAPP), which produced no literature on its own but "occupied itself with the production of writers."[60] The idea that established writers could train their proletarian colleagues had gained special currency by the early 1930s, and workers were to create literary works in which they themselves played the starring role. Dobrenko notes that during the mid-1930s in Moscow alone, for example, there were "more than ten regularly staffed 'lit consultancies'" at various journals and publishing houses in the city. During the years 1931 to 1935, sixty thousand manuscripts ostensibly passed through the offices of such literary consultants in the capital alone.[61]

Prevailing sentiment, Dobrenko argues, insisted that "professional writers (yesterday's fellow-travelers)" could not be counted on to train their working-class counterparts properly.[62] Nevertheless, there was no one else to whom beginning writers could turn. As a result, authors as diverse—and as politically compromised—as Andrei Belyi, Isaac Babel, Victor Shklovskii, and Boris Pilniak were officially engaged to help workers transform their day-to-day experiences into works of art.[63] The project to give workers a voice thus offered fellow-traveler authors the opportunity to combine *"priatnoe s poleznym,"* as the Russian saying goes. They could undertake the "pleasant" task of remaking themselves as they changed the face of literature and made themselves "useful" by training a new generation of writers.

The plan to build a subway in Moscow in the mid-1930s seemed to offer the perfect construction site on which such a transformation could take place. The metro was seen as the ideal stage for using construction as pedagogical spectacle, revolutionary weapon, and instrument of self-flagellation. Workers would be making a Soviet miracle with their own hands, and the structure they created was meant to reflect both the public goal of technological superiority and private advances in ideological and cultural awareness. The location of the proposed subway in the very heart of old Moscow made this a symbolically significant project, as the regime extended its reach to deep below the surface in the center of the capital. The importance of the undertaking was obvious from the slogan adopted to publicize its construction. The catch phrase— "The whole country is building the Metro!"—appeared endlessly in headlines and posters to announce the project and capture the populace's attention for this ostensibly life-changing event.

Documents retained in Russian state historical archives detail the special hopes invested in the creation of the history of subway construction in Moscow. Numerous meetings were arranged between established writers and metro workers in the hope that the two groups would work together as they built the subway and remade themselves. The goal of an editor in October 1934, for example, was to visit six reading groups (*litkruzhki*) from Metrostroi in order to find the most active and talented workers. These "worker authors" would commit to the production of sketches (*ocherki*) to be used in the planned history of the metro. The workers would also have a chance to meet with more established authors who were working on the "very same themes." An evening meeting between the two groups would be followed by more work and extensive editing of worker accounts of their participation in the construction project.[64]

The consultant in charge of this particular activity in October 1934 was S. Persov, and his evaluation of the manuscripts he received from worker-authors suggests the difficulty of turning laborers into writers overnight, his comments on his "work with beginning authors" telling evidence of the complexity of such collaborative projects. Persov's responses are interesting both for their lack of enthusiasm for the accounts and for his clear expectation that workers' contributions can be improved. Most of the accounts promise little, in Persov's opinion: "Weak. Common situations. Petty facts" is his consensus on quite a few of the manuscripts he is evaluating. "Individual moments are fairly interesting," he notes about the manuscript of a certain Tiukhtiaev, secretary of a Komsomol group at the site, "but in general the material is very raw." About another worker's account, Persov concludes harshly, "the piece needs complete reworking. The main ideas of the author are not obvious. There are no conflicts. Individual characters are not revealed." The contribution of a worker by the name of Solovev seems to present more promise, and Persov notes that it is "imagined very interestingly." Unfortunately, he continues, the "story is not from life at Metrostroi" and is "still not finished." The worker Bondarev submits his diary, but it is "very drawn out. The set of facts is interesting, but they need to be used by an experienced author."[65]

Such problems had already been foreseen by some. As early as 1931, for example, Lidiia Seifullina had wondered how such amateur colleagues would be integrated into the real business of creating literature. Her comments on the long-term viability of such colleagues were published in the journal *Novyi mir* in October of that year. Speaking at a discussion of the creative method at the All-Russian Union of Soviet Writers (*Vserossiiskii soiuz sovetskikh pisatelei*, or VSSP), Seifullina had noted the "nasty quality" (*skvernoe kachestvo*) that characterized the output of such colleagues. Complaining that the "name alone says it all," she drew laughter with her sarcastic reference to works like "Morning of the Young Shock-Worker . . ." Yet the shock-workers themselves were hardly to blame, as Seifullina noted.

What is going on with those shock-workers we drew into literature? We drew them in, and, in most cases, we gave them the title of writers immediately, without the needed verification, just because some of their works were already in press, some already published and so on. At the very same time they were given unwise directions for work, told that the novel and the novella are built thus: construction, Five-Year Plan, proletariat. That's all. That's enough. It is the castration of literature.[66]

Seifullina notes that her work at several editorial offices gave her plenty of exposure to the manuscripts of such inexperienced authors, most of which are "not fit for publication." Her skepticism even extends to the production novels of accomplished colleagues. Leonov's *River Sot'* and Shaginian's *Hydrocentral* "bring their authors no new laurels," Seifullina continues. "That is just standing in place."[67]

If Kataev shared such skepticism, he kept those views to himself. Three years after Seifullina's remarks, he and others apparently still had high hopes for proletarian efforts in literature. An editorial assistant on the Metro project, for example, was optimistic in his analysis of "manuscripts of worker authors of Metrostroi." A fragment from "Komsomol Coed on the Subway," for example, received his relatively enthusiastic endorsement: "Ask for the whole sketch! Not bad!" Others were described as "artistically literate." Some "needed only minor editing," although one diary was singled out as an "example of how not to write." The author of that diary, unfortunately, was "hindered by his partial literacy."[68]

The collaborative intent behind the volume is obvious from comments consultants and editors make in their evaluations; even the best workers' efforts were intended not for direct publication but for use by a more experienced writer. Describing the contribution of "Comrade Altukhov," for example, an editorial consultant notes that Altukhov's observations are written in "literary language" and characterized by "sincerity and authenticity." According to the consultant, very little additional work would be needed before Altukhov "could give the authors of the book about the subway extremely valuable material on a series of themes: 'Minorities on Site,' 'Relations between Young Men and Women,' 'Relations between Old-timers and Youth,'" and so on.[69]

Experienced writers were on hand to help. Sergei Budantsev, as we have seen, was ready to help with the new construction project and had particularly high hopes for the collective task that they faced on the subway project. The close contact with workers there would mean that "for the first time in a book, collective labor will be guaranteed." Budantsev, along with so many others, focused not only on the construction of the "most majestic industry," but also on the fact that "people are growing in the activity."[70]

Budantsev's enthusiasm at the January 11 meeting was seconded by the writer Ivanov, who expressed the firm conviction that the "writer was becoming an industrial writer in the full sense of the word." As both explanation and proof of his point, he noted that "five years ago it would have been difficult to imagine" that so many authors would turn out to participate in such an event. Growth for a writer means "adaptation to the spirit and mood of the era," Ivanov noted. Now that the "writer is located in a different environment," that growth can take place. "A healthy world rolls out before him and the methods of work themselves assume new forms." Confessing that "we writers are a lazy lot," Ivanov looks for help in collective work. He recommends that authors be assigned in small groups to particular shafts or areas on the construction site to ensure that the important task of writing about the project actually gets done: "I, for example, would find it boring to go to the shaft by myself, but two or three people would take one another in hand, and it would be useful to them all." Responding to a demand on the spot that he "speak out and explain what I have done for the Metro," he notes that he has promised to write a film scenario based on the subway project. He admits that work on the script is not going well (*stsenarii idet tugo*), but he argues that this collective work will still be of use. "It might be a bad scenario, maybe it will be a bad job, but all the same it will be useful to our common activity."[71]

Ivanov's remarks, like those of other participants in the January meeting, were met with applause, but it was clear even to the writers and the workers present on that occasion that a collective history of the construction of the Moscow subway was as complicated and politically charged an affair as the construction project itself. Unresolved issues of class, for example, continued to emerge on-site as largely uneducated laborers took directions about "their" metro from engineers whose training and social class seemed to put them at odds with both the project and the workers on it. Writers faced the problem of how to treat such issues without casting doubt on the entire enterprise. The poverty and inexperience of most of the workers, the primitive conditions in which they toiled, and the haste with which the project was being carried out were all sensitive questions that authors had to negotiate in their accounts of the construction.

Some writers used conflicts on-site to organize their thoughts in an easily interpreted scheme. The "task," commented Volynskii, "is to reveal the elements of class war on the construction site, to reveal and give artistic reflection." Volynskii thought writers should focus on such problems in part because that kind of social question was more comprehensible to authors than were technical issues of construction, which would "present big difficulties in the understanding of a writer." One of the questions he thought authors might usefully tackle was the problem of engineers on-site still clinging to "grandfatherly methods." His example of an "engineer who walked around the site in white trousers"[72] while ignoring the concerns of the rank-and-file appealed to some in its simplicity.

Others at the meeting, however, argued specifically against the simplicity of such a binary approach in which good and evil could be determined by the color of a character's clothing. Sokolov, for example, noted that "the point, of course, was not whether an engineer wore white or black trousers. The point was in fictional literature, in depicting people. After all, even engineers in white trousers aren't afraid to get them dirty at the crucial moment, to take up the job. The point is to reflect the growth of people on our construction projects, to reflect the growth of the builders of a socialist society. And we definitely have such people." Describing what he called "living creators of socialism," Sokolov noted that such fighters for the cause were "growing together with the growth of the Red Metro." Sokolov's belief in the necessity of a nuanced picture of Soviet construction included the conviction that writers should engage even the most technical questions in their work. "And the most important thing," he commented, "is not to reject technical elements" (*elementy tekhnizatsii*). Such "technicism" (*tekhnitsizm*) is "important because specific problems, technical problems . . . should be penetrated with ties to the person who will solve these specific, technical tasks."[73]

Sokolov and others like him seem genuinely convinced that literature of this era was an "operational affair," a strategic weapon that would be of "enormous help" in bringing the ambitious building projects of the time to fruition. Literary workers were understood as part of the joint project, workers as necessary to the creation of the production novel as writers were to the construction of the subway. A special "core of workers" was starting "to get control over not only technology but also the pen." With the publication of their "individual remarks for our newspapers," these people would form the necessary "supportive base" for "our Soviet writer." Together they would "create a monolithic work about the construction of the Red Metro."[74]

The worker-writers who were in attendance at that January meeting were no less enthusiastic about the possibilities of collaborative work, although they occasionally doubted their own abilities to produce what was needed. One of the workers from Shaft 21, a "tunneler" (*prokhodchik*) by the name of Savarskii, admitted that this was his first visit to a literary gathering, and, as such, it was "real news" (*bol'shaia novost'*). Hurrying to explain that he "couldn't write a book," Savarskii was nevertheless quite sure that the subject justified literary attention. "If I were a writer," he commented, "if I were a bit more literate, then I would absolutely write about how I came to master the work. It would be valuable material, which would describe how each one of us grew up" on-site. As he relates his own setbacks in the process, his gradual improvement, and his eventual comprehension that he was one of a group working toward commonly shared goals, Savarskii warms to the idea of creating a work of literature to reflect their joint progress. "Here 6 people are straining toward one point, I flow together with them and don't feel that I'm alone, but feel that I form one whole with them. Hey, that's what to show in artistic form. We could write the same way." Savarskii recalls moments of both joy and bitter disappointment on-site and remarks in a final burst of enthusiasm, "If you, comrade writers, came and taught us how to write this book, to write about these moments, hey, it would be classic."[75]

Worker Viktor Solovev from Shaft 12 had copious advice for the writers in attendance at the January 1934 meeting. Noting that he was speaking as a "reader," Solovev asked writers to reflect on the "bourgeoisie" who "thought about exploitation and profit" in regard to subways. "We are building not for profit," remarked Solovev, "but for the common good." He hoped that writers would investigate why "old land-owning Russia" could not build a subway and why America "wanted an electric volcano to run underground." In a flurry of eloquence, Solovev turned to "all writers with a request that every writer write a novella, novel, short story, and let them write about how we work underground, describe our accomplishments." Authors should consider writing about the role of the Komsomol on the project and the conservatism of engineering and technical personnel on the project, Solovev continued. "The most fundamental thing I want to say to writers" is "let them go down in the shafts more often, to live in the tunnels a bit more. That will be useful."[76]

Leopold Averbakh, the literary functionary who was intimately involved in both the Belomor Canal book and the subway project, professed wholehearted agreement with the worker's sentiment. In lengthy comments at the January meeting, Averbakh made a number of important propaganda points, but, more than any other, he hammered home the notion that writers needed to play a direct and active role in construction. "We need a history of the Metro that is saturated with living, concrete contents, so that people can learn from this book," Averbakh declaimed. "It is necessary to write the book as a part of the [construction] work. Writers should not be guests on this Metro, should not be raiders who fly in for a newspaper sketch, but should be in the tunnels and should feel responsibility for what is being done." The volume needed to be "directly merged with the masses, so that every writer is an organizer of a literary workshop [*gruppa literaturnogo aktiva*] and the voice of this writer is your voice."

Continuing in his direct appeal to the workers on-site, Averbakh noted that it would "not be enough" to meet on such solemn occasions and to treat authors on-site with the "respect our country affords writers." Instead, Averbakh continued, "you need to approach the writers with demands: 'If we can do a serious and difficult deed, then you writers can join in with the full responsibility needed to cope with such a large and difficult task.'" The subway was scheduled to open its first line on the seventeenth anniversary of the revolution, according to Averbakh, and writers should aim to publish the first volume of the subway's history at the same time. The "work should be a weapon of permanent mobilization of the masses and transfer of experience."[77]

A word of caution about the project was in order, according to comrade Matusov, who as a member of the organizing committee, was well aware of the potential for problems when too much public attention was turned toward the subway workers. Matusov counseled authors to focus on "experienced people," seasoned individuals who had proved themselves on the job and "endured the difficulties to the end." Noting that the "definition and identification of heroes" would be a challenge, Matusov cited cases in which "comrades had been included on the pages of the central press" and, then, "in celebration" the very next day "committed a disgrace on site." He was worried about the "excessive romanticism" that characterized myths about Metrostroi, mentioning in particular these "solemn meetings that spoil our folks." Complaining that "everywhere and anywhere our people come out like heroes," Matusov pointed out that it was time to move "from such meetings to actual work." The "comrade-builders need to fulfill the plan, and comrade-writers need to give [us] literature, the artistic works that they promise and that they also have not yet given."[78]

Matusov's words of caution may have been wise, but they fell on mostly deaf ears in this era of enthusiasm. If literature could be constructed the way any other building project was put together, then collective will and strong arms were all that was needed to produce literature worthy of the Soviet laborers who would read it in the new subway on their way home from work. Admittedly, some workers were reluctant to take on writing tasks in addition to their daily norms in the subway tunnels, and they had to be cajoled. One way to enlist participation was to publish workers' names in newspapers and to post them elsewhere. Such announcements made it clear that presence at these organized public meetings was required.[79] Higher ranking participants were sent personal summons, requesting that they appear at the editorial offices of the History of the Metro to arrange for a private meeting.[80] The most significant contributors, if they could not write their own accounts, were interviewed individually. Arrangements were made to conduct such exclusive interviews at the convenience of the "authors," who were freed from their other obligations during the "writing" of the interviews.[81] Other workers saw writing as a way to escape the hard labor and crushing poverty that would otherwise be their lot.[82] Archival holdings reveal the wide variety of people who applied to work on the literary Metro project. Former peasants and tradespeople, often with just a smattering of literary or journalistic experience, were willing to help turn subway stories into spun gold. Provincial teachers, professional historians, clerks, and Komsomol secretaries were also ready to serve.[83]

Numerous established authors, like Kataev, were invited to lend their talents to the ambitious joint endeavor. The archives contain various lists of the writers who were invited to attend meetings devoted to the project, the net to catch potential contributors cast very wide. Authors invited to meetings on the subject in the late summer and fall of 1934 apparently included Fedor Gladkov, Ilia Ilf, Evgenii Petrov, Viktor Shklovskii, Boris Pilniak, Demian Bednyi, Ilia Selvinskii, David Zaslavskii, Boris Kushner, Lev Nikulin, Boris Lapin, Sergei Budantsev, Mikhail Zoshchenko, Mikhail Prishvin, Ivan Kataev, Evgenii Gabrilovich, Nikolai Ognev, Sergei Tretiakov, Vladimir Lidin, Lev Kassil, Bela Illés, Efim Zozulia, and others, although it is unclear how many of these invited personages actually attended the meetings or ended up helping on the project.[84]

Others who were absent from the invitation list nevertheless appear elsewhere in archives from the project. Ilia Erenburg, for example, had already submitted his manuscript, a piece entitled "Old Moscow and transportation" (*Staraia Moskva i ee transport*) by October 15, 1934, although he is absent from the lists of authors invited to public meetings.[85] Isaac Babel, too, seems to have kept away from public discussions about the project, even though his wife, A. N. Pirozhkova, was a Metrostroi engineer. Babel is listed as a participant on work for the volume *Kak my stroili Metro* in late November 1934. The writer apparently had responsibility for several manuscripts to be included in the history of the subway's construction. The archives lend mute witness to his fall from favor and ultimate execution, however, when "comrade Babel's" responsibilities are crossed off the list or transferred quietly to Lev Kassil.[86]

Authorial responsibility on the project varied, depending in part on whether the writer was a well-known and politically reliable quantity or persona non grata struggling to eke out a living from such editorial projects. Certain participants had clearly defined obligations that were spelled out from the beginning. Ilia Selvinskii, for example, was supposed to deliver a "Poem about the Metro" by November 25, 1934, for the history. His task was to create a "general sketch [*ocherk*] of old and new." Ilf and Petrov, too, had clearcut responsibilities. Their "satirical sketchings [*zarisovki*] on the history of transportation in Moscow and contemporary transport (tram, taxi, horsecab)" were due by November 10. Other writers were to serve as both authors and editors. Viktor Shklovskii, for example, is listed as the author of articles on "Caisson Work" and "How Old Moscow Got Entangled," the coauthor or editor of various manuscripts taken from interviews with subway contributors, and a literary and layout editor for the history of the subway.[87] Many of the better-known authors worked with editorial assistants whose responsibility was to supply them with accounts by the workers themselves.

Why were authors drawn into the project? Is coercion the sole explanation, or were there other reasons that writers cooperated? Clearly, the justifications were as many and varied as the participants themselves. First of all, the work paid well.[88] An agreement in the archives between Lev Nikulin, for example, and the publisher of the History of the Metro bears witness to the fact that authors were well compensated for their efforts. Nikulin was to receive one thousand rubles for his "artistic reworking" of the autobiography of "comrade Gordon" for the volume *Kak my stroili Metro*. The resulting article was expected to take up two and one-half printed pages; Nikulin would receive 25 percent of his fee upon signing the contract, with an additional 35 percent to follow upon the receipt of acceptable material. The final 40 percent would be paid once the reworked manuscript was approved.[89] Numerous authors would have found such terms attractive enough to consider joining the project.

Other writers may have participated out of genuine belief in the long-term importance of Soviet construction projects. Plans to build both the new Soviet man and the authors to describe him reflected the continued hope in revolutionary ideals after nearly two decades of Soviet power. Ilf and Petrov, for example, seem to have been firm in their conviction that the Soviet system was still an improvement over former regimes, and they demonstrated their willingness to believe by contributing to the proposed metro volumes. There is little reason to doubt that the comedic coauthors were sincere in their desire to harness the "laughter of the victors" to aid a just cause, however much their enthusiasm may have been tempered by an understanding of the inevitable deviation of reality from dream.

Other writers may have tried to use the metro project to demonstrate a willingness to submit their talents to the common goal. The prospect of participation in an important official project would have been appealing to people interested either in currying favor or in updating their professional qualifications. While the actual construction work was far from glamorous, the idea of participating in a publishing venture that had the attention of both Gorky and

Kaganovich must have been attractive. Such motivations seem to have stirred the former aristocrat Dmitrii Sviatopolk-Mirskii, who had returned from exile abroad and was now deeply involved in chronicling Soviet construction.[90]And the dream of shared writing projects in which the unspoiled and authentic contributions of untrained authors would appear alongside those of experienced artists continued to appeal to many, just as it had to writers before the revolution. Authors like Boris Pilniak, who was fascinated with the idea of collaborative authorship from the beginning, were clearly motivated by a variety of such contradictory rationales.

Coauthorship was an ideal that publishers of the subway project initially worked hard to ensure. Archival documents about the "authorial collective" for the history of the Metro, for example, include a long list of authors expected to cooperate on the project. The list concludes with an important reminder to those involved in the enterprise: "writers will do a series of chapters together with worker-authors of Metrostroi. The majority of authors are required to use material from worker diaries widely. The best worker diaries should go into the book."[91] Editorial assistants were invested with "complete responsibility" for providing writers with material on particular themes of interest to the collective endeavor. Thus, Viktor Shklovskii's article on "Caisson Work" was to be facilitated by an assistant, N. F. Kartalov, who had responsibility for providing Shklovskii and several other authors with authentic information from the work site. The work of the assistants was to be checked every six-day work cycle at an official gathering at the publishing house, an arrangement intended to bring order to the chaotic job of recording history in the making.

How well or poorly the system worked can be gauged in part from meeting notes that remain in the archives of the History of the Metro. Documents there reflect the difficulty of such an undertaking. The scope of the writing project was problematic on its own, but the dramatic tempo at which it was expected to proceed made it even more complicated. Scores of individuals needed to carry out their tasks in a timely fashion in order for the venture to succeed, and, inevitably, there were countless reasons the work slowed. Although some of the authors could be listed as "working" at the six-day accountings of progress on the project, others were clearly not. Boris Kushner, for example, was described as having been "given a lot of m[ateria]l," but he was "dragging. Not going anywhere." The verdict on Shklovskii was "the same as Kushner." Lev Nikulin "was not working." Sergei Tretiakov objected that he "didn't like the press run" and thought "800 rubles was too little!" before he "departed." Efim Zozulia was waiting for a decision "about whom to write (Khrushchev, Bulganin, Kaganovich!)," and N. Bogdanov was "getting medical treatment." L. I. Gumilevskii's manuscript was described as "pretty dry," while Vladimir Stavskii had apparently given up on the project altogether. "I won't work" was the brief but eloquent quotation next to Stavskii's name on the list. Even willing writers were occasionally tempted to abandon ship. V. G. Fink apparently did, canceling his contract in "despair" of getting his subject, sluice-gate boss Ia. F. Tiagnibedy, to meet with him. Fink's comment about his subject's reluctance—"Tiagnibedy doesn't want to advertise himself"—hints at the many problems even sympathetic authors encountered in this supposedly collaborative effort.[92]

Such difficulties seem to have led to specific requests to reorganize the structure of the venture, with particular criticism directed at the publisher History of the Metro, whose work is described in a memorandum in the archives as "incorrect." The "authorial collective" bringing these charges seems to have included many of the secondary authors and editors whose work was essential to the publication of the volume. According to fragmentary archival documents, the group considered taking a stance on general complaints, arguing that the publisher had spent too much time and energy directed toward "mass measures" (*massovoe meropriatie*) and not enough on the real business at hand. Authors of the memorandum complained of "being deprived of any sort of material that could be used" in the actual volume, and in a statement that was apparently never sent, they noted with irritation that they "had to collect material from the very beginning at their own risk and responsibility." The group claimed to have earlier proposed the liquidation of the publisher "History of the Metro." Their suggestion was to turn the task and needed resources over to the publishing entity "History of Factories." It is unclear if such a proposal ever reached the Party hierarchy or elicited a response from either the Party or the administration of Metrostroi.[93]

The same archives contain other documents that testify to shoddy work and missed deadlines in work on the volume. Some authors were allowed to keep the advances they were paid, even when their written contributions to the volume were found wanting. Other tardy authors were sent final warnings that asked them to repay the advance if unable to produce an acceptable manuscript within the next three days.[94] Even diligent assistants must have occasionally found their work coming to naught. G. E. Kholin, for example, promised to gather material for an article on the role of women in the construction of the subway. He contracted to conduct a series of interviews, following the guidance of Sergei Tretiakov, for the piece and to "collect the necessary fictional, journalistic, and newspaper literature" as well as any "necessary documents" for the work. Kholin may have fulfilled his part of the bargain for 150 rubles, but Tretiakov's complaints about the press run and low pay made it unlikely that the work would proceed as expected in any case.[95]

Some writers were able to complete their assignments with much less trouble, however. Viktor Shklovskii, for example, was a reliable contributor whose willingness to participate in the undertaking committed him to articles on "How Old Moscow Became Entangled" and "Caisson Work." True to his word, Shklovskii submitted the article on "Caisson Work" on November 3, 1934, nearly two weeks ahead of schedule. In a letter in the archives, Shklovskii notes that work on the article convinced him of the need to devote more time to writing "about problems and people than about technology," but he submits his work with complete conviction that it will satisfy the terms of the contract and justify his four-hundred-ruble advance. In the letter to the publishing house "History of the Metro" that accompanied his manuscript, Shklovskii lists a number of illustrations that need to be included in the text and complains that he was never informed of the "plan for the book," making it likely that he has encroached on someone else's theme. As convinced as he is of the suitability of the material, Shklovskii, nevertheless, concludes his letter with the caveat that it is just a "rough draft, not edited from a technical standpoint." Since he was "sick with the flu and unable to investigate the site really well," Shklovskii concludes that his work needs to be shown to the technical editor.[96]

Shkovskii had fulfilled the contract faithfully, but his confession that he had been unable to investigate the construction site properly pointed out a problem common to the endeavor: writers were reluctant to get their hands dirty "at work." This was the point of S. Persov's comment in the meeting in January 1934. "The writer should be in the tunnel," archival documents quote Persov as saying. "I don't agree with writers studying the technology of this business from books." To work effectively, shoulder to shoulder with subway workers, "the writer needs to be not in the courtyard, not in the office, but there—under the ground."[97]

Similar accusations troubled even Kataev, whose pose as elder literary statesman was upset as a result. Although he had arrived at the meeting on March 30, 1934, expecting that his listeners

"would find something useful" from his experience in Magnitogorsk, he fairly quickly found himself fielding critical comments
from the floor.[98] Despite his relative seniority "at work," Kataev,
too, was questioned about the superficiality of his "chronicle." A
questioner asked Kataev pointedly what inadequacies he could
identify in his novel. "Don't you feel the superficiality?" the worker
wondered provocatively. After all, he continued, "it isn't possible
to find out what is going on in Magnitogorsk in 3 months."[99]

Kataev's self-defensive answer sheds fascinating light on the
long-term goals for this collective history. He explains to his audience that the "main theme now is construction. That is the mastery of technology. . . . But mastery of technology is successful only
when man is made richer, smarter. It's necessary to organize a new
human being. The old human didn't master technology. Now there
is a battle for a [new] human."[100] Kataev's explication of official
hopes for the project is itself masterful, but the workers remain
skeptical, in part, perhaps, because Kataev is clearly not the unal-
loyed literary celebrity he may have imagined himself to be for this
crowd. Convinced, for example, that "comrades, you have all here
read my novel," Kataev learns from a "voice from the floor" that "it
was on at the theater; some read [it], some saw" it.[101] Kataev insists on his own work qualifications, contending, for example, that
he was in Magnitogorsk "not in the capacity of a writer, but attached to a specific sector." In that special capacity, he "studied
how to lay cement, had to do some physical labor." Encouraged to
address a question about the book's deficiencies directly, Kataev
admits the text may be a bit wordy in places, but insists that "in regard to the superficiality of the novel, I don't agree with you."[102]
Nevertheless, the crowd remains skeptical. "Which do you think is
a better and more accurate way to gather material," asked another
challenging voice from the floor toward the end of their March discussion, "standing at the cement mixer for an entire month or
standing nearby as an observer?"[103]

Kataev's answer to such challenges is to insist on the importance
of the writer's special mission. "If I want to describe the creative
state of the worker," he notes, "then I should work as much as possible at the cement mixer myself." But "if I want to capture the
production state of the collective [*proizvodstvennoe sostoianie
kollektiva*], then I should probably be a foreman when I can move
freely around the shop, be now at the cement mixer, now watching
how the cement is poured."[104] Contending that the question of
"what every person thinks" is the most interesting, Kataev draws

an implicit connection between Soviet writers and those from the bourgeois world. "By far the most favorite theme" (*nailiubimei- shaia tema*) of "bourgeois literature," he notes, is "how a million- aire is made from some boot-black." Such an approach is "not rel- evant for us," obviously, so Soviet writers have to concentrate on those themes that are truly "topical." In this case, that means "a per- son backward, downtrodden" who then "becomes a real, fully en- franchised member of society, an intelligent person, an engineer."[105]

Kataev seems to imply that the process of creating literature re- mains eternal, although the details of the individual story may change, and it is clear that he takes pride in his ability to make the bourgeois boot-black into a hero of socialist labor, just as he makes Bunin's "little girl" into his own brigade leader at Magnitogorsk. Yet equally obvious is the connection the author draws between the transformation of actual physical spaces and the fundamental re- construction of the individual. Although he asserts that he would not follow such an approach again, Kataev admits that, like the fic- tional Georgii Vasilievich, he "gathered material unsystematically" because his "goal was to record the landscape." He insists that this emphasis on the details of the actual physical locations was justi- fied because of the historical importance of those very landscapes. The sense that he is recording a unique and essential history gives his work special meaning: "it was indispensable to describe the landscape because the construction of Magnitogorsk is history. Only three or four writers saw it in that state, and I wanted to reg- ister it at the time of construction."[106]

Kataev illustrates the importance of history and memory in the creative process in his description in *Time, Forward!* of Moscow, which is being de-constructed as Magnitogorsk is being built. Just as Kataev preserves his fictional author's comments while "removing" them from the text, so, too, he preserves the buildings of the city as he describes them being dismantled. In the time it takes for one of his characters to run an errand, the face of Moscow—a very recog- nizable face since Kataev sets the scene near the Kremlin—has changed completely. Margulies, the engineer from Magnitogorsk, has sent his sister to consult with experts about his construction work.[107] As she hurries from home to do his bidding, she passes the imposing Cathedral of Christ the Savior in the distance. The build- ing seems to dominate Moscow life even from afar, its authority over the immediate site, the river, and the distant landscape secure. "Like a feudal lord," Kataev notes, such history "still exercised its indivis- ible, self-assured authority over Red Square" (105).

By the end of the chapter, however, history is being rewritten, as walls are torn down, commercial buildings removed, statues relocated, and the cathedral itself dismantled.[108]

> Above Iberian Street stood columns of dry plaster dust. The famous gates were being torn down. At the corner of Tverskaia, Okhotnyi Riad was being wrecked. At the Prechistensky Gates, idlers were crowding. A cupola of the Cathedral of Christ the Savior was being taken apart. It was being taken apart in narrow golden segments. They disclosed a complex azure carcass, through which, like through the lattices of a gazebo, gleamed the greyish-blue summer sky which suddenly seemed strangely empty. Small cupolas of the belfry had also been stripped. They resembled wire cages. People were scurrying in the cages, like birds. (*Vremia, vpered!*, 1960, 97; my translation).

Construction has "turned Moscow into a purgatory" (107), but Kataev's character is unfazed: "the appearance of the cathedral which was suddenly being taken apart did not surprise her in the least. She merely glanced at it. She was in a great hurry" (108). When she reports to her brother, the engineer, he expresses absentminded approval of this reshuffling of the landscape.

> They are tearing apart the Cathedral of Christ the Savior. They are tearing down the Okhotnyi. They have just moved the monument of Minin and Pozharsky.
> "Do you understand?" she would shout quickly. "Can you hear me? Do you understand? On my way there, Minin and Pozharsky were in their place. On my return trip, there is only empty pavement. How do you like that?"
> "Good!"
> "And the cupola of Christ the Savior . . . do you hear me? I said that they've split the cupola of Christ the Savior in half. I never knew that it was so enormous. . . ."
> "Good," Margulies muttered.
> "Every section of the cupola was several feet wide. And by the way, from a distance, it looks like the rind of a melon . . . Do you hear me?"
> "Goo-o-od," Margulies roared. "Go on, go on!" (*Vremia, vpered!*, 1960, 126; my translation)

If these characters do not regret the passing of architectural history, it is because they are too busy building their own. Authors like Kataev chronicle the end of old traditions with little regret because their focus is on the new world coming into shape before their very eyes.[109] Bruno Iasenskii offers a similarly fascinating landscape of the new capital under construction in his own production novel,

Man Changes His Skin (*Chelovek meniaet kozhu*). Iasenskii begins that work with a panoramic view of the center of Moscow as it appears to his character Jim Clark, an American engineer who has just arrived in the bustling city. Clark, fleeing economic crisis and rampant unemployment in the United States, "did not believe in socialism." He is nevertheless profoundly curious about the "unheard-of contest" taking place in the Soviet Union, and as he makes his way from the train station to his hotel in the heart of the city, it is clear that he will soon be more than a skeptical outsider, who has come only "to work here, to take part in the carrying out of an experiment in which he did not believe."[110]

As a foreigner unfamiliar with the city, Clark is too slow and methodical to catch the single taxi that could have ferried him to his destination, and he finds himself relegated instead to a decidedly less contemporary horse-drawn droshky (*proletka*). This seeming disadvantage, however, allows him to imagine himself in a glowingly heroic light; as he passes under a giant triumphal arch, he draws a comparison between himself and the architectural feature above him, and his humble conveyance becomes a chariot with six horses readying itself "to go bounding along over the smooth resounding surface of the street" (6). The arch Clark passes is clearly the Moscow Triumphal Arch, built to commemorate Russian defeat of the French invaders from 1812 and topped by the figure of Victory, driving a chariot with six horses. The classical figure on top of the arch allows Iasenskii to draw an effortless parallel with the unfinished but portent Soviet space his character has just entered, imperial grandeur, and the magnificence of antiquity.[111]

As Jim Clark travels down a fictionalized Tverskoi Boulevard, all of Moscow rises to meet him. But "this was not a street like all the other streets in the world—an immovable defile of houses." Although Moscow's houses are "hunchbacked and stunted by nature," they expand upward in scaffolding that makes the street resemble a cheerful "parade of athletes—the houses were all in motion, new stories were scrambling acrobatically onto their broad shoulders" (8–9). The American's droshky soon passes an army detachment, which sends a "shiver" down Clark's spine before he "suddenly" feels "irrepressibly cheerful."[112] He drives by the famous monument to Pushkin, on the opposite side of the boulevard from its present-day location, although Clark knows nothing about the poet as yet and notices only a "bronze curly-haired man in an old-fashioned coat." The monument looks "in perplexity" across to a "strawberries-and-cream colored church." The Strastnoi Convent that Pushkin contemplates was scheduled for demolition as

part of the vast 1935 plan to reconstruct Moscow, and its imminent
demise is already obvious in Iasenskii's description; half of the
church's upper façade is obscured by the frame of a "little two-
seater automobile" attached to the building, "evidently . . . the ad-
vertisement of some Soviet automobile firm" (12).

The sight of the car bursting through the second floor of the
chapel causes Clark to "laugh out loud" (12), and the reader too is
continually invited to share in the amusement. Clark's sense of delight fades temporarily as he passes the Liberty Obelisk, which had
been installed in a burst of artistic fervor on the first anniversary
of the revolution. Clark "particularly disliked the stone maiden" at
the foot of the obelisk, which reminded him of "all the stone Muses
and Freedoms scattered over the various squares of the globe"
(16).[113] His dissatisfaction with finding such a recognizable and,
therefore, inappropriate monument disappears, however, when he
catches sight of places he recognizes from reproductions (St.
Basil's) or his exceptionally limited knowledge of Cyrillic (Lenin's
mausoleum). This kind of set piece is clearly part of the pleasure of
the production novel, as readers take command of the landscape
they survey in prose. Jim Clark's joyful naïveté finds its geographical center when he takes possession of Red Square itself. As he
comes up on to the "boundless square," it "suddenly seemed to
Clark, despite the correct geography he had learned in school, as if
his entire journey here from New York had led him up the steadily
rising curve of a semicircle until he arrived at this culminating
point." Clark's training as an engineer allows him to comprehend
the simple geometrical truth of such production novels. He had
made it to the "roof of the world" (17–18). His later journey to
Tadzhikistan, where he will take part in an important construction
project and be reforged himself, thus originates in Soviet space that
he and his readers have already recognized and made their own.[114]

Such written descriptions of reality suffice, in this transitional
period, for actual landscapes that do not yet live up to their literary portrayal. One such vision of the future was the colossal Palace
of Soviets, which was intended to honor the first Five-Year Plan
and projected for the very site of the razed cathedral that Kataev's
production novel marks only in passing. Out of scale with its intended surroundings, the colossal tower was never built, but, as
Sheila Fitzpatrick has argued, that fact scarcely mattered. In the
spirit of the era, the never completed Palace of Soviets nevertheless "was more familiar than most actual buildings."[115] Elaborate
plans for the architectural feat, like the descriptions of other construction projects included in transitional production novels, were

intended to substitute handily for a reality that was still all too often imperfect and incomplete. Such a "compensatory function" characterized much of the discourse and behavior during this period. A remarkable anecdote from a memoir by Wolfgang Leonhard makes the process clear; he describes the map he and his mother purchased in 1935 that showed projected architecture improvements already proudly ensconced on paper.[116]

Kataev's engineer imagines a "young Moscow" quite different, however, from that of either old Moscow or the monumental new version associated with the gargantuan Palace of Soviets. His focus is not an oppressive city being dismantled or a vision of utopian skyscrapers, but a city under construction. As B. E. Galanov has pointed out, in this sense *Time, Forward!* serves as a guidebook to the aspirations of the society Kataev wanted to inhabit and insisted he served. Its values, humane and life-affirming in Kataev's presentation, are ostensibly reflected in projects like the new stadium at Dynamo, the gardens of the big Park of Culture and Rest near the center of the city, and the new swimming pools and tennis courts now available to all the city's inhabitants.[117] Picturing a diver about to enter a swimming pool, Kataev imagines that "he spread out his arms as if he wanted to embrace everything that lay stretched before him in this fresh and miraculous morning world of young Moscow—the river, grey-blue, scarcely touched by the glowing flush of the dawn, the pavilions of flowers in the Park of Culture and Rest, the Crimean Bridge, the blue smoke of Sparrow Hills, a little tug and its barge, the wiring of the Shabolov radio station, a cloud, roses, tennis nets, a street car, a building in the process of construction" (78).

Substituting an alternate landscape to both the oppressive past and the undisciplined present, Kataev imagines a miraculous but relatively modest future. In one of many descriptions of Magnitogorsk that describe the city from the air, Kataev offers an aerial view of the site.[118] Arriving back at the Magnitogorsk construction site by airplane, the director of the construction site in *Time, Forward!* pictures a landscape that literally inverts the world: "the starry field of the earth swayed and turned. . . . The moon-white steam of trains swirled up. Dotted lines, strips of streets and roads stretch in all directions, clashing and crossing each other. . . . The bulging sides of hills, studded with lights, swam by." In the "starry geometry of his complex enterprise" (312), the engineer notices disorder, but is unfazed since he "knew that this was merely the preliminary sketch. He looked down on the space of the construction as if it were an illuminated blueprint. He saw it as it would look a year hence. In a year all these separate, torn details would be joined together, smoothed over, welded, integrated, polished. The construction would have become a factory, and the factory would spread out with all its rivets, pipes and cylinders" (312–13). Chaos is brought to order by standing the normal organization of space on its head. Just before returning from theory to reality, then, Kataev completes his metaphor and brings the very heavens down to earth: "before passing from the general to the particular, the airplane whisked up like the board of a swing, reversed the positions of the starry sky and the starry earth (the moon and the hotel), made one last circle, straightened out, and swooped down to the landing" (313).

6

Deconstructing Soviet Work:
Andrei Platonov and the
End of the Production Novel

MANY CRITICS WILL BE UNHAPPY TO FIND ANDREI PLATONOV (1899–1951) included in a discussion of the Soviet production novel. A clear-sighted observer of Stalinist totalitarianism and a victim of the regime's cruelty, Platonov is often excluded from the list of authors of production novels, as though inclusion in that group would taint his literary production and deny its genius. Yet Platonov's works, including *Chevengur, The Foundation Pit* (*Kotlovan*), and *Happy Moscow* (*Schastlivaia Moskva*), belong to the history of that particularly Soviet genre. An engineer turned author, Platonov understood better than most the importance of the construction site in building the new Soviet man. The author's personal background, his technical expertise, literary innovations, and artistic fate are essential additions to our understanding of how Soviet culture was constructed.

Platonov has been the subject of intense critical interest both East and West, especially since his strange, hypnotic, and tragic prose was "rediscovered" in the Soviet Union in the late 1960s and then again in the late 1980s. His tortured style can be confused with that of no other writer. He raises the tongue-tied narrative to an exquisite art form, and his characters, especially the self-taught engineers and builders that people his works, are unforgettable. This is particularly interesting for a Russian author of the late 1920s and early 1930s, of course. Working in a literary tradition that purported to transparency, comprehensibility, and optimism, Platonov produced literary works that were models of the convoluted and melancholic. In times that insisted literature be effortlessly accessible to the proletarian reader, Platonov offered difficult and unresolved dilemmas.[1]

It is all the more remarkable, then, to realize that the author continued to believe that his unwieldy prose was a worthy contribution to the edifice Soviet writers were constructing at the end of the 1920s and the beginning of the 1930s. Despite repeated remonstrance from the reigning literary politicians at the time, Platonov obstinately submitted his work as a legitimate addition to the communal literary effort. He turned repeatedly to the dean of Soviet letters, Maxim Gorky, as well as other literary functionaries for help and worked doggedly to publish his pieces even when those authorities failed to assist. The reasons for his stubborn insistence on a place in the ranks of proletarian literature were many, but perhaps the most trenchant argument was biographical: Platonov was a genuine member of the working class, and, as such, he felt justly entitled to status as a proletarian author.[2]

Other writers might have needed an introduction to the workaday world in order to become "engineers of the human soul," but Platonov had grown up there and needed no help imagining it. He was accustomed to the world of science and technology in a way that few of his fellow authors were, and at numerous points his technical life even overshadowed his literary activity. In comments from 1921, he illustrates the prejudice for action over contemplation that was common at the time: "how much one wants to say and how unnecessary it is to talk because warriors are needed now, not dreamers." Platonov's remarks from 1922 are equally telling. The "invention of machines," he insists, "the creation of new, working, iron constructions—that's proletarian poetry." Linking the technological and the human in an approach that would characterize his later work, too, he comments "every new machine is a genuine proletarian poem. Every great new work on altering nature for man—that's clear, proletarian, exciting prose." An interview that Viktor Shklovskii happened to conduct with Platonov in Voronezh in 1925 indicates a similar preference for direct action, which vied with Platonov's abiding interest in the literary world. The writer, who was working at the time as a technician to alleviate the drought that had stricken the area, spoke to Shklovskii "about literature . . . , about how it's impossible to describe a sunset and it's impossible to write short stories."[3] With years of seniority in the field, Platonov had practical and journalistic experience, scientific and technical articles, and even patents to back up theoretical understanding of the problems facing a country set on industrialization. An early and fervent supporter of the revolution, Platonov was ideally suited to participate in building the Soviet production novel.

And participate he did. Despite continued exclusion from official public discourse, Platonov was an intense and active contributor to the discussion of how to build the improved world in which new Soviet men and women would reside. His literary works are suffused with themes, vocabulary, plot elements, and philosophical musings related to the meaning of construction, and he wrote a number of journalistic works, including some that he was unable to publish, on pressing issues of public interest. Natal'ia Kornienko suggests, for example, that Platonov's "Fabrika literatury" was intended as a public response to Mayakovsky's piece on "How to Make Verse" that had appeared in the June 1926 issue of *Krasnaia nov'*. Even more compelling is his 1929 industrial sketch (*proizvodstvennyi ocherk*) found years later on the back of one of Platonov's fictional manuscripts; the author apparently hoped to publish it as part of the official campaign to send writers to factories that year.[4] What kept Platonov out of the debate, then, was not his unwillingness to contribute or his hostility to the process itself, but rather his exclusion by those who were setting the terms of the debate. His work belongs in an evaluation of the development of the production novel and the evolution of Socialist Realism itself. This is a point worth stressing since it contradicts the reading numerous scholars have given to Platonov's work.

Much of Platonov's oeuvre has been read as anti-utopian or parodic, with a number of scholars concluding that Platonov rejected the utopian dreams of universal brotherhood that were an explicit part of Stalinist rhetoric.[5] Nothing could be further from the truth. Platonov's opposition to events in Soviet Russia was directed against bureaucratic caprice and political hubris, not toward utopian aspirations themselves. The same "Fabrika literatury," for example, suggests the writer's continued interest in shared literary activity with its exhortation of writers to organize their craft on the basis of industrial production. Today's critic may view such suggestions with irony, but, as Tomas Langerak notes, the tone of Platonov's comments and the social context of his argument make it difficult to conclude that the author was arguing tongue-in-cheek.[6] Platonov's remarkable insight into the potential dangers of the totalitarian state convinced him of the need to speak out about those threats. But his opposition never extended to plans to construct a more perfect existence on earth. Although he was well acquainted with the imperfections of life on earth, Platonov continued to believe in the possibility of improvement. David Bethea notes that even Platonov's mature works are "neither fully utopian not fully anti-utopian." As his daughter comments in a posthumous edition of her father's work, "some people regard his main writings as more or less anti-Soviet, but as a writer Platonov was above crude ideology."[7]

Platonov relies on the metaphor of building to explore his characters' deepest motivations, and it provides him with a means to discuss both the noble aspirations and the fatal drawbacks of the elaborate plans to remake the world that characterized this period in Soviet Russia. Platonov himself was intimately involved in several Soviet construction projects, and he depicts a world in which architectural decisions have profound, occasionally even fatal consequences for its inhabitants. Despite the clear drawbacks, however, the author never abandons his search for a better built environment. Architecture itself, often reduced here to its most primitive incarnation, is thus both the elusive goal and the tragic by-product of human striving. The drive to build is an essential component of human existence in Platonov's universe, and his characters engage in the process at every opportunity.

Platonov's embrace of the material world and its built environment was decidedly ambivalent, however. One of the primary functions of the constructed universe in Platonov's work is to offer human beings temporary shelter from a natural world that is largely hostile to those very construction projects. The amorphous space, or *prostranstvo,* that surrounds his characters threatens to engulf them at almost any moment. Much of the action in Platonov's works takes place, therefore, at the decidedly uneasy nexus between the man-made universe and the natural world. Divisions that make sense in other contexts lose their teleological certainty in Platonov's universe, as the boundaries between natural and artificial, nature and man, even animate and inanimate begin to waver.

This is certainly the case in Platonov's work *Chevengur,* which had a number of provisional titles that reflect the author's interest in building a better world, including "Proiskhozhdenie mastera" (Origin of the Master) and "Stroiteli strany" (Builders of the Land).[8] The novel opens with a description of Zakhar Pavlovich, who like other such eccentric characters in Platonov, is a builder and self-taught inventor. In Zakhar Pavlovich's universe, obvious, seemingly immutable categories are dismantled by his creative activity alone. "He regarded people and fields with indifferent tenderness, not infringing upon the interests of either," and he spends the winter evenings making "unnecessary things such as towers of wire, ships cut from pieces of roofing tin, paper dirigibles, and so on."[9] Such inventions, which run contrary to expectations and against type, amaze Zakhar Pavlovich's contemporaries with their bold and visionary thrust. Thus, he fashions a frying pan out of wood, for example, a feat that is described as part of a "surrounding universal mystery," which transcends arbitrary divisions we might otherwise be tempted to make. Such experiments comprise the very meaning of life for Platonov's homegrown builders. "I'd die right now, myself," Zakhar tells a mortally ill peasant, "but you know how it is, when you're working on different things . . ." A believer in progress, at least initially, he thinks with satisfaction that "as long as any natural raw material goes untouched by human hands, people are far from having invented everything" (3, 5).

As an inventor, Zakhar Pavlovich can see beyond irrelevant categorization to a world of artistic potential. Platonov even uses the word "art" (*iskusstvo*) to describe the man's homemade but revolutionary excursions into the world beyond binary divisions. His collection of inventions—"a full assortment of agricultural tools, machines, instruments, and household devices" made entirely of wood—is "technological art," and it too erases the boundary between technology and nature. Platonov points out how strange it is that not a single item that Zakhar has fashioned from this ostensibly "natural" material "repeated nature" (5). The ability to transgress seemingly fixed borders is characteristic of all of Platonov's self-taught "masters," who inhabit a world of almost magical possibilities in which previously immutable laws of physics no longer hold sway. When Zakhar Pavlovich is taken on as a technician at the railroad, "a new and expert world arose before him, a world so long beloved it was as though he had always known it, and he decided to cling to it forever" (15).

Such trust in technology and a concomitant unwillingness to be restrained by "arbitrary" divisions was common enough in Stalin's Russia. Utopian dreams of electrifying the entire country that had arisen with Lenin, for example, were now to become reality, as more and more elaborate and previously unrealizable plans were set in motion. The energy, strength, and technical expertise to accomplish such goals had to come, in large part, from the next generation of newly minted specialists. Such homegrown "engineers," like Platonov himself in fact, sensed a world of human potential in Soviet plans to remake the visible universe. If Zakhar Pavlovich represents the first generation of such indigenous technical personnel, then the orphan Sasha Dvanov is his obvious descendent.

Sasha is one of the main characters of *Chevengur*, and it is his peripatetic wanderings that help give the book its erstwhile subtitles "Journey with an Open Heart" and "Journey with an Empty Heart."[10] Despite his prominence in the narrative, Sasha is largely a cipher, his indeterminate nature defined in part by a strange inability to distinguish clearly between objects of material culture and the natural world. This trait, which he shares with Zakhar Pavlovich, places him in the middle of the potent emptiness that is the site of Platonov's fictional universe. Sasha is the son of a fisherman who has died after throwing himself into a lake to satisfy his curiosity about the division between life and death. At the urging of Zakhar Pavlovich, the unlucky orphan is taken in by the Dvanov family, and his quiet observations of their yard indicate how the natural and the constructed world blend seamlessly with his own precarious existence. "Sasha watched the buildings, changed by the dusk but all the more familiar for that, the wattle fences, the shafts of the overgrown sled, and felt sorry for them, because they were exactly like him." The realization that such objects "must one day die for good" offers the boy no consolation; their resemblance to him makes his own fate only too comprehensible (26).

Sasha's seeming inability to categorize things definitively emerges, in the end, as a rejection of the binary system altogether. When he next looks at a fence, for instance, he sees neither boundary nor division, but an invitation to take up a position on the margin spanning both natural and artificial worlds. His own immediate attempt to "become" a fence suggests a synthesis of private and public that he attempts to effect through his own corporal body: "When he looked at the ancient fence, he often thought in an intimate voice, 'It stands for itself,' then he too went to stand someplace without the slightest need."[11] His identification with the fence is depicted as a natural extension of Sasha's interest in "machines" and "other moving and living things." He empathizes with the train engine at the depot where he works and with the chickens in the village where he lives. We are told that he "wanted more to feel them, to live their life with them, than to find them out," his act of solidarity with "the chickens or the locomotive" nevertheless deliberate. "Not conscious of himself as a firm independent object," Sasha lives in a universe in which even the boundaries between visible and invisible are blurred. Thus, he can conclude that "I am like it" when he "saw the wind." His sympathy for the immaterial even leads him to conclude that the invisible wind is the perfect proletarian, always laboring for a common cause. "I only work in the day," Sasha thinks with pity, but the wind "has to work in the night too. The wind has things even worse" (38).

This ceaseless wind that blows through the terrifying vacuum of Platonov's universe is connected directly to both the written word —literature itself, in fact—and to the amorphous individual self in a complicated metaphor that connects the process of reading with the loss of an essential oneness with the world. Platonov first introduces the metaphor in a surprising passage that features Zakhar Pavlovich, as well as Proshka Dvanov, a boy from Sasha's adoptive family who ends up playing a decisive role in the orphan's fate. Zakhar Pavlovich is shown reading a book aloud, but the narrative he is reciting could not be more divorced from his own reality. "Count Victor," he proclaims to all who will listen, "placed his hand upon his brave and dedicated heart and said, 'I love you, my dearest one.'" Such shopworn literary images are of no interest in postrevolutionary Russia, and Proshka, who listens at first, "thinking that this was a fairytale," soon becomes "disenchanted" and cuts Zakhar Pavlovich off (36). Proshka offers instead to bring the orphan Sasha to Zakhar Pavlovich for the price of a ruble, and the two are soon reunited.

When we next see them, they are living together, and it is now Sasha who is reading as Zakhar Pavlovich only watches. "What do you think?" Zakhar asks the boy. "Is it absolutely necessary for everybody to live or not?" (37). Sasha's own father has committed suicide, and so the boy's answer is fraught with meaning. The fisherman who saw death as nothing more than "another province" and sought to bridge the two worlds with his own sacrifice alludes directly to Christian mythology, of course, particularly in light of the man's "intention to live awhile in death" and then "return" (6). Sasha, who is described as "somewhat understanding the anguish of his father," nevertheless rejects the notion of a kingdom beyond this earth. He replies affirmatively to Zakhar's question: it is indeed necessary for "everybody" to live. With Sasha's conviction that everybody is condemned to this existence, Zakhar probes further. "But you haven't read anywhere how come or for what, have you?" he asks plaintively. Sasha replies to this existential query with a platitude taken straight from his own books: "I have read that the farther we go," he comments, "the better it will be to live" (37).

Zakhar wants to believe in such a tantalizing prospect, but he is not easily convinced. He has questioned the notion of endless progress before and now concludes that the idea is flawed. Technology is again the basis for his speculations. The spool of an engine forces him "to worry about the infinity of space," and he takes to stargazing "to see if the world is spacious, to see if there is enough space for the wheels to live and turn eternally." Using his own two hands as a "scale," he applies that human measure to the infinity of space, and his calculations lead him to conclude that the vast expanse is actually finite. He has "read that the world is endless," and he "wanted the world really to be endless, so that wheels would always be necessary, ever preparing the way for general happiness." Despite this fervent desire for endless progress, however, he "simply could not feel infinity," and he is skeptical. "The number of miles is unknown, because it is farther!" he comments. "But somewhere there's a dead end and the last mile stops. . . . if there really was infinity, then it would have spread out by itself in the great space, and there'd be no hardness . . . so how can there be infinity? There's got to be a dead end!" (27–28).

With this unnerving realization comes the even more disturbing thought that his own terminal life is the best proof of the infinite nature of existence. If the world can be made "to stretch," as Zakhar Pavlovich later claims to have discovered, and "space can also be heated and stretched, like steel banding" (28), the individual human life is much less elastic.

> No matter how much Zakhar Pavlovich lived, he noticed with surprise that he didn't change and didn't get smarter but stayed exactly as he had been at ten or fifteen years old. Only some of his former premonitions had become ordinary thoughts, but nothing had changed for the better because of that. Previously he had imagined his future life as a deep, blue space—so far away that it almost didn't exist. Zakhar Pavlovich knew in advance that the longer he lived, the smaller the space of unlived life would get, while behind him a dead, trampled road would stretch out. But he was mistaken: life grew and accumulated, but the future also grew and spread out, deeper and more mysterious than in youth, as though Zakhar Pavlovich had backed away from the end of his own life or had increased his hope and trust in life. Seeing his face in the locomotive's lanterns, Zakhar Pavlovich would say to himself: "How amazing. I'm going to die soon, but everything is just the same." (*Chevengur,* 1988, 57)

This understanding—that the future itself grows and expands while the individual stays in one place to face eventual decay and death—is cold comfort for Zakhar. It is the only solace available to Platonov and his generation as well.

The realization that they would never actually live in the endlessly retreating future was tragic for this generation of writers. They had sacrificed their youth and talents to the notion that life could be built anew, and the thought that the very premise for their suffering may have been mistaken was painful to contemplate. As we have seen, authors found a variety of ways to explain to themselves the huge costs they had been asked to bear. Olesha's retreat into "indifference," Shaginian's repeated willingness to relearn her lessons, and Pilniak's belief in the communal nature of literature, for example, were the authors' attempts to come to terms with the realization that individual contributions to a better world were decidedly ephemeral.[12]

Platonov's practical experience as a real engineer made him even more painfully aware of the difficulty of finding a lasting solution to common problems. Even if human beings as a group are able to make general progress, it is still impossible for that improvement to change the lot of each individual in the society. As Platonov comments in his provocative autobiographical story "The Motherland of Electricity," for example, it is "in youth" that "it always seems there is a great deal of life and that there will be enough of it to help every old woman."[13] With maturity and age, however, we have no choice but to accept human frailty and the insufficiency of the individual existence. Thus, as the older Zakhar Pavlovich stands near a dying foreman from the railroad depot, for example, he "noticed again that no matter how evil, intelligent, and brave the man, all the same he became pitiful and sad, dying from the weakness of his powers." This realization shakes him to the core. "So we'll die, it seems," Zakhar concludes, and "in the following years nothing touched him" (40–41). The aging man no longer hopes "for a general radical improvement—no matter how many machines were made, neither Proshka, nor Sashka, nor he himself would ever ride on them" (41).

Here, Platonov returns to the metaphor of reading, which appears in an expression of real skepticism over the possibility of individual improvement. Zakhar's realization that the individual is not perfectible results in a feeling of apathy that is disturbed "only in the evenings, when he glanced at Sasha reading." Only at such moments "would pity for the orphan rise up. Zakhar Pavlovich would have liked to tell Sasha not to torment himself with books, because if there had been anything serious in them, people long ago would have embraced one another" (41). The older man, who "had lived his entire life through on his own strengths," is nevertheless jealous of the younger generation. "I tortured myself," he comments enviously, "and he's reading" (42).

Zakhar's envy is misplaced, of course. Sasha, like his own mentor, is only too human. The kerosene used for his late-night reading sessions is wasted (*gorit zria*), "illuminating the soul-shaking book pages, which all the same he didn't follow later." The explanation for such failure is simple: the individual human vessel is inadequate for the infinite truths it tries to measure. "No matter how much he read and thought," Platonov tells us, "some kind of hollow place remained ever within him, an emptiness through which an undescribed and untold world passed like a startled wind."[14] Sasha initially perceives this empty space as creative potential, and he even tries to construct something there, again using his own body as the measure and the material for building. In "accustomed anguish," he

> imagined an emptiness inside his body, through which life would pass, entering and exiting ceaselessly, every day, neither pausing nor growing stronger, as even as a distant rumble, in which it is impossible to distinguish the words of a song. Sasha felt a coldness within, as though from a real wind, blowing in the spacious dark behind him, while in front, where the wind was born, there was something enormous, light, and transparent—mountains of living air, which needed to be transformed into his own breath and heartbeat. His chest seized up in advance with the presentiment, and the emptiness within his body expanded even further, preparing to seize future life. (*Chevengur*, 1988, 71)

This enormous potential seems to exist on an individual level, and each of Platonov's characters is initially "ready to seize that future life." In the end, however, the individual is unable to sustain building activity on such a momentous scale. "There it is—I!" Sasha exclaims joyfully at the end of the passage quoted above. He has recognized his potential and seems about to realize it. Just at that moment, however, he succumbs. His joyfully individualized construction cannot withstand the slightest external scrutiny. Zakhar Pavlovich follows Sasha's declaration with the simplest of inquiries—"Who are you?"—but Sasha instantly falls silent, "clutched by a sudden shame, which carried off the full joy of his discovery." The harsh light of common reality destroys his "mountains of living air" on contact, and Zakhar Pavlovich explains his failure by resorting to Platonov's original metaphor of reading. Zakhar answers his own question regarding Sasha's true identity, and the verdict is devastating: "You're a reader," Zakhar comments, and "nothing more" (*chtets ty i bol'she nichego*) (43).[15]

Platonov describes this tension between vast but amorphous possibility and intense but limited reality again and again in his production novels. His characters play out their individual lives on the border between the two modes of existence, and they attempt to resolve the tension between them by leaning now one way, now the other. The balance they achieve is precarious, and such individual solutions are ultimately unsustainable. The individual is finally powerless against overwhelming forces of entropy, and the author understands this, although he regrets that truth. All of Platonov's main characters, then, must confront the pitiless question of how to construct a new world in which they themselves will never thrive.

Zakhar Pavlovich abandons the quest, becoming "bitter in his old age." He now realizes the enormity of "that which he had lost in his life. He had lost everything, and the wide, open sky above him had in no way changed from his many years of activity. He had conquered nothing to justify his weakened body, in which beat some sort of important, shining strength, and that in vain" (47). The problem, for Zakhar and others, is again the difficulty of applying an individual measure to a societal task. Looking "with regret at the wattle fences, the trees, and at all other people to whom in fifty years he had brought no joy and no defense," he recalls a welder in the shop were he had worked. "Remember Fedka Bespalov?" he asks Sasha, to whom he is entrusting the struggle for a better world. "Used to be they'd send him somewhere to measure something," "and he'd go, measure it with his hands, and then come back holding the measure in the space between his palms. As he walked the feet turned into yards. 'What the hell, you son of a bitch!' they'd yell at him, and all he'd say is 'I need this real bad. All the same they won't fire me for it!' Only the next day did Alexander understand what his father wanted to say" (47).

Not surprisingly, part of Zakhar's realization of the hopelessly finite nature of the individual contribution comes from an experience with technology. He and Sasha are making a tour of the various political parties that promise salvation after the revolution. They interview and reject them all before finally arriving at the "very last party, which had the very longest name" and was "behind the last door in the corridor."[16] Zakhar inquires how quickly "the end of everything will come" and is assured that "socialism" will only take a year. Zakhar decides that "probably this would be the smartest power, which would within a year either completely build the world, or else raise up such a fuss that even a child's heart would grow tired." As they fill out the paperwork to become members, Zakhar notices a telephone in the party office. He investigates the phone with a "forgotten attraction." Remembering his own wooden constructions in sad comparison, he admits that he "never made such a thing in my life." Here, too, the personal viewpoint has been too narrow: "I overlooked that thing," he comments (46).

The encounter with the telephone underscores for Zakhar just how limited his own personal contributions to general progress have been. His inventions have now been far outpaced by society, and that fact helps cement his conviction that the individual measure is too limited for the new world under construction. His final advice to Sasha suggests a different synthesis of the particular and the general that will use the individual not as a measure but as a conduit for vast forces of change. "A Bolshevik has to have an empty heart," Zakhar insists, "so that he can make room in it for everything" (47). Shortly after receiving this advice, Sasha leaves Zakhar's company and the locale he has called home since childhood. It is his "journey with an empty heart" that occupies the rest of the narrative as Sasha travels across the vast space of Russia in a search for the "end of the world" (48).

The quest is an unusual one, and Sasha makes an unorthodox hero, tossed by the vagaries of civil-war Russia through what Platonov describes as the "dangerous expanse of the fields" and the "alarm of overgrown, forgotten space" (49–50). Nevertheless, his fate was common in Russia,[17] and Sasha fits easily into the long tradition of "Russian wanderers and pilgrims," who "trekked constantly, dissipating the weight of the people's grieving soul with their motion" (61). The image of the solitary beggar haunts Platonov's narrative, as it did Olesha's just a few years earlier. Thus, Platonov looks out onto the "barefoot unsown fields" and notes that "occasionally a lone man would appear there, stare at the city for a long time, his chin leaned on his walking staff, and then he would go away into the gulley somewhere, where he lived in the murk of his shack and hoped for something" (61).

It is from such people as these that Platonov and his characters expect socialism to emerge, to have "popped up somewhere unawares, because people had nowhere else to go once they had banded together in fear of poverty and the effort of want" (61). Sasha is soon dispatched to the provinces to "have a look around and see if maybe there aren't socialist elements of life out there" after all (62). He remembers how people had "wandered among the fields and slept in the empty buildings at the front" and concludes that "maybe those people in fact had already bunched up in a gulley somewhere, out of the wind and the government, and there they lived, content with their friendship. Dvanov agreed to look for communism in the initiative of the populace" (63).

His search consumes the rest of the novel, as Sasha looks for a more productive nexus of public and private across the vast expanses of Russia. Platonov again draws our attention to the importance of the spoken word to this search by noting that "in this guttering, bowing world, Dvanov spoke with himself. He loved to converse alone in the open spaces." Convinced that "only words can turn flowing feeling into thought," the "thinking man converses." But this private monologue, like the individual gesture it is, withers on contact with the larger world: "if anyone had heard him, Dvanov would have been ashamed, like a lover caught in the dark with his beloved." What is "art" in the private realm of the individual is only "entertainment" when it is translated by "conversing with other people" (69).

Sasha understands and regrets this inevitable simplification, but he understands, as well, the practical need to turn private thought into public action. Individual poetic sentiment is valuable in its own right, of course, but translating it into a public narrative is also a vital social need. "Nature is a businesslike thing," notes Sasha, speaking aloud "so that he could think." He wants to "put words back into the disjointed passages of the day's songs," which he can still hear in the air, but he notes that "these much-sung dales and rills are not just field poetry" since "you can also water the soil, the cows, and the people with them. They'll become productive, and it's better that way. People feed themselves from earth and water, and it's people that I have to live with" (69–70).

Sasha's continued search for the union of individual poetics and public practicality is difficult: he is shot and stripped naked, and his hopes of finding socialism often have more in common with a nightmare than with a cherished dream. Shortly after meeting Stepan Kopenkin, a Bolshevik field commander, with whom he will travel for most of the novel, Dvanov "frightened himself in a dream, thinking that his heart was stopping, and he sat on the floor as he woke up 'But where then is socialism?' Dvanov remembered and peered into the murk of the room, searching for his thing. It seemed to him that he had already found it, but then had wasted it in sleep among these strangers. Dvanov went outside in fear of the punishment to come, hatless and in his socks, saw the dangerous unanswering night, and dashed off through the village into his own distance" (79). This description is followed by a strange series of events that make it clear that Sasha is still dreaming, even as he closes "his eyes so as to disassociate himself from any spectacles" (79).

Following this sequence, Platonov turns to a lengthy digression about the nature of the mind. His discussion there suggests again the search for a public perspective on individual experience that haunted the writer throughout this period of his life. When Sasha wakes from his dream "two days later," he "remembered why he lived." He has now apparently realized that "there is within man also a tiny spectator who takes part neither in action nor in suffering, and who is always cold-blooded and the same. It is his service to see and be a witness, but he is without franchise in the life of man and it is not known why he exists in solitude." This tiny homunculus is presented in spatial terms in Platonov's universe, "like the doorman's room in a large building." Like the watchman in every Soviet building, this "heart doorman" was called upon only to bear witness to the real life that unravels before him. He "sits entire days at the entrance into man and knows all the inhabitants of his building, but not a single resident asks the doorman's advice." His "powerless knowledge" makes him the "eunuch of man's soul." The "spectator" within Sasha "saw everything, but it never warned him and never helped him, not once" (79–80).

This small spectator is watching when Dvanov loses his innocence with a peasant woman. The tiny "watchman burst into tears," after "losing his equilibrium in sympathy but a single time." After this remarkable event, Dvanov is tempted to abandon his quest. He even sends Kopenkin off alone initially, "towards the place where the living enemy of communism dwelt" (91). He comes to his senses shortly, however, and rejoins the "elderly warrior." His decision to join Kopenkin signals a commitment to developing a public aspect to his private dreams. Shortly after this passage, Sasha begins to offer advice on concrete actions they will need to take before "the villages are resettled in a Soviet way." Sasha's comments overlap with plans Platonov himself must have made as part of his activity as a reclamation engineer. "First we have to bring water out into the steppe," he muses. "Around here that's all dry, our watershed is an outcropping of the deserts beyond the Caspian" (92).

Sasha's commitment to "building socialism" develops further the next day when he attempts to convert the character "Fedor Dostoevsky" to adopt a revolutionary reorganization of space in the village. Advising Dostoevsky to break the village "up into five or six collectives," Sasha imagines a physical resettlement of the houses that will facilitate the new way of life. This picture parallels Stalinist plans to resettle the real rural populace of Russian all too realistically, of course, and Dostoevsky is soon fascinated by the concept as well. He, too, has it "within his mind to picture the empty steppe in some familiar place, move each household of his village there by name, and then look at how it had turned out" (95–96). As Stephen Kotkin has noted at length, this modular approach and the accompanying belief that human society was susceptible to rational planning were highly characteristic of modernism during the twentieth century.[18] Such "well-intended" experimentation colored many of the Stalinist projects of the late 1920s and 1930s, and the experimental notion of the plan to reorganize Russian rural life appeals to both Dostoevsky and Sasha. Sasha, in particular, finds the potential for development much more compelling than any completed work could ever be. Thus, Platonov notes that Sasha "loved ignorance more than culture, for ignorance is a bare field, while culture is a field already grown over with plants, so that nothing else can grow there. Dvanov was happy that in Russia the revolution had weeded absolutely clean the few spots where there had been sprouts of culture, while the people remained what they had always been, fertile space" (108).

In this universe, where Sasha serves as a conduit for timeless ebb and flow, the notion of endless possibility is much more compelling than a final product. Sasha is looking, after all, for the perfect balance between process and stability, and, as a result, he is in no particular "hurry to have anything sown" (108) on the vast field of potentiality. This is revealed in the "monument to the revolution" that he helps design for the commune that he and Kopenkin are visiting. The figure he draws for the monument is deceptively simple: "the eight on its side signifies eternity of time and the upright arrow with two heads means infinity of space," he tells the president of the commune. "There's both eternity and infinity here," agrees the president, "and that means there's everything. Couldn't think up anything smarter if we tried" (108).

This perfect balance of "everything" is altogether rare, but that does not dissuade Sasha and the others from seeking it continually. On occasion, Platonov's characters even achieve the perfect amalgam of process and stasis, feeling and thought, movement and stillness. Such moments bring happiness, but the experience of happiness is so fleeting and meager that it might easily be confused with its opposite. Here, too, Platonov reverts to the idea of an impartial watchman, or *storozh*, who stands apart from the fray and provides distance and perspective on the torments of the world as we know it. Sasha, sitting on Kopenkin's powerful horse, the appropriately named Proletarian Strength, seems to enter a kind of contemplative state that partakes of both emotion and rational thought in search of perfect unity.

The feelings rose up high with his heart and tumbled down behind it, already transformed into a stream of mitigating thought. But above the dam still burned the duty light of that watchman, who takes no part in man, only drowsing within him for very low pay. The light allowed Dvanov to see both spaces—the warm swelling lake of feelings and the long quickness of thought beyond the dam, cooling off from its own speed. And then Dvanov could outstrip the work of heart, which both fed and stifled his consciousness and he could be happy. (*Chevengur,* 1988, 161)

"There it is—the raw material for socialism!" Sasha notes shortly, his exclamation a conscious echo of the earlier "There it is—I!" (121).

This epiphany, if that is not too exceptional a term for such a quiet and ephemeral discovery, follows Sasha's clear-eyed evaluation of the Russian countryside. The landscape that spreads out before him is a humbled twentieth-century vision of the view Herzen and Ogarev had seen from their vantage point on Sparrow Hills in the preceding century. As Dvanov peers at the "poor landscape in front of him," he notices that "both earth and heaven were unlucky to the point of fatigue. Here people lived alone and took no action, dying like firewood set upon the bonfire." This seemingly inauspicious site nevertheless evokes hope, even joy, in Sasha and Kopenkin. Kopenkin points out the "dark and sad valley," while "rejoicing as though he had already ridden straight into the town." As they ride down the road, "it seemed as though if one were to build up some speed, it would be possible to break free and fly." This is the location on which Sasha and Kopenkin hope to build their own version of the future. As such, its desolate aspect is the perfect setting for a world that is always being completed, but will never be complete. "Not even a single building," Sasha concludes triumphantly, "just the misery of nature, an orphan!"[19]

Platonov advances a similar argument in a comment by his character Gopner, a welder who declares that "we are all comrades only when there is identical trouble for everybody. As soon as there is bread and property, why you'll never get a man out of it! What do you mean freedom, if everybody has bread fermenting in his belly and your heart is watching him like a hawk? Thought loves lightness and misery" (141). Desolation and emptiness provide these characters with a sense of individual possibility that is otherwise lacking. Gopner shares Sasha's fascination with the empty space that is the essential location for the nexus of thought and action. Only the barren void provides enough room for the individual performance of meaning: "My father wanted to see God with his own two eyes," he notes, "and what I want is some sort of empty space, damn it, so as to do everything over from the beginning, depending just on my own mind . . ." (148). This realization is followed by a pointed editorial comment: "Gopner wanted not so much happiness as precision."[20]

The vision Sasha and Kopenkin have of the future is never actually constructed, of course. Sasha soon parts company with Kopenkin and heads for the city instead. There he meets Chepurnyi, a resident of Chevengur, who describes his town as an idyllic destination, the location of "the end of everything," the end of "all of world history" (146). Sasha is fascinated by the notion of a place where artificial divisions have already been overcome, and he asks Chepurnyi to contact Kopenkin so that the elderly warrior can evaluate the town's success. When Chepurnyi and Kopenkin finally meet, however, it is in the open expanse of the steppe, which "stopped nowhere, running right up to the lowered sky in a smooth lingering slope that no horse had ever conquered entirely" (155). This amorphous location, where even the border between sky and land has been erased, is the most likely spot for communism to triumph. Only here can temporary boundaries be overcome and human beings comprehend their full, unfettered potential.

That potential, like reality itself, changes with every passing minute, as Platonov clearly understands, and, as a result, the inhabitants must react to continually changing conditions. The town itself is constantly "in turmoil." Platonov depicts its townspeople in perpetual motion, "wandering around the town among the clearings and the brush, some in pairs, some alone, but all without bundles or property." They are busy, too, rearranging the environment, dragging the buildings, even moving the gardens, which, like everything else in this location, are constantly being shifted, resettled from one location to another on a daily basis (159). "Trees grew on almost all the streets of Chevengur, giving their branches as staffs to the wanderers who roamed through Chevengur but did not stay the night," Platonov tells us, so that even the streets and boulevards must constantly realign themselves (161).[21] When told about an alleged "moral path to socialism," Chepurnyi scoffs. "What do you mean 'path,' when we've arrived? . . . Now, my friend, there are no paths. The people have arrived" (163).

Platonov understands what Chepurnyi does not, however: this location at the end of history is itself a temporary one. The "Chevengur pedestrian, Lui" is the most obvious expression of this problem. He has begun to realize that "communism meant the uninterrupted movement of people into the distance of earth," and he tries to convince Chepurnyi that "communism should be declared to be a journey and Chevengur removed from its eternal sedentarization" (*vechnaia osedlost'*). Lui's argument stems from his belief that stasis will inevitably be followed by oppression: "the wind has to pour over a fellow or else right off he'll take up oppressing the weak on you, or else he'll dry up on his own and get all despairing like." On the roads, however, "nobody can avoid friendship. And there'd be enough jobs for communism!" (172–73).[22] Lui's decision to leave Chevengur is entirely consistent with this belief that the revolution must be permanent. "There is no way communism will take place on a sedentarized spot, for it can have neither enemies nor joy!" he insists. From his own spot on Herzen's metaphorical hillside, Lui decides to join the navy and travel the world in the endless motion that a real search for perfection requires. Looking back down on the "Chevengur lowlands," he turns away from stability toward eternal movement: "Farewell, comrades and communism!" (173–74).

Kopenkin seems to dismiss Lui's contention initially, but as soon as he sees the pedestrian leave, he decides "finally today to test the whole communism of Chevengur and then take his measures." When he heads back to town to do so, even Proletarian Strength almost loses its way: "Because of the relocation of the houses the streets of Chevengur had disappeared, and all structures were in flight, not in place. Proletarian Strength, who was used to smooth street roads, grew anxious and sweaty from the frequent turns" (174). Kopenkin's conclusion, like that of Lui, looks for dissension in the midst of unity. "Hell, it's so good here in Chevengur," he says sadly. "But how is it that there's been no sorrow organized? Communism should be biting, just a tad poisonous even" (175). Although he "lived twenty-four hours confident in Chevengur," he "then grew weary of his stay in the town, for he did not feel any communism in it" (195). Like Lui, he soon realizes that "around Chevengur there was no communism, just transitional stages" (189), and he is forced to accept the dreary fact that the "end of everything" is itself only temporary.

Even more distressing is the realization that the much vaunted future must be endlessly crafted and re-crafted by those who wish to bring it to fruition. This seems to be the revelation that strikes Chepurnyi, for example, as he waits impatiently for the imposition of communism in Chevengur. Noting to himself that "flowers and perennial beds and gardens" are "swinish cultivations," Chepurnyi vows to have them "cut down and trampled on forever in Chevengur" (198). Only partially satisfied with this destructive impulse, Chepurnyi wants to balance that destruction with a constructive gesture, but he is hampered by the limited scope of his own individual resources. He notes with sadness that "nowhere, neither in books nor in fairytales, was communism written out as a comprehensible song that might be recalled for comfort in a dangerous hour" (199). Chepurnyi notices this lack of "art" (256), and he bemoans its absence since it "forced him to rely solely on his own inspired heart and its difficult strength in order to gain the future" (199–200). "Posters in Moscow and the provinces," Chepurnyi and Platonov note sadly, "depicted a hydra of counterrevolution and trains filled with calico and broadcloth chugging into villages that had cooperatives, but nowhere was there a touching picture of that future, for the sake of which the hydra's head had to be lopped off and the heavy freight trains had to be pulled" (199). In the end, Chepurnyi is comforted by the fact that the town "sat on a dreary even steppe beneath a sky that also resembled a steppe, so that no beautiful natural forces were visible anywhere, to distract people from communism and secluded interest for one another" (211).

The conundrum that Platonov has posed here is the one that gripped all of Stalinist Russia: there was no lasting place for the individual inside an endlessly evolving collective and no permanence to the human element in a universe at the end of time. Sasha Dvanov comprehends this tragedy when he visits Chevengur and realizes that "time comes ever into being and disappears, while man stays in one place with his hopes for the future" (273). This understanding gives Sasha insight into the "Bolsheviks of Chevengur," led now by his adopted brother Prokofii, who wants "the comrades to sacrifice truth, because all the same it won't live for long" (267). In a long conversation with clear allusions to the Grand Inquisitor scene from *Brothers Karamazov,* the brothers Sasha and Prokofii debate the merits of asking the populace to "take up some other happiness which will live for a long time, until the truest truth of all" finally arrives (267). Prokofii is planning "to hold all of communism and the happiness it would bring inside of some protective reserve." Such a plan will allow him the luxury of "doling it out to the masses in partial doses" and let him "thus protect the inexhaustibility of both property and happiness" (268).

Their conversation on this plan to gather power for the good of the masses has no end in the novel, but it is clear that Sasha will have no part in it. By the end of the narrative, he has accepted the fact that human beings are different from machines and realized that their progress toward perfection cannot be hurried. He tells a comrade, for example, that communism in Chevengur must develop naturally. "What we have here," he explains, "isn't a mechanism, it's people living here. You can't get them squared around until they get themselves arranged. I used to think of the revolution as a steam engine, but now I see that's not it" (272). He continues his attempts to build a better society for the inhabitants of the town, helping with projects to construct a dam, irrigation canals, a solar-powered electric plant, and a defense system. But in his personal search for resolution of the conundrum that Platonov has set for his characters, Sasha returns to the lessons his own father taught.

Sasha notices that "evening was gathering within him," a "time of maturity, a time of happiness or regret." This is precisely the "sort of sundown of life that Dvanov's father had hidden permanently in the depths of Lake Mutevo," and now Sasha, too, is reaching the end of his useful life. "My youth is ending," he notes. "Within me it is quiet, and dusk is gathering above all of history" (259). This growing sense of personal obsolescence is evidence that Sasha has learned to accept the harsh truth that his individual contribution to human progress will be limited. He clearly recognizes that his role as a conduit for universal forces is drawing to a close. Despite his "pang of loss" (273), he sees this approaching end in positive terms as a cycle completed. Mumbling in his sleep, Sasha seems to comment on another existence that he and his father will share beyond the boundaries of this life. "I'll wake up soon, father . . . sleeping is tiresome too . . . I want to live on the outside, I feel cramped in here. . . ." In his sleep, it seems, "Dvanov's perished father had wound his heart well with his own hopes" (275–76).

His father's image is connected with the tiny watchman who has offered a synthesis of process and stasis to Sasha before. Here, too, "the watchman opened the rear door of memory and Dvanov again felt the warmth of consciousness in his head. He was walking in the village at night, and he was a little boy" (319). This dream image evolves into and mingles with Sasha's discussion of the weapon he is attempting to fashion to protect Chevengur. That conversation is interrupted, in turn, by a conversation about his former love Sofia Aleksandrovna, and Sasha realizes with "shame and the sticky weight of memory" that "he might well have enclosed himself with the closeness of one person until death, and only now did he understand that terrible, unrealized life of his in which he might have remained forever, like in a house that had fallen down" (320).

In contrast to the horror of such a narrow, individual existence, his father's experience is presented as an optimistic example of how to meet life's challenges. The architectural metaphor—a "house that had fallen down"—is chosen carefully since it signals the loss that precedes new construction of a better future. The fisherman who sacrifices himself in an elusive but high-minded pursuit emerges in Platonov's final accounting as a role model, and Sasha's own release from the travails of this world becomes the natural fulfillment of a cycle. Their deaths allow the author to posit, finally, closure to the problem that has troubled him from the beginning of *Chevengur*. Only death brings an end to individual human striving, and, as such, it offers a potential moment of hope and a possible end to suffering. The faint possibility of gaining understanding, justice, meaning, or even simple human companionship drives the actions of both Sasha and his father. Their suicides are not self-centered, then, but evidence of their dying hope that something better can still be built. "Hope," Platonov explains to us, "cannot be realized and still beat within a man, for if it is realized the man dies, and if it is not, the man remains, but in torment, and the heart beats on in the middle of the man, in its place from which there is no escape" (276).

Hope and self-sacrifice are essential to Platonov's understanding of Soviet construction, as we see as well in *The Foundation Pit*, Platonov's short novel from late 1929 to early 1930. V. A. Chalmaev describes this novella (*povest'*) as Platonov's "most capacious work,"[23] and the construction site that provides the title for the work helps foster that sense of endlessly expanding space that characterized the Soviet imagination during these transitional years. Platonov's fictional creation embodies the narrative of a real-life Soviet factory in a literal sense: on the back of the manuscript for *Kotlovan*, archival researchers found the writer's description of his visit to the Kamenskaia Paper Factory in 1929. This remarkable discovery provides graphic demonstration of the way Platonov and others incorporated official discourse about Soviet production into their creative endeavors. As T. M. Vakhitova notes, Platonov's factory sketch "exactly follows the canonical genre" that was being established for such pieces during those years, yet, she comments, it seems that "complicated human fates, contradictory social processes fit poorly in [this] type of simplified sketch."[24]

What makes Platonov's production novels so fascinating, however—and so essential to this study of transitional examples of the genre—is that the "fit" seemed perfectly natural to the writer himself. Platonov saw no inherent contradiction between official discourse about the factory, which he himself intended to produce, after all, and his own fictional approach to the subject. Although Vakhitova sees a "sharp emotional, ideological, aesthetic division" between Platonov's "publicist writing and the artistic text," she eventually concludes that the two works demonstrate a "paradoxical closeness."[25] This seeming paradox is actually predictable, however, and creatively justified. The contradiction between public rhetoric about building and Platonov's prose on the topic existed

only in the minds of those who excluded him from the public forum. The fact that his two narratives literally bleed into one another, as one manuscript encroaches upon and overwrites the
other, demonstrates how pliant Platonov expected the production
novel in this transitional period to be. The author himself was entirely sympathetic to Soviet architectural projects and admired the
desire they evinced to organize human existence in a more just and
humane fashion. He was acutely aware of the high cost of such
projects, especially the price that had to be paid by individual
builders, and he focused naturally on the inevitable loss that the individual must bear in creating a better future for all. In the late
1920s and early 1930s, Platonov and others still believed that public discourse could accommodate such complexity.

The novella begins with the architectural metaphor in its title.
Particularly for readers of the time, the name carries connotations
of change, renewal, and improvement. These notions are implied in
the image of a foundation pit, the allusion to plans to "build socialism" inherent in the image. The building site serves as the locus for much of the action in this work, although Platonov's
attitude toward that site and toward architectural structures in general is as ambivalent as expected from this sophisticated author.
The event that opens this work is actually a negative one: the dismissal of one of the central characters, Voshchev, from his job at a
small factory on his thirtieth birthday. His age, the same as Christ's
at the beginning of his final ministry, is significant since it signals
the beginning of Voshchev's own quasi-religious journey.[26]

Like Christ, Voshchev is reluctant at first to begin his mission;
he has been let go from the factory "on account of weakening
strength in him and thoughtfulness amid the general tempo of
labour."[27] Platonov turns quickly to an architectural metaphor to
describe his character's plight. Voshchev gathers his belongings
from his room and goes "outside so as better to understand his future out in the air" (1). Thus, from the first words of the novel,
Platonov seems to be setting up a dichotomy between confining
structures and the relative freedom of open space. The author immediately subverts his own binary system, however, by complicat-
ing the opposition he has just established. The clarity Voshchev
expects from unconfined nature evades him: "the air was empty,"
and Voshchev "did not know where he felt drawn." This static moment is also reflected in all he surveys: "motionless trees were carefully holding the heat in their leaves, and dust lay boringly on the
deserted road—the situation in nature was quiet." Instead of of-

fering movement and release from confinement, the open air represents new imprisonment and stasis instead: the trees "hold" the heat; the road is motionless and "deserted" (1).

Voshchev's indecision soon finds him at another architecturally significant juncture: the moment of transition between city and the expanse beyond. He stops in confusion "at the end of the town" and leans, characteristically for Platonov, on a low fence. Fences, in this case *ograda,* serve as important, if ambiguous place markers in Platonov's universe. They are barriers, of course, but often curiously permeable ones. They define boundaries, but do not completely restrict movement. They fence undesirables in as easily as they keep them out. Thus, it is significant that Voshchev pauses briefly to lean on the low fence of "a large house where children with no family were being habituated to labor and use" (1).

The children (*besssemeinye deti*) are in transition, like Voshchev himself, and it is not surprising that they are located in this architecturally significant location. They are behind a fence, to be sure, but it is a low one. Their existence is in the public sphere, admittedly, but on its far edge. On this transitional spot, the children are being trained for life in the new world. A faint notion of coercion effortlessly accompanies the introduction of both the socialist vocabulary of work and the existence of a new generation in whose name current sacrifices will be made. Significantly, however, training of this future generation is taking place in a structure left over from the past. The *usad'ba* (country estate or farmstead) that houses the next generation seems to imply a return to the architectural dichotomy of town versus city. But in *The Foundation Pit*, this country dwelling marks not the beginning of rural pleasures but the end of a clearly defined existence. Children represent the future in Platonov's world, but their position is decidedly insecure.

Beyond the children's dwelling, "the town stopped" (*prekrashchalsia*). Again, the transitional location is important for Platonov, and he has his character linger in the moment of ambiguity. In this amorphous state between city and country, "there was only a beer room." Neither town nor country, the beer hall is artificial, imposed on the landscape but not indigenous to either side of the proposed architectural dichotomy. Its poor fit in its surroundings brings another comparison to the author's mind: the pub for migrants and "low-paid categories" stands "without any yard," "like some official building or other." This curious metaphor from the world of artificial structures is then mirrored by a comparison to the natural environment. Behind the beer hall is "a clay mound" with

"an old tree [that] grew on its own there amid bright weather" (1).
The tree, like the beer joint, marks the place where easy comparisons
end. It is the psychic location of most of Platonov's characters.

In this frightening no-man's-land, Voshchev finds respite from
both the rigors of life in enclosed structures and the terror of endless space. The beer hall shelters the rowdy (*nevyderzhannye liudi*), among whom Voshchev feels "more cut off and at ease" (*glushe
i legche*). Inside, he manages to exist (*prisutstvoval*) until evening,
"until the noise of a wind of changing weather" (1). Characteristically, Voshchev pauses at the window, another architectural divider,
to consider his options.[28] From the window—a barrier but transparent, an opening but restricted—Voshchev notices the tree,
which is being rocked by the change for the worst in the weather.

As we have already seen, the wind that brings about the transition plays an important role for Platonov as a signal of movement
from one state to another. Not surprisingly, the wind moves rest-
lessly back and forth between the city and the country, between the
world of man-made structures and pitiless nature. In Platonov's
universe, this movement back and forth suggests a far-reaching
transition between the world as it is and the world as it could be.
The wind that rocks the tree in this transitional location carries
sound as well. Voshchev hears a band droning in the distance. The
"monotonous music" was "getting nowhere" and the wind carries
it away, sweeping it across the barren emptiness that Voshchev inhabits to disappear into a nearby ravine, "and into nature" (2).

The ravine is itself an important topos in Platonov's world. It appears again and again in his work, particularly in *The Foundation
Pit*, where it will play a role in Platonov's attempt to synthesize the
world of man-made structures and the natural universe. Here as
elsewhere, the ravine marks the end of the built environment and
the symbolic beginning of a natural one, and it is soon pressed into
service as a temporary place of refuge for Voshchev. Sitting at the
window of the pub, Voshchev listens to the sounds of the night and
hears the artificial music of the distant band disappear into the
ravine. His respite at the edge of two worlds is fleeting. It ends
when he is unceremoniously sent out of the beer joint. "You paid
for a beverage, not for premises" (*Vy platili za napitok, a ne za
pomeshchenie!*), the waiter announces, underlining both the importance of the architectural metaphor for Platonov and the transitional nature of such structures in his universe (2). It is a mark
of Voshchev's desperation that he turns toward the ravine for shelter. Stretching out there on his stomach, he hopes for the oblivion

of sleep but is tormented instead by questions of existence, not knowing "whether he was of use to the world or whether everything would get along fine without him" (3). In this tortured state, his body itself becomes a hostile location, a "hard and stony" container for his anguished heart (2).

When Voshchev wakes in the morning, he starts a long, circuitous journey that will occupy him for the rest of the novella. The nearly ceaseless movement that characterizes him begins in the ravine and leads first back to the trade union committee. Asked why he had been thinking in the middle of the working day, Voshchev replies that he was considering a "plan for life" that was "something like happiness" (3). When he fails to convince the trade union of the reliability of his plan, Voshchev heads off again. This time his journey is both spatial and temporal: "His path on foot lay amid summer," we are told, time and space seemingly uniting at this crucial moment. "On either side work was now under way on technical improvements and housing blocks where the hitherto unsheltered masses would soon lead their speechless existence" (4).

The adverb Platonov uses—speechless or *bezmolvno*—adds a curious note of neutrality, if not indifference to architectural structures. Voshchev seems unable to comprehend the full significance of the structures within which he exists. His "body was indifferent to comfort," we are told. "He could live, without exhaustion, in an open space" (4). In fact, this physical ability to exist outside of a constructed environment seems to have been a handicap: "he had pined with an unhappiness of his own during the time of plenty, during the days of peace in his past lodgings." Yet, as he retraces his steps past the beer joint and irrevocably away from his old life, he seems equally detached, out of place in this new "natural" environment. At the site where he camped the previous night in the ravine, he notices that "something in common with his own life still remained there." Voshchev is poised, then, in no-man's-land. He "found himself in space, with only the horizon before him and the feel of the wind against his downbent face" (4).

Throughout *The Foundation Pit*, Platonov returns to this particular landscape—the distant horizon—to comment on the faint possibility of a better world in which the natural and the man-made will coexist in harmony. Like the future, this synthesis is always just out of reach. Here, as in *Chevengur*, Platonov searches for a balance between that imagined shared perfection and an immediate individual sacrifice. The solution he posits in *The Foundation Pit* is the same one he offered in that earlier work: movement forward toward an ever-receding goal. Voshchev, soon to be engaged in constructing the foundation pit of the title, has no choice but to participate.

In this world under construction, the individual must make continual sacrifices toward a common goal. Voshchev has just been fired from his previous job for contemplating a personal happiness, and he is soon hard at work on construction of a project for the common good that he will never see completed. Platonov offers us a view of Soviet construction as Voshchev wanders the town, "waiting for the world to become a matter of common knowledge." The construction site is lit up by electric lights that illuminate builders who are "separate from nature, in a bright place of electricity" (9–10). These construction workers toil "with a will, erecting brick partitions, striding with burdens of weight in the timber delirium of the scaffolding." As Voshchev watches the construction of a "tower that was unknown to him," he notices that "something had come about in the site and was drawing the building toward completion." An early version of the manuscript implies that this elusive architectural addition must come from the humans themselves: "Don't people get to feel smaller as their buildings get bigger?" he wonders. This process of building through de-construction fascinates Voshchev, and his understanding of the procedure is absolutely stark: "Man puts up a building and falls apart himself."[29] Although he hopes that this process will bring the desired social result, he nevertheless wonders about the individual fates of the builders themselves. "Who'll be left to live then" (9), he asks of the "All-Proletarian Home" they are building.[30]

Voshchev participates in the general construction by digging the foundation pit, which expands over the course of the novel to include the nearby ravine in a conscious attempt to overcome the unnatural dichotomy between nature and the man-made environment. Urged on by the reproaches of the unsavory Comrade Pashkin, the workers continually attempt to increase their pace, even though they realize that they will not benefit directly from its construction. "They stood and saw: the man was talking sense—it was necessary to hurry up and get the earth dug and the home built, or else they would die and be too late. Life might be ebbing away now like a flow of breath, but it could still be organized to future use through the structure of the building—for the sake of immovable happiness to come and for childhood" (22).

Their own lives are finite, but they build in the belief that their efforts will be useful to the future. These fictional sacrifices echo earlier thoughts that Platonov himself expressed in a polemical article from 1920. He notes there both the practical nature of the sacrifice workers make now and its teleological importance. "We have begun to build our truth from the bottom," Platonov argues. "We are only laying the foundation. First we will give life to the people and then we will demand that it have truth and sense in it" (*dadim zhizn' liudiam, a potom potrebuem, chtoby v nei byli istina i smysl*). The young Platonov already understood how difficult it would be to "give life to the people." His older self would realize, as well, that the life he gave would be his own and that later demands for "truth and sense" could barely compensate him for his personal sacrifice and inevitable loss. As Platonov argued in his unpublished production sketch from 1929, such "extra work always entails the abridgement of life; it substitutes for suicide."[31]

The amorphous future toward which these characters strive is personified in this particular case by Nastia, a child who comes to reside on the construction site. The fact that the actual child in question ends up dying in the foundation pit itself is not surprising in Platonov's universe.[32] Nastia, too, makes a sacrifice for the future, and her death stirs the building crew to continue their feverish activity at the end of the novel. "Communism's something for the kids," Platonov's character announces after Nastia's death; "that's why I loved" her. Voshchev himself makes a similar discovery. Although he at first feels that he "no longer knew: Where in the world was communism now going to be if it didn't first begin in a child's feeling and convinced impression," he then kisses her dead body, "with greed of happiness," finding in that final embrace rather "more than he was looking for" (148).

Platonov offers a further clue to this remarkable ending in his treatment of the figure of the engineer in *The Foundation Pit*. His character, Prushevskii, is guided both by the compelling urge to provide essential shelter for those around him and by the more utopian desire to create new structures in which new ways of life will be possible. Platonov's engineer attempts to give balance and symmetry to chaos, but he is painfully aware that his own individual efforts are doomed to failure. Platonov had noted with distress in *Chevengur* that there was no "touching picture" of the future to help workers visualize the destination toward which they are striving. He attempts to remedy that situation by being one of the only authors of a production novel to describe the dwellings of the future in any detail.[33] Is it any wonder, however, that he does so in order to reject them?

The engineer of the "All-Proletarian Home" believes that "in a year's time the entire local class of the proletariat would leave the

petty-proprietorial town and take possession for life of this monumental new home." The new building will itself eventually be replaced, notes Prushevskii, trying to picture the "tower in the
middle of the world" that another engineer would design "after ten
or twenty years" so the "laborers of the entire terrestrial globe"
could "be settled there for a happy eternity." Prushevskii thinks
that from the point of view of "both art and expediency," he can
"already foresee what kind of composition would be required in the
center of the earth." But he cannot "foresense the psychic structure" of the inhabitants (19). He peers voyeuristically through a
"former knot in the wood" into the workers' barracks, watching the
laborers sleep in an attempt to intuit "what kind of body" the youth
of the future would have, and "what agitating force" would stir
them, setting the "heart beating and the minds thinking" (18–19).
His inability to imagine those house dwellers of the future threatens Prushevskii's building plans in the present since he fears creating a building that is outdated before it is even completed: "He
was afraid of erecting empty buildings—buildings where people
lived only because of bad weather." Since he suspects that humans
will evolve in an unpredictable direction, he needs to know the
shape their future lives will take so that the "walls of his architecture should not be built in vain" (19).

Like Sasha Dvanov, Prushevskii at age twenty-five already "had
felt a constriction of his own consciousness and an end to any
further understanding of life." Here, too, Platonov imagines this
process of aging and obsolescence in spatial terms. Prushevskii
climbs down into the foundation pit, looking for inspiration, but he
instead feels "as though a dark wall had appeared straight in front
of his groping mind." He is in "torment" over this structure and
spends his time "moving about beside this wall of his and calming
himself with the thought that he had, in essence, already grasped
the true, innermost structure of the substance out of which the
world and people had been thrown together." He tries to convince
himself that "the essentials of science all lay on this side of the wall
of his consciousness, while beyond the wall could be found only a
boring place that there was really no need to struggle towards"
(20). But the imaginary structure continues to plague him, and he
is painfully aware of the press of time and the insignificance of his
own contribution to the shared cause.

Prushevskii returns to the workers' barracks and again peers
down at the nearest body, "hoping to notice on him something unknown in life." The proletariat is mute, however. The engineer can
see very little and all he can hear is the sound of "slow, flagging

breathing." Prushevskii is left only with a nagging suspicion that somebody else has already "managed to surmount the wall and move on forward beyond it" (20). Walking back to his own apartment, he catches sight of an "unclear star" that is "far away, suspended and without salvation." Realizing that it "would never come any closer," Prushevskii begins to suspect the limits of the individual in the process of inexorable but excruciatingly slow social progress. He wonders if he should "perish," finally understanding that "in place of hope, all that remained to him was endurance" (20–21).[34] This shift in focus—from dreams of individual achievement to resigned conviction in progress on a societal level—is typical of these transitional production novels. Once he accepts the inevitability of individual limits, his refuge is familiar too; "having decided to pass away," Prushevskii is left with the consolation of "indifference towards life" (27).[35]

In an effort to intuit the future beyond his own limited understanding, Prushevskii later wanders the countryside near the building site. Platonov's use of the metaphor of construction is typical of the transitional production novel. On one of Prushevskii's walks, he notices at the "end" of nature, some "peaceful white buildings" that "shone with more light than there was in the air around them." Although he does not "know a name for this completed construction" or "its purpose," Prushevskii can tell those distant buildings were erected "not only for use but also for joy."[36] This project amazes Prushevskii, but serves equally as a reproach since it awakens fears that his own building will substitute utilitarian purpose for utopian inspiration. He is overwhelmed by the "precise tenderness and the chilled, comprised strength of the remote monuments" he sees. The buildings seem to embody an enviable synthesis of the binary model, combining as they do the power of unrelenting logic and the force of elemental passion. "Not everything in these buildings was white," Prushevskii's reverie continues, in one of the few literary descriptions to provide any detail to the picture of a shared future. "In some places they possessed blue, yellow, and green colors, which lent them the deliberate beauty of a child's depiction" (60).

Yet as much as Prushevskii admires this synthesis of "faith and freedom in composed stone" (60), he ultimately rejects both it and the binary model that Katharina Hansen Löve and others have applied to Platonov's spatial universe.[37] Resorting to another architectural metaphor, Platonov likens the complex of buildings on the horizon to an "island," radiating "from peace" amid a "remaining world that was being newly constructed." Rather than accept this delineation of the universe into far and near, complete and incomplete, closed and open, however, Prushevskii rejects the binary notion altogether. But "when on earth was this built?" he asks "with bitterness" (60), objecting not to the buildings, which he has just admired, but to the binary structure they imply. After all, if the construction at nature's end already exists, his own struggles lose their significance, as they become just one side of an already decided equation.

The buildings, like "an alien and distant happiness," awaken in him only "shame and alarm." For that completed model, Prushevskii substitutes an indeterminate one, patterned after individual human life, which by its very nature is incomplete. Prushevskii looks once more at the "new city, not wanting to forget it or be mistaken." The buildings stand as "clear as before," as "if around them lay not the murk of Russian air but a cool transparency" (60–61). To such unchanging certainty, however, Prushevskii prefers "the sadness" of earth's burnt-out "star."[38] His final comment on these buildings from the future provides an unexpected, but fitting commentary on all the architectural projects of this literature. More than those beautiful buildings off on the horizon, Prushevskii, "without admitting it," really wanted "the whole world, forever under construction yet never constructed, to be like his own destroyed life" (60).[39]

It is little wonder, then, that Platonov's characters at the end of his novel are in the same *Foundation Pit* in which they began their work. Prushevskii is certain that he will "die before the building came to an end" (26), but he persists nevertheless, busying "himself with objects and mechanisms, so as to possess them inside his mind and empty heart in place of friendship and affection for people." The process of "engineering the peace and stability of the future building guaranteed Prushevskii the indifference of clear thought, an indifference close to delight." Scientific detachment and indifference to individual existence are exactly what is required for genuine participation in social life: "inside him it began to feel light and muffled, as though he were living not an indifferent life-before-death, but the very life his mother had once whispered to him about with her own lips" (26–27).

Like Prushevskii, Voshchev, too, looks for personal meaning in public action. His behavior on the construction site reflects the ethos of the monument that Platonov's characters erected in *Chevengur:* endless movement on a timeless path. Like everyone in Platonov's universe, Voshchev moves through an obscure present on the road to an only dimly imagined future. Ceaseless personal sacrifice in service to a vague general goal is the only activity available to this generation. "He looked around: everywhere the steam of living breath hung over space, creating a sleepy, stifling invisibility; endurance dragged on wearily in the world, as if everything living found itself somewhere in the middle of time and its own movement; its beginning had been forgotten by everyone, its end was unknown, and nothing remained but a direction to all sides. And so Voshchev disappeared down the only open road" (65–66).

Platonov continues his own endless journey on this single available path in his work *Happy Moscow* which he worked on from 1933 to 1936.[40] On a map where everything is being built from scratch, it is not yet obvious where top and bottom will lie, and even those who are unambiguously part of the new world must struggle for orientation. This becomes particularly clear in Platonov's haunting vision of the new world and its builder, Moskva Chestnova. The heroine of *Happy Moscow* participates fully in the construction of the new world. As a member of the parachute corps, she is one of the new Soviet elite, and she cements that reputation by contributing as well to the building of the Moscow subway system, one of the most visible and highly touted of Stalin's many construction projects. Yet she, too, is disoriented and finds it problematic to chart a course in the new Soviet universe.

As we have already seen, construction of the Moscow subway was perceived by politicians and literary authorities as a momentous opportunity to facilitate both personal change and collective literary labor. Writers of all stripes were to join the process of constructing Soviet culture, and it makes particular sense that Platonov, an engineer and writer who fervently hoped to join the public discourse, might have sought a way to make his manuscript relevant to that timely debate. Like the Belomor canal and its accompanying literary incarnation, the subway project was deemed essential to ongoing plans for building both the new Soviet man and the unique environment in which he would reside, and Platonov undoubtedly would have wanted to comment on that process.

We know from archival materials and the writer's own correspondence that Platonov had sought to be included in the writer brigades that played such a role during this period.[41] Documents from the secret police files from 1933, for example, indicate that he was interested in such a role on the Belomor project. He was ostensibly introduced to Semyon Firin, the head of construction at Belomor, by Leopold Averbakh in that year. The police informant who reported this information claimed that Platonov wanted to meet with Firin in order "to realize an interesting project for the electrification of water transportation" on the canal project. Although the constrained nature of such reports makes it necessary to treat these accounts with caution, it is quite likely that the author, a loyal Soviet citizen and man of science, did look for a way to be included in such a highly visible construction project.[42] Alexander Solzhenitsyn's moral certitude in condemning the Belomor literary project is unassailable, to be sure, but Platonov's example suggests, again, that there were myriad reasons for cooperation on such projects. As Mikhail Ryklin has argued, the metro project in particular was important as a symbolic "discourse," but for an engineer like Platonov, the technical aspects of such construction would have been equally as fascinating as its symbolic nature. Platonov was still active as an engineer and inventor during this period, and it seems likely that he would have been interested in both the subway "discourse" and its real-life incarnation.[43]

He hardly needed exposure to the construction site. As he noted in his answers to a pointed official questionnaire from the journal *Na literaturnom postu* in 1931, Platonov explained that his "primary profession was electrician" (*eletrotekhnik*) and that he was "familiar and I want to be even more familiar with construction." As he discreetly points out, "the environment in which I grew up and work experience in socialist construction gave me everything, although I have yet to master it completely." With such seniority, Platonov could afford to be skeptical of writers who traveled to the work site for short and inevitably superficial visits. Such trips were fine, if nothing else could be arranged, he argued, but the "best way to participate in socialist construction is straightforward, hard, shock work as a laborer, a technical specialist, and so on." The questionnaire wondered "What Kind of Author We Need," and Platonov's response was unequivocal: "It is impossible to be a 'pure' writer. It is necessary to get a technical education and dive into the thick of the republic. Art will find time to be born in free moments."[44]

Platonov's inclusion of a metro worker in his novel from this period, then, is predictable. His use of her there, however, is more evidence of his highly unusual treatment of themes that were common to early Stalinism. Moskva Ivanovna receives her iconic name in an orphanage where she has landed after the revolution and civil war leave her country in shambles. The story of her individual life begins with that historic event: her first memory is of a man running by her house with a revolutionary torch in his hand, and that image haunts her for the rest of her existence. Whenever she remembered it, we are told, she "would immediately change her life:

if she was dancing, she would stop dancing; if she was working, she would work more surely, with more concentration; if she was alone, she would cover her face with her hands."[45] Tied as her life is to the revolution, Moskva provides the perfect example of the new human being who will inhabit the new world under construction. Her participation in the plan to build a subway in Moscow in the mid-1930s offers the precise site for such a transformation to take place.

So fully identified with the capital city that she bears its name, Moskva is nevertheless able to achieve perspective on her society only by dangling her head upside down from the window of her multistoried apartment house. This prestigious "new building" houses the elite of the new world—"pilots, aircraft designers, engineers of all kinds, philosophers, theoretical economists, and members of other professions" (18). Suspended on the windowsill above the city, however, Moskva finds no vantage point from which to define space permanently. She is surrounded not by an endless frontier or by well-defined boundaries but by amorphous and poorly delineated space. Mysterious, artificial structures and brooding elements from the natural world create an architectural ensemble that makes the radiant future no more recognizable than the past. "The windows of her flat looked out over the neighboring city roofs while far off, in the faint, fading extremity of space, she could see thick woods and enigmatic watch-towers; at sunset some kind of strange disc would glitter there, reflecting the last of the sunlight onto the clouds and the sky. It was around 10 or 15 kilometers to this alluring land, but, were she to go down onto the street, Moscow would never find her way there . . ." (18).[46] Platonov's description here provides all of the elements we are used to in his picture of constructed Soviet space. Events take place in the same, slightly malevolent *prostransto* that we have seen before in his novels, the ancestral forests and strange towers (*zagadochnye vyshki*) only adding to our sense of foreboding. The strange, glittering disc reminds us of Prushevskii's tower; here, too, our impulse is to turn away from a future that is too remote even to be found.

From this vantage point, high above the metropolis, Moskva can see another world as well as the familiar one below. "From above" she notes a second layer of life on the city's rooftops. Entire families come out of their apartments to sleep in the fresh air, and couples in love spend the whole night long perched there, "beneath the stars yet above the multitude of humanity" (20). Moskva's bird's-eye perspective allows her entry into the lives of the late shift, as she watches night workers come home from their jobs just as others are waking. This perspective on "turbine operators and engine

drivers, radio technicians, scientific researchers, aircraft mechan-
ics manning early flights, and others" (20) gives her special insight
into the new universe under construction, and she empathizes with
all those laboring to build a better world. Her thoughts on the matter serve almost as a catalogue of Five-Year Plan projects, as she
itemizes the main industrial developments around her. Her "imagination was continually at work and had never yet tired."

> In her solitude she filled the whole world with her attention, watching
> over the flame in the street lights to make sure they went on shining,
> listening to the resounding thuds of the steam-pile drivers on the
> Moscow River to ensure the piles went securely down into the depths,
> thinking about the machines which exerted their power day and
> night so that light would burn in the darkness, so that the reading of
> books would continue, so that rye could be milled by electric motors
> for the early morning bake, so that water could be pumped through
> pipes into warm shower-rooms in dance halls and the conception of
> a better life could take place in people's ardent and firm embraces—in
> the dark, in privacy, face to face, in the pure emotion of a united, dou-
> ble happiness. (19)

Moskva's perspective on these grand events moves soon from
voyeurism and vicarious pleasure to a sense of participation and,
finally, responsibility for the activity. She wanted "not so much to
experience this life as to make sure that it came about," to "stand
night and day near the brake lever of the locomotive that was taking people to meet one another; she wanted to repair water mains,
to weigh out medicines on pharmaceutical scales" (19). Once
again, Platonov's character seeks balance between the individual
and the collective. Her altruism does not supplant Moskva's own
needs—"she too wanted somewhere to put her large body"—but
complements them. "She was not denying her own needs," the author tells us, "she was merely postponing these needs for a more
distant future." She was "patient and able to wait" (16).[47]
With her perspective thus set on the vast and far away, Moskva
has difficulty understanding a narrower point of view. She notes,
for example, that the corridor to the housing cooperative is always
crowded with people talking "about every subject under the sun."
Her description of such conversation captures some of the flavor
of quotidian existence, or *byt,* in Soviet Russia, but Moskva is mys-
tified as to why people would restrict themselves to conversations
about "food supplies, repairs to the toilets in the yard, the coming
war, the stratosphere, and the death of the local laundry-woman,
who had been deaf and insane." Moskva "could not understand

why people clung to the housing co-operative, to the office, to letters of reference, to the local needs of a small happiness, to wearing themselves out in trivialities, when the city had world-class theaters and there were still eternal enigmas of suffering to be resolved in life" (26–27). Her observations of the pettiness of normal existence in the corridor serve as warning and presentiment. She notices a poster with a "picture of a man shaped like the letter Я, one of his legs cut short by a road accident." The Cyrillic letter to which she refers is the letter used for the personal pronoun "I," of course. As Platonov's narrative and Moskva's story develop, this individual self will be cut short.

In this familiar Platonic setting, then, pitting everyday existence with eternal questions, Moskva's Soviet rags-to-riches story proceeds in orthodox fashion. Her patronymic—Ivanovna—reflects her connection to the "average Russian Red Army man," and her last name is said to reflect the "honesty of her heart" (4). Like Sasha Dvanov, Moskva barely escapes the narrow and constrained existence of individual life. Still a young woman, she marries a "chance" man, "forever spoiling her body and her youth." Her "large hands, fit for bold activity," are "taken up with embraces" instead. Her "heart, which had looked for heroism, began to love just one sly man, who kept a tight hold on her, as if she were some inalienable asset" (6). Despite this inauspicious beginning, however, Moskva manages to escape the lonely existence as an individual that will otherwise be her fate. One morning she feels so "achingly ashamed of her life, not quite knowing exactly why," that she leaves her husband, in the first of a series of restless departures she will make in the novel (6).

Newly homeless, Moskva is chosen almost at random for flight school, picked up off the street and offered the opportunity in magical fashion. Soon she is parachuting from airplanes and living among the elite. She eats the finest cuisine that the Stalinist 1930s have to offer, and she dresses in the newest fashions, crafted from material so fine that the very beat of her heart can be seen through its gossamer layers. Her rescuer is Viktor Bozhko, whose activity as an urban planner makes him one of many characters to share a vocation with the author. Bozhko, like nearly all the males in the narrative, is fascinated by Moskva, and he imagines the beating of her heart in "her large bosom" as a force powerful enough to "regulate the course of events" throughout the "whole world" (12).

Her connection with this life force places Moskva in the same position as Sasha Dvanov, who envisioned an empty space within his own body where external forces could meet and create.[48] Moskva, too, imagines herself as a vessel, a conduit for elemental powers that nearly overwhelm the individual receptacle. Jumping out of the airplane, she "felt she was an empty tube, with the wind blowing right through her," and she holds "her mouth constantly open so she would manage to breathe out this savage wind that was piercing right through her." Hurtling toward the ground after her dive out of the plane, she notices that the "wind tore harshly at her body, as if it were not the wind of celestial space but some heavy, dead substance," even "harder and still more merciless" than the earth itself. "So, world, this is what you're really like!" she thinks, just before being brought up short, both by the revelation and by the force of the cruel wind against her solitary parachute (16–17).

This notion of the human body as a passageway for nearly overwhelming natural forces also connects Moskva to Sambikin, another of Platonov's eccentric scientists. Sambikin is obsessed with a life force that he suspects is hidden in the deepest chambers of the human body. Looking for the source of this mysterious essence, he comes to believe the body serves as a reservoir for the "long-lasting power of life" for a short period of time after the individual dies. He becomes convinced that "at the moment of death some kind of hidden sluice must open in the human body, and that from there flows through the organism a special fluid" containing this elusive substance. Sambikin's research is intended to "transform the dead into a force that would nourish the longevity and health of the living," and he probes deep into the cavities of the human intestine in his search for the secret. Much as he tries, however, his success, like that of both Sasha Dvanov and Moskva, actually depends on finding "that hidden sluice," the passage that will join the eternal and the temporary forever (49–50). His belief that "life was only one of the rare peculiarities of eternally dead material" helps establish him as yet another character in Platonov's work attempting to avoid obvious binarities. He is convinced that "the dead needed as little to come back to life as they had previously needed in order to die" (98).

Sambikin is fascinated with Moskva, but he turns away from her consciously, in an attempt to conserve the energy he needs for his research and to spare her the experience of exchanging "all the noise of life for the whisper of a single human being" (45). A fanatic with little time for anything but his scientific endeavors, Sambikin nevertheless realizes that his own efforts are infinitesimal in light of the endless need for progress. He is driven to find the source of life, but he continues despite his clear understanding of "how much a human being was still a poorly constructed, homespun creature—no more than a vague embryo, or blueprint, of something more authentic." His dreams of future progress tie him explicitly to Moskva and her flight above earth: "how much more work was needed," he thinks, "in order for this embryo to develop into the soaring, lofty image that lies buried in our dream" (38).

Sambikin consciously rejects Moskva's considerable physical charms in order to devote himself to the soaring cause they both serve. The mechanic Semen Sartorius, however, is fascinated by Moskva as a woman, and he soon succumbs unwillingly to his physical desire, which he knows in advance will result in nothing "except foolishness and personal happiness!" (48). Moskva, too, expects nothing from such individual pursuits, and, as she rejects the notion of private happiness, she recalls for Sartorius a woman she once saw who was facing the wall and crying with bitterness over her own wasted past (60). Semen and Moskva consummate their physical relationship on the edge of the metropolis, where such individual desires can be met, but both know that their sexual relations represent only a "child-like, blissful joy" and cannot solve the more important problem of "drawing people into the mystery of a shared existence" (61). Moskva, in particular, rejects the possibility of immediate individual happiness. Instead "she wanted to go away into the incalculable life that had long tormented her heart with a premonition of unknown pleasure—into the darkness of people and crowds, so as to live out with them the mystery of her existence" (62).

Moskva's behavior in the rest of the novel puzzles many readers and some of her fellow characters, and, at times, even she herself seems to be perplexed by her choices. Yet her later actions mirror those identified in the passage above rather closely. She rejects the narrowness of private fulfillment in favor of a more generalized existence that partakes of shared emotion. Her decision to visit the failed artist and poet Komiagin, for example, and her willing humiliation at his hands (78–82) are examples of her attempt to experience the "darkness of people and crowds" and to comprehend in that fashion "the mystery of her existence." Moskva stands with her face to the wall in the corridor outside of Komiagin's apartment in a clear visual repetition of the image of the crying woman she has earlier rejected. Platonov follows this rehearsal of individual passions with an authoritative statement in the text, making it clear that the meaning of life lies elsewhere: "No, this was not the high road that led into the distance; the road of life did not pass through the poverty of love, or through the intestines, or through the zealous attempts of a Sartorius to comprehend precise trifles" (82).

His reference to "comprehension of precise trifles" is one of many biographical notes in this narrative. Throughout much of the time he was working on the manuscript, Platonov was employed by Rosmetroves, an institute charged with standardization of the system of weights and measures throughout the Soviet Union.[49] The job of weighing and measuring the results of the revolution fell to Platonov in a literal sense in his job at Rosmetroves, and it is not surprising, then, that he includes the same job in his narrative. It provides him with a rich avenue to discuss the metaphoric reckoning of the era that he and his fellow writers included in their production novels. He subscribes such activity in the novel to Sartorius, who is asked by Bozhko to develop some simple, precise, and inexpensive scales for "all the collective and state farms and for the whole of Soviet commerce." Here, too, the text reads like a manual on industrialization, explaining to the reader the many issues involved in the endless process of bringing rationality to the rapidly modernizing country. Bozhko explains to Sartorius about the "great and unnoticed problems of the national economy: the additional difficulties experienced by socialism on the collective farms, the reduced payments to collective farmers, kulak politics that exploited the inaccuracy of weights, scales and balances, and the massive, if involuntary, defrauding of working-class consumers in cooperatives and distribution centers . . ." (53).

Sartorius is skeptical of the project: Archimedes and Mendeleev had already worked on the problem of scales, after all. He even begins crying against his own will as he sits over his calculations, "covering sheet after sheet of paper with calculations of prisms, levers, deformation tensions, costs of materials and other data" (67). Sartorius has already understood that such equations will not bring him any closer to the real meaning of life, and his tears reflect his reluctant grief over that fact. He understands, too, what Sambikin with his search for the soul of life does not. There is no way to "ascend in one bound to a mountain peak from which times and spaces would become visible to the ordinary grey gaze of man" (68). Sartorius knows that nature is "too difficult" for such "instant victories and could not be confined within a single law" (69).

Even as a young man, Platonov seems to have shared Sartorius's mature skepticism toward the illusory aspects of the exalted perspective. In a polemical article from 1920, he railed against those who love "the unknown, the heavenly, the distant" and claimed that "we won't trade a lump of horse manure" for such "sky-blue heights" (*golubaia vys'*). His objection is practical here; at least the manure can be used as fertilizer. From "good, rich soil, much bread will grow and this bread will be used for feeding our many children, who will come out to fight for sense and the truth of the universe." With the "sky-blue heights," however, "we can do nothing."[50]

Unlike her male counterparts, who first seek their answers in a single, exalted location, Moskva quickly comprehends that the complexity of life demands a multivalent solution. "At times she felt so good that she wanted somehow to leave herself behind, to leave her body and dress, and become someone else" (44). At other moments "she wanted to take part in everything and she was filled by that indeterminacy of life which is just as happy as its definitive resolution" (87). With such thoughts, Moskva sees a poster inviting the Komsomol to "Help build the metro!" and she obeys this exhortation. Her work on the subway gives her an underground perspective to complement the bird's-eye view she had as a parachutist, and the move beneath the earth marks the beginning of her dissolution as a separate individual. She is soon wounded in a subway accident, and the dream she has while on the operating table suggests a grotesque version of her goal of participating in everything. As she runs down the street in her dream toward an "empty sea," she is torn, bit by bit, into pieces. The animals and people who attack her begin gradually to reduce her torso and limbs, but she is willing to endure this, "anything not to return to the terrible place she had run away from, anything to survive, even if only as a worthless creature composed of a few dry bones" (100). When she awakes, she finds that Sambikin has amputated her injured leg, and, with this singular deformation, she is well on her way to disappearing into the masses.

As her recuperation continues, Moskva makes plans to return to Komiagin: "I'm lame now—I'm a lame woman!" she comments with certainty. "I'll go away, I'll go away somewhere," she whispers repeatedly as she "looks for hours into irrevocable space" (102–3). Sambikin takes her to recuperate on the Black Sea, where the "movement of water in space reminded Moskva Chestnova of the great destiny of her life: the world really was infinite and there was nowhere its ends would ever meet" (105). Once she leaves Sambikin's care, she is reunited with Komiagin, and she begins her final disintegration as an individual, losing her individual personality and, eventually, even her name.

Sartorius, standing in the corridor outside of Komiagin's apartment listening to Moskva live out the "mystery of her existence" among the people, finally himself understands how "impoverished he was to have only a single torso that was closed in from every side" (114). When he hears that Moskva is "lost somewhere in the space of this city and of humanity," he becomes "merrier" and soon begins "imagining of other souls," experiencing "unknown sensations of being in a new body." He thinks about the "thoughts in other people's heads," and begins to "walk with a gait that was not his own" (127). Before long he, too, has taken on a new name and identity, and the novel ends with this new persona ready to overcome a final dichotomy between animate and inanimate existence. It is a fitting end to the collectively imagined production novel to see its last heroine disappear without a trace into the people, its last hero confusing "every object," all of which "seemed to him to become a likeness, or a distortion, of someone familiar, someone they all knew—and that might even have been his own self" (136–37).

In the increasingly monologic universe in which Platonov labored over *Happy Moscow*, such polyphonic solutions would meet with only growing hostility. By the time he finished working on the manuscript in 1936,[51] the purges were already carrying away colleagues in both the technical and the literary world. For decades afterward, Platonov's narrative would remain an almost unknown experiment on the margins of Soviet literature. But this long forgotten work carried invaluable information about the master narrative that crowded it off the stage, suggesting the multiplicity of voices that were asking to be heard even as a single state soliloquy threatened to drown them out permanently. In the end, Platonov and other authors of transitional production novels offered a lesson that transcended their Stalinist times: literature would survive not through administrative fiat or official mandate but by the efforts of single authors who envisioned their individual endeavors as part of an enduring cultural tradition that changed form over time but retained its essential significance.

A Conclusion and a Beginning

THE TRAGIC TONE THAT ANDREI PLATONOV ADOPTS WHEN SPEAKing of Soviet construction is appropriate to the era that this transitional production literature describes. Platonov saw and understood the enormous losses that accompanied great Soviet hopes, and he employed a sorrowful register as the only one suitable to describe that unique misery. For his part, Olesha counseled a pitiless indifference to approach the future, but he followed his own advice poorly, and his work is characterized by anguish and torment as often as the requisite optimism. Shaginian saw the construction of Soviet culture as an assignment to be completed; her approach to loss and failure was dogged persistence, a trait she shared with many of her fellow writers. Ilf and Petrov suggest a similar tack, though with a lighter touch and more humor. The continued popular success of their work demonstrates a human longing for comic relief even in the most dire of circumstances, though it shows, as well, how willing we are to pay nearly any cost in service to a distant but fondly held dream. Even Kataev, perhaps the most enthusiastic of any of these authors, later revealed his understanding of the price of such utopian aspirations. Pilniak, too, chronicled the guilt such authors felt for their role in building such elaborate and costly human construction projects.

Like Platonov's engineer Prushevskii, these writers turned away from the castles of the future, rejecting the fantasy of science fiction to catalog their own times. Infinitely more complex than later examples of the genre suggest, these early production novels dealt as often with collapsed bridges as they did with palaces of labor, and emptiness played as big a role as erected structures. Attempting to build more authentic selves along with the new world they were constructing, the authors struggled as well to give meaning to the societal losses they could clearly perceive. They saw their own roles as important contributors to a process that was painful but necessary to achieve a much desired goal. In their minds, the end justified their means.

As we attempt to reconstruct the history of this particular period of Russian literature, we need to work hard at overcoming the limitations of our own expectations. Although the projects that are detailed in these production novels led in the end to a Soviet Union permanently *na remonte,* permanently under repair, that end was not a foregone conclusion. Both those engaged in the work of construction and those tasked with chronicling that process believed they were building a new and better world. To understand the production novel, we need to explore the alternative space that its earliest examples imagined. On closer inspection, that space reveals a landscape devoid of the easy dichotomies we have associated with this genre and the period. By building a better metaphor for the writers of this complex era of literary history, we have a chance at understanding what Platonov called their "destroyed lives" much better.

As the Moscow conceptual art group Gnezdo pointed out in 1976, the iron curtain that separated the "West" from the "East" was itself a concept. Like one of Platonov's walls, it hid the future that constantly recedes from us. When that curtain was finally drawn, it revealed a world without clear boundaries or easy solutions. It makes sense, then, that the production novel might even be revived as we enter a new century with new problems that resemble very old dilemmas. It should no longer be surprising to learn that author Kseniia Buksha produced *Veroiatnost',* a new "production novel" published in St. Petersburg in 2002, or that Boris Akunin, one of the most popular writers on Russia's vigorous commercial market, should announce plans for his own version of the genre. They, like countless writers at work before them, are looking for answers to the grand questions that continue to bedevil us, searching for ways to unite human society rather than surrender to artificial divisions. The hope of finding such answers is what drove the earliest authors of production novels in their quest to construct what they hoped would be a better and more just Soviet world. By looking carefully at their fragile successes and their tragic failures, we can learn much of use for our own continued search.

Notes

INTRODUCTION

1. Speer, *Inside*, 58–59.
2. See Igor Golomstock, *Totalitarian Art*, for a discussion of characteristics and genres thought to be typical of totalitarian art. Katerina Clark, who argues that the more a regime is "in need of legitimization and aggrandizement, the more likely it has been to appropriate neoclassical architecture and symbols," suggests that such a state characterized both Stalinist Russia and Fascist Europe (Clark, *Petersburg*, 65). Geyer and Fitzpatrick, *Beyond Totalitarianism*, is one of numerous scholarly comparisons of Nazism and Stalinism to appear this century.
3. The scale model and Hitler's similar fascination with it are discussed in Speer, *Inside*, 132–34.
4. Irina Gutkin identifies the production novel as the "most common literary form" in *Cultural Origins*, 1. Katerina Clark's definition of the genre as "the most common type of Stalinist novel" can be found in *Soviet Novel*, 256; emphasis Clark.
5. According to Marsh, "no clearly definable boundaries" distinguish the "conventional 'production novel' and the rather more interesting 'science novel'" that it ostensibly also resembles (*Soviet Fiction*, 23, 24). Nina Kolesnikoff argues that such works, which she calls "industrial" novels, "developed under the influence of two Western authors, Pierre Hamp and Bernhard Kellermann" (*Bruno Jasieński*, 93–94), although the similarities she notes are primarily thematic.
6. Clark, *Soviet Novel*, 99; emphasis Clark. In a later assertion of the importance of the early production novel to the development of Socialist Realism, Clark argues that the production novel was the "pro-obraz sotsialisticheskogo romana" (Klark, "RAPP," 221).
7. Stephen Kotkin, "Modern Times," 130; emphasis Kotkin.
8. See Clark, *Soviet Novel* and Gutkin, *Cultural Origins* in particular. Regine Robin takes issue with Clark's unusual periodization of the Stalinist era in Robin, *Socialist Realism*, especially 254–55. Classic early discussions of the period include Harriet Borland, *Soviet Literary Theory*, and Edward Brown, *Proletarian Episode*. The end of Soviet power has led, naturally, to a welcome reevaluation of the literature from 1917 to 1991, as archival material and long hidden facts come to life. A recent Russian forum on literature written to order is further evidence of the ongoing need to reexamine the Soviet period (see "1920–e: Sotsial'nyi zakaz i strategii samorealizatsii," *Novoe literaturnoe obozrenie* 78 [2006]: 7–84). This is particularly true for the Stalinist period. Andreas Guski's extended study of the production novel focuses on the literature of the First Five-Year Plan (*Literatur und Arbeit*). Karen McCauley offers an interesting approach to the genre

in "Production Literature," where she argues that the foundations of production literature lie in critical developments from the end of the nineteenth century. Compelling studies of the diary genre under Stalin are welcome additional contributions to our understanding of literature during the period; see, for example, Hellbeck, *Revolution*, and Garros, Korenevskaya, and Lahusen, *Intimacy and Terror.*

9. The term "cultural revolution," commonly used to describe and explain events in Soviet society during approximately the years of the First Five-Year Plan, has been called into question. See, for example, the discussion in Fox, "What is Cultural Revolution?" and Fitzpatrick, "Cultural Revolution Revisited."

10. This is the title of an article by Fredric Jameson devoted to issues of postmodern architecture.

11. Boris Groys has been a leader in describing this Soviet development as the legacy of the prerevolutionary avant-garde. He notes, for example, that culture under Stalin "inherited the avant-garde belief that humanity could be changed and was driven by the conviction that human beings were malleable" ("Utopian Mass Culture," 13).

12. Tolstoy's comment is the final sentence in his contribution to *Pisateli ob iskusstve i o sebe*, 19.

13. Jeffrey Brooks, in his study of the official press of this era, particularly the newspaper *Pravda*, notes that the "schema of socialist building gained sway" around 1927 (see Brooks, *Thank You, Comrade Stalin!*, 23 and 24–27, 38, 48–49, 54–59). Rolf Hellebust explores the industrial metaphor in early Soviet society in *Flesh to Metal: Soviet Literature and the Alchemy of Revolution* (Ithaca: Cornell University Press, 2003).

14. For these and other statistics, Milka Bliznakov, "Soviet Housing," 85. As Bliznakov notes in an article on the architectural avant-garde, "architecture . . . was in the forefront of the new Soviet culture from the beginning of its development in the 1920s. Actual construction, however, was limited because of lack of funds until the Five-Year Plan" (Bliznakov, "Nietzschean Implications," 174).

15. See David Cowling, *Building the Text*, 140–42, for a longer discussion of the importance of the author/builder metaphor to classical literature. See Dobrenko's comment in *Making of the State Writer*, 372. As historian Sergei Zhuravlev has pointed out, one of the many crimes of Stalin's regime was its "parasitic use of the sincere enthusiasm" that people felt during this period (Zhuravlev, *Fenomen*, 5). Gorky's epistle to Stalin can be found in Artizov and Naumov, *Vlast'*, 125.

16. According to Sergei Zhuravlev in his outstanding overall history of the venture *Istoriia fabrik i zavodov SSSR*, the idea for the publishing house arose almost spontaneously (*Fenomen*, 5). One clear indication of the significance of the publishing venture is the number of prestigious publications it put out; see Bouvard, *Le Metro de Moscou*, 119.

17. Zhuravlev, *Fenomen*, 5.

18. Stephen Hanson suggests that such an approach was distinctly Soviet. Hanson sees the Soviet concept of time as a combined "charismatic-rational" approach borrowed from Marx that attempted to use "rational time discipline to master time itself" (ix). Echoes of this attempt to constrict or control time can be heard particularly in the project to document construction of the Moscow subway.

19. This concept of reforging, or *perekovka*, enjoyed its greatest currency at the end of the 1920s and the beginning of the 1930s. The camp newspapers for the Belomor Canal, for example, and for the subsequent construction of the Moscow-Volga Canal (1933–37) were both named *Perekovka*. For a more com-

plete discussion of reforging, see Ruder, *Making History for Stalin*, 142–53, and *"perekovka"* in Mokienko and Nikitina, *Tolkovyi slovar'*, 432. Viacheslav Polonskii, who visited the famous Magnitogorsk construction site in the Urals in 1931, described the connection between construction and humans succinctly: "Not only are the mountain and the steppe being rebuilt in Magnitogorsk. Man himself is being rebuilt" ("Magnitostroi," 152).

20. Stalin's caustic remark was reported by literary functionary Valerii Kirpotin, who noted that "Stalin emphasized: on the basis of successes in socialist construction, an enormous increase in the number of writers should be expected. He said: 'The writers will come like little fishes'" (Kirpotin, *Rovesnik*, 183). Stalin compared the writers to the common roach (*plotva*).

21. Newer approaches reflected, for example, in the volume *Socialist Spaces*, consciously "call into question the absolute status of the dichotomy of the great and the ordinary sites of socialism" throughout the eastern bloc (Crowley and Reid, *Socialist Spaces*, 5). This follows, of course, the path-breaking work done by Sheila Fitzpatrick, Stephen Kotkin, and others.

22. Gumbrecht's comments are from his study of the year 1926, where he notes that clear distinctions between "Center" and "Periphery" give "people the impression that they inhabit a homogeneous world space." Gumbrecht argues that such binary oppositions are prized by "geopoliticians," Hitler included, who want to "neutralize the ambivalences typically found in border spaces and transitions" (Gumbrecht, *In 1926*, 277–78). Jan Plamper has argued that a binary definition of censorship and cultural production has been remarkably resilient in studies of Soviet practices in the 1930s, perhaps because it is at the core of the self-definition of contemporary producers of texts, scholarly ones included (Plamper, "Abolishing Ambiguity," 526–27). See Alexei Yurchak, *Everything Was Forever*, 4–8, for another critique of the binary model, particularly as it is applied to the post-Stalinist period.

23. See Tony Pinkney's introduction to Raymond Williams, *The Politics of Modernism*, 16.

24. Jochen Hellbeck's study of the diary genre in the Stalinist period questions the utility of a binary structure in approaching the era, although he relies on it in parts of his own argument (see Hellbeck, *Revolution*, 86–97). Katerina Clark argues that a binary between eternal and ephemeral—or sacred and profane—is at the heart of Socialist Realism (Klark, "Sotsrealizm," 123). As we will see, however, many of the early production novels, although they were important forerunners of Socialist Realism, explicitly reject the spatial binary on which Clark bases her argument.

25. Vladimir Papernyi, *Kul'tura Dva*. Papernyi's work was published in English as *Architecture in the Age of Stalin: Culture Two* (New York: Cambridge University Press, 2002).

26. See, for example, Sergei Medvedev's reliance on Papernyi's categories in his essay "A General Theory," 33–43. Papernyi identifies 1932 as the "major turning point in Soviet cultural history, and architecture in particular" because of the restructuring of official artistic organizations in that year (Papernyi, "Men, Women, and the Living Space," 149, 150).

27. Elizabeth Papazian describes this problem in approaches to Gorky after the demise of the Soviet Union, noting a Gorky scholar's identification of the "principle of opposites" that followed the breakup of the country. "Everything that under Soviet power had been evaluated positively was automatically perceived as negative, and vice versa" (*Manufacturing Truth*, 129).

28. Todorov, *Facing the Extreme*, 138.

29. See Kotkin, *Magnetic Mountain*, for a compelling treatment of the way ordinary people learned to gain access to power in Stalin's Russia. Pile's comment comes in his discussion of the greater usefulness of Michel de Certeau's terminology when it is "wrenched from a narrowly dichotomized account, in which the powerful occupy and control space, and the powerless do the best they can" (Pile, "Introduction," 23).

30. Boym, *Common Places*, 30; emphasis Boym. The classic discussion of the importance of binary models in Russian culture is by Iurii Lotman and Boris Uspenskii, "Binary Models."

31. See Davies, "'Us Against Them,'" as well as her monograph *Popular Opinion*. Platonov's comment can be found in his industrial sketch "V poiskakh," 364. See also Igor' Smirnov's comment that "in the Stalinist empire, which is based on the Hegelian 'removal' of contradictions . . . , the place of the universal subject is occupied by the builder of 'socialism in a single country'" ("Sotsrealizm,"19).

32. N. Meshcheriakov, "O sotsialisticheskikh gorodakh,"161. According to Meshcheriakov, the answer lay in the "destruction of the opposition between the city and the village."

33. Groys, "The Art of Totality," 98.

34. See Stephen C. Hutchings, *Russian Modernism*.

35. Buchli uses the shift to a more contextualized approach toward the question of which items would be deemed "petit-bourgeois" to date the ascendancy of Stalinism. He calls the time of the First Five-Year Plan "the height of *byt* activism" (*Archeology*, 51, 119, and 55–56).

36. Clark, *Soviet Novel*, 256. Clark notes that Gladkov "has not divided his characters into 'positive' and 'negative,'" and she points out that when *Cement* "actually deals with agents of authority and control, the reader encounters ambiguity, sketchy development, and fuzziness" (ibid., 80, 82). Focused on developing her notion of the Stalinist "master plot," she largely ignores such ambiguities, however, concluding only in passing that *Cement* is "a text that can help us perceive that Stalinist culture was put together from a variety of preexisting elements" (ibid., 70). Curiously, in *Soviet Novel* Clark mentions the production novels by Boris Pilniak, Marietta Shaginian, and Valentin Kataev only in passing. She and Evgeny Dobrenko later identify *Hydrocentral* as a "model" production novel, implying that their characterization of the novel as a work which "glorified the heroic labor of the participants in the First Five-Year Plan" needs no clarification (*Soviet Culture*, 116).

37. Oleg Kharkhordin, "Reveal and Dissimulate," 340; emphasis Kharkhordin.

38. N. N. Kozlova describes such a viewpoint in her article on methodological approaches to the question of political power in literature in the Stalinist era (see Kozlova, "Soglasie").

39. Irina Gutkin, *Cultural Origins*, 1, 57, 71.

40. Regine Robin, *Socialist Realism*, 13. As Robin notes elsewhere "Soviet society in the 1930s was less monolithic, more complex and heterogeneous than the 'totalitarian' model leads us to believe" (Robin, "Stalinism and Popular Culture," 26).

41. Boris Groys, *The Total Art of Stalinism*.

42. Iu. K. Shcheglov, *Romany I. Il'fa i E. Petrova*, 11.

43. The NKVD report can be found in Artizov and Naumov, *Vlast'*, 238–39. Naturally, it is necessary to use information from secret police informants with ex-

treme caution. Complaints about writer compensation are reported in Babichenko, *"Schast'e literatury,"* 153.

44. See Joachim Klein's argument that even many of the political leaders who pressed authors into service were acting from real conviction, rather than expediency, as late as the mid-1930s. He makes his case in a study of the Belomor Canal album, where he concludes that the "line between lies and self-suggestion was vague" (*"Belomorkanal,"* 235).

45. Gladkov was ostensibly writing from the construction site at Kuzbass, which he argued would soon be "one of the cultural centers of our Union" ("Pisateli na krupneishie stroiki," 2).

46. Hans Gunter notes that fellow travelers were particularly likely to take up the production novel during the years of the First Five-Year Plan, when the genre assumed "particular significance" as a genre of "conversion" (*perekliuchenie*), although he argues that such writers were frequently "simulating" their enthusiasm ("Khudozhestvennyi avangard," 104–5). Following Andreas Guski, Gunter explains the formal intricacy of many production novels from this time as the result of authorial insincerity rather than as expected generic complexity during a transitional period.

47. Widdis, "Viewed from Below," 69.

48. Evgeny Dobrenko makes a similar argument in his assertion that the function of Socialist Realism was "to fill the space of 'socialism' with images of reality" (Dobrenko, *Political Economy*, 6).

49. This concept of "reforging," or *perekovka*, fascinated foreign observers too. André Gide, for example, in his account of an orchestrated trip to the Soviet Union in the late 1930s, regrets his inability to linger on the descriptions of certain charming tourist spots he visited in the country, but reminds us that "but it is not for this that I travelled to the U.S.S.R. The important thing for me here is man—men—what can be done with them, and what has been done." The often fatuous Gide was unimpressed by the actual building projects around him. Remarking that "Moscow is changing from month to month and is a town in process of formation," he nevertheless comments that "I am afraid it has started badly. On all sides buildings are being cut through, pulled down, undermined, suppressed, rebuilt, and all apparently at haphazard." He much preferred the "harmonious blending" and "perfectly proportioned" classicism of "St. Petersburg" (Gide, *Return*, 14–16).

50. Ilf died of tuberculosis in 1937. Pilniak was arrested in that same year and executed in 1938. Petrov died as a war correspondent in 1942. Platonov contacted tuberculosis from his dying teenaged son, who returned from arrest already ill with the disease. He died in 1951. Olesha, who became a hopeless alcoholic, died in 1960. Shaginian lived until 1982, while Kataev, apparently suffering pangs of conscience, made it until 1986.

51. Halfin and Hellbeck, "Rethinking," 460. As Halfin and Hellbeck note, the Stalinist period in particular has been colored by western reliance on the existence of this "transhistorical subject." See also Jochen Hellbeck's argument for the existence of "an illiberal, socialist subjectivity" in *Revolution*, 9. Choi Chatterjee and Karen Petrone provide an overview of shifting approaches to the Soviet self in Chatterjee and Petrone, "Models."

52. According to Krylova, an intellectual shift in the West "circumscribed interpretive possibilities within a set of binary categories: indoctrination/resistance, belief/disbelief, faith/cynicism" (120).

53. Selim Khan-Magomedov in Latour, *Rozhdenie metropolii,* 287. This is a recurring question when confronting totalitarian regimes, of course, and explains much of the interest in "everyday" life under both Stalin and Hitler. See, for example, such studies as Sheila Fitzpatrick, *Everyday Stalinism;* Lewis Siegelbaum and Andrei Sokolov, *Stalinism as a Way of Life;* N. B. Lebina, *Povsednevnaia zhizn';* Valentina Antipina, *Povsednevnaia zhizn';* and Timo Vihavainen, *Normy i tsennosti,* as well as the importance of *Alltagsgeschichte* in scholarship on the Nazi period, as evidenced by such studies as Johnson and Reuband, *What We Knew,* 2005. The appearance of numerous previously unpublished diaries written under both Nazi and Stalinist regimes makes it clear that the question was topical even for contemporary observers. See, for example, Victor Klemperer's many puzzled attempts to fathom either public sentiment or intellectual support for Hitler (*I Will Bear Witness,* 386 and throughout). Elizabeth Papazian's study of the "documentary moment" in early Soviet culture includes a similar attempt to understand what motivated the "humanist" Gorky and his "Stalinist" self (Papazian, *Manufacturing Truth,* 125–66, especially 132–33).

Chapter 1. *Envy*

1. V. O. Pertsov, for example, noting that Leonov's *River Sot'* and Marietta Shaginian's *Hydrocentral* appeared only at the beginning of the 1930s, argues that *Envy* was perhaps the first novel in Soviet literature to treat industrial motifs. Pertsov describes Olesha's "whimsical, artistic refraction" of the theme (see Pertsov, "Iurii Olesha," 288). Gladkov's *Cement* predated all of these works, of course, but it was primarily concerned with restoration rather than new construction. Kirill Postoutenko sees distant echoes of Tommaso Campanella's 1602 *City of the Sun* in images from Olesha's "Strogii iunosha" ("Istoricheskii optimizm," 485). As Galina Belaia astutely points out, formal complexity was usually the first thing to catch the notice of representatives of Soviet power looking for aberrant content, and on that point, Olesha stood out ("Stilevoi regress," 556).

2. *Pervyi vsesoiuznyi s"ezd,* 235–36.

3. Ibid., 236. See Gleb Struve for a discussion of Olesha's difficulty with contemporary themes and his "dialogue with himself" in Struve, *Russian Literature,* 242–44.

4. *Pervyi vsesoiuznyi s"ezd,* 234. For Olesha, the notion of bifurcation was inherent in intellectual life. In his 1930 diaries, for example, he describes a character in a novel he is planning as an individual who "hates himself for his intellectualism, 'Hamletism,' bifurcation (*razdvoennost'*)" and sees the Russian intellectual as someone who "doubts, suffers, bifurcates." Olesha declares that his dream is to "stop being an intellectual" (see Olesha, *Kniga proshchaniia,* 41, 55). Olesha continues this theme in several places, arguing, for example, in 1930 that intellectuals "should write only about themselves. It's necessary to write confessions, not novels" (see Gudkova, *Iurii Olesha,* 37).

5. The phrase is Katerina Clark's in *Soviet Novel,* 256.

6. *Pervyi vsesoiuznyi s"ezd,* 235. According to Veniamin Kaverin, Olesha very quickly, "about six years before the congress," became convinced that *Envy* marked the end of his career (quoted in Viktor Vasil'ev, "Prince Faberge," 9).

7. As Andrew Barratt notes about Olesha's 1929 story "The Cherry Pit," Olesha's anxiety included "fear that his own willingness to serve the new Russia

might simply be ignored" (see Barratt's comment in his short but interesting study *Yurii Olesha's Envy*, 60). This fear, which Olesha shared with so many of his generation, seems to have haunted him for most of his life, engendering or exacerbating a long-lasting artistic crisis for the author. Olesha's example supports Igor Smirnov's contention that a fundamental characteristic of totalitarian systems is the erasure of the boundary between law breakers and obedient citizens, leaving everyone equally afraid of punishment (see Smirnov, "Sotsrealism: antropologicheskie izmerenie," 17). Boris Wolfson argues that Olesha turned to the diary form in 1930 in order to "reinvent himself as a Soviet writer" ("Escape from Literature," 609).

8. *Pervyi vsesoiuznyi s"ezd*, 235. The beggar is just one of the literary doubles Olesha creates for himself. As Elizabeth Klosty Beaujour points out in her elegant study of Olesha's work, another of the writer's creations, author and fellow traveler Zand, ends up repeating some of Olesha's own speeches nearly verbatim (see Beaujour, *Invisible Land*, 102).

9. *Pervyi vsesoiuznyi s"ezd*, 236. The significance of the ovation for Olesha did not escape the attention of the secret police; an informant reported to them, for example, the comments of delegate P. Sletov, who complained that although "90 percent of what was said at the congress was the typical made-to-order banality" (*kazennaia poshlost'*), the heartfelt ovations for Pasternak and Olesha "could not be suppressed by anything" (Artizov and Naumov, *Vlast'*, 241).

10. On the sense of ostracism that nonparty writers, or fellow travelers, felt during this time, see Vera Inber's comments, for example, in her published diaries from the early 1930s. Inber describes herself as literature's "stepdaughter," a designation she received as a result of her identification as "petty bourgeois." Inber notes that her "stepdaughter" status disappeared with the April 23 Central Committee announcement that did away with RAPP hegemony in literature (Inber, *Sobranie sochinenii*, 4:423, 426). Inber's comments on Olesha after his death in 1960 make use of a still timely architectural metaphor to explain the writer's continued importance in Russian literature. She notes that Olesha's central work, *Envy*, correctly identified the ominous influence of the past on plans for the future. Now that we stand on the threshold of the "bright, shining building of communism," Inber comments, "we need to enter that building without taking any of the assortment of obsolete feelings" with us. Olesha, Inber argues, understood that architectural imperative well in advance of his contemporaries (Inber, 4:326). Like other fellow travelers, Inber seems to have used the construction site to cement her loyalty to the regime; see her inclusion, for example, in a writers' brigade in 1931 ("Pisateli na krupneishie stroiki," 2).

11. Olesha's sense of being old before his time was common among writers of his generation, particularly among fellow travelers whose social background, moral scruples, psychological makeup, or stylistic approach alienated them from writers who claimed to be in better touch with the times.

12. *Pervyi vsesoiuznyi s"ezd*, 235. The brilliantly lit construction site that Olesha mentions in passing was a popular trope of the early production novel. It is used to effect in the preface to David Saslavsky's journalistic *Dnieprostroi*, published in 1932 for foreign readers (5–6).

13. *Pervyi vsesoiuznyi s"ezd*, 235.

14. As Peter Burke notes in his study of historical images, such an image of a landscape inevitably "evokes political associations" as well (Burke, *Eyewitnessing*, 43).

15. Lefebvre, *The Production of Space*, 164.

16. In later reminiscences of Vladimir Mayakovsky, Olesha notes that the poet feigned confusion of the Russian title for the proposed novel—"*Nishchii*"—with the philosopher Nietzsche. When Olesha corrects Mayakovsky, explaining that he is writing about a beggar, not about the philosopher, Mayakovsky replies "It makes no difference" (see Olesha, *Kniga proshchaniia*, 145).

17. Olesha, *Kniga proshchaniia*, 57. Olesha's disgust with the "brown swill" of a Soviet intellectual's life was shared by many others, who periodically swore off their "overfed," drunken, disreputable way of life. See, for example, Ivan Gronskii's promises to Stalin to swear off drinking, which he describes as a necessary part of his work with writers. Gronskii's description of his literary colleagues is entirely unflattering: "they bicker among themselves, plot, gossip, fawn, gather together all kinds of groups and gangs in their own interests" (see Gronskii's letter to Stalin, reprinted in part from archival documents, in Maksimenkov, "Ocherki," 55). Kornelii Zelinskii's description of the meeting of a group of well-known writers with Stalin, Kaganovich, Molotov, Voloshilov, and Postishev on October 26, 1932, portrays many of the authors as undisciplined, dissolute, and emotionally unstable. According to Zelinskii's account, by the time Stalin uttered his famous phrase "You are engineers of human souls," many of the writers he was addressing were so engaged in drinking they were not even listening to the leader (Zelinskii, "Odna vstrecha," 166).

18. *Kniga proshchaniia*, 97.

19. Ibid., 102–3. Olesha includes this image and his reworking of this text in a short story entitled "Zapiski pisatelia" from *Vishnevaia kostochka*, 48–62. Real-life beggars were a common sight in postrevolutionary Russia, wracked, as it was, by civil war, famine, and shortages. According to Natal'ia Lebina, for example, shortages even in the late 1920s and early 1930s made it difficult for nearly everyone to dress themselves (see Lebina, *Povsednevnaia zhizn'*, 218).

20. *Pervyi vsesoiuznyi s"ezd*, 235–6.

21. Pertsov, "Iurii Olesha," 288. Guski, too, includes Olesha in his discussion of *Literatur und Arbeit*.

22. *Pervyi vsesoiuznyi s"ezd*, 289.

23. Ibid., 287, 289.

24. See, for example, Libedinskii, *Rasskazy tovarishchei*, 1933, which was based on Libedinskii's interviews with workers. According to Katerina Clark, Libedinskii was criticized by RAPP (Russian Association of Proletarian Writers) members for his earlier novel *Rozhdenie geroia* from 1930, and his apology for alleged mistakes was followed by such "production sketches" (Klark, "RAPP i institutsializatsiia," 218).

25. See Evgeny Dobrenko, *Making of the State Writer*. As might be expected, the reality of this push to include newcomers into the ranks of Soviet authors differed significantly from the theory. Even party stalwart Valerii Kirpotin admitted that the numbers of shock-worker writers and literary circles organized for them were inflated. Kirpotin notes, for example, that RAPP claimed to have two hundred such circles, when in fact the actual number was closer to forty (Kirpotin, *Rovesnik*, 173–74).

26. *Pervyi vsesoiuznyi s"ezd*, 289.

27. Iurii Olesha, *Zavist'*, 10–11. All further quotations will be cited in the text from the 1977 Ardis reprint of this edition. Translations are my own. Olesha's sharp-eyed observation of the class war in miniature that was taking place around him should be read in the light of encroaching totalitarianism even in 1928. Compare, for example, Boris Groys's comment that the "aim of totalitarian art" is to

"fill the largest possible territory with specific signs that are identifiable as 'our' signs" (see Groys, "The Art of Totality," 98).

28. Their resemblance is physical, intellectual, and behavioral. See, for example, Makarov's letter to Andrei, in which he compares Andrei's pity for Kavalerov to Ivan and his feelings (*"Slovno ne ty eto, a Ivan Petrovich," Zavist'*, 57). Kavalerov and Andrei are connected on several occasions, either in mirrored reflections (*Zavist'*, 121) or in responses that one character unexpectedly provides for the other (*Zavist'*, 12, 130). Perhaps the best example of this character confusion is the well-known scene in which Kavalerov's reflection is combined with that of Ivan in a mirror (*Zavist'*, 66).

29. Olesha noted the psychological difficulty of hearing his character Kavalerov, with whom he identified closely, criticized. Olesha's early days as a soccer player and his lifelong interest in the game, both of which tie him to Makarov, have been noted by numerous commentators, including Valentin Kataev in *Almaznyi moi venets*.

30. Later attempts by Olesha to redefine the self include his invention of an alter ego, a Soviet white-collar worker by the name of Grigorii Ivanovich Stepanov, who appears briefly in Olesha's published diaries from 1934 (see Olesha, *Kniga proshchaniia*, 116). These fragmented selves recall Katerina Clark's passing assertion that Gladkov's *Cement* "can help us perceive that Stalinist culture was put together from a variety of preexisting elements" (*Soviet Novel*, 70).

31. A related attention to the seamy side of life is common in Russian literature from the 1920s and early 1930s, especially work by Andrei Platonov and Boris Pilniak. Eric Naiman has discussed Platonov's fixation on the underside of life in *Happy Moscow*, for example. See his introduction to *Happy Moscow*, xxvi–xxx.

32. William Harkins suggests a partially Freudian reading of *Envy* that sees the male characters as uniformly sterile while the females are castrators. He notes, however, Olesha's recognition of the possibility of a "third way" involving a synthesis of dichotomous organic and technological forces (Harkins, "Sterility," 78).

33. Perhaps predictably, it is reflected in real life as well; in 1931, when Olesha takes temporary possession of a hotel room secured for him by Leopold Averbakh, the room comes equipped with a "green lamp" that seems destined to shine on his new authorial triumphs (Olesha, *Kniga proshchaniia*, 107). Olesha's association of a green lamp with the creative process is connected both to Aleksandr Pushkin and to the "Green Lamp" literary group to which he, Kataev, and other writers from Odessa belonged in 1918 (see Skorino, *Pisatel'*, 104–8).

34. Among other studies of the difficulties of fitting into life in the new Soviet Union, see Alexopoulos, *Stalin's Outcasts*, for a discussion of the many issues individuals faced. Alexopoulos's study deals with those on the fringes of Soviet society, but even writers who were clearly part of the establishment were under enormous psychological pressure, occasionally self-imposed, to fit in and "believe." See, for example, Tamara Ivanova's description of her husband, the writer Vsevolod Ivanov, on the organized writers' trip to the Belomor Canal. Ivanova's retrospective account of the trip, on which she accompanied her husband, suggests that the supposed rehabilitation of criminals on the construction site was an obvious sham, in which Ivanov and his colleague Mikhail Zoshchenko nevertheless "wanted to believe!" (Ivanova, "Eshche," 6).

35. See Michel de Certeau, *Practice of Everyday Life*, 92, on the pleasure of the bird's-eye view, "this pleasure of 'seeing the whole,' of looking down, totalizing the most immoderate of human texts."

36. The comparison in the narrative of Andrei Babichev to the Buddha (here and page 23) suggests that Kavalerov identifies him with a profound, if inscrutable truth. A much later passage from Olesha's fellow writer, Valentin Kataev, indicates the power such a comparison might have held for this generation. In his autobiographical work "Grass of Oblivion," Kataev imagines an ant crawling up his arm. Unable to create a whole picture from the "paltry" pieces with which he has contact, the ant cannot "imagine my immeasurably gigantic, complex body, all of its mysteries, the thousands, millions of nerve connections, visual, olfactory mechanisms, the brain centers—in a word, all of me as a work of art, as a personality, as something unique, like a galaxy. He doesn't know what I am called, what my name is, and that is tortuous: for him I am nothing more than a depersonalized Buddha, deprived of animate meaning and any kind of idea" (Kataev, "Trava zabveniia," 203). Although Kataev has reversed the location of the authorial voice, his sympathies, nevertheless, remain with the insect.

37. See *Zavist'*, 23–24, 121, and 38.

38. Ivan's compromised identity as an engineer reflects Olesha's own conflict—internal and familial—with the possibility of a career in that field. He describes the problem at length in his story "Human Material," which was included in his 1931 collection *Cherry Pit*. Stalin's identification of Soviet writers as "engineers of the human soul" dates from 1932, in one more example of the close interweaving of individual fates and social trends at the time (see Cynthia Ruder, *Making History*, 44, for discussion of Stalin's use of the phrase).

39. Chukovskii, *Dnevnik*, 409–10.

40. Olesha's comment was reported by B. V. Bobovich as quoted in Skorino, *Pisatel'*, 104. Other interesting examples of eavesdropping and window peeking can be found in Ilia Erenburg's production novel, *Second Day* and, as we will see, Andrei Platonov's work, even for the quintessential proletarian, Moskva Chestnova. An eerily similar example from real life is offered by American Margaret Wettlin, who emigrated to the Soviet Union in the early 1930s. She describes her acquaintance with writer Maurice Hindus, who in an attempt to help her understand what she was seeing, "took me for a walk after dark and we peered into basement windows and saw people sleeping on the floor in rows." Wettlin describes herself as "lucky to have arrived in Russia at the tail end of a period of revolutionary fervor that lasted, with diminishing force, from 1917 to 1936." According to her, understanding of this "vibrant period" is necessary to comprehend the "extent to which hopes were betrayed and it explains behavior, my own in particular, that is otherwise inexplicable" (Wettlin, *Fifty Russian Winters*, 10, 13).

41. Shaginian's comments are from *Gidrotsentral'*, 115. In a footnote to his description of the kolkhoz, Gide hypothesizes that "the people who sleep in dormitories suffer less from the promiscuity and the absence of privacy than if they were capable of individuality." He offers his opinions in *Return*, 25.

42. The very curious figure of a "respectable old man in a cream-colored vest" who appears prone on the ground of the stadium before the soccer match in *Envy* suggests a similar confusion of space by the author himself. This unexpected and unexplained figure may signify the presence of the older writer as his younger selves hash it out, indicating that the mature Olesha, unlike his younger incarnation, is well aware of the possibility of injury, aging, and death for the artist. The incongruous old man, breathing heavily and stretched out in front of a grandstand full of spectators who ignore his presence, is repeated later when the character,

dissatisfied, suspicious, and now slightly rumpled, reappears near the snack stand with an ice cream cone (*Zavist'*, 124, 131).

43. Olesha connects the balcony with a sense of mastery he experienced even in childhood. In diary notes, for example, he describes his childhood sensation that "life . . . is endless summer. Balconies are hanging in the azure under striped marquises, covered with vegetation. I'm going to study, I'm talented—and if the fact that I'm poor right now calls up some bitterness, then it's a pleasant bitterness, because I see up ahead the day on which my dreams will be fulfilled" (Olesha, *Kniga proshchaniia*, 27).

44. In a marvelous demonstration of Olesha's technique, Makarov uses his letter to describe a calf he has seen running after the local inspector (*uchastkovyi nadziratel'*), who is trying to keep his briefcase out of the calf's eager mouth. Makarov's emphatic declaration—"I just hate those calves" (59)—speaks to the colorful image of backward rural Russia as it simultaneously evokes the Russian phrase *"teliach'e nezhnosti,"* or calf-like tenderness, an expression still used pejoratively to describe overly sweet sentiments. Makarov's rejection of the notion of such emotional entrapment suggests the new Soviet man's firm disavowal of the "conspiracy of feelings" that Ivan and Andrei both represent. His statement comes just before he declares himself a "man-machine," noting with a diligence familiar to all who struggled to remake themselves in this era, "I've turned into a machine. And if I haven't yet turned into one, then I want to" (59).

45. The reference is to Varvarskaia ploshchad' near the center of historic Moscow. The square, now renamed Slavianskaia Square in honor of a recent memorial to Cyril and Methodius, probably got its earlier name from the nearby church of St. Barbara, or Varvara, a proper name which is related to the Russian word for barbarian. A shift in stress changes the meaning from Barbara's to barbarian. Babichev also refers to the location as Nogin Square, after the Bolshevik activist Viktor Nogin, whose name marked the square and eventually a prominent subway stop during the Soviet period.

46. The blanket from Kharkov is another connection between Kavalerov and the real-life author Olesha, who spent the hungry years of 1921–22 in that city with his colleague Valentin Kataev. As Irina Panchenko points out in her publication of Olesha's propagandistic play from this time, Olesha's Kharkov period is relatively little studied (Irina Panchenko, "Iurii Olesha," *Zerkalo*, April 2005, 4). I am grateful to Irina Panchenko for her generosity in sharing this article with me. Kataev has written about their stay in Kharkov and their employment as political agitators there in *Almaznyi moi venets*.

47. In this context, it is interesting to note that Olesha identifies his father, too, as a "beggar." In a "letter" to his father from the diaries, he compares the fate of his father, who has emigrated, to his own. "We are both beggars, you there in your homeland, and I here, in the new world. No, no, not in a metaphorical sense, but literally: I'm a real live beggar, a professional" (*Kniga proshchaniia*, 97).

48. *Zavist'*, 57–58. His harshness comes as no surprise to some commentators. See, for example, A. Belinkov's sardonic conviction that "in the year 1937 comrade A. P. Babichev was illegally repressed" in his study *Sdacha i gibel'*, 207. Belinkov's comment resembles the fate Valentin Kataev allegedly foresaw for his character Margulies—"convicted for espionage and wrecking" (see B. Galanov, *Kataev*, 5). According to Stephen E. Hanson, the tragedy of the First Five-Year Plan is that Kataev's character, Nalbandov, the more conservative engineer, and not Margulies "turned out to be right" (Hanson, *Time and Revolution*, 160). As

Kevin Platt and David Brandenberger note, during the "Great Terror" of the late 1930s, "at times, it must have seemed as if only Socialist Realism's *fictional* heroes . . . did not risk arrest," and even they were chastised (Brandenberger and Platt, "Tsarist Heroes," 11 and 14, note 17).

49. *Kniga proshchaniia*, 100.

50. Olesha's identification of the color green as something non-Russian can be found as well in another diary entry, where the color, along with the color blue, is specifically tied to the "West" (ibid., 27–28).

51. Ibid., 45.

52. Ibid., 44–45.

53. See, for example, his insistence to that effect in ibid., 28, 33, 35, and 36.

54. Ibid., 58.

55. Ibid., 35. Olesha would no doubt have been sad to learn that fellow writer Valentin Kataev eventually concluded that the diary genre could not serve such an exalted purpose. Kataev's much later ruminations on the topic are largely pessimistic. He complains, for example, in his aptly named autobiographical fiction, "Grass of Oblivion," that he cannot identify the genre of the "tale" he is crafting. ". . . if it's not a memoir and not a novel, then what is it that I'm writing now? Fragments, remembrances, pieces, thoughts, subjects, sketches, notes, citations . . . And all the same I don't have the strength to fill that immense and eternal abyss of time and space with this pathetic wreckage from my own and others' memory" (Kataev, "Trava zabveniia," 212).

56. *Kniga proshchaniia*, 36.

57. Ibid.

58. Ibid., 46, 65.

59. Pilniak's article "Zakaz nash" appeared in *Novaia russkaia kniga* in 1922, and he refers to it as "programmnoi" in a letter to the journal's publisher A. S. Iashchenko (*Russkii Berlin*, 193, 198–99). His comments on his departure from *belles lettres* can be found in "Materialy k romanu," *Krasnaia nov'*, 1, no. 18 (1924): 3. Shaginian's resolution from January 10–20, 1928, is included in *Dnevniki*, 256. See David Shepherd, "Canon Fodder?" for a compelling discussion of the genre-bending *Kik* and its relation to *Hydrocentral*.

60. For Shklovskii on Platonov, see *Tret'ia fabrika*, 125–31, where Shklovskii describes his meeting with Platonov and other technical specialists in Voronezh. Shklovskii's comment about Remizov can be found in *Zoo, ili Pis'ma ne o liubvi* in *Sobranie sochinenii*, vol. 1 (Moscow, 1973), 182. Kataev discusses Bunin's advice on the subject in "Trava zabveniia," 141–42. His comments from "Porogi" are quoted in Galanov, 52. As Katerina Clark notes, this was common during the First Five-Year Plan, too, when writers rejected "as 'bourgeois' the old concept of literature as aesthetic, literature as the product of individual genius, literature as a privileged or distinctive language" ("Little Heroes," 194). As early as 1915, Vasilii Rozanov noted in *Fallen Leaves* that "sometimes it seems that the decomposition of literature, *of its very being*, is taking place inside me. . . . And a strange feeling flashes through my mind—that I am *the last* writer, and after me all literature will come to an end, except the trash, which will also soon come to an end. People will begin just *to live*, and will consider it funny and unnecessary and repulsive to indulge in literature" (Rozanov, *Apocalypse*, 186).

61. "Nerozhdennaia povest'," *Sobranie sochinenii*, 5:202.

62. Ibid. Pilniak would apparently claim later that Soviet writers had "introduced scientific clarity into our metaphors, which after all are the substance of style. Someone has said that our style has become the skin rather than the dress

of the content. That is true." The comments can be found in Joseph Brainin's "transcription" of a meeting between Pilniak and Theodore Dreiser, during the writer's trip to America (Pilnyak, "Human Nature," 116).

63. *Kniga proshchaniia*, 28.

64. Ibid., 43.

65. Ibid., 43–44. For an interesting history of the image of the city in western literature, see Richard Lehan, *The City in Literature*. Lehan's contention that the "city is the end product of the evolution of capitalism" includes the observation that most studies of the subject "treat the city as a matter of dichotomy: country versus city, static city versus city of flux, or as private versus public space" (Lehan, *City*, 286, 289).

66. Gudkova, *Iurii Olesha*, 12. The desire to support the cause they had shared since before the revolution is hardly surprising, although authorial support for revolutionary ideals that were rapidly being corrupted still evokes comments from critics, even those quite sympathetic to the authors they study. See, for example, Irina Panchenko's remark, in her study of Olesha's very early "agitprop" play, "Slovo i delo," that "the writer at the time imagined that it was possible to divide creation into functional activities (to satisfy the needs of Agitprop, for the enlightenment of the uneducated masses) and those which were aesthetically refined" (Panchenko, "Iurii Olesha," *Zerkalo*, May 2005, 28). The wall that separates the old from the new in Olesha reappears, as we will see, in a slightly different guise in Andrei Platonov's *Foundation Pit*.

67. The comment, taken from a secret police report on Pavel Solomonovich Karaban, needs to be treated with care, but the repetition of Olesha's favorite theme of the "beggar" suggests its likely veracity. According to the same NKVD report, poet Vladimir Ivanovich Narbut complained that writers were being ordered to show the "extraordinary nature" (*neobychainost'*) of life even though there was no longer anything exceptional about their times. Narbut continued: "Olesha himself grew up on the fact that he longed for and envied extraordinariness, while simultaneously demonstrating that no such extraordinariness existed" (Artizov and Naumov, *Vlast'*, 313).

68. Quoted from archival sources in Gudkova, *Iurii Olesha*, 20–21. The passage, like most of the rest of the archival page, is crossed out.

69. See, for example, an entry in his diary in which he claims that it is "shameful" to be a writer before admitting, a few lines later, that such a claim is itself an act of "fiction" (*sochinitel'stvo*) (*Kniga proshchaniia*, 41). In a chilling exchange with a KGB interrogator in 1944, Mikhail Zoshchenko was asked "whose fate do you consider tragic of the writers alive today." According to the secret police protocol, which naturally must be used with care, Zoshchenko said that "the fate of Iurii Olesha worries me particularly. He said that he faced ruin" (Artizov and Naumov, *Vlast'*, 516). According to notes from an interrogation included in Shentalinsky, Babel' agreed with Zoshchenko's dire assessment (*Arrested Voices*, 47).

70. See, for example, his defensive comments in his diary from 1937: "When they say that I'm not writing, obviously, they are expressing their dissatisfaction with the fact that I am not putting out books. They have in mind the publication of a ready, completed product. . . . Really, I do have relatively few completed products." Nevertheless, Olesha points out, "in the space of ten years I published two novels—*Zavist'* and the children's novel "Tri tolstiaka," and then three plays, a book of short stories, two screenplays, and a number of newspaper and journal articles" (*Kniga proshchaniia*, 155). In light of such creative activity, accusations of Olesha's lack of productivity seem largely unfair, as Victor Peppard points out

in his study, *The Poetics of Yury Olesha*, 13. In a letter to Stalin dated January 2, 1936, the secretary of the Writer's Union, A. S. Shcherbakov, noted that a number of writers who had not been heard from recently were about to publish. In that list, he included Olesha, Marietta Shaginian, and Isaak Babel', who could be expected, Shcherbakov insisted, "to give us new works in the next half year" (see Babichenko, *"Schast'e literatury,"* 205).

71. Olesha, "Vishnevaia kostochka," *Vishnevaia kostochka*, 84–85; translations are my own.

72. Ibid., 85.

73. Ibid., 85–86.

74. Ibid., 95.

75. Olesha's seeming acceptance of the notion that he must yield to the new generation is made clear by his use of the metaphor of the tree, which will take time to grow, and by his reference to "vashe derevo" where he uses the polite form of the word "your" to indicate that the tree is no longer his individual contribution but belongs to others, particularly to the next generation, including Natasha's as yet unborn son, whom he invites to the site (ibid., 91).

76. Ibid., 96.

77. Ibid.

CHAPTER 2. *HYDROCENTRAL*

1. Naturally, it is important to approach Shaginian's diaries, written between 1917 and 1931 and published in 1932, with care. S. V. Iarov makes this general point in his article "Intelligentsiia," 17. Iarov's article is part of a forum devoted to "sotsial'nyi zakaz" and strategies of self-realization in the 1920s. The publication of Shaginian's diaries is cited by the head of Glavlit in a letter to the Politburo from April 1933 as a failure of censorship; V. Volin notes that there are still problems (*proryvy*) with the censorship process and notes ruefully that Shaginian's diaries had mistakenly been allowed to appear with "politically odious entries" (Artizov and Naumov, *Vlast'*, 196).

2. Marietta Shaginian, *Kak ia rabotala*, 7.

3. Jeffrey Brooks, *Thank You, Comrade Stalin!*, 8. See Dobrenko, *Making of the State Writer*, for a discussion of the contributions of both established writers and worker-writers in training. Shaginian also participated in the Belomor Canal project as a member of the official delegation (see Ruder, *Making History*, 214).

4. Marietta Shaginian, *Dnevniki*, 153, entry for January 6, 1926. Her use of the verb "to build" (*postroit'*) to describe her intentions helps reveals the importance of the building metaphor to this period.

5. *Dnevniki*, 155, January 13, 1926.

6. *Dnevniki*, 155, January 17, 1926.

7. *Dnevniki*, 155, January 20, 1926. She calls the archival material "great" (*zamechatel'nyi*).

8. On this point, see Lidiia Seifullina's 1931 defense of Shaginian, who had just been accused of joining the train of Soviet literature by "climbing onto the train car with her lady's needlework" (*damskoe rukodelie*) ("Diskusskia v VSSP," 126). Seifullina was disdainful of claims that Shaginian had remade herself with the publication of *Hydrocentral*, noting that the author had actually joined the ranks of Soviet literature years earlier, when to do so had meant "a rupture with

tradition, with most of the intelligentsia and a terrible break with one's entire worldview." In light of the difficulty of that earlier transformation, Seifullina continued, *Hydrocentral* itself looked more like a piece of "needlework . . . that Shaginian had brought on board so as not to be late to the exhibit of writers' handicrafts from the era of reconstruction." She makes a similar point about Leonov's *Sot'*, though, as we will see, she was skeptical of both works.

9. *Dnevniki*, 281, October 6, 1928.

10. "Gidrotsentral'," *Novyi mir*, 1930, 1–7, 10 and 1931, 2–4, and *Gidrotsentral': Roman* (Leningrad: Izdatel'stvo pisatelei, 1931).

11. Unfortunately, Shaginian's diaries from her second, extended visit on-site, as well as the first rough draft of *Hydrocentral*, are apparently no longer extant. According to Shaginian, they were stolen in 1929 (*Dnevniki*, 254–55). Nevertheless, it is clear from the materials that remain that Shaginian's participation in the project was significant and sustained, including, for example, work on-site, research trips to scientific institutes, participation in engineering experiments, and so on. Additional information about the trip and her work on the novel can be found in *Dnevniki*, especially 256–406. Shaginian's later writings on the significance of the Five-Year Plans and literature are also of interest. See, for example, Shaginian, *Literatura i Plan* (Moscow: Moskovskoe tovarishchestvo pisatelei, 1934) and *Po dorogam piatiletki: ocherki* (Moscow: Profizdata, 1947).

12. S. V. Laine, *Marietta Shaginian*, 27. See Konstantin Fedin's similar comments about poet Maria Shkapskaia and her intensive work on the history of the five-year plans after her seemingly incongruous start with "erotic-mystical and physiological verses" (Antipina, *Povsednevnaia zhizn'*, 96).

13. "*Trud—krasiveishee i gratsiozneishee, chto est' u cheloveka*" (*Dnevniki*, June 1, 1926, 195). The factory that Shaginian visited in Stalingrad, Krasnyi Oktiabr', was a former French holding, nationalized after the revolution. It was the scene of fierce fighting during the battle for Stalingrad in World War II.

14. *Kak ia rabotala*, 13.

15. See, for example, incidents in *Dnevniki*, 174, 182.

16. This comment occurs in her diary from 1926 after she is denied a hotel room and has to raise a ruckus to secure a place ("*ia prirozhdennaia skandalistka*") (*Dnevniki*, 188).

17. *Kak ia rabotala*, 10, 22. American John Scott provides a contemporary account of such an attitude. Scott, who had left the unemployment of the United States to work in Magnitogorsk in the 1930s, describes a trip he makes to France and the United States in 1937. Although he is shocked to see how "incomparably higher" living standards were in those two countries when compared with the Soviet Union, he is horrified to see "two able-bodied French working men, obviously unemployed" come through the restaurant where he is eating to ask for alms. "The Russian worker" could take comfort in this purge year, Scott argues, in the fact that while he "may not have had much . . . he felt that he would have more the next year" and "he was, therefore, inclined to be essentially cheerful and optimistic" (Scott, *Behind the Urals*, 226–27).

18. *Dnevniki*, 262.

19. See, for example, her seemingly laconic comment about Shusha, which she notes "was burned down 6 years ago. The boulevard has become a field. Out of 28,000 or 29,000 inhabitants, 5,000 or 6,000 remain" (*Dnevniki*, 211).

20. Her comment—"*ne khochu sdelat' polnogo perekhoda v tvorchestvo*"—comes after a futile attempt to start a novel that she refers to in the diary as "The Smell of Rain" (*Zapakh dozhdia*). She notes her own stubborn insistence on an

"egotistical experience of life" and explains her reluctance to create as the result of "either laziness or infatuation." She concludes finally that such inertia is "disgusting" (*Dnevniki,* 186–87).

21. Ibid., 260.

22. Ibid., 261. Shaginian was most likely reading from a brand-new copy of Blok's *Dnevnik,* which had just been published that year in a two-volume set in Leningrad.

23. Ibid.

24. Ibid.

25. Ibid.

26. The felicitous phrase belongs to David Shepherd, "Canon Fodder?" 55. Such textual realities make it difficult to continue to claim, as Clark and Dobrenko nevertheless do, that *Hydrocentral* is "a model 'production novel'" (Clark and Dobrenko, *Soviet Culture and Power,* 116). See Guski, *Literatur und Arbeit,* 3–41, for additional discussion of the generic implications of the production novel.

27. *Gidrotsentral',* 24. Further quotations will be cited in the text; translations are my own.

28. The phrase comes from Shaginian's diary from 1926 in which she describes a visit to Nizhnyi Novgorod where "*byt eshche ne vpolne sovetizirovan*" (everyday existence is not yet completely Sovietized).

29. In her diary from February 8, 1928, Shaginian describes Ryzhii as an "*uslovnaia figura*" whose example, "organizational skills," and "personal magnetism" are meant to "energize the reader with the will to work" (*Dnevniki,* 260). The real hero is undoubtedly the "picture of the country (that is, of the population)" unfolding before the reader (ibid.).

30. The career of hairdresser is particularly interesting as it figures prominently in a complicated subplot to the novel in which Ryzhii is confused with a criminal gang operating in the area. According to Golfo Alexopoulos, numerous individuals who had been cast aside by the system worked as hairdressers and barbers in Stalin's Russia (see Alexopoulos, *Stalin's Outcasts,* 130).

31. *Dnevniki,* February 8, 1928, 260. Shaginian uses the term "*neprisposoblennost'*" to describe Arshak's awkwardness. His further identification as "*skandalist*" recalls her own self definition as "*prirozhdennaia skandalistka.*"

32. Ibid.

33. *Dnevniki,* 198.

34. Cf. Valentin Kataev's "engraving" simile as his character looks out on the construction site in *Time, Forward!,* 99. Shaginian's use of architectural shadow is also reminiscent of Olesha's frequent play with light and dark in *Envy.*

35. Shaginian's description of a deserted village she encounters in her travels through Armenia is somewhat more explicit. She describes the unnerving experience of passing through a village that has been completely abandoned, noting parenthetically that it was "(probably during the civil war)," *Dnevniki,* 207. The village is completely untouched, but there is not a soul in it, and only a stream of water sounds as it passes though an iron faucet somewhere nearby.

36. The form the roof eventually takes is based on vernacular architectural forms that Shaginian saw on her travels in Armenia. See, for example, her approving description of Armenian roofs in her diary from February 23, 1926 (*Dnevniki,* 162). She is enchanted by the architectural forms she sees throughout Armenia during this period, particularly by the appropriateness of vernacular forms to the material that shapes them. Her observations convince her that "every form should emerge from the material itself" (161).

37. Arshak's comments reflect the curious process by which writers whose output was deemed old-fashioned or out of favor were thought to be much older than their contemporaries. Boris Pilniak (b. 1894), Osip Mandelstam (b. 1891), and Iurii Olesha (b. 1899) are a few examples of this widespread "premature aging."

38. Ryzhii's use of the phrase "fundamental break" echoes Stalin's declaration of the "Year of the Great Break" and has the effect of linking his monologue to later official notions of state building. Stalin announced the *"god velikogo pereloma"* in November 1929.

39. This seems to have been exactly the case in Stalinist Russia. See Sheila Fitzpatrick's claim, for example, that the never-built Palace of Soviets was more familiar to inhabitants of Moscow than real buildings of the time (Fitzpatrick, *Everyday Stalinism*, 69–70).

40. Shaginian expands on these ideas about new methods of communication in a diary entry from July 29, 1928, where she notes "there's a crisis of literary form now. Why? Because writing, as a physical process, is becoming obsolete [*izzhevaet sebia*], should stop (something like the way printing in the Middle Ages suddenly stopped the process of transcription and, probably, was the main impulse supporting conversational vernacular language over Latin). In general, thingness [*veshchost'*] is discontinuing, sublimated in fluid construction (film and radio broadcasting). Those who are not able to overhaul their apparatus [*perestroit' svoi apparat*] are formally doomed. From what will come salvation? From poetry, music, from logically dependent elements of fluid construction. Poets and musicians will survive in the word" (*Dnevniki*, 277).

41. Kirportin, *Rovesnik*, 194. He was describing Stalin's October 26, 1932, meeting with writers at Gorky's residence.

42. *"Ia dolzhna zasest' na novoe i naiti novuiu—svoiu formu."* Shaginian then states decisively that "with that I decided to return to Dzorages (at one time I had firmly decided to break off with it) (*Dnevniki*, 256, January 10–20, 1928). See David Shepherd, "Canon Fodder?' for a compelling discussion of *Kik* and its relation to *Hydrocentral*. Shaginian's dissatisfaction with the tropes of conventional fiction was typical, as we have seen, of writers even in the early 1920s.

43. *"Perekovka"* and *"pererodit'sia/pererozhdenets/pererozhdenie"* in V. M. Mokienko and T. G. Nikitina, *Tolkovyi slovar' iazyka sovdepii*, 432–33.

44. The teacher describes her class as composed of the children of the *"vydvizhentsy,"* workers promoted during this period to new positions of responsibility and leadership, whose personal advancement made them a strong source of support for Soviet power. Shaginian's description of the group is interesting in its slightly unorthodox nature: "the land had sent here children of the *'vydvizhentsy,'* of those who had already moved out of poverty into petty trading, into small plot ownership. In front of her was the real, not imagined social element" (*Gidrotsentral'*, 54).

45. See a similar technique being used in Mikhail Bulgakov's journalistic report "1–aia detskaia kommuna" from 1923, where Bulgakov reports on a miniature town with tram line and working elevators that the orphaned children of a "commune" in Moscow have built with the help of an electrician (Bulgakov, "1–aia detskaia," 2:276).

46. See Widdis, *Visions*, especially pages 66–69.

47. The incident is likely based on Shaginian's visit in March of 1926 to a home in Tbilisi, where she is charmed by her host, a self-made geologist who has turned his home into a geological museum of "incredibly interesting material" (*Dnevniki*, 168).

48. Harley, "Maps," 278. Harley characterizes his analysis as an attempt to move away from "traditional cartographical criticism with its string of binary oppositions between maps that are 'true and false,' 'accurate and inaccurate,' 'objective and subjective,'" and so on.

49. Gor'kii, *Belomorsko-Baltiiskii Kanal imeni Stalina*, frontispiece.

50. Ibid., 19.

51. *Gidrotsentral'*, 115.

52. Gaston Bachelard, *The Poetics of Space*, xxxvii. Bachelard describes his concept of an "esthetics of hidden things" and notes that for those of us who "must describe what we imagine before what we know, what we dream before we verify, all wardrobes are full" (xxxviii).

53. See Sergei Zhuravlev, *"Malen'kie liudi,"* 243–47. Zhuravlev quotes at length the amazing documents related to the case that he found in Moscow's Central Municipal Archive.

54. Zhuravlev, *"Malen'kie liudi,"* 244.

55. Ibid., 245.

56. The meeting is reported in the State Archive of the Russian Federation (Gosudarstvennyi Arkhiv Rossiiskoi Federatsii). GARF materials are cataloged in descending order, according to *fond* (fund), *opis'* (inventory), *delo* (file), *edinnoe khranenie* (individual file), and *list* (page). See GARF, f. 7952, op. 7, d. 240, l.1. The beginning of this meeting on January 11, 1934, was not recorded.

57. A. V. Lavrov provides fascinating evidence of Belyi's efforts to produce his own production novel in "Proizvodstvennyi roman." Lavrov implies that there was a strong element of calculation in Belyi's numerous plans to visit construction sites in the Caucasus, although he concludes that any "attempt to answer the question [of such cold calculation] definitively" would "undoubtedly be inadequate and inaccurate" (Lavrov, "Proizvodstvennyi roman," 118). K. N. Bugaeva's occasional exasperation with her husband Belyi's inability to exploit his connections suggests that strategic calculation played a smaller role in the writer's production attempts than Lavrov indicates. See, for example, Bugaeva, "Dnevnik," 256, in which she notes that Belyi has letters of introduction and addresses of people who can help them on their tour of Erevan, but "he is so unaccustomed to 'using' anything that we decided to look around first ourselves upon arrival." Belyi's protest after his archive was confiscated during a 1931 search of Bugaeva's apartment can be found in Artizov and Naumov, *Vlast'*, 150–51. For more on Belyi's intentions to participate in Socialist Realism, see the intriguing article by Monika Spivak, "'Sotsialisticheskii Realizm,'" especially page 270 where Spivak discusses Belyi's attempts to relate the word Soviet (*sovet*) to the Russian word for conscience (*sovest'*).

58. GARF, f. 7952, op. 7, d. 240, l. 3. Budantsev was apparently referring to Belyi's participation in the construction of the first Anthroposophist Goetheanum, erected in Switzerland between 1913 and 1919.

59. Lavrov offers convincing proof that Belyi followed the publication of Shaginian's production novel and her subsequent receipt of a medal for her role in "helping to speed the completion of construction" (Lavrov, "Proizvodstvennyi roman," 119–20). Belyi's correspondence from the time indicates that the writer was genuinely hopeful that a construction project would aid him in his "search for new forms." Kirpotin claims that "Andrei Belyi amazed everyone" at a late 1932 meeting of the committee to organize the first Writers' Congress with the "enthusiasm with which he spoke about Soviet reality, about socialism as a final

refuge in which he had found the solution to the contradictions that had tormented him" (Kirpotin, *Rovesnik,* 209).

60. Bugaeva, "Dnevnik," 271–72. Just how touching this new fascination with physical labor could be is clear from Bugaeva's description of a flat tire they have on their journey a few days before the factory visit. "We had to see the mastery of the chauffeur," she notes of the occasion on May 20, 1928. "Our tire got a flat. And in a matter of just ten minutes or so he had changed it for another one. We all openly watched his work. It was so very interesting to follow the series of quick, well coordinated movements. . . ." (Bugaeva, "Dnevnik," 269; ellipsis Bugaeva). Her comment later about their mutual dislike of being photographed, a distaste they supposedly shared with "the majority of our friends," further underlines their estrangement from contemporary technology (Bugaeva, "Dnevnik," 281).

61. Shaginian's friendship with Belyi dates to 1908 when she, in a rush of school-girlish emotion, wrote the older poet a sympathetic letter. Her gesture, as well as a second letter she sent with a bouquet of flowers, drew Belyi's attention and led to an "affair/novel in letters" (*roman v pis'makh*) that Shaginian published in 1982. Judging from Belyi's responses, the bulk of which date from late 1908 and early 1909, Shaginian was infatuated with the poet but eventually accepted friendship rather than requited love from Belyi (see Shaginian, *Chelovek i vremia,* 237–52).

62. *Dnevniki,* 271.

63. Shaginian, *Dnevniki,* 272. The reference to *"nemota"* is somewhat ironic in the case of Shaginian, who was quite deaf. Describing the discussions as "lively and interesting," Bugaeva noted that Belyi was "boiling and shouting at the top of his lungs" to accommodate Shaginian's hearing problem. She "doesn't hear," Bugaeva continued, "and he was trying. Plus, the themes really agitated him. Many misunderstandings from a host of years were hashed out. But the shouting was friendly and reciprocal" (Bugaeva, "Dnevnik," 269).

64. The notion of personal sacrifice is particularly important to Platonov, who, following Fedorov, was also profoundly interested in the possibility of overcoming physical death, an idea that fascinated a number of writers in the 1920s and 1930s.

65. *Dnevniki,* 272.

66. *Dnevniki,* 321. It is tempting to read Shaginian's "N" here as the mathematical symbol indicating the nearly endless number of friends in such a predicament at the end of the 1920s.

67. *Gidrotsentral',* 119.

68. The role of such propaganda and show trials in Stalinist Russia is discussed at length by Julie Cassiday, *The Enemy on Trial,* and Elizabeth Wood, *Performing Justice.* Valentin Kataev admits using *"pokazatel'nye sudy"* as a part of his journalistic propaganda work in Magnitogorsk in 1931 while he was gathering material for his production novel, *"Time, Forward!"* (see his statement in archival documents from a meeting with Moscow subway workers in GARF, f. 7952, op. 7, d. 239, l. 88). In his industrial sketch from 1931, Petr Vorob'ev depicts an emergency meeting called to address the "hooliganism" of a Russian worker tormenting a young Chechen on-site. The Chechen's fondest wish is to learn to "work like a Russian!" The meeting ends with a unanimous vote to expel the troublemaker from the production site ("Parafin," 126–27).

69. Elizabeth Wood argues that the "Cultural Revolution" and the initiation of the First Five-Year Plan resulted in such trials no longer being able to serve as "a place for discussion of social ideas." Defendants during this time, according to

Wood, "were made into objects of hatred" and "no one is ever found innocent after 1928" (Wood, *Performing Justice,* 196, 200). The publication of Shaginian's novel in 1931 suggests, however, that the process Wood describes was far from complete even toward the end of the First Five-Year Plan.

70. The allusion is to the ubiquitous posters that papered Soviet walls during the postrevolutionary period, when every surface was made to serve the pedagogical moment. Ryzhii refers to posters with advice on "how to transport packages without spilling the contents, how to plaster, how to pick up loads" or, from the public cafeterias, the admonitions "Wash your hands," "Insects transfer disease," or "The fly is the communicant of death." Both Ryzhii and writers Ilf and Petrov find the entreaty that "By carefully masticating your food, you help society" ludicrous (*Gidrotsentral',* 140, and Il'f and Petrov, *Twelve Chairs,* 61).

71. Shaginian's diary account of her visit to the archives ends with her recount of a "marvelous dream" she has after her visit there. Set in the next millennium, her dream depicts a wonderful existence, where "people have overcome death by utilizing everything that they ingest. Metabolism is complete," Shaginian concludes happily, "and there are no by-products" (*Dnevniki,* 155–56).

72. Shaginian is careful not to dispense entirely with the "old borrowed" forms, of course. An elaborate and entertaining subplot in which Ryzhii is misidentified as a suspect in a series of crimes ensures that the genre of the detective story continues to be of use. That is one of David Shepherd's points in "Canon Fodder?"

73. *Gidrotsentral',* 188–93.

74. Jochen Hellbeck notes a similar sentiment in Kornei Chukovskii's diary from a trip he took in 1932 (Hellbeck, *Revolution on my Mind,* 100). This strange desire to look back on the present from the yet unseen but perfectly imagined future is the key to Boris Pilniak's short story "Povest' o spetsovke." Pilniak is writing about metro builders in March 1934, but the focus of his "tale" is the conversation between two "former" builders that he sets in 1964. Pilniak, who was one of the experienced authors called in to help metro workers put their "reminiscences" about the work onto paper, describes these veterans from "mine shaft 21–bis" as "old men" (see "Povest' o spetsovke," in Pilniak, *Rozhdenie cheloveka,* 56–58). Pilniak accomplishes a similar sleight of hand in his letter to the émigré journal *Nakanune* when he expresses his belief that the "new Russia is coming, has arrived" (*idet, prishla novaia Rossiia*) (Hoover Institution, Nikolaevsky archives, box 741, folder 11). Mikhail Ryklin notes a similar shift in time in official discourse about the new Moscow subway; he describes it as a "paradoxical grammatical time, the anticipatory future, the future-in-the-present" ("Metrodiskurs," 725). The same nostalgia for the present can be found in sketches in the journal *30 dnei* about the new way of life (*novyi byt*) by Ilf and Petrov, Konstantin Paustovskii, and especially Kataev, who offers his material from 1930 to the "future novelist" as raw material of how he and others lived. A copy of the journal can be found in the Russian State Archive for Literature and Art [*Rossiiskii gosudarstvennyi arkhiv literatury i iskusstva*], or RGALI. RGALI materials are cataloged in descending order of size and category, according to *fond* (fund), *opis'* (inventory), *delo* (file), *edinnoe khranenie* (individual file), and *list* (page). See RGALI f. 2208, op. 2, ed. kh. 41.

75. *Dnevniki,* 169–70.

76. The archival discovery is included in Artizov and Naumov, *Vlast',* 147.

77. The cellophane letter is described in Gumilevskii, "Sud'ba i zhizn'," 71. Clark and Dobrenko cite this incident as evidence of Shaginian's naïveté, but such

special pleading was common among writers during this era. Clark and Dobrenko discuss Shaginian's belief in her "safe conduct" in *Soviet Culture and Power*, 117.

78. Kirpotin, *Rovesnik*, 252, 253.

79. Ibid., 228. According to a report from Party functionary Pavel Iudin, by August 15, 1934, Anna Akhmatova was the only writer who had not filed the paperwork to join the Writers' Union (Antipina, *Povsednevnaia zhizn'*, 29).

80. The report, retained in State Security archives, is reprinted in Artizov and Naumov, *Vlast'*, 216.

81. Ibid. A secret police report from the end of 1931 crystallizes the problem, claiming that 1931 had been marked by "the rout of counterrevolutionary organizations of the intelligentsia, formed at the beginning of the reconstructive period . . . and the appearance of a new type of counterrevolutionary formation of the intelligentsia characterized, first of all, not only by a deeply clandestine mode of anti-Soviet activity, but also by conscious, carefully coded anti-Soviet activity in the guise of 'ideological purity,' 'advanced social activism,' [and] 'irreproachable fealty to the party'" (ibid., 160). The burden of proving loyalty just as every gesture of commitment became newly suspect must have been considerable.

82. Shaginian's comments are included in her letter to Ordzhonikidze, sent to the newspaper *Pravda* on February 20, 1936 (see Babichenko, *"Schast'e literatury,"* 211, for the complete letter). According to Valentina Antipina, who quotes documents from the Writers' Union, Shaginian complained to the union on February 27, 1936, about the one-room apartment she was sharing with an emotionally disturbed relative. It was apparently not until February 20, 1940, that the union took action intended to improve her situation (Antipina, *Povsednevnaia zhizn'*, 126).

83. Babichenko, *"Schast'e literatury,"* 212; emphasis and capital letters are Ordzhonikidze's.

84. There is little reason to doubt that Shaginian was correct in her estimation of the edifying effect her example would have on others. In a letter from Gorky to Stalin around this same time, Gorky relates André Malraux's concern for both Shaginian and Dmitrii Shostakovich. Gorky is scathing in his dismissal of Malraux's "deficiency . . ., his 'for the individual, for the independence of his creation, for freedom of individual growth' and so on, typical of all of the intelligentsia of Europe" (Artizov and Naumov, *Vlast'*, 301). At a meeting of Party members of the Writers' Union just a week later, it was noted that "entire groups" had visited Shaginian with "expressions of sympathy." Her sympathizers, V. Stavskii commented indignantly, had even "brought her flowers." Displaying a level of knowledge about the author's personal life that was common in the increasingly totalitarian state, Stavskii admitted that Shaginian, however, was "clever enough to turn them away." The archival notes from the meeting are quoted in Babichenko, *"Schast'e literatury,"* 213.

85. Just two months before Shaginian's calamitous decision to leave the union, the secretary of the organization had written to Stalin, promising that several authors, including Shaginian, were about to produce new works of interest (see Babichenko, *"Schast'e literatury,"* 205).

86. Andreev's report to Stalin can be found in Artizov and Naumov, *Vlast'*, 413.

87. The Politburo resolution can be found in ibid., 414, 776.

88. Awards for Shaginian and the others are listed in ibid., 700–702. Inber received the order *"Znak Pocheta."* Complete lists of the literary awards from 1932 to 1953 are included in ibid., 692–730.

CHAPTER 3. "NOVYE VASIUKI"

1. Various commentators have noted Ostap Bender's suspicious background. See, for example, the assertion by commentators M. P. Odesskii and D. M. Fel'dman that Bender's clothing and behavior mark him clearly as a recidivist criminal in Il'f and Petrov, *Dvenadtsat' stul'ev: pervyi polnyi variant*, 464–66. Iu. K. Shcheglov, who identifies a number of literary precedents for Bender, includes in that list Aleksandr Ametistov, the criminal hero of Mikhail Bulgakov's story "Zoia's Apartment" (Shcheglov, *Romany*, 136–38). Anxious to defend Ilf and Petrov against all possible criticism, Ia. S. Lur'e argues that Bender would have been a political prisoner and not a common criminal (Lur'e, *V kraiu*, 25). Although Ilf and Petrov may have been disillusioned in the late 1930s by events in the Soviet Union, as some have argued, their early and continuing support for the system seems equally clear. Like their many colleagues, they had great hopes for positive change in the Soviet Union, participated in an official capacity in projects involving the Belomor Canal, Turk-Sib construction, and the Moscow subway, and wrote at least briefly about all three events. See Nakhimovsky, "Death," 211–12, for an interesting interpretation of their comments on Belomor.

2. Vakhitova's compelling comments can be found in "Oborotnaia storona," 374. See the corresponding confusion of space in Andrei Platonov's *Chevengur*, for example, when revolutionaries move their lodgings and reorganize the streets of the town on a daily basis. Work done by Marina Balina on travel literature in Stalinist Russia suggests the travel sketch as one of the sources for the production novel genre (Balina, "Literatura," 898–99).

3. Il'f and Petrov, *Dvenadtsat' stul'ev: avtorskaia redaktsiia* (Moscow: Tekst, 2004), 57 and Ilf and Petrov, *Twelve Chairs*, trans. John H. C. Richardson (New York: Vintage Books, 1961), 34–35. Unless otherwise noted, further quotations will be cited in the text from the Richardson translation, with only minor emendations as necessary. Ilf's daughter, Aleksandra Ilf, has published definitive Russian editions of both novels, as well as her father's notebooks and Petrov's memoirs. Bender's association with the astrolabe and his transfer of the object to a plumber hints at the expansion of Soviet territory to the world underground. Keith Livers has argued that such motifs recall the "triumph of technology and civilization over feminine nature that was the stock-in-trade of Stalinist mythology" (Livers, *Constructing the Stalinist Body*, 217).

4. Odesskii and Fel'dman document the image of the roll of paper in Il'f and Petrov, *Dvenadtsat' stul'ev: pervyi polnyi variant*, 466. According to J. B. Harley, "in modern times the greater the administrative complexity of the state—and the more pervasive its territorial and social ambitions—then the greater its appetite for maps" ("Maps," 280). The USSR, endlessly touted in Soviet times as an impressive one-sixth of the world's land mass, would certainly have qualified as an administratively complex space.

5. As Aleksandra Ilf notes, *Zolotoi telenok*, written in 1929 and 1930, was first published serially in 1931. The original name for the novel was "Velikii Kombinator," nicely translated by John Richardson as "Smooth Operator," but the name was changed to *Zolotoi telenok* for publication in the journal *30 dnei*, and that title stuck (see Aleksandra Ilf's introduction to Il'f and Petrov, *Zolotoi telenok: Avtorskaia redaktsiia*, 5).

6. Fitzpatrick, "The World of Ostap Bender," 557. Kharkhordin, "Reveal and Dissemble," 350.

7. See Petrov's comments in *Moi drug,* 134–39 and 23. Cf. Boris Pilniak's similar statement, in a letter to friend and mentor Aleksei Remizov, that "in Russia the geological layers have yet to settle, there are still no norms, each person is like a seafarer when each day it's necessary to discover a new America, always a tortuous one, when it is in the realm of morals" (Pil'niak, *Mne vypala gor'kaia slava,* 211).

8. The phrase belongs to Stanislav Rassudin, *Samoubiitsy,* 13. Bender's untimely death at the end of the first novel suggests the original fate Ilf and Petrov had imagined for their character. His popularity as a figure of fun caused the authors to resurrect him for the second novel where they commented that their goal was "satire of precisely those people who don't understand the reconstructive period," implying their intent to help the "construction of socialism" (Il'f and Petrov, *Zolotoi telenok,* 12).

9. Even Lunacharskii held out hope, albeit slim, that Bender could be rehabilitated enough to help construct the new world. See his comment that for Bender to "end up a builder of the new future would be very, very difficult, although with the enormous purifying power of revolutionary fire similar facts are possible" (Lunacharskii, *30 dnei,* 1931, 8:66, quoted in Petrov, *Moi drug,* 255).

10. "Stul" in S. I. Ozhegov, *Slovar' russkogo iazyka* (Moscow: Russkii iazyk, 1978).

11. Cf. the reference in Boris Pilniak's *The Volga Falls to the Caspian Sea* where the degenerate engineer Poltorak muses about the number of "beds and towels there must be in a million-peopled city" (Pilniak, *Volga,* 84). Bruno Iasenskii includes a fascinating digression on the revolutionary possibilities of the material substrate of culture in his production novel *Man Changes His Skin.* His character, the American engineer Jim Clark, is learning to read and write in Russian, and Clark's teacher gives him an extended dictation entitled "The Table" that imagines a socialist revolution among the furniture (see *Man Changes,* 595–99; *Chelovek meniaet,* 392–95). This *diktovka* from Clark's young female instructor is followed shortly by the engineer's own composition, in which he uses his new fluency in Russian to reveal his love for her.

12. Odesskii and Fel'dman speculate on the significance of this date in Il'f and Petrov, *Dvenadtsat' stul'ev: pervyi polnyi variant,* 13–15.

13. Iu. K. Shcheglov notes that the conventional nature of this beginning provided the authors with exactly the standard opening that they needed (Shcheglov, *Romany,* 107). For an interesting compilation of the uses of this convention, see its use by the little known but extremely talented Leonid Dobychin in Belousov, "Khudozhestvennaia toponimiia," 8–15.

14. Odesskii and Feldman, in Il'f and Petrov, *Dvenadtsat' stul'ev: pervyi polnyi variant,* 444.

15. Shcheglov, *Romany,* 121, and Odesskii and Feldman, in Il'f and Petrov, *Dvenadtsat' stul'ev: pervyi polnyi variant,* 450, agree that this is a reference to the removal of the Red Gates, or Krasnye vorota, from Moscow in 1927. A similar lack of sentimentality seems to have characterized the reaction of Ilf to the destruction of the Christ the Savior Cathedral in the center of Moscow, which he captured with his new camera in 1931. See Colton, *Moscow,* 269–70 for a contrasting description of the process. The collection of Ilf's photographs published in 2002 documents that his apartment at the time looked out on the square in front of the cathedral (see *Il'ia Il'f—fotograf,* 90–97). Ilf may have been relatively indifferent to most architectural monuments of the past; that is the impression his description of Rome—*"tri kolonny s karnizom"*—from 1933 gives (see Il'f,

Zapisnye knizhki, 380). The Empire State Building, however, and other master-pieces of modern technology seemed to impress the coauthors. They describe their awe at catching sight of the Empire State Building in 1935 ("a noble, clean build-ing, sparkling like a beam of artificial ice"), noting that "New York skyscrapers evoke a feeling of pride for the people of science and labor who built such mag-nificent buildings" (Il'f and Petrov, "Odnoetazhnaia Amerika," 18).

16. This is much like the "hole from the *bublik*" that Mayakovsky and Man-delstam made famous with their debate over the enduring qualities of "space" in a vacuum.

17. According to N. V. Kornienko, such "renaming of space" in the new Soviet Union was most typical of the 1920s. As Kornienko points out, however, "the mythology of the new geography in the 1920s and 1930s was not especially rich" (Kornienko, "Moskva vo vremeni," 215).

18. See, for example, Viola's compelling study of disastrous Stalinist plans to rationalize the Russian peasantry in Viola, *Unknown Gulag*.

19. See Odesskii and Fel'dman in Il'f and Petrov, *Dvenadtsat' stul'ev: pervyi polnyi variant*, 528.

20. Ibid., 370. Bender himself suggests the name "Four Knights Chess Club." The Russian word for the knight chess piece is *kon'*, or steed, which recalls the Olympian perspective of the Quadriga atop the Bolshoi Theater, with its depic-tion of Apollo and four horses yoked to his chariot.

21. Ibid., 375. The coauthors suggest the real-life potential of Bender's utopian plans when Bender returns to Chernomorsk at the end of *Zolotoi telenok* and finds that his deceptive front company "Horns and Hooves" has become a thriving con-cern. The real-life, present-day town of Novye Vasiuki, built in Elista, Kalmykia by the eccentric leader there, Kirson Iliumzhinov, suggests that the potential for utopian dreams lives on in contemporary Russia.

22. Richardson's translation—"We'll have to get some funds"—eliminates the allusion to Marxist terminology that characterizes the original *Tut material'nuiu bazu podvodit' nado* (*Dvenadtsat' stul'ev*, 150).

23. Other than noting that "professional cement experts" had to be imported for the project from Leningrad, Ilf and Petrov say little about the workers them-selves (113).

24. In light of such realistic moments here and in other production novels, it may be easier to comprehend Andrei Platonov's belief that his highly critical de-scriptions of Soviet construction would also be welcome additions to the literary history of the creation of the new Soviet world.

25. This expression of *otvrashchenie k brat'iam-pisateliam* suggests that Ilf and Petrov are expressing their own feelings here since Treukhov is an engineer and not a "brother journalist."

26. It was common to stage the formal opening of building projects to coincide with official holidays. See, for example, Malte Rolf, who notes that "the comple-tion of construction of factories, roads, power plants, and cultural facilities . . . all took place on Soviet holidays." Rolf explains this as the result of the "target date mentality" that characterized the Five-Year plans (Rolf, "Constructing a Soviet Time," 457–58).

27. Michael Gorham gives a different interpretation, arguing that episodes with such tongue-tied characters reflect a general shift of importance from oratory to written documents. Gorham believes that this change became typical of the "offi-cial literature of the early 1930s" (Gorham, *Speaking in Soviet Tongues*, 157). The examples from Ilf and Petrov in the late 1920s suggest once again, however, that

the supposedly sharp division between the two decades is partially an artificial convenience.

28. Ilia Erenburg uses the device repeatedly in his production novel, *Den' vtoroi*, to establish his own narrative as an authentic one that contrasts with ostensibly less reliable accounts of other writers.

29. Il'f and Petrov, *Zolotoi telenok*, 12.

30. Widdis, *Visions*.

31. Ilf and Petrov, *Little Golden Calf*, 3. Unless otherwise noted, further quotations will be cited in the text from this edition with only minor emendations as necessary.

32. Compare this to O. A. Lavrenova's contention that Russia "seemed to be gradually moving to the south-east" in Russian poetry by the beginning of the twentieth century (Lavrenova, *Geograficheskoe prostranstvo*, 29).

33. One of the best examples of this is a comment in Valentin Kataev's play "Squaring the Circle" from 1927 that reflects the most fraught political discussion of the time: whether communism could be built in only one country. The two couples who must share a single room in that play decide to divide the space by drawing a line down the center. "An unusual experiment," notes the character Abram, "building a household in one room" (see Kataev, "Squaring the Circle," 118).

34. Skhlovskii, *Zhili-byli*, 442. In a similar passage from *Khod konia,* he notes his willingness to burn his arms and legs as well, if only they had been wooden (Quoted in Papernyi, *Architecture*, 14).

35. Eisenstein, *Immoral Memories*, 60. The episode Eisenstein recounts is significant in many ways, reminding us simultaneously of the everyday violence this generation endured as part of their commitment to the revolutionary cause and of the enduring effects such turmoil had on the material culture that surrounded them. Eisenstein, who seems to draw a lesson from the reflection of self he sees in the mirror of his memory, leaves the image incompletely defined instead. "Heavens," he concludes the autobiographical passage somewhat disingenuously, "how I would like to make some profound metaphor or image of this! But nothing comes. So let us leave me lying on a straw mattress placed between myself and the mirrored surface of a wardrobe door . . ." (ibid.). In an interesting article about domesticity in the 1920s, Olga Matich interprets Eisenstein's wardrobe as a "prefiguring [of] the constructivist concept of multifunctional furniture" ("Remaking the Bed," 69).

36. See, for example, the long list of "the art of Russian furniture" with which Pil'niak begins *Krasnoe derevo* (Pilniak, *Rasplesnutoe vremia*, 110–11).

37. These sets of elephants are discussed at length in Buchli, who describes them as "good luck charms." He is convinced of the "power of individuals to effect arbitrary normative control over the domestic realm" during the Stalinist era (Buchli, *Archeology*, 79, 89–91). The unofficial artist Vadim Zakharov included a similar set of elephants in his late Soviet work "Sloniki" from 1982, where they represent a convergence of mythological models (see Zakharov, *25 let*). As we shall see, the appearance of an elephant in Valentin Kataev's production novel *Time, Forward!* serves a different purpose.

38. Il'f and Petrov, *Zolotoi telenok*, 88–89.

39. "Nikuda nel'zia bylo uiti ot sovetskogo stroia," *Zolotoi telenok*, 88–89; my translation. If Khvorobev was counting on greater distance to provide him with Olympian detachment to the situation, then he soon finds that Ilf and Petrov have already divested this location of any possible exalted perspective; see Bender's comments as he views the city and valley below: "A valley in Paradise," said Ostap.

"It is pleasant to rob such cities early in the morning before the sun begins to bake. Less tiring" (ibid., 85).

40. Ibid., 90.

41. Ibid., 91.

42. Ibid., 99.

43. On this point, see the amazing anecdote about the supposedly effortless transition of convinced Soviet architects from urbanism to anti-urbanism. According to a story that Selim Khan-Magomedov told Vladimir Papernyi, Moisei Ginzburg, the head of the Soviet construction committee (*Stroikom*) in 1929 and a staunch and committed urbanist, transformed into an anti-urbanist in a process that took only ninety minutes (Papernyi, *Architecture*, 37).

44. *Zolotoi telenok*, 151; my translation. Bender provides a low-brow expression of the same sentiment for his fellow con artist Kozlevich a bit later in the novel when he debunks the Polish Kozlevich's fear of exclusion from heaven: "Heaven?" he comments disbelievingly. "Heaven is now in a state of neglect. This is a different epoch, a different slice of time. Angels want to come down to earth now. It is good on earth, because you have communal advantages here, and observatories where you can look at the stars while you listen to an anti-religious lecture" (201).

45. Il'f and Petrov, *Zolotoi telenok*, 252; my translation.

46. The original Russian contains an unmistakable allusion to Lenin in its formulation "Kto kogo?" (*Zolotoi telenok*, 277).

47. Bruno Iasenskii uses a similar device in his production novel *Man Changes His Skin*, when his character, a "foreign writer," takes the homegrown Tajik engineer for a visiting Italian specialist (*Man Changes,* 690; *Chelovek meniaet,* 450).

48. Il'ia Erenburg, *Den' vtoroi*. Quotations from the 1934 edition are included in the text; translations are my own.

49. Oleg Kharkhordin's distinction between the concepts of *chastnoe* and *lichnoe* sheds interesting light on Bender's use of the phrase *chastnoe litso* here (Kharkhordin, "Reveal and Dissimulate," 344). Kharkhordin argues that "Soviet dissimulation was instrumental in constructing the Soviet individual" (350), a point of view similar to Sheila Fitzpatrick's suggestion that "impersonation" may have been the "flip side" of Soviet "self-construction" (Fitzpatrick, "The World of Ostap Bender," 557). Both Fitzpatrick and Kharkhordin emphasize a conscious will to dissemble that is at odds with the well documented desire of most of the populace to be part of the collective. Authors of production novels, in particular, were anxious to join, a fact that no doubt played a significant role in their individual decisions to work in that genre.

50. Il'f and Petrov, *Zolotoi telenok*, 352.

51. G. V. Andreevskii in his impressionistic but entertaining history of everyday life under Stalin lists the house manager as one of the "highly significant" figures in life at the time (Andreevskii, *Povsednevnaia zhizn'*, 447).

52. See the republication of photographs from that trip in Wolf, *Ilf and Petrov's American Road Trip*.

53. Such a comment casts doubt on statements like that of Milne (212), who argues that Ilf and Petrov were not "seduced" by the Belomor project. Ia. S. Lur'e also voices his conviction that the two writers "refused" to work on the Belomor volume because of their objection to participation in such morally questionable projects (*V kraiu*, 142, 159–61). For a further discussion of the authors' involvement in Soviet projects of collective authorship, see Nicholas and Ruder, "In

Search." Documents in the State Archives of the Russian Federation indicate that Fedor Gladkov, Ilia Erenburg, Demian Bednyi, Ilia Selvinskii, Lev Nikulin, Nikolai Ognev, Viktor Shklovskii, Boris Lapin, and numerous other well-known authors were initially expected to join Ilf and Petrov in the subway venture (GARF, f. 7952, op. 7, d. 370, ll. 8, 38). Shklovskii's experience editing the Belomor canal volume apparently qualified him for continued service here. On a document dated October 15, 1934, he, Gladkov, and Mikhail Koltsov were listed as "literary editors," apparently expected to be in charge of "montage of the book" (GARF, f. 7952, op. 7, d. 370, l. 88).

54. The piece was submitted in late 1934 and apparently earned the writers one thousand rubles (GARF, f. 7952, op. 7, d. 348, l. 88 and d. 405, l. 11, 17).

55. GARF, f. 7952, op. 7, d. 405, l. 11.

56. Ibid., l. 17.

57. Corney, *Telling October*, 153. It comes as little surprise that the written history of the construction of Moscow's subway ended somewhat before the official opening of the first line on May 15, 1935. Sergei Zhuravlev notes that an atmosphere of secrecy had overwhelmed the construction site by early February 1935, and an order that month forbade the publication of materials "relating to the use of the Metro, the cost of a ride, and so on" (*Fenomen*, 203, note 179). See Nicholas and Ruder, "In Search," for a fuller discussion of the Belomor and subway collective histories during this period. A general discussion of issues involved in collective authorship in the Soviet Union can be found in the forum on "monumental Stalinist publications" in the journal *Kritika* 6.1 (Winter 2005): 5–106. The forum includes Elaine MacKinnon's study of the creation of Civil War history and an article by Brian Kassof on the first edition of the Soviet encyclopedia. See also the discussion of the role of literature in cultural mobilization projects of the Stalinist 1930s in *Novoe literaturnoe obozrenie* 71.1 (2005): 229–89.

58. For a full discussion of the intersection of life and narrative during this period, see Thomas Lahusen, *How Life*.

59. Their short story "How Robinson was Created" (*Kak sozdavalsia Robinzon*) from 1932 indicates their obvious understanding of the dangers of too much pressure from above on any sort of creative writing.

60. "M," *Sobranie sochinenii*, vol. 3, 354–57.

CHAPTER 4. *MAHOGANY*

1. See Gary Browning's comment on the novel as the first Five-Year-Plan novel in *Boris Pilniak: Scythian*, 171. Irene Masing-Delic repeats the claim in "Boris Pilniak's *The Volga*," 414. Igor Shaitanov offers the information about Pilniak's stay at Dneprostroi in his introduction to Boris Pil'niak, *Romany*, 20. Pilniak's remarks are part of a personal letter he wrote to Stalin in late 1930 requesting permission to travel abroad. The letter is included in a collection of Pilniak's letters from 1915 to 1937 prepared by the writer's youngest son and his granddaughter. See Boris Pil'niak, *Mne vypala*, 345.

2. His claim appears in his letter to the editor of *Literaturnaia gazeta* in August 1929, reprinted in full in Pilniak, *Mne vypala*, 333–39. T. A. Nikonova describes the wait for the "first Soviet novel" in her discussion of the "mass-hero" (*geroi-massa*), singling out V. Zazubrin's 1921 novel *Two Worlds* in *Novyi chelovek*, 106–8. Pilniak seems to have captured the attention of the party hierarchy

early in his career. A decree of the Politburo in August 1922, for example, specifically directs party leaders Rykov, Kalinin, Molotov, and Kamenev to read Pilniak's story "Ivan da Mar'ia" and requests that all the members of the Politburo read "Metel'" in connection with the confiscation of the author's early volume *Smertel'noe manit*. Whether they all did so or not, the confiscation order was lifted a week later (see the associated Politburo documents in Artizov and Naumov, *Vlast'*, 41–42 and 736, note 46). This early incident, about which the well-connected Pilniak would certainly have heard, helps explain his apparent belief later that sympathetic higher-ups would support his work, even when it was deemed unacceptable at lower levels of the power structure.

3. See Vera T. Reck, *Boris Pil'niak*, for an early "post-Thaw" interpretation of events. Reck also discusses the scandals involving Pilniak's story "Povest' nepogashennoi luny" from 1925.

4. Pil'niak, *Mne vypala*, 334.

5. Writers were actually assisted in this process by the government agency VOKS, as Pilniak pointed out in a letter of protest to the newspaper *Literaturnaia gazeta*. The agency *Vsesoiuznoe obshchestvo kul'turnykh sviazei s zagranitsei*, or VOKS, was organized in 1925 to facilitate ties between Soviet writers, artists, and so on with scholarly and cultural institutes abroad. Authors were apparently surprised by the virulence of the sudden attack against Pilniak, which was initiated in an article by B. Volin in *Literaturnaia gazeta*, August 26, 1929. See sketchy but suggestive information about an earlier run-in Pilniak had with Volin (Boris Mikhailovich Fradkin) in Pil'niak, *Mne vypala*, 284–85.

6. Pilniak's son and granddaughter describe the event at some length in their notes to Pilniak's letter of protest about the affair (see Pil'niak, *Mne vypala*, 337–39). They include archival evidence suggesting that Pilniak, his friend Boris Pasternak, Zamiatin, and their colleague and friend Anna Akhmatova all resigned from the writers' union in protest over the events (ibid., 337–38). See ibid., 341, for Zamiatin's reaction to the "panic" that resulted from the attacks and his comment on the "campaign against the writers' union." *Krasnoe derevo* first appeared in the Soviet Union only in 1989.

7. Kenneth Brostrom's article "Enigma" is an exception to such an approach, as is the work of Gary Browning. See Browning's argument, for example, that the inclusion of *Mahogany* into the later novel was "mainly in response to *artistic* considerations" (Browning, *Boris Pilniak: Sythian*, 168; emphasis Browning).

8. See Eastman's comments in Eastman, *Artists in Uniform*. See fascinating documents related to Eastman's involvement in the story in Fleishman, "V polemike." Clark and Dobrenko argue that Pilniak's "dissidence" was "always for show" (Clark and Dobrenko, *Soviet Culture and Power*, 116). See, as well, the introductory essay to *Mne vypala* by Pilniak's granddaughter, Kiri Andronikashvili-Pilniak, who passes over *The Volga Falls to the Caspian Sea* in silence.

9. Many writers objected to the over-politicization of art, but most accepted that art and literature played a political role in both pre- and postrevolutionary Russia. Even such demonstratively apolitical writers as Boris Pasternak, for example, played a significant role in literary politics, although in some instances this activity was forced upon them.

10. "Povest' nepogashennoi luny" appeared in the journal *Znamia* only in 1987. Pilniak's story about Frunze was especially provocative, of course, but when other stories received the same allegorical treatment they proved to be equally disturbing to his official readers at the time. In a letter from June 11, 1926, to V. M. Molotov and S. I. Gusev, for example, the head of the state publishing house noted

with dissatisfaction that GIZ had mistakenly concluded a contract with Pilniak to publish a book of short stories that included "Povest' nepogashennoi luny," "Zhenikh vo polunochi," and others. The stories, described as "extremely weak in the artistic sense," are said to demonstrate the "much refined methods of counterrevolutionary poison in the area of fictional literature." According to the terms of the contract, Pilniak received 3,450 rubles for the proposed volume. See Babichenko, *"Schast'e literatury,"* 28–29.

11. Pilniak's literary endeavors during the 1920s included, for example, his work with the publishing house "Krug," his correspondence with authors about their unsolicited manuscripts, his participation in the All-Russian Writers' Union, his indefatigable overseas travel, and so on. His correspondence from the time shows a playful, energetic author actively involved in literary affairs of all sorts (see *Mne vypala*, 184–333 throughout). Kornei Chukovskii includes a short description of Pilniak's wheeling and dealing in *Dnevnik*, 238–39.

12. Pilniak's letter, saved in his family's private archive, was first published in 1990 (see B. Pil'niak, *Rasplesnutoe vremiia*, 591–93). It is also included in the anthology *Mne vypala*, 304–9.

13. Quoted in B. B. Andronikashvili-Pilniak, "Pil'niak, 37–i god," in Pil'niak, *Rasplesnutoe vremiia*, 592–93. Not surprisingly, this kind of claim seems to have been standard in such apologies. See Pavel Postyshev's very similar contention about his "Bolshevik soul" while under attack by members of the Politburo in 1938 (Khlevniuk, *Master*, 211).

14. Boris Groys's study of the role of political will in Russian avant-garde art and literature is an invaluable tool for understanding the behavior of Pilniak and other such writers throughout the 1920s and 1930s. See Groys, *Total Art*.

15. Pilniak's letter to Lutokhin, dated November 9, 1924, is included in *Mne vypala*, 285–86. Lutokhin lived in emigration from 1923 to 1927, although he considered returning as early as 1924, when Pilniak offered to help him with the necessary bureaucratic steps (see ibid., 169, 260).

16. *Mne vypala*, 211. This echoes Evgenii Petrov's comment about his sense of the "postrevolutionary emptiness when it was unclear what is good and what is bad" (Petrov, *Moi drug*, 23).

17. *Mne vypala*, 216.

18. Ibid. Pilniak's reference to his grand theme and his novel would be repeated frequently over the next decade or so.

19. Pilniak resided in Kolomna with his first wife, a rural physician, for much of the early 1920s. He makes clear in comments elsewhere that Kolomna served in part as a place to hide from literary politics. See, for example, his comment to Dalmat Lutokhin that "Moscow allies from the Union of Writers . . . are looking at me askance (and at my comrades, especially at them, you can't get a good hold on me in Kolomna)" in ibid., 167. He describes his stay in an isolated forester's hut near the Volga in a 1924 letter to Andrei Belyi. That trip, which resulted in his novella *"Mat' syra-zemlia,"* was followed shortly by his trip to Arkhangelsk and beyond (see ibid., 280–81). At numerous junctures throughout his correspondence, Pilniak mentions day-to-day conversations with workers and peasants that provide him with insight into the thoughts and reactions of the Russian "Everyman."

20. Ibid., 168, 228. Pilniak's frequent claims in his correspondence to have abandoned his involvement with the publisher "Krug," for example, are interspersed with business letters to colleagues on the editorial board (see ibid., 220, 244, 287–88).

21. A. K. Voronskii, "Iz perepiski," 555.

22. *Mne vypala*, 166; emphasis Pilniak.

23. *Ia liubliu russkuiu kul'turu, russkuiu—pust' nelepuiu—istoriiu . . . Ia liubliu russkii, muzhichii, buntovshchichii—oktiabr', v revoliutsii nashei metelitsu, ozorstvo.*

24. Ibid., 166.

25. *Mne vypala*, 167, 169. Pilniak would repeat this sentiment in the introduction to his eight-volume set published in 1930. He notes in the foreword there that a "very great deal of what was written by me, I would no longer write" before concluding that he will nevertheless leave the work untouched "because it is history" (*Sobranie sochinenii*, 1:30).

26. *Mne vypala*, 185; emphasis Pilniak.

27. Ibid.

28. Pilniak asks Gorky to send them "Pustynnik," an apparent reference to the older writer's "Otshel'nik," which appeared in a Berlin journal in 1923 (see ibid., 185, 187).

29. Ibid., 186. Pilniak's relative optimism about the material state of writers was apparently short lived. He notes in a letter to the Central Committee from 1924 that their position is "extremely difficult" and complains that "salaries are miserly" and writers have nowhere to live [*beskvartir'e*] (ibid., 278).

30. Ibid., 186.

31. Ibid.; emphasis Pilniak. Part of the reason for turning to Gorky would undoubtedly have been for the status his name could offer writers. According to Kornei Chukovskii's account, Pilniak had already relegated Gorky to the past by mid-1921. See his comment that Gorky is "a good person, but as a writer he's passé," reported in Chukovskii, *Dnevnik*, 163.

32. *Mne vypala*, 234–35.

33. Ibid., 235.

34. Ibid., 214; emphasis Pilniak. On Zamiatin's plans to emigrate at the time, see Kornei Chukovskii, who offers a sarcastic interpretation (*Dnevnik*, 243). Chukovskii calls Zamiatin's opposition to the government "window-dressing and ersatz" (*Dnevnik*, 217).

35. *Mne vypala*, 214. Pilniak's emphasis on the phrase "in my conscience" suggests his realization that some of his actions may have been interpreted by those in the émigré community as harmful, but that such an interpretation violates his original intent. Chukovskii's 1922 account of Pilniak's recent trip to Berlin suggests that the author's attempts to play all sides of the ideological debate made everyone suspicious (Chukovskii, *Dnevnik*, 216).

36. See, for example, Pilniak's request to Lutokhin to send any useful books to the Russian assistant trade consul in London, who would see that Pilniak received them (*Mne vypala*, 228–29). In a letter to Ivan Kasatkin from the same period, Pilniak notes that he and Nikolai Nikitin are working in London for the Soviet information bureau. He asks Kasatkin to help publicize their study of the economic situation in Russia and to gather material himself (ibid., 221). In another letter to Lutokhin from October 1923, Pilniak passes along greetings to friends of his parents, now living abroad (ibid., 237–38). In the unpublished essay "Zagranitsa," Pilniak notes that it is improper to divide literature into "émigré and non-émigré branches" (the essay is quoted extensively by Peter Jensen, *Nature as Code*, 47 and elsewhere).

37. Stylistic peculiarities make it clear that the letter was penned by Pilniak. According to Pilniak's son and granddaughter, the original manuscript contains

corrections by P. Oreshin, which were incorporated in the final typescript (see *Mne vypala*, 277–78).

38. Ibid., 277.

39. The use of prison labor on the Belomor canal presented particular ethical problems for writers asked to join the writers' project, as Aleksandr Solzhenitsyn noted and Cynthia Ruder details in her study of the volume.

40. *Mne vypala*, 277. Numerous accounts testify to the prestige of the profession of writer in Soviet times. See, for example, the diary of a young man who noted in 1932 that "the engineer is the highest form of human study. . . . That thought didn't abandon me until 1932" when "it was crowded out by the word Writer" (the diary, from unnumbered archives located in the "Narodnyi arkhiv" Documentation Center, is quoted by N. N. Kozlova, "Soglasie," 195). Sof'ia Chuikina notes that the creative world was a favorite realm for "former" people looking for employment in postrevolutionary Russia (Chuikina, "Dvoriane," especially pages 164–65).

41. *Mne vypala*, 233–34. Pilniak's comments were in response to his participation in the volume *Pisateli ob iskusstve i o sebe*, planned by Voronskii for "Krug" in 1924.

42. *Mne vypala*, 234.

43. Ibid., 235.

44. Ibid., 288.

45. Ibid., 288–89. Gorky was legendary for helping authors rework their writings. On Pilniak's work with other authors, see, in particular, his collaboration with Andrei Platonov on the sketch "Che-Che-O." His letter to Polonskii, can be found in *Mne vypala*, 311. See a revealing episode in which Kataev discusses helping an older "beginning" author in Antipina, *Povsednevnaia*, 58.

46. Pilniak's colleague and coauthor Andrei Platonov demonstrated a similarly incredulous response when he wrote to Maxim Gorky to ask, disbelievingly, if he was really going to be denied a role in Russian literature. See Platonov's letter to Gorky in *"Mne eto nuzhno"*, 180. Chronicles from Ginzburg to Solzhenitsyn make it clear that Soviet labor camps were full of such disbelief up until Stalin's death.

47. See, for example, Avdeenko's conviction that a full and immediate confession of his "guilt" for involvement in the film *"Zakon zhizn'"* would have helped him in 1940 (Avdeenko, "Otluchenie," 94–98).

48. Pilniak, *Mne vypala*, 334.

49. Viktor Shklovskii, for example, accused Pilniak of reusing his works because he lacked a creative imagination. Pilniak relies on themes traditional to Russian literature, Shklovskii complains, because he is "not an original master." Other critics implied that Pilniak's pattern of repetition was a stylistic borrowing that tied Pilniak's work to writers like Andrei Belyi. Shklovskii was writing in *LEF* in 1925 ("O Pil'niake," 127). Much has been written about Pilniak's indebtedness to Belyi, which he himself acknowledged.

50. *Mashiny i volki*, 6.

51. Ibid. Pilniak highlights the easy communality of literary endeavors in his "Story about the Year 1920," included in his 1935 collection *Rozhdenie cheloveka*. The story describes the activity of a writer of fiction from Kolomna, who is pressed into service by the local newspaper "Voice of a Communist." Protesting that he cannot sign his own name to columns he writes for the newspaper, he suggests that he and the editor cosign each piece ("Rasskaz o dvadtsatom gode," *Rozhdenie cheloveka*, 71). Pilniak's career included numerous incidents of co-

authorship, including cases in which Pilniak published entire diaries or the fragments of diaries that he had obtained from other individuals. These include diary accounts in *Kitaiskaia sud'ba cheloveka: povest'*, which he published with A. Rogozina in 1931, sections of *Machines and Wolves,* "Fragments from a Diary," and others. Iurii Annenkov describes Pilniak's attempts to publish "Dnevnik Jean'a Sukhova," allegedly a diary Pilniak obtained from his neighbor in Koloma (see Annenkov, *Dnevnik moikh vstrech,* 289–91).

52. Shklovskii's failure to understand Pilniak was just one reflection of a general failure by avant-garde critics to include writers like Pilniak in their conception of Russian modernism. For more on the context for this debate, see Mary Nicholas, "Formalist Theory." Pilniak's appropriation of shared images suggests a technique that would become widespread in Russia only in the 1970s, as part of developments now called postmodernism.

53. *Mashiny i volki,* 6.

54. Pilniak, "Problema obraza," 2.

55. Ibid.

56. Ibid.

57. The 1924 declaration, signed by Pilniak, Esenin, Mandelstam, Babel, Zoshchenko, and numerous others, can be found in the collection *Voprosy kul'tury,* 137–38. It was also reprinted in Osip Mandel'shtam, *Sobranie sochinenii,* 3:295–96. Pilniak's early comment can be found in *Nikola-na-Posad'iakh.*

58. "Red wood" is the literal Russian for "mahogany." Leonov's comment comes in a September 1931 discussion of creative methodology at the All-Russian Union of Soviet Writers. His remarks, along with those of Lidiia Seifullina, V. Polonskii, and others, were published in *Novyi mir,* 10 (1931): 123–65. This comment, from page 124, comes at the end of Leonov's criticism of writers who visit construction sites or collective farms and then attempt to substitute poorly written reportage about their trips for the difficult work of real literature.

59. Pilniak's name appears on an archival list of authors assigned to assist with specific worker accounts. Among other names, Pilniak is listed as working with N. A. Ermolaev, S. A. Sokolin, P. N. Gurov, V. L. Makovskii, and I. N. Kuznetsov, all of whom contributed to the volume *Kak my stroili metro.* The archival documents can be found in GARF, f. 7952, op. 7, d. 348, ll. 21, 22, 60, 77.

60. Leone argues that Western scholarship has overstated the discontinuity between the RAPP-dominated years of 1928–1931 and the years after 1932. He notes that there was actually "great continuity in leading personnel and literary doctrine" between RAPP and the Writers' Union that followed. Leone makes an interesting case for the influence of RAPP and mass journalism on the development of the Stalinist literary canon, but he bases much of his argument on Valentin Kataev's work *Time, Forward!* while underplaying or ignoring the novels of Marietta Shaginian, Boris Pilniak, and others (see Leone, *Closer to the Masses,* 294 and 212–44).

61. See Kornelii Zelinskii, "Odna vstrecha u Gor'kogo," especially page 166.

62. Stalin's comments to Party writers were reproduced in a stenographic record of the meeting on October 20, 1932, by writer Feoktist Berezovskii. Berezovskii's account was reprinted from archival documents by Leonid Maksimenkov, "Ocherki," 224–34. The better known meeting on October 26, 1932, is described by Kornelii Zelinskii in "Odna vstrecha u Gor'kogo."

63. According to biographical information published in 2001, for example, Pilniak had enough influence in the early 1930s to place his older son Andrei in the prestigious school where Stalin's son Vasilii studied. In a later twist of fate, An-

drei studied civil engineering and worked in construction, earning particular professional distinction after Stalin's death and Pilniak's eventual rehabilitation (V. S. Krasnoshchekov, "Pokolennaia rospis'," 154). According to V. A. Panov, Pilniak was considered the "best author" at the journal *Novyi mir* in late 1929, and Panov, an aspiring young author himself, had memorized entire sections of Pilniak's prose ("Vstrechi s Pil'niakom," 176). Letters from Pilniak's family archives indicate that the writer was performing organizational duties for authors scheduled to receive summer homes in the writers' colony Peredel'kino as late as 1936. Another epistle describes his efforts to trade two rooms in an apartment on Pravda Street for two others on Gorky Street in the center of Moscow in mid-1936 to accommodate his complicated family situation. Pilniak's access to overseas travel, foreign cars, and a summer home in Peredelkino make his status as respected writer clear, although he had more and more difficulty publishing as the 1930s wore on (*Mne vypala*, 375–76, 379–80).

64. *Mne vypala*, 235.

65. Pilniak's essay "Otryvki iz dnevnika" can be found in *Pisateli ob iskusstve*, 77–89. This passage is also included in *Rasplesnutoe vremia*, 586, from which I have quoted.

66. *Rasplesnutoe vremia*, 587.

67. Ibid., 587.

68. The discussion about social directives was published in *Pechat' i revoliutsiia*, 1929, 1. This quotation can be found on page 70.

69. Pilniak's 1926 short story "Rasskaz o tom, kak sozdaiutsia rasskazy" depicts a Japanese writer who betrays his non-Japanese-speaking Russian wife by writing explicitly about their sexual relations. This story is one of the clearest examples of Pilniak's understanding of the traitorous nature of the authorial craft. Pilniak's comments about his methods as a young child were included in his answers to a questionnaire distributed to a number of famous writers by the printing house Izdatel'stvo pisatelei and published in 1930 (see Andrei Belyi, *Kak my pishem*, 124–25). Pilniak's discussion of "disloyalty" can be found in "Orudiia proizvodstva," *Babranie sochinenii*, 5: 259.

70. "Pisateli o sotsial'nom zakaze," 71; emphasis Pilniak.

71. Pilniak's comments on future Pushkins and Shakespeares were part of a discussion entitled "O novom tipe pisatelei," from *Literaturnaia gazeta*, June 11, 1933. The meeting of the presidium of the Writers' Union in 1936 was reported by Ia. Eidelman, who criticizes Pilniak for merely repeating "words about the chosen status of the writer, about his inability to write 'differently than he writes,' about 'sensations,' as the decisive and determining factor in creation and so on and so forth" (see Eidelman, "V Prezidiume," 4). Lazar Fleishman gives an interesting account of the significance of this meeting, particularly for Pasternak, in Fleishman, *Pasternak v tridtsatye gody*, 377–83.

72. The article in *Izvestiia* appeared as "Sias'skii kombinat," *Izvestiia TsIK*, March 16, 1928, 4. Pilniak's correspondence with Radek in early March 1928 is one more piece of evidence of his belief that an inclusive approach would dominate both literature and politics. At the time of Pilniak's letter, Radek had already been expelled from the party and exiled to Tobol'sk. He would be arrested in 1936. Pilniak's assistance to Radek's family was used to incriminate the writer after his own arrest in 1937 (see *Mne vypala*, 323–24). Boris Frezinskii quotes an archival letter from Pilniak's then wife Olga Sherbinovskaia that mentions his trip to "some kind of factory under construction" (Frezinskii, *Pisateli i sovetskie vozhdi*, 129).

73. Pilniak,"O novom tipe pisatelei," 3. Since he himself had already visited several construction sites and seemed to be genuinely impressed, Pilniak's comments must be intended to establish the importance of imagination and reflection over political fervor in the artistic endeavor. He was clearly setting himself against prevailing sentiment by making such a statement in 1933 in the very public forum of *Literaturnaia gazeta*.

74. I have included quotations from the 1930 edition of *Volga vpadaet v Kaspiiskoe more* directly in the text, emended where necessary with reference to the edition included in volume 2 of the 1994 *Sochineniia*. Translations are my own. Pilniak's interest in the confluence of rivers near Kolomna far predated his work on the production novel. He writes in a letter to A. S. Iashchenko in April 1922, for example, that "literature is like a river, into which different streams fall, like the Volga, perhaps, into which fall the Oka and the Kama and the Karaman, and it all flows, entangles the flow, changes the river bed, washes the shores, carries shoals to previous depths, freely, awkwardly, pointlessly, and the subterranean water of all Russia feeds all of that river (all of that Volga)" (Pilniak's letter is part of the Nicolaevsky Collection at the Hoover Institution in Stanford, California, box 26, folder 24. It is also included in *Mne vypala*, 160–63, and in *Russkii Berlin*, 191–94).

75. See Chekhov's comment in "Uchitel' slovesnosti," 364. Lotman's reference to the truism can be found in *Semiotics of Cinema*, 13. Velosipedkin's comment occurs in "Bania," Mayakovskii, *Sobranie sochinenii*, 7:67.

76. Pilniak catalogs the antique dealers' visits in *Volga vpadaet*, 46–51. The conversation with the old woman occurs on 46–47. His comment about his willingness to sacrifice the old for the new—*zhertvuiu starym trudom*—is from *Mashiny i volki*, 6. Pilniak's allusion to the endless numerical succession can be found in *Volga vpadaet*, 51.

77. See Christina Kiaer, *Imagine No Possessions*, for a discussion of some of the "socialist objects" that Russian constructivism envisioned for the new world.

78. Dasha's actions suggest that Victor Buchli is too categorical in his argument that such an approach characterizes the ascendancy of Stalinism.

79. The scene from *The Volga Falls to the Caspian Sea* echoes one in *Mahogany* where the character Akim, a Trotsky sympathizer, misses the "train of time" when his carriage (*tarantas*) becomes stuck in the provincial Russian mud ("Krasnoe derevo," *Rasplesnutoe vremia*, 288–89).

80. *Volga vpadaet*, 46. The description is included almost verbatim in *Krasnoe derevo*, 276.

81. One of Pilniak's earliest admirers, Aleksandr Voronskii, referred to him as chronicler (*bytopisatel'*), an epithet Pilniak seems to have accepted (see Voronskii, *Na styke*, 42).

82. "Rasplesnutoe vremia," in *Sobranie sochinenii*, 5: 5–6. Pilniak raises a similar issue in his short story "Prostranstvo i vremia" (Space and Time), published in *Novyi mir* in 1934 and then included in his collection *Rozhdenie cheloveka* from 1935. The story concerns the transfer of old letters from a now famous author to a literary museum. The author is shocked to learn that his correspondence and, by analogy, he himself, are now part of history: "Of course, they are right . . . , the letters need to be placed in a literary museum of the revolution, but I, I, I?! . . . Am I history? . . . But I'm alive, after all! . . . What, is history alive!? Yes-ter-da-aa-ay!" (*Rozhdenie cheloveka*, 68).

83. Olesha's Babichev brothers, particularly Andrei, are classic examples of the problem, as is the aging engineer in Ilia Erenburg's production novel *Den' vtoroi*.

As we will see, the dilemma is also central to Platonov's understanding of the revolution and the new world to come.

84. The *okhlomony* have all adopted last names that incorporate Russian roots meaning fire or burning, including Ozhogov, Podzhogov, Plamia, Pozharov, and so on.

85. Pilniak's letter to Stalin can be found in Artizov and Naumov, *Vlast'*, 139–41. A rough draft of the letter was published in *Znamia* in 1994 and included in *Mne vypala*, 345–49. The rough draft claims that "all of my authorial mistakes" arose from such a conviction; the final version has been amended to make that claim only for "many of my mistakes." Pilniak's sketches on Tadzhikistan were published in *Izvestiia* in 1930 and later expanded into a book entitled *Tadzhikistan, sed'maia sovetskaia*, which found little favor with the literary authorities (see Pilniak's complaints to Kaganovich on the subject in *Mne vypala*, 351).

86. In a rhetorical flourish typical of the time, the draft of Pilniak's letter described the potential profit as the equivalent of "four-five tractors a year" (*Mne vypala*, 46).

87. Artizov and Naumov, *Vlast'*, 140–41. The rough draft of Pilniak's letter had outlined his project as the "history of the last two decades of the world" (*Mne vypala*, 347).

88. Stalin's answer to Pilniak's letter was a classic in the genre of veiled threats. He notes that the "surveillance organs" (*organy nadzora*) originally "hesitated" to approve Pilniak's trip before eventually deciding to agree to it. The phrase granting permission—"the organs have no objection"—first read "the organs have no objection at this time" (see Artizov and Naumov, *Vlast'*, 141).

89. The rough draft, dated January 23, 1932, can be found in *Mne vypala*, 350–55. The final version to Stalin, dated January 28, is included in *Bol'shaia tsenzura*, 229–31. "Glavlit" refers to the government censorship agency *Glavnoe upravlenie po delam literatury i izdatel'stv*. The final version of the letter claims that Pilniak's contract was canceled on January 27, but the rough draft already complains about that fact on January 23.

90. Pilniak's letter asks for help publishing "Korni i kamni: kommentarii," an apparently alternate title to the work that was serialized in *Novyi Mir* in 1933 and published in separate editions in 1934 and 1935. The letter was first published in *Mne vypala*, 362–64.

91. Pilniak, *Kamni i korni*, 60. Pilniak's remark refers to the seventh volume of his eight-volume *Sobranie sochinenii*, published by Gosudarstvennoe izdatel'stvo in 1930.

92. Stalin's comments are taken from Berezovskii's stenographic record of the leader's remarks to writers at Gorky's house on October 20, 1932, reprinted in Leonid Maksimenkov, "Ocherki," 224–34. The comments on Pilniak are on 227. Stalin's second meeting with writers on October 26 provided a slightly more developed definition of the newly recommended method of socialist realism.

93. Zelinskii, whose diary entry is the source for most of our information about the meeting, testifies that "Pilniak came to see A. M. Gorky to have it out as to why he hadn't been invited to the meeting." According to Zelinskii, Lidiia Seifullina was also excluded originally, but added later at Gorky's initiative. He seems to have regretted his addition since Seifullina was outspoken in her criticism of the continued influence of RAPP on Soviet literature, to Gorky's dissatisfaction (see Zelinskii, "Odna vstrecha," 169, 149–50).

94. Maksimenkov, *Bol'shaia tsenzura*, 231. In the rough draft of the letter, Pilniak claimed that his circumstances were already straitened. That earlier version

of the letter notes that his fate is permanently tied to the revolution, but does not mention the "general'naia liniia" (*Mne vypala*, 353). A letter to the Writers' Union in May 1937 asking for a loan of six thousand rubles to tide him over until he can publish something suggests the relative difficulty of Pilniak's position at that late date. He notes in his letter that his request has already been rejected by Litfond (*Mne vypala*, 387–88). See further evidence of Pilniak's isolation in Dagmar Kassek's interesting article on Pilniak's late film scenario ("Maloizvestnii stsenarii,"42).

95. Their commentary can be found in *Mne vypala*, 378. According to Pilniak's son and granddaughter, Mikoyan was not satisfied with sections of the serialized publication in *Novyi mir* and asked that it be amended. When Pilniak refused or was unable to meet Mikoyan's demands, the work was dropped from publication. An account of a discussion of *Miaso* in the Sovetskii pisatel' publishing house in July 1936 is in RGALI, f. 631, op. 2, ed. khr. 160. Kassek argues that Pilniak's film scenario "The Earth Blooms Anew Every Spring" (*Kazhduiu vesnu no novomu tsvetet zemlia*) from the same time period is a parody ("Maloizvestnyi stsenarii," 52). Masing-Delic seems more inclined to take Pilniak seriously. She sees *Volga* as part of Pilniak's depiction of a world in which "rivers and humanity have become harmoniously 'androgynous'" ("Boris Pilniak's *The Volga*," 429).

96. *Mne vypala*, 377.

97. Ibid.

98. Kataev's statement can be found in "Trava zabveniia," 192.

99. See Pilniak's comment in *Mashiny i volki*, 6. If the horrifying accounts from the secret police files can be believed, Pilniak's final words echoed this sentiment. "I very much want to work," Vitaly Shentalinsky reports him as saying on April 20, 1938, before his execution the following day. "I want to live, to work hard, I want to have paper in front of me on which I could write something of use to Soviet people . . ." (*Arrested Voices*, 156). Shentalinsky's presentation of this difficult material is problematic in many respects, but this alleged quotation from Pilniak certainly rings true.

CHAPTER 5. *TIME, FORWARD!*

1. Richard Borden describes Kataev as the "archetypal Fellow Traveler, a consummate survivor of Soviet historical vicissitudes." In his compelling study of "mauvism" of the late Soviet era, Borden argues that Kataev should also "occupy a place near the center of post-Stalin literary history" (Borden, *Art of Writing Badly*, 8, 9, 10).

2. *Vremia, vpered!* appeared in 1932, and an English translation was published a year later as Valentine Kataev, *Time, Forward!*, trans. Charles Malamuth Bloomington: Indiana University Press, 1933). Unless otherwise noted, I follow Malamuth's translation, and page numbers are included in the text.

3. For a detailed description of the Magnitogorsk project, see Stephen Kotkin's master work, *Magnetic Mountain* (37), from which this description is quoted.

4. "Trava zabveniia," 179. IugROSTA, the Odessa branch of the Russian state telegraph agency (*Rossiiskoe telegrafnoe agentstvo*, or ROSTA), had an ambitious agenda that supposedly involved "information" and "propaganda" on the "war against speculation, an enrollment drive for the Red Army, the war with

Poland, Petlura, Vrangel, Bulakhovich, Savinkov and bandits, the campaign against kulaks, help for sick and wounded servicemen, labor mobilization, public schooling, a general sanitation week, the town-countryside," and so on. The IugROSTA mandate even involved helping with the introduction of new revolutionary holidays such as "Bastille Day, the anniversary of the International, and Engel's centenary" (Skorino, *Pisatel'*, 159–60). In an extended study of the author, L. Skorino treats Kataev's biography, including, for example, his service as a young ensign just after the February revolution in World War I, in the context of the general social history of the time (see Skorino, *Pisatel'*, 90–95 and throughout).

5. "Trava zabveniia," 180.

6. "Almaznyi moi venets," 358. See Richard Borden's detailed description of *My Diamond Crown* for a discussion of the complexity of this and other later autobiographical writings by Kataev (*Art of Writing Badly*, esp. 112–21).

7. Skorino, *Pisatel'*, 165.

8. "Almaznyi moi venets," 358–59. Skorino provides fascinating additional details on Kataev's work for IugROSTA. The Russian state telegraph agency, ROSTA, was made famous by Mayakovsky's work for the group in Moscow, where he produced slogans, window designs, and building displays, some of which are still famous. Perhaps the best known of these advertising poems, for example— *Nigde krome kak v Mossel'prome*—was resurrected on the side of a building in the center of Moscow during the 1990s. ROSTA had various divisional branches, including those in Kharkov (UkrROSTA), where Bagritskii, Olesha, Ilf, Petrov, Vera Inber, and others found work, and the Caucasus, where Velimir Khlebnikov, Aleksei Kruchenykh, T. V. Tolstaia, and others were employed. See Skorino, *Pisatel'*, 158–65, and Lidiia Libedinskaia, *"Zelenaia lampa,"* 7.

9. See "Almaznyi moi venets," 362–65. The devastating effects of famine on the Russian and Ukrainian populace throughout the early Soviet period have been chronicled at length, casting Kataev's anecdote in a flip and cynical light. These early experiences were clearly formative for both Kataev and Olesha, however, and affected their sense of commitment to their roles as Soviet writers. See Elizabeth Wood, *Performing Justice*, 93–96, for interesting material on agitational trials related to the famine.

10. A. M. Leites, from an interview in 1962 with Skorino, *Pisatel'*, 165.

11. Kataev, "Trava zabveniia," *Almaznyi moi venets*, 177. The autobiographical "Grass of Oblivion" is subtitled "Povest'," or "Tale." Pchelkin's assignment was to enlist both "district" (*volostnye*) and "rural" (*sel'skie*) correspondents for "daily bulletins." According to Kataev, members of the "rural intelligentsia" were the most likely to respond to the request, especially rural clerks and teachers or young men who had finished school and were just returning from a stint at the front line (ibid., 182). Kataev uses the device of mixing real figures with fictional characters extensively, here and elsewhere; see, for example, Skorino, *Pisatel'*, 85–86. His coy identification of a younger self with the fictional Pchelkin serves important private ends, too, since it allows the older writer to obfuscate a spotty past that apparently included service in both the Tsarist and the White Volunteer armies (see Borden, *Art of Writing Badly*, 10). Kataev's work in Odessa on such propaganda exercises as "flying concerts," "talking newspapers," and so on would have primed him for agitational activity of this sort, although, in his later account, it is Olesha who is the first to respond to the officer's proposal to write the commemorative verses (Skorino, *Pisatel'*, 162, and Kataev, "Almaznyi moi venets," 362–65).

12. "Trava zabveniia," 181. Kataev's account includes a fascinating portrait of a "red priest," who is killed by the same group of bandits Pchelkin has just es-

caped. See Shcheglov, *Romany*, 123–24, for a brief but interesting note on the role such breakaway clergy played in Russia in the early 1920s. Iurii Olesha's *Envy* hints at a similarly dangerous episode in the history of his character Babichev, who was once "saved" by Volodia Makarov as they ran from danger through a star-filled ravine one night (see *Zavist'*, 100).

13. "Trava zabveniia," 196.

14. See Bunin's reported accusations in ibid., 118. Kataev would go on to achieve the fame and wealth that was the privilege of the most loyal Soviet writers, including a summer home in Peredelkino, access to scarce consumer goods, and permission to travel abroad, while, according to many accounts, losing his soul in the process. See Natal'ia Ivanova's introduction to Kataev, *Almaznyi moi venets*, 5–26 for a brief but pointed discussion of both the rewards Kataev reaped as a respected Soviet writer and the damage his behavior caused his reputation. Richard Borden argues that Kataev was actually "denied the full complement of official laurels normally accorded" the most orthodox of Soviet writers. He simultaneously notes slights of Kataev by western scholars (Borden, *Art of Writing Badly*, 10, 339–40).

15. "Trava zabveniia," 165.

16. In her study of the end of "mass utopia," Susan Buck-Morss makes an interesting case that "in class warfare, space is merely tactical, not the practical goal, whereas for the nation-state, time is tactical and space is everything." Nevertheless, she admits that "the terrain of class war, as civil war, is spatial confusion" (see Buck-Morss, *Dreamworld*, 22, 23, and 37). During the first Five-Year Plan, in particular, the present becomes "an obstacle to overcome," a task that is understood, at least in part, spatially.

17. See Joseph Backstein's contention that Russian pictorial art has "always been conceptual," making the accompanying essay even more necessary. According to Backstein, in Russian art, for example, the titles of paintings are "as important as their depictions, if not more" (Backstein, "History of Angels," 18).

18. "Trava zabveniia," 99.

19. See Ilf and Petrov's helpful aid for writers, "Torzhestvennyi komplekt," in *Zolotoi telenok*, 286–89. The crib includes, among other "useful" nouns, the words for laborers, dawn, life, lighthouse, hour, mistakes, and enemies, as well as heart and past. For reliance on the notion of a galvanizing image in literature of this period, see Boris Pilniak's essay in *Literaturnaia gazeta* from 1934, "Problema obraza." Such an episodic approach characterized much of the literature of the 1920s and early 1930s, much to the chagrin of critics who demanded a more heroic form of art to describe the revolutionary era.

20. See a fascinating discussion of the Claude glass in Malcolm Andrews, *Landscape*, 115–20.

21. Numerous commentators have remarked on the militarization of Soviet society. See, for example, Karen Petrone's comment that the order of parades through Red Square was determined by the "overarching symbolic and strategic importance" of the military to Soviet power (Petrone, *Life Has Become More Joyous*, 28).

22. This rhetoric is from a February 1931 resolution of the board of directors for RAPP, the Russian Association of Proletarian Writers that dominated the literary political scene from 1928 until 1932. The resolution is quoted in Dobrenko, *Making of a State Writer*, 206. Editor and critic Viacheslav Polonskii provides a real-life example of Kataev's literary type. Writing in *Novyi Mir* about his 1931 visit to Magnitogorsk, Polonskii views the city from the air as he lands at night,

but confesses his disorientation on site the next day, noting "in the morning when I left the hotel, I was astounded. The city had disappeared" ("Magnitostroi," 109).

23. Dobrenko, *Making of a State Writer*, 210.

24. This is the approach implied, for example, by Kataev's sympathetic biographer L. Skorino, who suggests that Bunin could have been on the side of Bolshevik power if only he had had the "strength and courage to look this historical innovation in the eyes, understand it, and accept it with his heart, as Aleksandr Blok had done" (Skorino, *Pisatel'*, 149).

25. Golfo Alexopoulos makes an interesting point in her suggestion that those "most vulnerable to political attack" were often the most vociferous in their model Soviet activism (Alexopoulos, *Stalin's Outcasts*, 132).

26. Kataev's own difficulty with the tasks the new world had given him is demonstrated vividly in manuscript pages retained in Russian literary archives. Hard at work on a story about the construction of an apartment building by a young Komsomol brigade, Kataev covers several pages with attempts at inspirational verse with many false starts. Much of the back of one page is covered with variations on the theme "for" and "against." Manuscript pages are retained in the Russian State Archive for Literature and Art (*Rossiiskii gosudarstvennyi arkhiv literatury i iskusstva*), or RGALI. RGALI materials, like those in other Russian archives, are cataloged in descending order of size and category, according to *fond* (fund), *opis'* (inventory), *delo* (file), *edinnoe khranenie* (individual file), and *list* (page). Thus, references to materials from RGALI are classified in terms of f., op., d., ed. kh., or l. See RGALI f. 1723, op. 1, ed. kh. 4.

27. The acronym was apparently an established part of unofficial Soviet culture. According to a recent anthology of memoirs from the Solovetskii camp, a song from inmates there refers to the "red elephant" (*krasnyi SLON*) in the White Sea (Babicheva, *V Belom more*, 3). A roughly contemporaneous use of the image of an elephant appears in Andrei Platonov's industrial sketch "V poiskakh budushchego," where an old worker at the paper factory Platonov is visiting tells him "a working man can become a fly or an elephant—whatever he wants; but any spider can deal with a fly, while the elephant can take out trees by itself" ("V poiskakh," 368). See Benedikt Sarnov for a discussion of other contemporary uses, including the sarcastic "Rossiia—rodina slonov" by Viktor Shklovskii and Ilia Erenburg (Sarnov, "Rossiia—rodina mamontov," http://www.lechaim.ru/Arhiv/137/Sarnov.htm [accessed July 13, 2009]).

28. Evidence for this comes from Aleksandr Avdeenko, who describes Kataev's behavior in an account published long after the events in question (Avdeenko, "Otluchenie," 17–22).

29. According to Richard Borden, such "creeping empiricism" with its emphasis on "thingliness" was one of the key devices Kataev used at the end of his career in developing an experimental "mauvist" style, which, Borden argues, influenced an entire generation of late Russian modernists (Borden, *Art of Writing Badly*, 104–5).

30. *Time, Forward!*, 340. See Umberto Eco, "Architecture and Memory," 89.

31. "Trava zabveniia," 244. Skorino reports a conversation with Kataev, in which Mayakovsky's generosity is partially explained by his comment that he is a poet rather than a novelist: "*Ia romanov ne pishu*" (Skorino, *Pisatel'*, 219).

32. Kataev's depiction of Bunin himself is relatively balanced, although he subjects Bunin's aged widow to a scathing gaze that seeks to set her isolated last years in emigration in contrast to the more integrated life she ostensibly would have had under Soviet power. In his nuanced treatment of Kataev's later career, Richard

Borden argues that Kataev "slanderously fabricates a life of émigré squalor for Bunin," perhaps to justify his own "decision to remain in the Soviet Union after the Revolution" (*Art of Writing*, 160). As Skorino notes, Kataev's early depictions of Bunin are much less sympathetic than the later one from "Trava zabveniia" (Skorino, *Pisatel'*, 153–55). The older Kataev, with much to account for in his own compromised past, may have been searching for the quiescence that, according to Bachelard, is incompatible with profound dichotomy. See Bachelard's notion that "formal opposition is incapable of remaining calm" in *Poetics of Space*, 212. That was the opinion of Kataev's contemporary Evgenii Zamiatin too, of course, who based much of his early novel *We* on the instability of such a formal dichotomy.

33. "Trava zabveniia," 204.

34. See, for example, Ingulov's letter to Stalin, Kaganovich, Andreev, Ezhov, Zdanov, Molotov, and Mekhlis, of December 7, 1937, in which he denounces a story written by Arkadii Perventsev that was to have been included in the November 1937 issue of the journal *Oktiabr'*. Ingulov calls Perventsev's story about a sick horse "counterrevolutionary" and claims it could have done as much damage with its "anti-Soviet sorties" as Boris Pilniak's scandalous "Povest' nepogashennoi luny," if not for Ingulov's own intervention to remove the issue from circulation (Babichenko, *"Schast'e literatury,"* 265–67). In "Trava zabveniia" Kataev has Ingulov serve as the person who sends Riurik Pchelkin to the countryside to raise revolutionary consciousness among the peasants ("Trava zabveniia," 183).

35. "Trava zabveniia," 264.

36. Ibid.

37. Ibid., 265.

38. Ibid., 275.

39. Ibid., 273.

40. Ibid., 262.

41. See the entire passage, on which Kataev expends considerable literary pathos, in ibid., 274. As we will see, the bird's-eye view will be essential to Kataev's resolution of past, present, and future in *Time, Forward!* itself. Bruno Iasenskii provides an interesting contrast to Kataev's view from above in his production novel *Man Changes His Skin*. The American engineer Jim Clark endures a series of airplane flights on his way to Tadzhikistan from Moscow, but he rejects the bird's-eye view provided there. Gazing out of the plane's window he "saw a town, all neatly laid out, like a game of patience on a revolving table. Clark's head was awhirl. He decided not to look any more, and did not open his eyes until the plane touched earth." Once the plane lands, he throws himself on the grass patch, "hugging the ground tight, his whole body drinking in the blessed sensation of stability. For an instant the thought flashed through his mind that immobility is an illusion—the earth, too, revolves around the sun. At this thought he began to feel sick again" (*Man Changes*, 37; *Chelovek meniaet kozhu*, 24–25).

42. *Literaturnaia gazeta*, October 4 and November 5, 1930, quoted in Skorino, *Pisatel'*, 214–15. The intended relationship is described as *shefstvo*. The enthusiasm authors found for such activities did not always relate directly to the industrial feats they were to describe. Valerii Kirpotin notes, for example, that on his trip to Dneproges with Leonid Leonov, Fedor Gladkov, and others, Leonov "for some reason wasn't interested in industrialization but rather cactuses. He was constantly dragging us to one conservatory or another, which turned out to be just small hothouses" (Kirpotin, *Rovesnik*, 169).

43. Skorino, *Pisatel'*, 216–17.

44. Ibid.

45. Documents related to Stalin's early criticism of Bednyi are included in Babichenko, *Schast'e literatury*, 85–93. The affair leading directly to his ouster from the Writers' Union is discussed in A. M. Dubrovsky, "Chronicle," in *Epic Revisionism*, 77–98. Responses to Bednyi's censure were cataloged by the secret police, whose report is included in Artizov and Naumov, *Vlast'*. Writers' reactions ranged from the typical *zloradstvo* to mild pity. A translation of the NKVD reports, or *svodki*, can be found in *Epic Revisionism*, 99–114.

46. Details about the trip and Kataev's participation in it can be found in Ruder, *Making History*. For a recent discussion of some of the general issues involved in collective authorship in the Soviet Union, see the forum on "monumental Stalinist publications" in the journal *Kritika: Explorations in Russian and Eurasian History*, Winter 2005, 6, 1: 5–106.

47. The encounters of Firin with both Kataev and former aristocrat Dmitrii Sviatopolk-Mirskii are described by Aleksandr Avdeenko in "Otluchenie," 17–22. Mirskii was included in the official Belomor writers' brigade, and he reports similar official visits to Central Asia, the Urals, and even the subway construction site (G. S. Smith, *D. S. Mirsky*, 220, 244). He perished in the purges in 1939. Avdeenko's remarkable account of the trip and his gradual disenchantment with the Stalinist regime was published only many years later in "Otluchenie."

48. Avdeenko, "Otluchenie," 3:22.

49. Avdeenko, "Otluchenie," 3:19, 22. Orlando Figes, who uses some of Avdeenko's account, leaves this incident out of his retelling of the trip. Figes, quoting Tamara Ivanova's retrospective description of the "Potemkin Village" aspects of the journey, fails to include her comments about her conviction that her own husband Vsevolod Ivanov believed in the possibility of reforging "with all sincerity" (see Figes, *Whisperers*, 192–94). Cynthia Ruder offers a fuller account of Ivanova's comments about both her husband and Mikhail Zoshchenko in *Making History*, 81–83. Avdeenko qualifies his opinion of Kataev later in his essay. Noting the unusual noise and cheerfulness with which Aleksandr Fadeev and Kataev hurry down an otherwise terrified Moscow street in the purge year of 1938, Avdeenko asks accusingly "what makes them so cheerful?" ("Otluchenie," 90). Avdeenko notes Kataev's participation in a meeting to attack his film "Zakon zhizni" in 1940, but spares him special criticism for that incident, noting that Kataev had just been under attack himself at the time ("Otluchenie," 4:104).

50. Avdeenko, "Otluchenie," 23.

51. Ibid., 59. Avdeenko was one of the many living connections between the early production novel and its later incarnations. Rosalind Marsh singles out his 1978 work "By the Sweat of his Brow" for notice in her study of the genre in the post-Stalinist period (*Soviet Fiction*, 124).

52. Quoted in Figes, *Whisperers*, 204. According to Figes, Simonov, "another 'proletarian writer' to make his name through the White Sea Canal," was sent to visit the canal by the state publishing house and "lived in the barracks with a team of prisoners" for a "month" (*Whisperers*, 195–96). If Simonov's account is true, it contradicts other suggestions that direct contact between writers and the prison-camp laborers was extremely limited.

53. The reference to the "edge" (*gran'*) comes from an article in *Na literaturnom postu* in May 1930, criticizing Kataev's deviations from literary orthodoxy, quoted in Skorino, *Pisatel'*, 223.

54. B. Galanov, *Kataev*, 313–14.

55. According to an order published in *Literaturnaia gazeta* in October 1930, authors who agreed to be "adopted" by a factory were to be officially enrolled and placed on the list of regular employees (*"vydany raschetnye knizhki i tabel'nye nomera"*) during their service to the factory (see Skorino, *Pisatel'*, 215–16.)

56. For an excellent introduction to the overall venture, see S. V. Zhuravlev, *Fenomen*.

57. According to Mikhail Ryklin, this subway project was "the only large-scale construction project of the Stalin era for which practically no prison labor was used" (Ryklin, "'The Best in the World,'" 264). Ryklin gives no source for his claim.

58. According to the stenographic report of the meeting, the gathering was part of the official preparations for the First All-Union Congress of Writers. Information about the meeting can be found in the State Archive of the Russian Federation (*Gosudarstvennyi Arkhiv Rossiiskoi Federatsii*), or GARF. GARF materials, like those in RGALI, are cataloged in descending order of size and category, according to *fond* (fund), *opis'* (inventory), *delo* (file), *edinnoe khranenie* (individual file), and *list* (page). See GARF, f. 7952, op. 7, d. 239, l. 132.

59. Archival documents from GARF on the Metro project list dozens of established authors identified as possible participants, including, for example, Fedor Gladkov, Mikhail Zoshchenko, Sergei Tret'iakov, Ilia Selvinskii, Lev Kassil', Viktor Shklovskii, and many others. See GARF, f. 7952, op. 7, d. 370, l. 34–41.

60. Evgeny Dobrenko, *Making of the State Writer*, 212.

61. Ibid., 329, 332.

62. Ibid., 321.

63. A. V. Lavrov notes Andrei Belyi's intentions to work with a group of "writers-shock workers" in March 1933 (Lavrov, *"Proizvodstvennyi roman*, 117). Babel, Shklovskii, and Pilniak all participated in work on worker manuscripts for the volume "Kak my stroili Metro," and many other well-known writers were invited to participate on the volume, including Demian Bednyi, Fedor Gladkov, Ilia Selvinskii, and others. Shklovskii offered his work "O tom, kak zaputalas' staraia Moskva" for the third volume of the history of the construction of the subway. See GARF, f. 7952, op. 7, d. 348 and d. 370. Marietta Shaginian was also active in her work with aspiring writers, as her work "Kak ia rabotala nad Gidrotsentraliiu" testifies.

64. A sample plan for the work of one such "lit consultant" can be found in GARF, f. 7952, op. 7, d. 223, where S. Persov details his intended activity on October 2, 1934.

65. Ibid.

66. Seifullina's remarks were part of a general discussion that included Leonid Leonov, Viacheslav Polonskii, and others ("Diskussiia v VSSP," 127). Seifullina's outspoken stance was also evident at the October 26, 1932, meeting of writers with Stalin and other members of the government. One of the only women to attend the gathering, at which Stalin pronounced the authors "engineers of human souls," Seifullina was one of the first to speak. She sharply criticized plans to include three former RAPP members—Averbakh, Ermilov, and Makar'ev—as part of the leadership of the organizing committee for the new writers' union, sarcastically shouting down accusations from her colleagues: "Yeah, I'm that kind of a counterrevolutionary. I don't believe what Averbakh promises. Can I not believe?" (Zelinskii, "Odna vstrecha," 150). Stalin defended her later that evening, noting that "she turned out to be braver than everyone. She blurted out the truth that everyone was thinking" (Zelinskii, "Odna vstrecha," 164).

67. "Diskussiia v VSSP," 127.

68. GARF, f. 7952, op. 7, d. 225, l. 7, 11, 13, 23.
69. GARF, f. 7952, op. 7, d. 225, l. 20.
70. GARF, f. 7952, op. 7, d. 240.
71. Ibid.
72. Ibid.
73. Ibid. White trousers like these turn up as well in Bruno Iasenskii's production novel, *Man Changes His Skin*, where Iasenskii uses them to demonstrate how collective work can inspire human beings to overcome such outdated binary distinctions. Iasenskii's sympathetic character, the American engineer Jim Clark, pauses briefly to contemplate his "snow-white trousers" before jumping onto the work site to replace a worker whose sudden illness has threatened the completion of an essential irrigation project (*Man Changes*, 400; *Chelovek meniaet kozhu*, 271). Clark's willingness to join in the actual process of physical labor wins him the sympathy of everyone else on site and facilitates the breakdown of unhelpful distinctions between management and labor, foreign and Soviet.
74. GARF, f. 7952, op. 7, d. 240, l. 9.
75. Ibid., l. 10.
76. Ibid., l. 11.
77. Ibid., l. 13.
78. Ibid., l. 14.
79. See GARF, f. 7952, op. 7, d. 348, l. 67 for sample lists of individuals "invited" to such meetings in October. The invitation to attend was extended by the publisher "Istoriia metro." Another archival document lists "authors who had been given an order (*zakaz*) to write about individual facts from the life of the caissons" (d. 226, ll. 19–20).
80. See the copy of such a request in the form of a "telephonogram" in ibid., l. 13.
81. See lists of such personages in ibid., ll. 14, 17. According to notes from a meeting kept at ibid., d. 370, l. 12, interviews could be "at the hotel or in the country" at the request of the interviewee, who was to be "completely released" from work obligations for "2–3 days."
82. Dobrenko asserts that the "percentage of unemployed people who saw the writing profession as a sort of way out of 'everyday troubles' was extremely high" (Dobrenko, *Making of the State Writer*, 228).
83. See sample work applications, for example, in GARF, f. 7952, op. 7, d. 232.
84. Ibid., d. 370, l. 38.
85. For notice of Erenburg's manuscript, see the "authorial collective" listed in ibid., 88. According to one of his biographers, Erenburg was in Russia for part of the summer and fall of 1934, although he apparently returned to France through Odessa after the writers' congress (Rubenstein, *Tangled Loyalties*, 134–38).
86. See GARF, d. 348, ll. 22, 80, 84. A chilling July 1936 denunciation by a secret police informant who had somehow gained the confidence of Pirozhkova and Babel can be found in Artizov and Naumov, *Vlast'*, 316–17. In a similarly incongruous moment, see the identification of Osip Mandelstam as a "*nomenklaturnyi poet,*" whose name was included in the list given to Stalin in April 1932 for consideration as a member of the organizing committee of the incipient Writer's Union (Maksimenkov, "Ocherki," 250).
87. For evidence of Shklovskii's extensive involvement in the project, see GARF, f. 7952, d. 348, l. 21, 22, 24, 100 and d. 370, l. 88, 90.
88. Literary functionary Valerii Kirpotin complained at how well authors were compensated for their "collective 'feat'" on the similarly valued Belomor project,

grumbling that writers of "sketches" from that trip received "significantly elevated" honoraria. Kirpotin describes the "unheard-of conditions" for writers on the Belomor volume—"free rooms at the 'Metropol' [hotel], restaurant privileges throughout work on the chapters" (Kirpotin, *Rovesnik*, 180).

89. See a copy of Nikulin's contract in GARF, f. 7952, op. 7, d. 370, l. 92.

90. A letter Mirskii wrote to an English acquaintance at the time suggests the limits of even the most fervent enthusiasm: "they are building an underground in Moscow. I went down into the shaft the other day. But at home I suffer a great deal from it because a stone-breaking machine stands under my very window and works 24 hours a day" (G. S. Smith, *D. S. Mirsky*, 220).

91. GARF, f. 7952, op. 7, d. 370, l. 62.

92. GARF, f. 7952, op. 7, d. 370, ll. 64–65. In the published volume, Tiagnibedy's contribution is confined to a mere two pages of text, filled with generic statements about the important role played in the construction by Comrade Kaganovich and so on (*Kak my stroili metro*, 105–6).

93. GARF, f. 7952, op. 7., d. 370, ll. 67, 68.

94. Ibid., l. 74.

95. For the agreement between Kholin and the publisher "History of Factories and Foundries," see GARF, f. 7952, op. 7, delo 349, l.19. Tret'iakov's apparent unwillingness to participate in the venture farther is suggested in ibid., d. 370, l. 65.

96. Ibid., d. 440, l. 1.

97. Ibid., d. 240, l. 3. This is apparently the same S. Persov, whose signature as "literary consultant" appears on the October 1934 plan for work with "the working-class author" (*rabochii avtor*) devised by the editors of "History of the Metro" (GARF, f. 7952, op. 7, d. 223). This may in fact be Shmuel Persov (1890–1952), author of a number of books translated from Yiddish and published in Moscow in the late 1920s and 1930s, including *Rzhanoi khleb* [Rye Bread] (1929), *Kontraktsiia* (1931), and *Viva Stalin!* (1938).

98. GARF, f. 7952, op. 7, d. 239, l. 64.

99. Ibid., l. 75. The hostile question may be a reflection of the relative sophistication of this particular audience. An archival document indicates that most members of the audience were either Komsomol or Party members (ibid., d. 226, l. 32). The challenge to Kataev was typical. Although even activist authors usually limited their actual time on site, this was ostensibly a sore point with workers. Matthew Lenoe describes the experience of Vladimir Stavskii, who was reporting from a railroad car factory in Tver where he had gone to collect material for a book on "socialist competition." Stavskii soon realizes that his original plan to stay at the factory for only a few days will not yield the insights he needs, and he extends his stay. Although he uses his own experience to urge writers to take up jobs on-site, he himself worked at the factory for only a month and a half (see Lenoe, *Closer to the Masses*, 233). A brief exchange at the meeting between Kataev and subway workers in which a member of the audience challenges Kataev about the meaning of *siuzhet* and *fabula* suggests that the group he addressed was fairly sophisticated. Surprisingly, Kataev contends that the two literary concepts are identical: "*siuzhet eto i est' fabula*" (GARF, f. 7952, op. 7, d. 239, l. 80).

100. Ibid., d. 239, l. 77.

101. Ibid., l. 69.

102. Ibid., ll. 72, 76.

103. Ibid., l. 90.

104. Ibid.

105. Ibid., l. 84.

106. Ibid., ll. 72, 77.

107. Kataev adds an intriguing footnote to the story of this character, whom he identifies at the rally as a real-life engineer by the name of Tamarkin. Describing a conversation he has had with a "certain Chekist acquaintance" about *Time, Forward!*, Kataev notes that the agent from the secret police recognizes the personality type from his reading of the novel: "Your engineer is so similar to one working at our shop," the Chekist comments. When they compare notes, they realize they are both talking about the same real-life individual. Apparently this same Moisei Aleksandrovich Tamarkin, now transferred to Nizhnii Tagil, is later the feature of an article entitled "An Engineer of Three Epochs" in *Pravda*. The author of that article was Aleksandr Avdeenko, Tamarkin's former coworker from Magnitogorsk. Avdeenko reports the engineer's 1937 suicide in "Otluchenie," 54–55.

108. As we know, the cathedral's destruction was captured in photographs by Ilia Ilf, who seems to have shared Katia's nonchalant reaction to the event.

109. Rosalind Marsh notes that *Time, Forward!* expresses "genuine enthusiasm" for the "technological progess and rapid social change" that Kataev depicts (*Soviet Fiction*, 7). As Timothy Colton points out, no architectural monument from the past was too precious to be above consideration for demolition. He reports discussions about removing St. Basil's Cathedral to facilitate holiday parades, and apparently there was even talk of obliterating the Kremlin (Colton, *Moscow*, 268, 277).

110. Bruno Jasienski, *Man Changes*, 14–15. I use this translation throughout with only minor emendations.

111. The arch was constructed according to plans by prerevolutionary architect Osip Bove and formally dedicated in 1834. Located near the Belorussian train station at the end of Tverskoi Boulevard, it was dismantled to make way for Stalinist renovations in 1936 and relocated in 1968 to its current site near the memorial complex at Pokolonnaia gora in Moscow (Schmidt, *Architecture*, 183). Greg Castillo makes the interesting point that the general plan for Moscow reconstruction, which he calls the "seminal document for Socialist Realism's urban aesthetic," allowed Stalin's architects to "pull off a brilliant sleight-of-hand." By focusing on the city's main thoroughfares and "giving priority to monumental curtains of street-defining buildings," they were able to complete "only a fraction" of the new construction that had been planned while still presenting the city as "having been relentlessly reconstructed" (Castillo, "Cities," 265, 278).

112. Iasenskii, *Chelovek meniaet kozhu*, 7–8. Clark's droshky driver recognizes the army detachment as part of the internal security forces, and his laconic comment "G-P-U" in an unmistakable "international language" first makes the American "shiver" before he becomes inexplicably happy (*neuderzhimo veselo*). The police have the same indisputable effect on the rest of the populace. The detachment is singing a catchy song, and passersby soon begin to walk in step "without noticing it themselves" (8). Iasenskii would die in the custody of the security organs, summarily executed in 1938.

113. Intended as a "symbol of emancipated Russia," the obelisk was included on Moscow's coat of arms until it was demolished in 1941. Colton includes a photograph of it in his description in *Moscow* (108–10).

114. Iasenskii made several trips to Central Asia, including a trip as part of an international brigade of writers in the spring of 1931 ("Internatsional'naia pisatel'skaia brigada," 1). He would be made an honorary citizen of Tadzhikistan for his work in that country. V. Oskotskii in an afterword to a 1969 Russian edi-

tion of Iasenskii's, novel draws a distinction between this early production novel and later versions from the "end of the 1940s—beginning of the 1950s." Discussing Iasenskii's descriptions of the technical aspects of construction, Oskotskii claims that the "purposeful, life-affirming spirit" of *Chelovek meniaet kozhu* "has little in common with the technical descriptions that are far from art" found in later production novels ("Bruno Iasenskii," 592). Dmitrii Sviatopolk–Mirskii traveled to Tadzhikistan with Iasenskii in the spring of 1933 (G. S. Smith, *D. S. Mirsky*, 244). Like his colleague, Mirskii died at the hands of the system he had served, executed in 1939.

115. This monumental structure, an example of what William Brumfield calls "stupendous megalomania," was to tower over the surrounding landscape, though it seems unlikely that it could have organized and controlled the site in the same organic sense the more "earthbound" cathedral did (and now does again) (Brumfield, *History*, 398, 485). Sona Hoisington gives a detailed description of the evolution of plans for the palace in "'Ever Higher.'" Fitzpatrick makes her point in *Everyday Stalinism*, 69–70.

116. Leonhard describes this incident from his childhood in *Child of the Revolution*, 13–14. Emily Johnson describes a very different, but related connection between image and printed text in her study of depictions of St. Petersburg by scholar Nikolai Antsiferov. She notes Antsiferov's tendency to fix architectural sites with famous literary descriptions of them, "as if a reference to or the incantation of a literary citation can help to spiritualize" the site ("Transcendence," 114). The notion of a "compensatory function" is advanced by Mikhail Ryklin, who argues that Soviet communism itself played the role of "totalized compensation for a real trauma, the only role that it, in fact, filled completely" ("Metrodiskurs," 719). See Evgeny Dobrenko's similar argument that Socialist Realism functioned "to produce reality by aestheticizing it" (Dobrenko, *Political Economy*, 4).

117. B. Galanov, *Kataev*, 38–39. Galanov first became acquainted with Kataev in his capacity as "child correspondent" during the First Five-Year Plan. His description of the "raid" he helped carry out on Kataev to encourage him to write for and about contemporary children is one of the interesting anecdotes included in this impressionistic discussion of Kataev's long career. The "raid," an unexpected visit by activists to check on progress in a particular industry, was a common tactic used throughout those and subsequent years to raise visibility for campaigns of propagandistic significance (see *"reid,"* Mokienko and Nikitina, *Tolkovyi slovar'*).

118. Viacheslav Polonskii's 1931 description captures the site at night and illustrates the continuing novelty of air travel at this early point in aviation history ("Magnitostroi," 109).

CHAPTER 6. ANDREI PLATONOV

1. Research by a veritable army of talented scholars helped bring Platonov back to life, as the series *"Strana filosofov" Andreia Platonova*, for example, testifies. The editor of that series, N. V. Kornienko, has been a particular leader in restoring Platonov's oeuvre to its original state, though certain questions about his work remain, including many textological issues. See, for example, Kornienko's comment that "the question of Platonov's evolution" is "an eternal ques-

tion for Platonov studies" ("O nekotorykh urokakh," 5). Much of Platonov's most important work was published only long after his death, and his method of working with variants of a single narrative makes the already complicated question of what constitutes a final text even more complex. V. Iu. V'iugin has argued that Platonov relied on multiple readings of a single text to compress his narrative into its final succinct form (V'iugin, "Kak pisal Platonov"). According to E. Taratuta, typists demanded three times the normal rate to work on Platonov's complicated manuscripts ("Povyshennoe soderzhanie sovesti," 101).

2. Evidence of the continued trouble Platonov experienced trying to get his work published is copious. Early correspondence makes it clear, for example, that he was mistaken in his 1921 hopes that comrades in the capital would understand him better than the provincials and their "enormous sluggishness" with which he had been dealing (see Subbotin, "Andrei Platonov," 440 and elsewhere). Most telling, perhaps, is his later correspondence with Gorky, which can be found in *"Mne eto nuzhno."* A letter from 1934 is all too typical; Gorky describes the "thunderous" effect Platonov's story "Musornyi veter" had on him before repeating that it is absolutely unpublishable (see *"Mne eto nuzhno"*). Proletarian writer Aleksandr Avdeenko described his own conviction that a connection with the working class gave him special authorial status in "Otluchenie," 29. Avdeenko, like Platonov, learned the hard way that "authentic" working-class voices were to be strictly controlled in Stalin's Russia.

3. Platonov's remarks about machines from 1921 and 1922 articles are quoted in Langerak, "Andrei Platonov v 1926 gody," 202. The relationship of Shklovskii's "Tret'ia fabrika" to Platonov's *Chevengur* is discussed in Golovanov, "K razvalinam," 230. See also Galushkin, "K istorii," who notes that Platonov "answered" Shklovskii in his 1926 story "Antiseksus" and, following Kornienko, in "Fabrika literatury" (180, 183). Frequently unable to publish his literary works, particularly in later years, Platonov was often forced to rely on his experience as an engineer and inventor in order to make a living. In his request to resign from official duties in 1935, Platonov nevertheless announces that he will continue his technical work since he cannot bear to leave the project on which he has spent a year and a half "without continuation and completion" (quoted in Kornienko, "'Dobrye liudi,'" 4). A letter to his wife from 1936 suggests that he saw both activities as essential parts of his self-image. He tells her that the "passion for scientific truth has not only not died in me; it's gotten stronger as a result of artistic contemplation" (*Vzyskanie pogibshikh,* 627). Fascinating documents from Platonov's time as a technician in Voronezh can be found in Nemtsov and Antonova, "Gubmeliorator."

4. See Kornienko's comments in "Chevengurskie mechtaniia," 484. Platonov's production sketch, "V poiskakh budushchego," details his trip to a paper factory; it was found on the back of the manuscript of *Kotlovan.* It is included in *Kotlovan,* 364–71. T. M. Vakhitova, who prepared the sketch for publication, offers fascinating background information in "Oborotnaia storona."

5. See I. Rodnianskaia's discussion of critics' tendency to dismiss or downplay Platonov's more "orthodox" works or to reinterpret them as satire ("*Serdechnaia ozadachennost',*" 332–35). Natal'ia Duzhina describes the "image of the 'builders of socialism'" in *Fountain Pit* as the "object of bitter authorial irony," noting only in passing that the role of the architectural engineer, "ideologist for all the construction," is "exceptional" (Duzhina, "Stroiteli," 461). Thomas Seifrid contends that *Fountain Pit* can be read as a "parody of the Five-Year Plan novel," although he concedes that the satire is "complex and ambivalent" (Seifrid, *Andrei Platonov,* 140–42). He modifies hs argument further in *A Companion,* 105–11.

Lola Debuser argues in "Tainopis' romana" for an interpretation of *Happy Moscow* as a parody of fundamental Soviet texts from the late 1920s through the 1930s. Platonov himself continually argued against such an interpretation; see, for example, his negative reaction in 1932 to the suggestion that his work is satirical and his rejection of that classification again in 1934 in "Stenogramma tvorcheskogo vechera," and "Anketa gruppkoma," *Andrei Platonov: Vospominaniia sovremennikov*, 299–300 and 318.

6. Langerak points out that it is often our own hindsight that provides the ironic note: such detached skepticism was mostly missing from the culture at the time (Langerak, *Andrei Platonov: Materialy*, 86). "Fabrika literatury" was reprinted in *Oktiabr'*, 1991, 10.

7. Bethea, *Shape of Apocalypse*, 158. Maria Platonova's comments are included in her preface to Andrey Platonov, *The Foundation Pit* (1996), viii.

8. See E. A. Iablokov, *Na beregu neba*, for a detailed discussion of the variants of *Chevengur*, including its numerous variants, fragments, and alternative titles.

9. Andrei Platonov, *Chevengur* (1978), 3. Platonov's dense, allusive, and difficult prose presents numerous problems for the translator, particularly when early translations were crafted from texts that later proved to be incomplete. With the nearly insurmountable difficulty of rendering Platonov into English in mind, I have quoted from the most widely available translations, with only minor emendations unless otherwise noted. Unless otherwise noted, quotations from *Chevengur* are taken from the 1978 Olcott translation and are included in the text. The eccentric Russian that Platonov uses in his prose works can also be found in his notebooks, unpublished writings, and even his correspondence. Such distinctive use of language is part of Platonov's unique style, but it may reflect his milieu as well. See, for example, the Platonovian utterance of a real-life peasant soldier that Vasilii Grossman reported in August 1941: "I've got a simple soul, as simple as a balalaika. It isn't afraid of death. It's those with precious souls who fear death" (reported by Grossman, *Writer at War*, 14).

10. See alternate subtitles *Puteshestvie s otkrytym serdtsem* and *Puteshestvie s pustym serdtsem* in Iablokov, *Na beregu neba*.

11. Sasha's idiosyncratic attempt to "become" a fence finds an echo in the dream of one of Anton Chekhov's own eccentric characters. The "hero" of "The Dangers of Tobacco," Chekhov's one-act monologue from 1902, describes a similar ambition. Ivan Ivanovich Niukhin fantasizes about running away from his tawdry existence. When he gets "far, far away," he announces, he'll "stop in a field somewhere and stand there like a tree or a fence post, like a scarecrow, under the great wide sky, stand there all night gazing at the moon, the clear, quiet moon, and forget it all, forget . . ." (see Chekhov, "O vrede," 605). For a different interpretation of the image of the fence in Platonov, see, for example, Heli Kostova, "Moskovskoe prostranstvo," 649–50. M. Ryzhkova notes Platonov's understanding of the connection that binds seeming opposites, quoting his comment from the newspaper *Krasnaia derevnia* that "there's a tie between the burdock, hobo, and field song and electricity, the locomotive, and the factory whistle that shakes the earth—a similarity, the same birth mark" (283).

12. Jochen Hellbeck's discussion of Soviet diaries from the 1920s and 1930s offers further evidence of the difficult psychological struggles necessary to negotiate this period. See, in particular, playwright Aleksandr Afinogenov's diary, which illustrates yet another author's pained response to complicated reality (Hellbeck, *Revolution*, 285–345).

13. The story describes events from the summer of 1921, but it was written significantly later, probably after 1926.

14. Wind is a significant symbol for Platonov, as we will see, and it was a trait he shared with his contemporaries who used winds, snowstorms, and explosions to represent the revolution. Grigory Kaganov suggests that this had an effect on representations of physical reality after 1917, arguing that "spatial representations" after the revolution depict a "new world" that is "seen as almost weightless; it will not so much lean on the earth as hang in the air" (Kaganov, *Images of Space*, 156).

15. This deprecating attitude toward reading and, by extension, to writing was an approach bequeathed to Russian literature from its most utilitarian proponents. The fear that reading was an unworthy pastime and writing an ineffectual retreat from the real problems of the day infected even nineteenth-century giants like Lev Tolstoy. Platonov would have been particularly susceptible to such guilt, both because of his practical education and experience and because of his repeated inability to find acceptance for his creative writing.

16. The reference seems to indicate the Bolsheviks, the *Rossiiskaia sotsial-demokraticheskaia rabochaia partiia (bol'shevikov)*, in 1917.

17. Peter Gatrell describes the upheaval that shook Russia in the first part of the century in his study, *A Whole Empire Walking: Refugees in Russia During World War I* (Bloomington: Indiana University Press, 1999).

18. See Stephen Kotkin, "Modern Times," for a detailed discussion of the many processes that affected all modern societies in the interwar period.

19. See *Chevengur*, 1988, 162; my translation.

20. This last sentence is missing from the Olcott translation, but is included in the 1988 edition of *Chevengur*, 193.

21. As I. Savel'zon points out, the result of this constant reshuffling is that readers know no more about the actual location of events by the end of the story than they do at the beginning in the novel ("Kategoriia prostranstva," 236). The unclear landscape that results is a feature of the transitional production novel, as we have seen.

22. Compare this to Ilf and Petrov's notion of the pedestrian as the pinnacle of human existence as well as their later journey from one side of America to another as if in restless search of something constantly on the move.

23. See his remark about this *"naibolee emkoe proizvedenie"* in *Chevengur, Sovetskii pisatel'*, 1989, 652.

24. Vakhitova, "Oborotnaia storona," 374, 375.

25. Ibid., 376, 378.

26. As Chalmaev points out in his commentary to the novella, Voshchev's age may also relate to Platonov's personal biography: he was thirty in 1929 when he was writing the work. That autumn Platonov had problems with his colleagues on the irrigation project for Narkozem, and those difficulties may also be reflected in Voshchev's dealings with his former workplace (Platonov, *Sobranie sochinenii*, 2:535).

27. Andrey Platonov, *The Foundation Pit* (2009), 1. Further translations from this edition will be included in the text. A definitive Russian edition, with a careful scholarly apparatus, was published by Nauka in 2000.

28. See Georg Simmel's essay "Bridge and Door" for a provocative discussion of such architectural dividers. Simmel's approach to the division of space has relevance to Platonov's work. In a similar vein, see Esaulov's interesting work on gates, doors, and windows in Platonov's *Happy Moscow* (Esaulov, "Vorota").

29. See early versions of the passage, including Voschev's question "Ne uby-vaiut li liudi v chuvstve svoei zhizni, kogda pribyvaiut postroiki?" in *Kotlovan*, 121. Mirra Ginsburg's translation here—"Man will make a building and unmake himself"—echoes the original "dom chelovek postroit, a sam rasstroitsia" (Plato-nov, *The Foundation Pit* [1994], 12).

30. As Elizabeth Markstein notes, this house is "not only an image-symbol," but also has "an absolutely real prototype in actuality." Numerous plans for "House-commune," "Apartment-commune," "City-commune," and so forth indi-cate the fascination of this concept for the Soviet builders of this era (see Mark-stein, "Dom i kotlovan," 288).

31. The quotation from Platonov's 1920 polemic about the new meaning of "re-ligion" can be found, along with a contemporary critic's view of it, in Subbotin, "Andrei Platonov," 458. Platonov identifies work as an alternative to suicide in "V poiskakh budushchego," 368, where he notes "*lishnii trud vsegda vlechet sokrashchenie zhizni, on zameniaet samoubiistvo.*" This is just one of many pas-sages in the essay reminiscent of *Kotlovan*, which was written during the same period.

32. The child of Dasha and Gleb in Gladkov's *Cement* also dies in the inhos-pitable conditions that she shares with others in a children's home to which she has been taken. Her death is presented as a regrettable, individual instance of the hardships all must suffer as her parents and others work tirelessly to build a more just society.

33. These production novels apparently share their lack of concrete architec-tural detail with medieval manuscripts. Commenting about architectural descrip-tions in late medieval and early modern texts, David Cowling notes that "disappointingly . . . developments in real architectural styles . . . are not reflected in descriptions of buildings in literary texts in any clearly demonstrable manner." Tellingly, Cowling points out that the "main interest of the building as an object for elaboration in allegory lay elsewhere" (*Building*, 6–7).

34. Prushevskii's question is still ambiguous at this point in the Russian text: he asks "*libo mne pogibnut'?*" (Platonov, *Kotlovan*, 33). But Platonov's stark as-sertion that "extra work . . . substitutes for suicide" in "V poiskakh budushchego" (368) suggests the need for inevitable self-sacrifice. Prushevskii's habit of wan-dering the work site and the surrounding countryside, particularly at night, seems to tie him to Platonov. The author notes in the unpublished production sketch that the "factory works day and night" which meant that he "didn't want to sleep at night." Complaining that he was "troubled by the surrounding energy," he notes that he stepped out "in search of the truth of highly productive labor" ("V poiskakh budushchego," 368).

35. The original tells us that Prushevskii falls asleep *so schast'em ravnodushiia k zhizni* (*Kotlovan*, 34), which Ginsburg calls the "happiness of indifference to life" (27).

36. The passage in the original Russian reads *Prushevskii tikho gliadel na vsiu tumannuiu starost' prirody i videl na kontse ee belye spokoinye zdaniia, svet-iashchiesia bol'she, chem bylo sveta v vozdukhe. On ne znal imeni tomu za-konchennomu stroitel'stvu i naznacheniia ego, khotia mozhno bylo poniat', chto te dal'nye zdaniia ustroeny ne tol'ko dlia pol'zy, no i dlia radosti* (*Kotlovan*, 59).

37. Löve, for example, argues that a "dualistic world-view" characterizes *Kot-lovan*, marked by oppositions between "*svoi-chuzhoi*" (us-them), "ideal and re-ality," "dream and deed," and others (*Evolution of Space*, 152).

38. Ginsburg translates the phrase—"*skorb' na zemnoi potukhskei zvezde*"—as "sorrow on the extinct terrestrial star" (65).

39. The original reads: *On by khotel, ne soznavaia, chtoby vechno stroiashchii-sia i nedostroennyi mir byl pokhozh na ego razrushennuiu zhizn'* (*Kotlovan*, 59). Ginzburg's translation of "the world, eternally under construction and never finished" (65) nicely captures both Platonov's meaning and the sense these transitional production novels have of the endless process of constructing self and reality.

40. Platonov apparently finished this innovative and quirky novel in 1936, but, like most of his work, it was rejected as stylistically and ideologically unacceptable and first published only decades after his death in 1951.

41. See N. Kornienko's contention that Platonov was interested in developing "his—personal—theme" of "proletarian Moscow" and therefore asked Gorky three times to include him in one of the writers' brigades (Kornienko, "'Proletarskaia Moskva," 367). Compare the case of the entirely untested Konstantin Simonov, who was reportedly successful in his request to be sent to the Belomor Canal to collect materials for his poetry (Figes, *Whisperers*, 195). Kornienko sees the Belomor canal volume as the incarnation of a project mentioned in Platonov's story "Nadlezhashchie meropriiatiia" ("Soveshchaniie v Soiuze," 327). See Robert Chandler's fascinating reading of the story "Among Animals and Plants" as Platonov's commentary on the Belomor Canal volume and the complex position of Soviet writers ("Introduction," xxii–xxvii).

42. See the police report (*svodka*) in Goncharov and Nekhotin, "Andrei Platonov," 853. Naturally, the veracity of information in such secret denunciations is suspect. As Natal'ia Kornienko notes, a copy of the Belomor volume, *Ocherki po istorii stroitel'stva Belomorsko-Baltiiskogo kanala imeni Stalina*, was part of Platonov's personal library (Andrei Platonov, *Vzyskanie pogibshikh*, 639), and Platonov had apparently offered it to his young son as edification. His written dedication from February 19, 1935, read "to a little bandit about big bandits" ("Soveshchanie o Soiuze," 327). Critic Iogann Al'tman's handwritten dedication from January 31, 1934, on another copy of the Belomor volume suggests sentiments common among the literary intelligentsia at the time: "With great joy for our life, with great regret that I didn't participate in this book, with great hope for participation in future books." Frustrated by his exclusion from such trips and from Soviet literature in general, Platonov was eventually included in a less prestigious official journey to Central Asia, which was reflected in his later work *Dzhan*. Natal'ia Kornienko provides fascinating information on Platonov's trip to Turkmenistan in her commentary to his notebooks (Platonov, *Zapisnye knizhki*, 364–65).

43. Ryklin, "Metrodiskurs," 714. For a fascinating account of Platonov's life as an engineer during this time, see Elena Antonova, "A. Platonov—inzhener."

44. Platonov's answers are included in "Otvet na anketu," 286–87. See also Kornienko's useful introduction to the document and the subject of Platonov in the 1930s in "Ne otkazyvat'sia."

45. Andrey Platonov, *Happy Moscow*, 3. Further quotations from this edition will be included in the text. A scholarly edition of the Russian text, with variant readings and a small scholarly apparatus, can be found in *"Strana filosofov" Andreia Platonova*, vol. 3.

46. This image of a woman dangling her head from the window sill of an apartment house is part of *Chevengur* as well, where the heroine, Sofia Alexandrovna, drowses on the window sill of her own apartment. These images help justify I.

Esaulov's contention that windows in Platonov's work are associated with contemplation and thoughtfulness ("Vorota," 252).

47. The unusual Russian *mogla ozhidat'* suggests that Moskva can "expect or hope" as well as "wait."

48. In this connection see V. Iu. V'iugin's compelling description of "emptiness" (*pustoe*) in *Chevengur* as a "readiness to absorb, to 'pass the world through one's self'" ("Povest'A. Platonova," 339–40, note 27).

49. Archival research has revealed that Platonov and his brother were both employed and active there for a number of years. See Elena Antonova, "A. Platonov—inzhener," throughout.

50. See Platonov's early skepticism and the reaction of a 1920 critic in archival materials discussed in Subbotin, "Andrei Platonov," 458. The metaphor of authors as human fertilizer for future generations can be found in later comments by both I. L. Sel'vinskii ("I'm afraid that we—our contemporary literature, just like medieval [literature]—are only manure, fertilizer for the literature that will come with communism") and Fedor Gladkov ("We are all manure for future literary harvests. Literature will arise only in 20 or 30 years"). Their alleged comments can be found in a secret police memorandum from V. N. Merkulov to Andrei Zhdanov in 1944 (Artizov and Naumov, *Vlast'*, 526, 530).

51. According to work by N. V. Kornienko and others, Platonov worked on the novel between 1933 and 1936 (see Kornienko, "Podgotovka teksta," 7, 105).

Select Bibliography

PRIMARY SOURCES

Erenburg, Il'ia. *Den' vtoroi*. Moscow: Sovetskaia literatura, 1934.

Iasenskii, Bruno. *Chelovek meniaet kozhu: roman*. Moscow: Izvestiia, 1969.

Il'f, Il'ia. *Il'ia Il'f—fotograf: Fotografii iz sobraniia Aleksandry Il'f, 1930–e gody*. Moscow: Moscow Art Center, 2002.

———. *Zapisnye knizhki: 1925–1937 (pervoe polnoe izdanie)*. Moscow: Tekst, 2000.

Il'f, Il'ia, and Evgenii Petrov. *Dvenadtsat' stul'ev: avtorskaia redaktsiia*. Compilation and commentary by A. I. Il'f. Moscow: Tekst, 2004.

———. *Dvenadtsat' stul'ev: pervyi polnyi variant*. Commentary by M. P. Odesskii and D. M. Fel'dman. Moscow: Vagrius, 1998.

———. *Sobranie sochinenii*, 5 vols. Volume 3: *Rasskazy, fel'etony, stat'i, rechi* and Volume 4: *Odnoetazhnaia Amerika*. Moscow: Gosudarstvennoe izdatel'stvo khudozhestvennoi literatury, 1961.

———. *Zolotoi telenok: Avtorskaia redaktsiia*. Compilation and commentary by A. I. Il'f. Moscow: Tekst, 2003.

Ilf and Petrov. *The Twelve Chairs*. Translated by John H. C. Richardson. Introduction by Maurice Friedberg. New York: Vintage Books, 1961.

Ilf, Ilya, and Eugene Petrov. *The Little Golden Calf: A Satiric Novel*. Translated by Charles Malamuth. New York: Frederick Ungar, 1932, reprinted 1961.

Jasienski, Bruno. *Man Changes His Skin*. Translated by H. G. Scott. New York: International Publishers, 1936.

Kataev, Valentin. "Almaznyi moi venets" and "Trava Zabveniia." In *Almaznyi moi venets*. Moscow: Eksmo, 2003.

———. "Squaring the Circle." In *Eight Twentieth-Century Russian Plays*. Edited and translated by Timothy Langen and Justin Weir. Evanston: Northwestern University Press.

———. *Time, Forward!* Translated by Charles Malamuth. New York: Farrar & Rinehart, 1933.

———. *Vremia, vpered!* Moscow: Federatsiia: 1932.

———. *Vremia, vpered!* Moscow: Khudozhestvennia literatura, 1960.

Kosarev, A. *Kak my stroili metro*. Moscow: Istoriia fabrik i zavodov, 1935.

———. *Rasskazy stroiteli metro*. Moscow: Istoriia fabrik i zavodov, 1935.

Libedinskii, Iurii. *Rasskazy tovarishchei*. Moscow: Sovetskaia literatura, 1933.

Olesha, Iurii. *Kniga proshchaniia*. Moscow: Vagrius, 1999.

———. *Vishnevaia kostochka*. Moscow: Federatsiia, 1932.

———. *Zavist': Roman*. Moscow: Zemlia i fabrika, 1928. Reprinted by Ardis Publishers, Ann Arbor, Michigan, 1977.

Petrov, Evgenii. *Moi drug Il'f*. Compilation and commentary by A. I. Il'f. Moscow: Tekst, 2001.

Pil'niak, Boris. *Kamni i korny*. Moscow, 1935.

———. *Mne vypala gor'kaia slava: Pis'ma 1915–1937*. Moscow: Agraf, 2002.

———. "O novom tipe pisatelei." *Literaturnaia gazeta*, June 11, 1933, 3.

———. "Pisateli o sotsial'nom zakaze." *Pechat' i revoliutsiia*, 1929, 1:71.

———. "Problema obraza." *Literaturnaia gazeta*, December 18, 1934, 2.

———. *Rasplesnutoe vremia: Rasskazy, povesti, romany*. Moscow: Sovetskii pisatel', 1990.

———. *Nikola-na-Posad'iakh. Rasskazy*. Moscow: Krug, 1923.

———. *Romany*. Moscow: Sovremenniki, 1980.

———. *Rozhdenie cheloveka*. Moscow: Khudozhestvennaia literatura, 1935.

———. *Sobranie sochinenii*. 8 vols. Moscow-Leningrad: Gosudarstvennoe izdatel'stvo, 1930.

———. *Sochineniia*. 3 vols. Vol. 2: *Volga vpadaet v Kaspiiskoe more*. Moscow: "Lada M," 1994.

———. *Tadzhikistan, sed'maia sovetskaia: ocherki, materialy k romanu*. Leningrad: Izdatel'stvo pisatelei, 1931.

———. *Volga vpadaet v Kaspiiskoe more: Roman*. Moscow: Nedra, 1930.

———. "Zakaz nash." *Novaia russkaia kniga*, 1922, 2: 2.

Pilnyak, Boris, and Theodore Dreiser. "Human Nature in a Crucible." *Jewish Standard*, September 30, 1932, 115:166–67.

Platonov, Andrei. *Chevengur: Roman i povesti*. Moscow: Sovetskii pisatel', 1989.

———. *Chevengur*. Moscow: Khudozhestvennaia literatura, 1988.

———. *Chevengur*. Translated by Anthony Olcott. Ann Arbor: Ardis, 1978.

———. *Kotlovan. Tekst, materialy tvorcheskoi istorii*. St. Petersburg: Nauka, 2000.

———. "Mne eto nuzhno ne dlia 'slavy . . .' (Pis'ma M. Gor'komu)." *Voprosy literatury*, 9 (1988): 174–83.

———. "Otvet na anketu 'Kakoi nam nuzhen pisatel'." In *Andrei Platonov: Vospominaniia sovremennikov. Materialy k biografii*, edited by Kornienko and Shubina. Moscow: Sovremennyi pisatel', 1994, 286–88.

———. *Schastlivaia Moskva*. In N. V. Kornienko, ed. "*Strana filosofov"Andreia Platonova: Problemy tvorchestva*. Vol. 3. Moscow: Nasledie, 1999.

———. *Sobranie sochinenii*. Vol. 2: *Chevengur. Kotlovan. Vprok*. Moscow: "Informpechat'," 1988.

———. *V poiskakh budushchego (Puteshestvie na Kamenskuiu pischebumazhnuiu fabriku)*. In *Kotlovan. Tekst, materialy tvorcheskoi istorii*. St. Petersburg: Nauka, 2000.

———. *Vzyskanie pogibshikh: Povesti, rasskazy, p'esa, stat'i*. Edited by M. A. Platonova. Moscow: "Shkola–Press," 1995.

————. *Zapisnye knizhki: Materialy k biografii*. Moscow: IMLI RAN, Nasledie, 2000.

Platonov, Andrey. *The Foundation Pit*. Translated by Robert Chandler and Geoffrey Smith. London: Harvill Press, 1996.

————. *The Foundation Pit*. Translated by Robert and Elizabeth Chandler and Olga Meerson. New York: New York Review Books, 2009.

————. *The Foundation Pit*. Translated and introduction by Mirra Ginsburg. Evanston: Northwestern University Press, 1994.

————. *Happy Moscow*. Translated by Robert and Elizabeth Chandler et al. Introduction by Eric Naiman. London: Harvill Press, 2001.

Rogozina, A., and Boris Pil'niak. *Kitaiskaia sud'ba cheloveka: povest'*. Leningrad: Izdatel'stvo pisatelei, 1931.

Shaginian, Marietta. *Chelovek i vremia: Istoriia chelovecheskogo stanovleniia*. Moscow: Sovetskii pisatel', 1982.

————. *Dnevniki, 1917–1931*. Leningrad: Izdatel'stvo pisatelei, 1932.

————. *Kak ia rabotala nad "Gidrotsentral'iu."* Moscow: Profizdat, 1933.

————. *Literatura i Plan*. Moscow: Moskovskoe tovarishchestvo pisatelei, 1934.

————. *Po dorogam piatiletki: ocherki*. Moscow: Profizdata, 1947.

Secondary Sources

Alexopoulos, Golfo. *Stalin's Outcasts: Aliens, Citizens, and the Soviet State, 1926–1936*. Ithaca: Cornell University Press, 2003.

Andreevskii, G. V. *Povsednevnaia zhizn' Moskvy v stalinskuiu epokhu 1920–1930-e gody*. Moscow: Molodaia gvardiia, 2003.

Andrews, Malcolm. *Landscape and Western Art*. Oxford: Oxford University Press, 1999.

Andronikashvili-Pil'niak, B. B. "Pil'niak, 37-i god." In *Rasplesnutoe vremiia: Rasskazy, povesti, romany*, by Boris Pil'niak. Moscow: Sovetskii pisatel', 1990, 582–604.

Andronikashvili-Pil'niak, Kira Borisovna. "Mne vypala gor'kaia slava . . ." In *Mne vypala gor'kaia slava: Pis'ma 1915–1937*, by Boris Pil'niak. Moscow: Agraf, 2002, 5–12.

Annenkov, Iurii. *Dnevnik moikh vstrech: Tsikl tragedii*. Vol. 1. New York: Mezhdunarodnoe literaturnoe sodruzhestvo, 1966.

Antipina, Valentina. *Povsednevnaia zhizn' sovetskikh pisatelei 1930–1950e gody*. Moscow: Molodaia Gvardiia, 2005.

Antonova, Elena. "A. Platonov—inzhener tresta 'Rosmetroves.'" In *"Strana filosofov" Andreia Platonova: Problemy tvorchestva*, edited by N. V. Kornienko, Vol. 4. Moscow: Nasledie, 2000, 787–804.

Artizov, Andrei, and Oleg Naumov, eds. *Vlast' i khudozhestvennaia intelligentsiia: Dokumenty TsK RKP(b)—VKP(b), VChK-OGPU-NKVD o kul'turnoi politike, 1917–1953 gg*. Moscow: Mezhdunarodnyi fond "Demokratiia," 1999.

Babichenko, D. L., ed. *"Schast'e literatury." Gosudarstvo i pisateli. 1925–1938 gg. Dokumenty*. Moscow: Rossiiskaia politicheskaia entsiklopediia, 1997.

Babicheva, M. E., ed. *"V Belom more krasnyi SLON . . ." Vospominaniia uznikov Solovetskogo lageria osobogo naznacheniia i literatura o nem.* Moscow: "Paskov dom," 2006.

Bachelard, Gaston. *The Poetics of Space.* Translated by Maria Jolas. Boston: Beacon Press, 1994.

Backstein, Joseph. "History of Angels." In *Angels of History: Moscow Conceptualism and its Influence,* by Joseph Backstein and Bart De Baere. Brussels: Mercator Funds, 2005.

Balina, Marina. "Literatura puteshestvii." In *Sotsrealisticheskii kanon,* edited by Gunter and Dobrenko. St. Petersburg: "Akademicheskii proekt," 2000, 896–909.

Barratt, Andrew. *Yurii Olesha's Envy.* Birmingham Slavonic Monographs, 12. Birmingham: University of Birmingham, n.d.

Beaujour, Elizabeth Klosty. *The Invisible Land: A Study of the Artistic Imagination of Iurii Olesha.* New York: Columbia University Press, 1970.

Beevor, Antony, and Luba Vinogradova, ed. and trans. *A Writer at War: Vasily Grossman with the Red Army 1941–1945.* New York: Pantheon Books, 2005.

Belaia, Galina. "Stilevoi regress: o stilevoi situatsii v literature sotsrealizma." In *Sotsrealisticheskii kanon,* edited by Gunter and Dobrenko. St. Petersburg: "Akademicheskii proekt," 2000, 556–68.

Belinkov, A. *Sdacha i gibel' sovetskogo intelligenta. Iurii Olesha.* Prepared by Natalia Belinkov. Madrid, 1976.

Belousov, A. F. "Khudozhestvennaia toponimiia rossiiskoi provintsii: k interpretatsii romana 'Gorod En.'" *Pervye dobychinskie chteniia.* Daugavpils, 1990, 1:8–15.

Belyi, Andrei, et al. *Kak my pishem.* Leningrad: Izdatel'stvo pisatelei, 1930.

Bethea, David M. *The Shape of Apocalypse in Modern Russian Fiction.* Princeton: Princeton University Press, 1989.

Bliznakov, Milka. "Nietzschean Implications and Superhuman Aspirations in the Architectural Avant-Garde." In *Nietzsche and Soviet Culture: Ally and Adversary,* edited by Bernice Glatzer Rosenthal. Cambridge: Cambridge University Press, 1994, 174–210.

———. "Soviet Housing During the Experimental Years, 1918 to 1933." In *Russian Housing in the Modern Age: Design and Social History,* edited by William Craft Brumsfield and Blair A. Ruble. Cambridge: Woodrow Wilson Center Press and Cambridge University Press, 1993, 85–148.

Borden, Richard C. *The Art of Writing Badly: Valentin Kataev's Mauvism and the Rebirth of Russian Modernism.* Evanston: Northwestern University Press, 1999.

Borland, Harriet. *Soviet Literary Theory and Practice during the First Five-Year Plan, 1928–1932.* New York: King's Crown Press, Columbia University, 1950.

Bouvard, Josette. *Le Metro de Moscou: La construction d'un mythe sovietique.* Paris: Editions du Sextant, 2005.

Boym, Svetlana. *Common Places: Mythologies of Everyday Life in Russia.* Cambridge: Harvard University Press, 1994.

Brandenberger, David, and Kevin M. F. Platt. "Tsarist Heroes in Stalinist Mass Culture and Propaganda." In *Epic Revisionism: Russian History and Litera-*

ture as Stalinist Propaganda, edited by Platt and Brandenberger. Madison: University of Wisconsin Press, 2006, 3–14.

Brooks, Jeffrey. *Thank You, Comrade Stalin! Soviet Public Culture from Revolution to Cold War.* Princeton: Princeton Universty Press, 2000.

Brostrom, Kenneth N. "The Enigma of Pil'njak's *The Volga Falls to the Caspian Sea.*" *Slavic and East European Journal,* 18, no. 3 (1974): 271–98.

Brown, Edward J. *The Proletarian Episode in Russian Literature, 1928–1932.* New York: Octagon Books, 1971.

Browning, Gary. *Boris Pilniak: Scythian at a Typewriter.* Ann Arbor: Ardis, 1985.

Brumsfield, William, and Blair A. Ruble, eds. *Russian Housing in the Modern Age: Design and Social History.* Cambridge: Woodrow Wilson Center Press and Cambridge University Press, 1993.

Brumsfield, William Craft. *A History of Russian Architecture.* Cambridge: Cambridge University Press, 1993.

Buchli, Victor. *An Archaeology of Socialism.* Oxford: Berg, 1999.

Bugaeva (Vasil'eva), K. N. "Dnevnik. 1927–1928." Foreword, publication, and notes by N. S. Malinina. *Litsa: Biograficheskii al'manakh,* vol. 7. Moscow and St. Petersburg: Feniks/Atheneum, 1996, 191–316.

Bulgakov, Mikhail. "1–aia detskaia." In *Sobranie sochinenii v 5–ti tomakh.* Vol. 2. Moscow: Khudozhestvennaia literatura, 1989.

Burke, Peter. *Eyewitnessing: The Uses of Images as Historical Evidence.* Ithaca: Cornell University Press, 2001.

Cassiday, Julie. *The Enemy on Trial: Early Soviet Courts on Stage and Screen.* Dekalb: Northern Illinois University Press, 2000.

Castillo, Greg. "Cities of the Stalinist Empire." In *Forms of Dominance: On the Architecture and Urbanism of the Colonial Enterprise,* edited by Nezar Al-Sayyad. Aldershot: Avebury and Ashgate Publishing, 1992, 261–87.

Chandler, Robert. "Introduction." In *Soul and Other Stories,* by Andrey Platonov. Translated by Robert and Elizabeth Chandler with Katia Grigoruk, Angela Livingstone, Olga Meerson, and Eric Naiman. New York: New York Review Books, 2008, vii–lvii.

Chatterjee, Choi, and Karen Petrone. "Models of Selfhood and Subjectivity: The Soviet Case in Historical Perspective." *Slavic Review* 67, no. 4 (2008): 967–86.

Chekhov, A. P. "O vrede tabaka." In *Sobranie sochinenii v dvenadtsati tomakh.* Vol. 9. Moscow: Khudozhestvennaia literatura, 1963.

———. "Uchitel' slovesnosti." In *Sobranie sochinenii.* 8 vols. Moscow: Izdatel'stvo Pravda, 1970, 5:346–68.

Chuikina, Sof'ia. "Dvoriane na sovetskom rynke truda (Leningrad, 1917–1941)." In *Normy i tsennosti povsednevnoi zhizhi: Stanovlenie sotsialisticheskogo obraza zhizni v Rossii, 1920–30–e gody,* edited by Timo Vikhavainev. St. Petersburg: Neva, 2000, 151–92.

Chukovskii, K. *Dnevnik, 1901–1929.* Moscow: Sovetskii pisatel', 1991.

Clark, Katerina. "Little Heroes and Big Deeds: Literature Responds to the First Five-Year Plan." In *Cultural Revolution in Russia, 1928–1931,* edited by Sheila Fitzpatrick. Bloomington: Indiana University Press, 1978, 189–206.

————. *Petersburg: Crucible of Cultural Revolution.* Cambridge: Harvard University Press, 1995.

————. *The Soviet Novel: History as Ritual.* 3rd edition. Bloomington: Indiana University Press, 2000.

Clark, Katerina, and Evgeny Dobrenko, eds. With Andrei Artizov and Oleg Naumov. *Soviet Culture and Power: A History in Documents, 1917–1953.* New Haven: Yale University Press, 2007.

Colton, Timothy J. *Moscow: Governing the Socialist Metropolis.* Cambridge: The Belknap Press of Harvard University Press, 1995.

Corney, Frederick. *Telling October: Memory and the Making of the Bolshevik Revolution.* Ithaca: Cornell University Press, 2004.

Cowling, David. *Building the Text: Architecture as Metaphor in Late Medieval and Early Modern France.* Oxford: Clarendon Press, 1998.

Crowley, David, and Susan E. Reid, eds. *Socialist Spaces: Sites of Everyday Life in the Eastern Bloc.* Oxford: Berg, 2002.

Davies, Sarah. *Popular Opinion in Stalin's Russia: Terror, Propaganda and Dissent, 1934–1941.* Cambridge: Cambridge University Press, 1997.

————. "'Us Against Them': Social Identity in Soviet Russia, 1934–41." *Russian Review* 65 (January 1997): 70–89.

Debuser, Lola. "Tainopis' romana 'Schastlivaia Moskva': Parodiia stalinskikh tekstov." In *"Strana filosofov" Andreia Platonova: problemy tvorchestva,* edited by N. V. Kornienko. Vol. 5. Moscow: Nasledie, 2003, 787–804.

De Certeau, Michel. *The Practice of Everyday Life.* Translated by Steven Rendall. Berkeley: University of California Press, 1988.

Degot, Ekaterina. "The Collectivization of Modernism." In *Dream Factory Communism: The Visual Culture of the Stalin Era,* edited by Boris Groys and Max Hollein. Frankfurt: Schirn Kunsthalle, 2003, 85–102.

"Diskussiia v VSSP." *Novyi mir,* 10 (1931): 123–165.

Dobrenko, Evgeny. *The Making of the State Writer: Social and Aesthetic Origins of Soviet Literary Culture.* Translated by Jesse M. Savage. Stanford: Stanford University Press, 2001.

————. *Political Economy of Socialist Realism.* Translated by Jesse M. Savage. New Haven: Yale University Press, 2007.

Dubrovsky, A. M. "Chronicle of a Poet's Downfall: Dem'ian Bednyi, Russian History, and *The Epic Heroes.*" In *Epic Revisionism: Russian History and Literature as Stalinist Propaganda,* edited by Kevin M. F. Platt and David Brandenberger, Madison: University of Wisconsin Press, 2006, 77–98.

Duzhina, Natal'ia. "Stroiteli 'obshcheproletarskogo doma' v kontekste politicheskoi povsednevnosti 1929–1930-x gg." In *"Strana filosofov" Andreia Platonova: Problemy tvorchestva,* edited by N. V. Kornienko. Vol. 6. Moscow: IMLI, 2005, 461–70.

Eastman, Max. *Artists in Uniform: A Study of Literature and Bureaucratism.* New York: Octagon Books, 1972.

Eco, Umberto. "Architecture and Memory." *VIA: Architecture and Literature* 8 (1986): 89–94.

Eidelman, Ia. "V Prezidiume Pravleniia SSP." *Literaturnaia gazeta,* October 30, 1935, 4.

Eisenstein, Sergei M. *Immoral Memories: An Autobiography.* Translated by Herbert Marshall. Boston: Houghton Mifflin, 1983.

Esaulov, I. "Vorota, dveri i okna v romane *Schastlivaia Moskva.*" In *"Strana filosofov" Andreia Platonova: Problemy tvorchestva,* edited by N. V. Kornienko. Vol. 3. Moscow: Nasledie, 1999, 252–60.

Figes, Orlando. *The Whisperers: Private Life in Stalin's Russia.* New York: Picador, 2007.

Fitzpatrick, Sheila. "Cultural Revolution Revisited." *Russian Review* 58 (April 1999): 202–9.

———. *Everyday Stalinism: Ordinary Life in Extraordinary Times: Soviet Russia in the 1930s.* New York: Oxford University Press, 1999.

———. "The World of Ostap Bender: Soviet Confidence Men in the Stalin Period." *Slavic Review* 61, no. 3 (Fall 2002): 535–57.

Fleishman, Lazar. *Pasternak v tridtsatye gody.* Jerusalem: Magnes Press, 1984.

———. "V polemike s Maksom Istmenom." *Materialy po istorii russkoi i sovetskoi kul'tury: Iz Arkhiva Guverovskogo Instituta.* Stanford Slavic Studies. Vol. 4. Stanford, 1992, 191–219.

Fox, Michael David. "What is Cultural Revolution?" *Russian Review* 58 (April 1999): 181–201.

Frezinskii, Boris. *Pisateli i sovetskie vozhdi: Izbrannye siuzhety 1919–1960 godov.* Moscow: Ellis Lak, 2008.

Galanov, B. *Valentin Kataev: Razmyshleniia o Mastere i dialogi s nim.* Moscow: Khudozhestvennaia literatura, 1989.

Galushkin, A. Iu. "K istorii lichnykh i tvorcheskikh vzaimo-otnoshenii A. P. Platonova i V. B. Shklovskogo." In *Andrei Platonov: Vospominaniia sovremennikov. Materialy k biografii,* edited by Kornienko and Shubina. Moscow: Sovremennyi pisatel', 1994, 172–83.

Garros, Veronique, Natalia Korenevskaya, and Thomas Lahusen, eds. *Intimacy and Terror: Soviet Diaries of the 1930s.* Translated by Carol A. Flath. New York: New Press, 1995.

Genette, Gerard. *Paratexts: Thresholds of Interpretation.* Cambridge: Cambridge University Press, 1997.

Geyer, Michael, and Sheila Fitzpatrick, eds. *Beyond Totalitarianism: Stalinism and Nazism Compared.* Cambridge: Cambridge University Press, 2009.

Gide, André. *Return from the U.S.S.R.* Translated by Dorothy Bussy. New York: Alfred A. Knopf, 1937.

Golomstock, Igor. *Totalitarian Art in the Soviet Union, the Third Reich, Fascist Italy and the People's Republic of China.* Translated by Robert Chandler. New York: IconEditions, 1990.

Golovanov, Vasilii. "K razvalinam Chevengura." In *"Strana filosofov" Andreia Platonova: Problemy tvorchestva,* edited by N. V. Kornienko. Vol. 6. Moscow: IMLI, 2005, 220–41.

Goncharov, Vladimir, and Vladimir Nekhotin. "Andrei Platonov v dokumentakh OGPU-NKVD-NKGB. 1930–1945." In *"Strana filosofov" Andreia Platonova: Problemy tvorchestva,* edited by N. V. Kornienko. Vol. 4. Moscow: Nasledie, 2000, 848–84.

Gorham, Michael S. *Speaking in Soviet Tongues: Language Culture and the Pol-*

itics of Voice in Revolutionary Russia. DeKalb: Northern Illinois University Press, 2003.

Gor'kii, M., L. L. Averbakh, S. G. Firin, eds. *Belomorsko-Baltiiskii kanal imeni Stalin: Istoriia stroitel'stva.* Moscow: "Istoriia fabrik i zavodov," 1934.

Groys, Boris. "The Art of Totality." Translated by Mary A. Akatiff. *The Landscape of Stalinism: The Art and Ideology of Soviet Space.* Edited by Evgeny Dobrenko and Eric Naiman. Seattle: University of Washington Press, 2003, 96–122.

———. *The Total Art of Stalinism: Avant-Garde, Aesthetic Dictatorship, and Beyond.* Translated by Charles Rougle. Princeton: Princeton University Press, 1992.

———. "Utopian Mass Culture." *Dream Factory Communism: The Visual Culture of the Stalin Era.* Edited by Boris Groys and Max Hollein. Frankfurt: Schirn Kunsthalle, 2003, 20–37.

Gudkova, Violetta. *Iurii Olesha and Vsevolod Meierkhol'd v rabote nad spektaklem "Spisok blagodeianii": Opyt teatral'noi arkheologii.* Moscow: Novoe literaturnoe obozrenie, 2002.

Gumilevskii, L. "Sud'ba i zhizn'." In *Andrei Platonov: Vospominaniia sovremennikov. Materialy k biografii,* edited by N. V. Kornienko and E. D. Shubina. Moscow: Sovremennyi pisatel', 1994, 52–73.

Gumbrecht, Hans Ulrich. *In 1926: Living at the Edge of Time.* Cambridge: Harvard University Press, 1997.

Gunter, Hans. "Khudozhestvennyi avangard i sotsialisticheskii realizm." In *Sotsrealisticheskii kanon,* edited by Gunter and Dobrenko. St. Petersburg: "Akademicheskii proekt," 2000, 101–8.

Gunter, Hans, and Evgenii Dobrenko, eds. *Sotsrealisticheskii kanon.* St. Petersburg: "Akademicheskii proekt," 2000.

Guski, Andreas. *Literatur und Arbeit, Produktionsskizze und Produktionsroman im Russland des 1. Fünfjahrplans (1928–1932).* Wiesbaden: Harrassowitz Verlag, 1995.

Gutkin, Irina. *Cultural Origins of the Socialist Realist Aesthetic: 1890–1934.* Evanston: Northwestern University Press, 1999.

Halfin, Igal, and Jochen Hellbeck. "Rethinking the Stalinist Subject: Stephen Kotkin's 'Magnetic Mountain' and the State of Soviet Historical Studies." *Jahrbücher für Geschichte Osteuropas* 44 (1996): 456–63.

Hanson, Stephen E. *Time and Revolution: Marxism and the Design of Soviet Institutions.* Chapel Hill: University of North Carolina Press, 1997.

Harkins, William E. "The Theme of Sterility in Olesha's *Envy.*" In *Olesha's* Envy: *A Critical Companion.* Edited by Rimgaila Salys. Evanston: Northwestern University Press and the American Association of Teachers of Slavic and East European Languages, 1999.

Harley, J. B. "Maps, Knowledge and Power." In *The Iconography of Landscape: Essays on the symbolic representation, design and use of past environments,* edited by Denis Cosgrove and Stephen Daniels. Cambridge: Cambridge University Press, 1988, 277–312.

Harris, Steven. "In Search of 'Ordinary' Russia: Everyday Life in the NEP, the Thaw, and the Communal Apartment." *Kritika* 6, no. 3 (Summer 2005): 583–614.

Hellbeck, Jochen. *Revolution on My Mind: Writing a Diary under Stalin*. Cambridge: Harvard University Press, 2006.

————. "Working, Struggling, Becoming: Stalin-Era Autobiographical Texts." *Russian Review* 60, no. 3 (July 2001): 340–59.

Hellebust, Rolf. *Flesh to Metal: Soviet Literature and the Alchemy of Revolution*. Ithaca: Cornell University Press, 2003.

Hoisington, Sona Stephan. "'Ever Higher': The Evolutions of the Project for the Palace of Soviets," *Slavic Review* 62, no. 1 (Spring 2003): 41–68.

Hutchings, Stephen C. *Russian Modernism: The Transfiguration of the Everyday*. Cambridge: Cambridge University Press, 1997.

Iablokov, E. A. *Na beregu neba (Roman Andreia Platonova "Chevengur")*. Studiorum Slavicorum monumenta. Vol. 22. St. Petersburg: Dmitrii Bulganin, 2001.

Iarov, S. V. "Intelligentsiia i vlast' v Petrograde 1917–1925 godov: konformistskie strategii i iazyk sotrudnichestva." *Novoe literaturnoe obozrenie* 78 (2006): 7–31.

Il'f, Aleksandra et al. *Il'ia Il'f—fotograf, 1930–e gody*. Moscow: Moskovskii tsentr iskusstva, 2002.

Inber, Vera. *Sobranie sochinenii*. 4 vols. Moscow: Khudozhestvennaia literatura, 1966.

"Internatsional'naia pisatel'skaia brigada na front." *Literaturnaia gazeta*, April 19, 1931, 1.

Ivanova, Tamara. "Eshche o 'nasledstve,' o 'dolge,' i 'prave.' Byl li Vsevolod Ivanov 'zhdanovtsem'?" *Knizhnoe obozrenie*, 1989, 34, 6.

Jensen, Peter Alberg. *Nature as Code: The Achievement of Boris Pilnjak, 1915–1924*. Copenhagen: Rosenkilde and Bagger, 1979.

Johnson, Emily. "Transcendence and the City: Nikolai Antsiferov's *Dusha Peterburga* as an Aesthetic Utopia." In *Moscow and Petersburg: The City in Russian Culture*, edited by Ian K. Lilly. Nottingham: Astra Press, 2002, 103–16.

Johnson, Eric A., and Karl-Heinz Reuband. *What We Knew: Terror, Mass Murder, and Everyday Life in Nazi Germany, An Oral History*. New York: Basic Books, 2005.

Kaganov, Grigory. *Images of Space: St. Petersburg in the Visual and Verbal Arts*. Translated by Sidney Monas. Stanford: Stanford University Press, 1997.

Kassek, Dagmar. "Maloizvestnyi stsenarii Borisa Pil'niaka, ili igra v sotsrealizm." In *Boris Pil'niak: Opyt segodniashnego prochteniia*. IMLI. Moscow: Nasledie, 1995, 42–55.

Kharkhordin, Oleg. "Reveal and Dissimulate: A Genealogy of Private Life in Soviet Russia." In *Public and Private in Thought and Practice: Perspectives on a Grand Dichotomy*, edited by Jeff Weintraub and Krishan Kumar. Chicago: University of Chicago Press, 1997, 333–63.

Khlevniuk, Oleg V. *Master of the House: Stalin and His Inner Circle*. Translated by Nora Seligman Favorov. Hoover Institution, Stanford University. New Haven: Yale University Press, 2009.

Kiaer, Christina. *Imagine No Possessions: The Socialist Objects of Russian Constructivism*. Cambridge: MIT Press, 2005.

Kirpotin, Valerii Iakovlevich. *Rovesnik zheleznogo veka: Memuarnaia kniga*. Moscow: Zakharov, 2006.

Klark, Katerina. "RAPP i institutsializatsiia sovetskogo kul'turnogo polia v 1920–x—nachale 1930–x godov." In *Sotsrealisticheskii kanon*, edited by Gunter and Dobrenko. St. Petersburg: "Akademicheskii proekt," 2000, 209–24.

———. "Sotsrealizm i sakralizatsiia prostranstva." In *Sotsrealisticheskii kanon*, edited by Gunter and Dobrenko. St. Petersburg: "Akademicheskii proekt," 2000, 119–28.

Klein, Joachim. "Belomorkanal: Literatura i propaganda v stalinskoe vremia." *Novoe literaturnoe obozrenie* 71, no. 1 (2005): 231–58.

Klemperer, Victor. *I Will Bear Witness: A Diary of the Nazi Years, 1933–1941.* Translated by Martin Chalmers. New York: Modern Library, 1999.

Kolesnikoff, Nina. *Bruno Jasieński, His Evolution from Futurism to Socialist Realism.* Waterloo, Ontario: Wilfrid Laurier University Press, 1982.

Kornienko, N. V. "Chevengurskie mechtaniia o 'novom cheloveke' v stat'iakh Platonova 1920–x gg." In *"Strana filosofov" Andreia Platonova: Problemy tvorchestva*, edited by N. V. Kornienko. Vol. 6. Moscow: IMLI, 2005, 483–518.

———. "'Dobrye liudi' v rasskazakh A. Platonova kontsa 30–40–x godov: Predvaritel'nye tekstologicheskie zametki." In *Tvorchestvo Andreia Platonova: Issledovaniia i materialy*, edited by V. Iu. V'iugin. Vol. 2. St. Petersburg: Nauka, 2000, 3–24.

———. "Moskva vo vremenii (Imia Peterburga i Moskvy v russkoi literature 10—30–x gg. XX v." *Moskva v russkoi i mirovoi literature: Sbornik statei*. Rossiiskaia Akademiia Nauk: Institut mirovoi literatury im. A. M. Gor'kogo. Moscow: Nasledie, 2000, 210–47.

———. "'Ne otkazyvat'sia ot svoego razuma' (Vvedenie v gody tridtsatye)." In *Andrei Platonov: Vospominaniia sovremennikov. Materialy k biografii*, edited by Kornienko and Shubina. Moscow: Sovremennyi pisatel', 1994, 204–14.

———. "O nekotorykh urokakh tekstologii." In *Tvorchestvo Andreia Platonova: Issledovaniia i materialy. Bibliografiia*. St. Petersburg: Nauka, 1995, 4–23.

———. "Podgotovka teksta i vstupitel'naia stat'ia." *"Strana filosofov" Andreia Platonova: Problemy tvorchestva*. Vol 3. Moscow: Nasledie, 1999, 7–105.

———. " 'Proletarskaia Moskva zhdet svoego khudozhnika' (K tvorcheskoi istorii romana)." *"Strana filosofov" Andreia Platonova: Problemy tvorchestva*. Vol 3. Moscow: Nasledie, 1999, 357–71.

———. "Soveshchanie v Soiuze pisatelei. Chetenie i obsuzhdenie rasskaza A. Platonova 'Sredi zhivotnykh i rastenii' dlia zhulnala *Liudi zheleznodorozhnoi derzhavy*." In *Andrei Platonov: Vospominaniia sovremennikov. Materialy k biografii*, edited by Kornienko and Shubina. Moscow: Sovremennyi pisatel', 1994, 327–47.

Kornienko, N. V., and E. D. Shubina, eds. *Andrei Platonov: Vospominaniia sovremennikov. Materialy k biografii*. Moscow: Sovremennyi pisatel', 1994.

Kostova, Heli. "Moskovskoe prostranstvo v romane 'Schastlivaia Moskva.'" In *"Strana filosofov" Andreia Platonova: Problemy tvorchestva*, edited by N. V. Kornienko. Vol. 4. Moscow: Nasledie, 2000.

Kotkin, Stephen. *Magnetic Mountain: Stalinism as a Civilization*. Berkeley: University of California Press, 1995.

———. "Modern Times: The Soviet Union and the Interwar Conjuncture." *Kritika* 2, no. 1 (Winter 2001): 111–64.

Kozlova, N. N. "Soglasie, ili obshchaia igra (metodologicheskie razmyshleniia o literature i vlasti)." *Novoe literaturnoe obozrenie*, 1999, 40, 193–209.

Krasnoshchekov, V. S. "Pokolennaia rospis' roda Vogay." In *Boris Pil'niak: Issledovaniia i materialy*, edited by A. P. Auer. Mezhvusovskii sbornik nauchnykh trudov. Vols. 3–4. Kolomna: KGPI, 2001, 144–58.

Kritika: Explorations in Russian and Eurasian History 6, no. 1 (Winter 2005): 5–106.

Krylova, Anna. "The Tenacious Liberal Subject in Soviet Studies," *Kritika* 1, no. 1 (2000): 119–46.

Lahusen, Thomas. *How Life Writes the Book: Real Socialism and Socialist Realism in Stalin's Russia*. Ithaca: Cornell University Press, 1997.

Laine, S. V. *Marietta Shaginian (100 let so dnia rozhdeniia)*. Moscow: Znanie, 1988.

Langerak, Tomas. *Andrei Platonov: Materialy dlia biografii, 1899–1929*. Amsterdam: Pegasus, 1995.

——. "Andrei Platonov v 1926 godu." In *Andrei Platonov: Mir tvorchestva*. Moscow: Sovremennyi pisatel', 1994, 193–211.

Latour, Alessandra. *Rozhdenie metropolii. Moskva 1930–1955: Vospominaniia i obrazy*. Moscow: Iskusstvo—XXI vek, 2002.

Lavrenova, O. A. *Geograficheskoe prostranstvo v russkoi poezii XVIII–nachala XX vv. (geokul'turnyi aspect)*. Moscow: Nasledie, 1998.

Lavrov, A. V. "Proizvodstvennyi roman—poslednii zamysel Andreia Belogo." *Novoe literaturnoe obozrenie*, 2002, 4, 56, 114–34.

Lebina, N. B. *Povsednevnaia zhizn' sovetskogo goroda: Normy i anomalii, 1920/1930 gody*. St. Petersburg: Izd. Kikimora, 1999.

Lefebvre, Henri. *The Production of Space*. Oxford: Blackwell, 1991.

Lehan, Richard. *The City in Literature: An Intellectual and Cultural History*. Berkeley: University of California Press, 1998.

Lenoe, Matthew. *Closer to the Masses: Stalinist Culture, Social Revolution, and Soviet Newspapers*. Cambridge: Harvard University Press, 2004.

Leonhard, Wolfgang. *Child of the Revolution*. Translated by C. M. Woodhouse. Chicago: Henry Regency, 1958.

Libedinskaia, Lidiia. *"Zelenaia lampa" i mnogoe drugoe*. Moscow: Raduga, 2000.

Literaturnoe nasledstvo. Vol. 70: *Gor'kii i sovetskie pisateli: neizdannaia perepiska*. Moscow: Izd. Akademii nauk, 1963.

Livers, Keith A. *Constructing the Stalinist Body: Fictional Representations of Corporeality in the Stalinist 1930s*. Lanham: Lexington Books, 2004.

Lotman, Iurii M., and Boris A. Uspenskii. "Binary Models in the Dynamics of Russian Culture (to the End of the Eighteenth Century)." In Iurii M. Lotman, Lidiia Ia. Ginsburg, and Boris A. Uspenskii. *The Semiotics of Russian Cultural History*. Translated by Boris Gasparov. Edited by Alexander D. Nakhimovsky and Alice Stone Nakhimovsky. Ithaca: Cornell University Press, 1985, 30–66.

Lotman, Jurij. *Semiotics of Cinema*. Translated and foreword Mark E. Suino. Michigan Slavic Contributions, no. 5. Ann Arbor: University of Michigan Press, 1981.

Löve, Katharina Hansen. *The Evolution of Space in Russian Literature: A Spatial Reading of the 19th and 20th Century Narrative Literature*. Studies in Slavic Literature and Poetics, vol. 22. Amsterdam: Rodopi, 1994.

Lur'e, Ia. S. *V kraiu nepuganykh idiotov: Kniga ob Il'fe i Petrove*. St. Petersburg: Evropeiskii universitet, 2005.

Maiakovskii, V. V. "Bania." In *Sobranie sochinenii*. 8 vols. Moscow: Izdatel'stvo Pravda, 1968, 7:66–135.

Maksimenkov, Leonid. "Ocherki nomenklaturnoi istorii sovetskoi literatury (1932–1946). Stalin, Bukharin, Zhdanov, Shcherbakov i drugie." *Voprosy literatury*, 4 (2003): 212–58.

Maksimenkov, L. V., ed. *Bol'shaia tsenzura: pisateli i zhurnalisty v strane sovetov, 1917–1956*. Series Rossiia XX vek. Dokumenty. General editor A. N. Iakovlev. Moscow: Materik, 2005.

Markstein, Elisabeth. "Dom i kotlovan, ili Mnimaia realizatsiia utopii." In *Andrei Platonov: Mir tvorchestva*. Moscow: Sovremennyi pisatel', 1994, 284–302.

Marsh, Rosalind J. *Soviet Fiction Since Stalin: Science, Politics, and Literature*. Totowa, New Jersey: Barnes and Noble Books, 1986.

Masing-Delic, Irene. "Boris Pilniak's *The Volga Falls to the Caspian Sea* as Trotskyite Sophiology." *Slavic and East European Journal* 52, no. 3 (2008): 414–38.

Matich, Olga. "Remaking the Bed: Utopia in Daily Life." In *Laboratory of Dreams: The Russian Avant-Garde and Cultural Experiment*, edited by John E. Bowlt and Olga Matich. Stanford: Stanford University Press, 1996, 59–78.

McCauley, Karen A. "Production Literature and the Industrial Imagination." *Slavic and East European Journal*, 42, no. 3 (1998): 444–66.

Medvedev, Sergei. "A General Theory of Russian Space: A Gay Science and a Rigorous Science." In *Beyond the Limits: The Concept of Space in Russian History and Culture*, edited by Jeremy Smith. Studia Historica 62. Helsinki: Finnish Historical Society, 1999, 15–47.

Meshcheriakov, N. "O sotsialisticheskikh gorodakh SSSR." *Novyi mir* 8 (1931): 8:161–74.

Milne, Lesley. *Zoshchenko and the Ilf-Petrov Partnership: How They Laughed*. Birmingham Slavonic Monographs no. 35. Birmingham, England: University of Birmingham, 2003.

Mokienko, V. M., and T. G. Nikitina, *Tolkovyi slovar' iazyka sovdepii*. Sankt-Peterburg: Folio-Press, 1998.

Nakhimovsky, Alice. "Death and Disillusion: Il'ia Il'f in the 1930s." In *Enemies of the People: The Destruction of Soviet Literary, Theater, and Film Arts in the 1930s*, edited by Katherine Bliss Eaton. Evanston: Northwestern University Press, 2002, 205–28.

Nemtsov, M. and E. Antonova. "'Gubmeliorator tov. Platonov.' Po materialam Narkomata zemledeliia. 1921–1926 gg." In *"Strana filosofov" Andreia Platonova: Problemy tvorchestva*, edited by N. V. Kornienko. Vol. 3. Moscow: Nasledie, 1999, 476–508.

Neutatz, Dietmar. *Die Moskauer Metro: Von den erten Planen bis zur Grossbaustelle des Stalinismus (1897–1935)*. Cologne: Böhlau Verlag, 2001.

Nicholas, Mary A. "Formalist Theory Revisited: On Shklovskii 'On Pil'niak.'" *Slavic and East European Journal* 36, no. 1 (1992): 68–83.

Nicholas, Mary A., and Cynthia A. Ruder. "In Search of the Collective Author: Fact and Fiction from the Soviet 1930s." *Book History* 11 (2008): 221–44.

Nikonova, T. A. *"Novyi chelovek" v russkoi literature, 1900–1930-x godov: Proektivnaia model' i khudozhestvennnaia praktika*. Voronezh: Izd. Voronezhskogo gosudarstvennogo universiteta, 2003.

Oskotskii, V. "Bruno Iasenskii: Posleslovie." In *Chelovek meniaet kozhu: roman*, by Bruno Iasenskii. Moscow: Izd. Izvestiia, 1969, 583–600.

Panchenko, Irina. "Iurii Olesha. 'Slovo i delo.' Pervaia publikatsiia neizvestnoi ranee p'esy." *Zerkalo*, April 2005: 4–7 and May 2005: 26–28.

Panov, V. S. "Vstrechi s Pil'niakom (otryvok iz rukopisi 'U poroga Moskvy')." In *Boris Pil'niak: Issledovaniia i materialy*, edited by A. P. Auer. Mezhvusovskii sbornik nauchnykh trudov. Vols. 3–4. Kolomna: KGPI, 2001, 174–90.

Papazian, Elizabeth. *Manufacturing Truth: The Documentary Moment in Early Soviet Culture*. DeKalb: Northern Illinois University Press, 2009.

Papernyi, Vladimir. *Architecture in the Age of Stalin: Culture Two*. New York: Cambridge University Press, 2002.

———. *Kul'tura Dva*. Moscow: Novoe literaturnoe obozrenie, 1996.

———. "Men, Women, and the Living Space." In *Russian Housing in the Modern Age: Design and Social History*, edited by William Craft Brumfield and Blair A. Ruble. Cambridge: Woodrow Wilson Center Press and Cambridge University Press, 1993, 149–70.

Pervyi vsesoiuznyi s"ezd sovetskikh pisatelei 1934. Stenograficheskii otchet. Moscow: Khudozhestvennaia literatura, 1934. Reprint, Moscow: Sovetskii pisatel', 1990.

Peppard, Victor. *The Poetics of Yury Olesha*. Gainesville: University of Florida Press, 1989.

Pertsov, V. "Iurii Olesha," in *Poety i prozaiki velikikh let*. Moscow: Khudozhestvennia literatura, 1969, 284–306.

Petrone, Karen. *Life Has Become More Joyous, Comrades: Celebrations in the Time of Stalin*. Bloomington: Indiana University Press, 2000.

Pile, Steve. "Introduction: Opposition, Political Identities and Space of Resistance." In *Geographies of Resistance*, edited by Steve Pile and Michael Keith. London: Routledge, 1997, 1–32.

"Pisateli na krupneishie stroiki CCCP." *Literaturnaia gazeta*, April 24, 1931, 2.

Pisateli ob iskusstve i o cebe. Sbornik statei, No. 1. Moscow-Leningrad: Krug, 1924.

Plamper, Jan. "Abolishing Ambiguity: Soviet Censorship Practices in the 1930s." *Russian Review* 60 (October 2001): 526–44.

Polonskii, Viacheslav. "Magnitostroi: Ocherk." *Novyi Mir* 8 (1931): 109–52.

Postoutenko, Kirill. "Istoricheskii optimizm kak modus stalinskoi kul'tury." In *Sotsrealisticheskii kanon*, edited by Gunter and Dobrenko. St. Petersburg: "Akademicheskii proekt," 2000, 481–91.

Rassudin, Stanislav. *Samoubiitsy: Povest' o tom, kak my zhili i chto chitali*. Moscow: Tekst, 2002.

Reck, Vera. *Boris Pil'niak: A Soviet Writer in Conflict with the State*. Montreal: McGill-Queen's University Press, 1975.

Robin, Regine. *Socialist Realism: An Impossible Aesthetic*. Translated by Catherine Porter. Stanford: Stanford University Press, 1992.

———. "Stalinism and Popular Culture." In *The Culture of the Stalin Period*, edited by Hans Gunther. New York: St. Martins' Press, 1990, 15–40.

Rodnianskaia, I. "Serdechnaia ozadachennost'." In *Andrei Platonov: Mir tvorchestva*, edited by N. V. Kornienko and E. D. Shubina. Moscow: Sovremennyi pisatel', 1994, 330–54.

Rolf, Malte. "Constructing a Soviet Time: Bolshevik Festivals and Their Rivals during the First Five-Year Plan. A Study of the Central Black Earth Region." *Kritika*, 1, no. 3 (Summer 2000): 447–73.

Rosenthal, Bernice Glatzer, ed. *Nietzsche and Soviet Culture: Ally and Adversary*. Cambridge: Cambridge University Press, 1994.

Rozanov, V. V. *The Apocalypse of Our Time, and Other Writings*. Edited by Robert Payne and translated by Robert Payne and Nikita Romanoff. New York: Praeger, 1994.

Rubenstein, Joshua. *Tangled Loyalties: The Life and Times of Ilya Ehrenburg*. New York: Basic Books, 1996.

Ruder, Cynthia A. *Making History for Stalin: The Story of the Belomor Canal*. Gainesville: University of Florida Press, 1998.

Ryklin, Mikhail. "Metrodiskurs." In *Sotsrealisticheskii kanon*, edited by Gunter and Dobrenko. St. Petersburg: "Akademicheskii proekt," 2000, 713–28.

———. "'The Best in the World': The Discourse of the Moscow Metro in the 1930s." Translated by Abigail Evans. In *The Landscape of Stalinism: The Art and Ideology of Soviet Space*, edited by Evgeny Dobrenko and Eric Naiman. Seattle: University of Washington Press, 2003, 261–76.

Ryzhkova, M. "'On shel svoei dorogoi odin i nezavisim . . .'(Chelovek i tekhnika v khudozhestvennom mire Platonova)." *"Strana filosofov" Andreia Platonova: Problemy tvorchestva*. Moscow: Nasledie, Nauka, 1994.

Salys, Rimgaila, ed. *Olesha's* Envy: *A Critical Companion*. Evanston: Northwestern University Press and American Association of Slavic and East European Languages, 1999.

Saslavsky, D. [David Iosifovich Zaslavskii]. *Dnieprostroi: The Biggest Dam in the World*. Moscow: Co-operative Publishing Society of Foreign Workers in the USSR, 1932.

Savel'zon, I. " Kategoriia prostranstva v khudozhestvennom mire A. Platonova." *"Strana filosofov" Andreia Platonova: Problemy tvorchestva*. Vol. 3. Moscow: Nasledie, 1999, 233–43.

Schmidt, Albert J. *The Architecture and Planning of Classical Moscow: A Cultured History*. Philadelphia: American Philosophical Society, 1989.

Scott, John. *Behind the Urals: An American Worker in Russia's City of Steel*. Bloomington: Indiana University Press, 1973.

Seifrid, Thomas. *Andrei Platonov: Uncertainties of Spirit*. Cambridge: Cambridge University Press, 1992.

———. *A Companion to Andrei Platonov's* The Foundation Pit. Boston: Academic Studies Press, 2009.

Shaitanov, I. O. "Kogda lomaetsia techenie." In *Romany*, by Boris Pil'niak. Moscow: Sovremenniki, 1980, 5–24.

Shcheglov, Iu. K. *Romany I. Il'fa i E. Petrova: Sputnik chitatelia*. Vol. 1. Vienna: Wiener Slawistischer Almanach Sonderband 26/1, 1990.

Shentalinsky, Vitaly. *Arrested Voices: Resurrecting the Disappeared Writers of the Soviet Regime*. Translated by John Crowfoot. Introduction by Robert Conquest. New York: Martin Kessler Books, The Free Press, 1993.

Shepherd, David. "Canon Fodder? Problems in the Reading of a Soviet Production Novel." In *Discontinuous Discourses in Modern Russian Literature*, edited by Catriona Kelly, Michael Makin, and David Shepherd. New York: St. Martin's Press, 1989, 39–59.

Shklovskii, Viktor. *"O Pil'niake." LEF* 3, no. 7 (1925): 126–36.

———. *Tret'ia fabrika.* Moscow: Krug, 1926.

———. *Zhili-byli: Vospominaniia, memuarnye zapisi, povesti o vremeni s kontsa XIX v. po 1964 g.* Moscow: Sovetskii pisatel', 1966.

———. *Zoo, ili Pis'ma ne o liubvi* in *Sobranie sochinenii,* vol. 1. Moscow: Khudozhestvennia literatura, 1973.

Siegelbaum, Lewis, and Andrei Sokolov. *Stalinism as a Way of Life: A Narrative in Documents.* New Haven: Yale University Press, 2000.

Simmel, Georg. "Bridge and Door." In *Rethinking Architecture: A reader in cultural theory,* edited by Neil Leach. London: Routledge, 1997, 66–69.

Skorino, L. *Pisatel' i ego vremia: Zhizn' i tvorchestvo V. P. Kataev.* Moscow: Sovetskii pisatel', 1965.

Smirnov, Igor. "Sotsrealism: antropologicheskie izmerenie." In *Sotsrealisticheskii kanon.* edited by Gunter and Dobrenko. St. Petersburg: Akademicheskii proekt, 2000, 16–30.

Smith, G. S. *D. S. Mirsky: A Russian-English Life, 1890–1939.* Oxford: Oxford University Press, 2000.

Smith, Jeremy, ed. *Beyond the Limits: The Concept of Space in Russian History and Culture.* Studia Historica 62. Helsinki: Finnish Historical Society, 1999.

Speer, Albert. *Inside the Third Reich: Memoirs.* Translated by Richard and Clara Winston. Introduction by Eugene Davidson. New York: Macmillan, 1970.

Spivak, Monika. "'Sotsialisticheskii realizm' Andreia Belogo: Istoriia nenapisannoi stat'i." *Novoe literaturnoe obozrenie* 40 (1999): 260–72.

Struve, Gleb. *Russian Literature under Lenin and Stalin, 1917–1953.* Norman: University of Oklahoma Press, 1971.

Subbotin, S. "Andrei Platonov i Gosudarstvennoe izdatel'stvo RSFSR v 1921–1922 godakh." In *"Strana filosofov" Andreia Platonova: Problemy tvorchestva,* edited by N. V. Kornienko. Vol. 3. Moscow: Nasledie, 1999, 439–62.

Taratuta, E. "Povyshennoe soderzhanie sovesti." In *Andrei Platonov: Vospominaniia sovremennikov. Materialy k biografii,* edited by Kornienko and Shubina. Moscow: Sovremennyi pisatel', 1994, 100–104.

Todorov, Tzvetan. *Facing the Extreme: Moral Life in the Concentration Camps.* Translated by Arthur Denner and Abigail Pollack. New York: Henry Holt, 1996.

Vakhitova, T. M. "Oborotnaia storona *Kotlovana.* Ocherk Andreia Platonova 'V poiskakh budushchego (Puteshestvie na Kamenskuiu pischebumazhnuiu fabriku).'" In *Kotlovan. Tekst, materialy tvorcheskoi istorii.* St. Petersburg: Nauka, 2000, 372–79.

Vasil'ev, Viktor. "Prince Faberge." In *Izbrannoe,* by Iurii Olesha. Series "Grand Libris." Moscow: Gud'ial Press, 1999.

Vihavainen, Timo, ed. *Normy i tsennosti povsednevnoi zhizhi: Stanovlenie sotsialisticheskogo obraza zhizhi v Rossii, 1920–30–e gody.* St. Petersburg: Zhurnal "Neva," 2000.

Viola, Lynne. *The Unknown Gulag: The Lost World of Stalin's Special Settlements.* Oxford: Oxford University Press, 2007.

V'iugin, Valerii. "Kak pisal Platonov (na materiale rukopisi "Chevengur")." In *"Strana filosofov" Andreia Platonova: problemy tvorchestva,* edited by N. V. Kornienko. Vol. 6. Moscow: Nasledie, 2005, 564–602.

V'iugin, V. I. "Povest' A. Platonova 'Stroiteli strany.' K rekonstruktsii proizvedeniia." In *Iz tvorcheskogo naslediia russkikh pisatelei XX veka: M. Sholo-khov, A. Platonov, L. Leonov.* St. Petersburg: Nauka, 1995, 309–89.

Voronskii, A. K. *Na styke: Sbornik statei.* Moscow-Petrograd, 1923.

———. "Iz perepiski s sovetskimi pisateliami." In *Literaturnoe nasledstvo: Iz is-torii sovetskoi literatury, 1920–1930–x godov. Novye materialy i issledovaniia.* Moscow: Nauka, 1983, 531–616.

Vorob'ev, Petr. "Parafin belyi: ocherk." *Novyi mir* 11 (1931): 120–27.

Wettlin, Margaret. *Fifty Russian Winters: An American Woman's Life in the So-viet Union.* New York: Pharos Books, 1992.

Widdis, Emma. "Viewed from Below: Subverting the Myths of the Soviet Land-scape." In *Russia on Reels: The Russian Idea in Post-Soviet Cinema,* edited by Birgit Beumers. London: Tauris, 1999, 66–75.

———. *Visions of a New Land: Soviet Film from the Revolution to the Second World War.* New Haven: Yale University Press, 2003.

Williams, Raymond. *The Politics of Modernism: Against the New Conformists.* Edited and introduced by Tony Pinkney. London: Verso, 1989.

Wolf, Erika. *Ilf and Petrov's American Road Trip: The 1935 Travelogue of Two Soviet Writers Ilya Ilf and Evgeny Petrov.* New York: Cabinet Books, 2007.

Wolfson, Boris. "Escape from Literature: Constructing the Soviet Self in Yuri Ole-sha's Diary of the 1930s." *Russian Review* 63 (October 2004): 609–20.

Wood, Elizabeth A. *Performing Justice: Agitation Trials in Early Soviet Russia.* Ithaca: Cornell University Press, 2005.

Yurchak, Alexei. *Everything Was Forever, Until It Was No More: The Last Soviet Generation.* Princeton: Princeton University Press, 2006.

Zakharov, Vadim. *25 let na odnoi stranitse.* Gosudarstvennaia Tret'iakovskaia galereia. Moscow: "Interros," 2006.

Zelinskii, K[ornelii]. "Odna vstrecha u M. Gor'kogo (Zapis' iz dnevnika)." *Vo-prosy literatury* 5 (1991): 144–170.

Zhuravlev, S. V. *Fenomen "Istorii fabrik i zavodov": Gor'kovskoe nachinanie v kontekste epokhi 1930–x godov.* Moscow: Russian Academy of Sciences, Insti-tute of Russian History, 1997.

———. *"Malen'kie liudi" i "bol'shaia istoriia": inostrantsy moskovogo Elektro-zavoda v sovetskom obshchestve 1920-kh—1930-kh gg.* Moscow: ROSSPEN, 2000.

ARCHIVAL MATERIALS

Gosudarstvennyi Arkhiv Rossiiskoi Federatsii, or GARF (State Archives of the Russian Federation), fond 7952, opis' 7, dela 223, 224, 225, 226, 232, 239, 240, 348, 349, 370, 405, 440

Rossiiskii Gosudarstvenni Arkhiv Literatury i Iskusstva, or RGALI (Russian State Archives of Literature and Art), fond 1433, opis' 2; fond 1723, opis' 1; fond 2208, opis' 2

Hoover Institution, Nicolaevsky Collection, box 126, folder 24 and box 741, folder 11.

Index